WARLORDS OF REPUBLICAN ROME

CAESAR VERSUS POMPEY

Nic Fields

CASEMATE
Philadelphia

Published in the United States of America in 2010 by
CASEMATE
908 Darby Road, Havertown, PA 19083

ISBN 978-1-935149-06-4

Cataloging-in-publication data is available from the Library of Congress.

Printed and bound in the United States of America.

10 9 8 7 6 5 4 3 2 1

Also published in the United Kingdom by
Pen & Sword Books, Ltd
47 Church Street
Barnsley
South Yorkshire
S70 2AS

For a complete list of Casemate titles, please contact:

Casemate Publishers
Telephone (610) 853-9131, Fax (610) 853-9146
E-mail casemate@casematepublishing.com
Website www.casematepublishing.com

Contents

To Esther

Without you
Who am I
But a simple, ordinary guy

Acknowledgements

Like many other small boys of my generation I soon grasped that 'the Romans were top nation on account of their classical education, etc.' I consider myself fortunate to have had a classical education, albeit as a 'mature' student, and in particular I owe a debt of gratitude to Jeremy Paterson for illuminating the rather tortuous political life of the late Republic. Though I still treasure the wit and eloquence of Sellar and Yeatman, I now appreciate that Caesar did more than just land 'at Thanet'.

I offer my thanks and appreciation to Rupert Harding of Pen & Sword for his enthusiasm, encouragement and, above all, heroic patience. Likewise to all those students who had to endure my boisterous zeal for the subject during the course of my brief academic career at Edinburgh, with special thanks being offered to Brian Marshall for his professional help and continued friendship. Finally, my greatest thanks go to *ma femme* (*d'esprit*), Esther, who has been with me on this project all along the way.

Chronology

During their official year, which was named after them, the two consuls were irresponsible and irremovable. Originally the consular year had begun on the Ides of March (the month named for Mars, the god of war), resulting in the consuls remaining in office for the first few months of the following year, but from 153 BC the beginning of the civil year was altered from 15 March to 1 January. Numerals in brackets after a name signify whether the man held the consulship before, while the abbreviation *cos. suff.* denotes *consul suffectus*, a consul elected to replace another who had either died in office or resigned before completing his term.

Date	Consuls	Events
107 BC	L. Cassius Longinus C. Marius	Marius enlists *capite censi*
106 BC	Q. Servilius Caepio C. Atilius Serranus	Battle of the Muluccha. Cicero born
105 BC	P. Rutilius Rufus Cn. Mallius Maximus	Iugurtha captured. Battle of Arausio
104 BC	C. Marius (II) C. Flavius Fimbria	Marius' army 'reforms'
103 BC	C. Marius (III) L. Aurelius Orestes	Saturninus' first tribunate
102 BC	C. Marius (IIII) Q. Lutatius Catulus	Teutones defeated at Aquae Sextiae
101 BC	C. Marius (V) M'. Aquilius	Cimbri defeated at Vercellae
100 BC	C. Marius (VI) L. Valerius Flaccus	Metellus exiled. Saturninus lynched
99 BC	M. Antonius A. Postumius Albinus	Metellus recalled. Marius in Asia
98 BC	Q. Caecilius Metellus Nepos T. Didius	Mithridates invades Cappadocia
97 BC	Cn. Cornelius Lentulus P. Licinius Crassus	Sertorius military tribune in Iberia
96 BC	Cn. Domitius Ahenobarbus C. Cassius Longinus	Sulla propraetor of Cilicia
95 BC	L. Licinius Crassus Q. Mucius Scaevola	*Lex Licinia Mucia*

94 BC	C. Coelius Caldus L. Domitius Ahenobarbus	Rutilius legate in Asia
93 BC	C. Valerius Flaccus M. Herennius	Clodius born
92 BC	C. Claudius Pulcher M. Perperna	Trial and condemnation of Rutilius
91 BC	L. Marcius Philippus Sex. Iulius Caesar	Drusus' tribunate. Social War begins
90 BC	L. Iulius Caesar P. Rutilius Lupus	Enfranchisement of Italy
89 BC	Cn. Pompeius Strabo L. Porcius Cato	Destruction of Asculum Picenum
88 BC	L. Cornelius Sulla Felix Q. Pompeius Rufus	Sulla marches on Rome. Marius flees
87 BC	L. Cornelius Cinna Cn. Octavius	Marius returns. Marians take Rome
86 BC	L. Cornelius Cinna (II) C. Marius (VII) Cn. Papirius Carbo (*cos. suff.*)	Death of Marius. Battle of Chaironeia
85 BC	L. Cornelius Cinna (III) Cn. Papirius Carbo	Sulla settles Asia. Sertorius praetor
84 BC	L. Cornelius Cinna (IIII) Cn. Papirius Carbo (II)	Cinna murdered. Peace of Dardanus
83 BC	L. Cornelius Scipio Asiagenus C. Norbanus	Sulla lands in Italy
82 BC	Cn. Papirius Carbo (III) C. Marius minor L. Cornelius Sulla Felix (*dict.*)	Battle of Porta Collina. Proscriptions
81 BC	L. Cornelius Sulla Felix (*dict.* II)	Curbs on tribunician power
80 BC	L. Cornelius Sulla Felix (*cos.* II) Q. Caecilius Metellus Pius	Sertorius controls Iberia
79 BC	P. Servilius Vatia Ap. Claudius Pulcher	Sulla retires. Cicero tours east
78 BC	M. Aemilius Lepidus Q. Lutatius Catulus	Sulla dies. Lucullus praetor
77 BC	D. Iunius Brutus Mam. Aemilius Lepidus Livianus	Rebellion and death of Lepidus
76 BC	Cn. Octavius C. Scribonius Curio	Successes for Sertorius in Iberia
75 BC	L. Octavius C. Aurelius Cotta	Sertorius–Mithridates pact
74 BC	L. Licinius Lucullus	Lucullus sent against Mithridates

	M. Aurelius Cotta	
73 BC	M. Terentius Varro Lucullus	Spartacus' revolt. Sertorius killed
	C. Cassius Longinus	
72 BC	L. Gellius Poplicola	Crassus commands in Slave War
	Cn. Cornelius Lentulus Clodianus	
71 BC	P. Cornelius Lentulus Sura	Defeat and death of Spartacus
	Cn. Aufidius Orestes	
70 BC	Cn. Pompeius Magnus	Cicero prosecutes Verres
	M. Licinius Crassus	
69 BC	Q. Hortensius	Battle and sack of Tigranocerta
	Q. Caecilius Metellus Creticus	
68 BC	L. Caecilius Metellus	Lucullus' soldiers mutiny
	Q. Marcius Rex	
67 BC	C. Calpurnius Piso	Mithridates defeats Romans at Zela
	M'. Acilius Glabrio	
66 BC	M'. Aemilius Lepidus	Lucullus replaced by Pompey
	L. Volcacius Tullus	
65 BC	L. Aurelius Cotta	Trial and acquittal of Catiline
	L. Manlius Torquatus	
64 BC	L. Iulius Caesar	Cato quaestor
	C. Marcius Figulus	
63 BC	M. Tullius Cicero	Catilinarian conspiracy
	C. Antonius Hybrida	
62 BC	D. Iunius Silanus	Battle of Pistoia. Death of Catiline
	L. Licinius Murena	
61 BC	M. Pupius Piso Calpurnianus	Trial and acquittal of Clodius
	M. Valerius Messalla Niger	
60 BC	Q. Caecilius Metellus Celer	The 'first triumvirate'
	L. Afranius	
59 BC	C. Iulius Caesar	Clodius elected to tribunate
	M. Calpurnius Bibulus	
58 BC	L. Calpurnius Piso Caesoninus	Cato in Cyprus. Cicero exiled
	A. Gabinius	
57 BC	P. Cornelius Lentulus Spinther	Battle of the Sabis. Cicero recalled
	Q. Caecilius Metellus Nepos	
56 BC	Cn. Cornelius Lentulus	
	Marcellinus	Conference of Luca. Cato returns
	L. Marcius Philippus	
55 BC	Cn. Pompeius Magnus (II)	Warlords extend their commands
	M. Licinius Crassus (II)	
54 BC	L. Domitius Ahenobarbus	Unrest at Rome. Cato praetor
	Ap. Claudius Pulcher	

53 BC	Cn. Domitius Calvinus	Battle of Carrhae. Crassus killed
	M. Valerius Messalla Rufus	
52 BC	Cn. Pompeius Magnus (*cos. sine collega*)	Unrest continues. Clodius killed
	Q. Caecilius Metellus Pius Scipio (*cos. suff.*)	
51 BC	Ser. Sulpicius Rufus	Cicero proconsul of Cilicia
	M. Claudius Marcellus	
50 BC	L. Aemilius Paullus	Pompey asked to save Republic
	C. Claudius Marcellus	
49 BC	C. Claudius Marcellus (II)	Battle of Ilerda
	L. Cornelius Lentulus Crus	
	C. Iulius Caesar (*dict.*)	
48 BC	C. Iulius Caesar (*cos.* II)	Dyrrhachium. Battle of Pharsalus
	P. Servilius Vatia Isauricus	
47 BC	Q. Fufius Calenus	Battle of Zela
	P. Vatinius	
	C. Iulius Caesar (*dict.* II, *in absentia*)	
46 BC	C. Iulius Caesar (*dict.* III, *cos.* III)	Battles of Ruspina and Thapsus
	M. Aemilius Lepidus	
45 BC	C. Iulius Caesar (*dict.* IIII, *cos. sine collega*)	Battle of Munda
	Q. Fabius Maximus (*cos. suff.*)	
	C. Trebonius (*cos. suff.*)	
	C. Caninius Rebilus (*cos. suff.*)	
44 BC	C. Iulius Caesar (*dict.* V, *cos.* V)	Ides of March. Octavianus returns
	M. Antonius	
	P. Cornelius Dolabella (*cos. suff.*)	
43 BC	C. Vibius Pansa Caetronianus	Mutina battles. Second Triumvirate
	A. Hirtius	
	C. Iulius Caesar Octavianus (*cos. suff.*)	
	Q. Pedius (*cos. suff.*)	
	C. Carrinas (*cos. suff.*)	
	P. Ventidius (*cos. suff.*)	
42 BC	M. Aemilius Lepidus (II)	Philippi battles. Suicide of Brutus
	L. Munatius Plancus	

The Careers of Pompey and Caesar

Pompey

106 BC	Born
89 BC	Member of father's staff at siege of Asculum Picenum
83 BC	Raises private army and joins Sulla. Command in Gallia Cisalpina
81 BC	Command in Sicily. Command in Africa
80 BC	Triumph. Divorces Antistia and marries Aemilia, step-daughter of Sulla
79 BC	Marries Mucia Tertia, uterine sister of Metellus Celer
77 BC	Propraetorian command against Lepidus. Propraetorian command against Sertorius
71 BC	Returns to Rome from Iberia. Triumph
70 BC	Consul
67 BC	Proconsular command against pirates (*lex Gabinia*)
66 BC	Proconsular command against Mithridates (*lex Manilia*)
64 BC	Establishes Syria as province
62 BC	Returns to Rome from east. Divorces Mucia Tertia
61 BC	Triumph
60 BC	Member of 'first triumvirate'
59 BC	Land for veterans and eastern *acta* ratified. Marries Iulia, daughter of Caesar
55 BC	Consul
54 BC	Proconsul of Iberian provinces. Death of Iulia
52 BC	Sole consul. Marries Cornelia, daughter of Metellus Scipio
49 BC	Proconsular command against Caesar
48 BC	Assassinated in Egypt

Caesar

100 BC	Born
87 BC	Nominated *flamen Dialis*
84 BC	Marries Cornelia, daughter of Cinna
81 BC	Envoy to Nikomedes of Bithynia. Wins *corona civica*
78 BC	Returns to Rome from Asia and Cilicia
75 BC	Captured by pirates
72 BC	Military tribune
69 BC	Quaestor in Hispania Ulterior. Death of Cornelia
67 BC	Supports *lex Gabinia*. Marries Pompeia, granddaughter of Sulla

66 BC	Supports *lex Manilia*
65 BC	Curule aedile
63 BC	Elected *pontifex maximus*. Speaks against execution of Catilinarian conspirators
62 BC	Praetor. Divorces Pompeia after Bona Dea scandal
61 BC	Propraetor of Hispania Ulterior. Victory against Lusitani
60 BC	Returns to Rome. Forfeits triumph. Member of 'first triumvirate'
59 BC	Consul. Marries Calpurnia, daughter of Calpurnius Piso. *Lex Vatinia*
58 BC	Proconsul of 'Two Gauls' and Illyricum. Campaigns against Helvetii and Ariovistus
57 BC	Campaign against Belgae
56 BC	Campaigns against Veneti and Aquitani. Attacks Morini and Menapii
55 BC	Crosses Rhine and Channel. Incursion of Usipetes and Tencteri. *Lex Licinia Pompeia*
54 BC	Second expedition to Britannia. Loss of *legio XIIII*. Campaign against Eburones
53 BC	Second crossing of Rhine. Campaign against Treveri. Incursion of Sugambri
52 BC	Revolt of Vercingétorix. Siege and surrender of Alésia. Law of Ten Tribunes
51 BC	Revolts of Bellovaci and Carnutes. Siege and fall of Uxellodunum
49 BC	Crosses Rubicon. Leaves Rome for Iberia. Mutiny of *legio VIIII*. Dictator
48 BC	Consul. Crosses Adriatic. Alexandrian sojourn
47 BC	Dictator. Mutiny of *legio X Equestris*. Crosses to Africa
46 BC	Dictator and consul. Quadruple triumph. Leaves Rome for Iberia
45 BC	Dictator and consul. Returns to Rome. Triumph. Publishes *Anti-Cato*
44 BC	Dictator and consul. Declared dictator in perpetuity. Assassinated
42 BC	Deified

Key to Forenames

Roman families were grouped into large clans or *gentes* (e.g. the Cornelii, the Licinii and the Sextii). Members of a *gens* might be rich or poor, and may not be related, in the same way that two people named Smith or Macdonald need not be related. Even so, among the aristocratic members of the same *gens* there was often a blood-tie (comparable with the Rothschilds today). A man's *gens* was indicated by his *gentilicium*, one of the two names (the other was his *praenomen*) used by all Roman male citizens. In the early Republic, and already in the Regal period, the *praenomen* was a personal name, while the *gentilicium* was a hereditary name, much like modern surnames, which are passed on from father to son.

By our period the legal name and description of a male citizen consisted of six elements. First, the forename (*praenomen*), usually abbreviated to the first letter only, as in A. (Aulus), C. (Caius), and Cn. (Cnaeus). Next came the family or clan name (*nomen gentilicium*), which usually ended in *-ius*, as in Hirtius, Iulius and Pompeius, but rare forms may end with -anus or -enus, such as Norbanus or Alfenus. Following this was the filiation or patronymic, consisting of the father's *praenomen* and the word filius, 'son'. Next appeared the name of the voting tribe (thirty-five in total) to which the man belonged, usually abbreviated, as in COR (Cornelia), GAL (Galeria) or VOL (Voltinia). The tribe was an essential part of a Roman citizen's name. The fifth element was the third part of the citizen's personal name, the cognomen. Some cognomina derived from personal peculiarities (e.g. Scipio 'stick', Cicero 'chickpea' and Crassus 'thick') but others were honorific, perhaps recalling personal military achievements in other countries, such as Africanus, Numidicus or Macedonicus. The final element of the legal description recorded a man's place of origin (*origo*) or domicile (*domus*).

A.	Aulus	M'.	Manius
Ap.	Appius	P.	Publius
C.	Caius	Q.	Quintus
Cn.	Cnaeus	Ser.	Servius
D.	Decimus	Sex.	Sextus
L.	Lucius	Sp.	Spurius
M.	Marcus	T.	Titus
Mam.	Mamius	Ti.	Tiberius

Key to Legionary Titles

In addition to their number, some legions at the end of our period were distinguished by a particular cognomen. The adoption of titles is hardly surprising when we consider the existence in rival armies of legions with the same numerals. The cognomen itself may reflect one of the following: a nickname; a god; a geographical area; a success; or an origin.

Alaudae	'Larks'
Antiqua	'Ancient'
Augusta	reconstituted by Augustus
Equestris	'Knightly'
Ferrata	'Ironclad'
Fulminata	'Thunderbolt-carrier'
Gallica	'Gallic' – served in Gaul
Gemella	'Twin' – one legion made out of two
Germanica	'Germanic' – served on the Rhine
Macedonica	'Macedonian' – served in Macedonia
Martia	'Sacred to Mars'
Sabina	'Sabine' – raised in Sabine country
Sorana	'Soran' – formed at the Latium town of Sora
Urbana	'Urban'

Maps

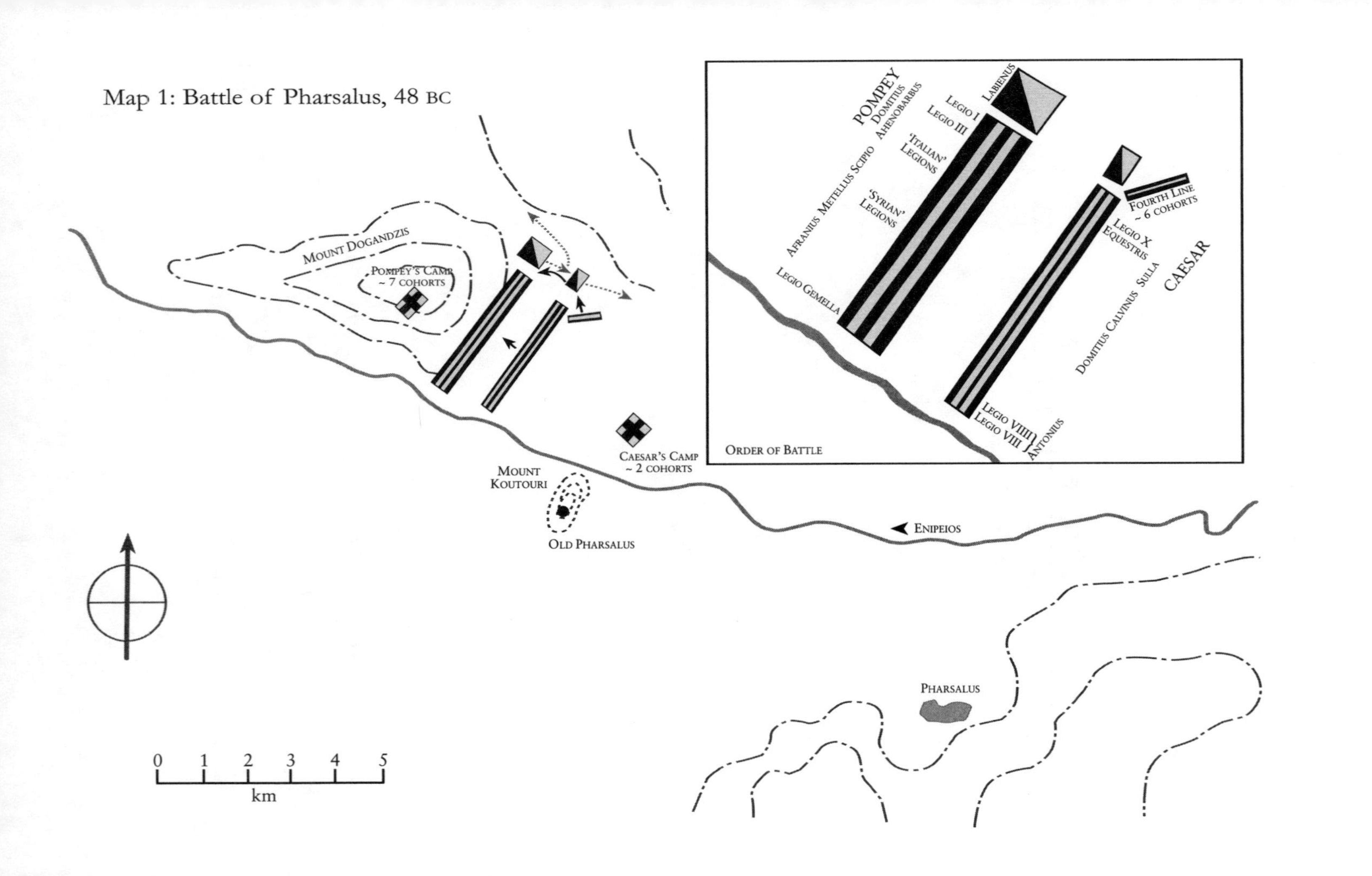
Map 1: Battle of Pharsalus, 48 BC
Mount Dogandzis
Pompey's Camp
~ 7 cohorts
Caesar's Camp
~ 2 cohorts
Mount
Koutouri
Old Pharsalus
Enipeios
Pharsalus
0
1
2
3
4
5
km
Pompey
Domitius
Ahenobarbus
Labienus
Legio I
Legio III
'Italian'
Legions
'Syrian'
Legions
Afranius Metellus Scipio
Legio Gemella
Fourth Line
~ 6 cohorts
Legio X
Equestris
Caesar
Domitius Calvinus Sulla
Legio VIIII
Legio VIII
Antonius
Order of Battle

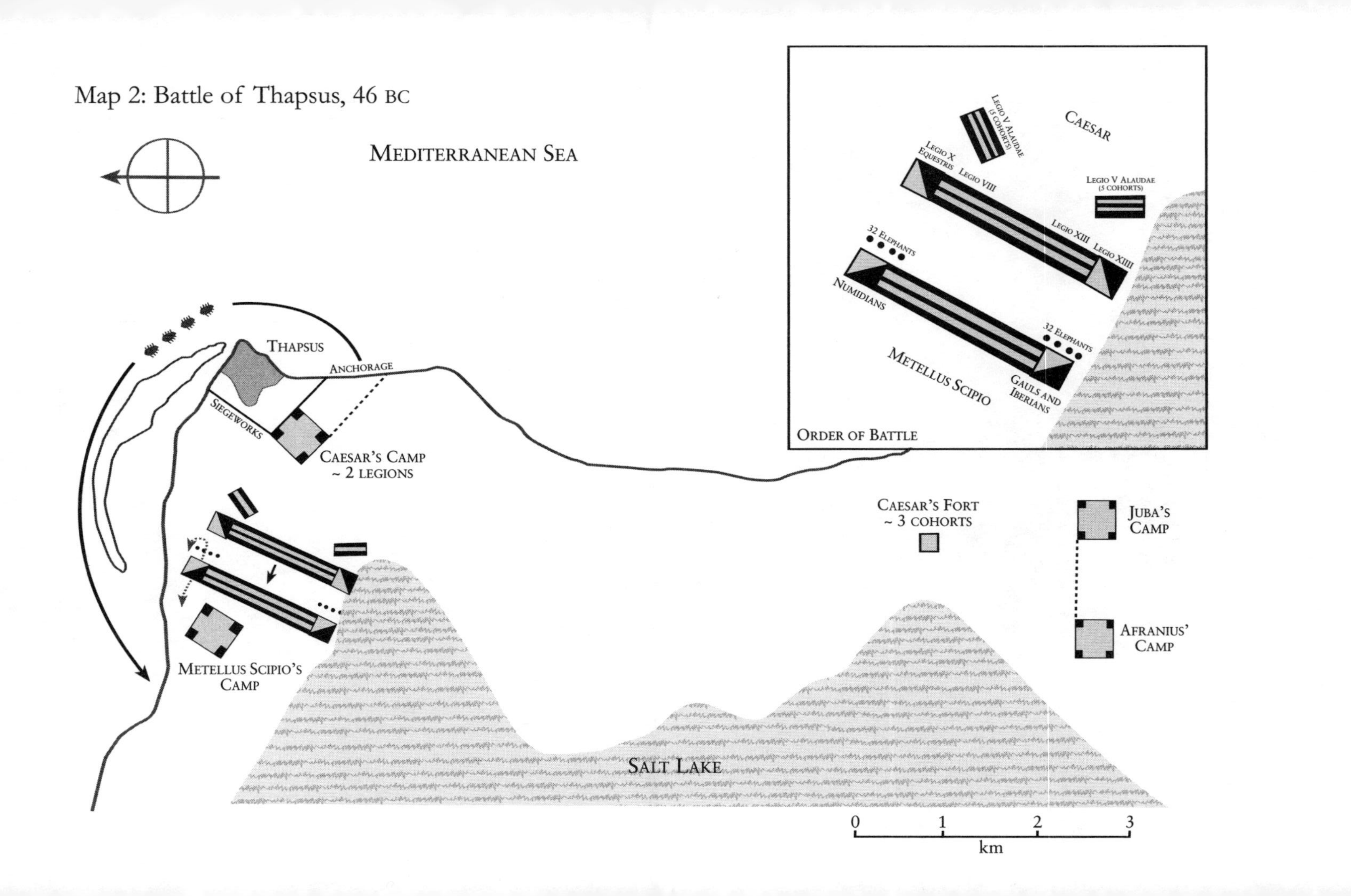
Map 2: Battle of Thapsus, 46 BC
Mediterranean Sea
Thapsus
Anchorage
Siegeworks
Caesar's Camp
~ 2 legions
Metellus Scipio's Camp
Salt Lake
Caesar's Fort
~ 3 cohorts
Juba's Camp
Afranius' Camp
0
1
2
3
km
Caesar
Legio V Alaudae
(5 cohorts)
Legio X Equestris
Legio VIII
Legio XIII
Legio XIIII
Legio V Alaudae
(5 cohorts)
32 Elephants
Numidians
32 Elephants
Metellus Scipio
Gauls and Iberians
Order of Battle

Map 3: The Roman Empire, *c.* 44 BC

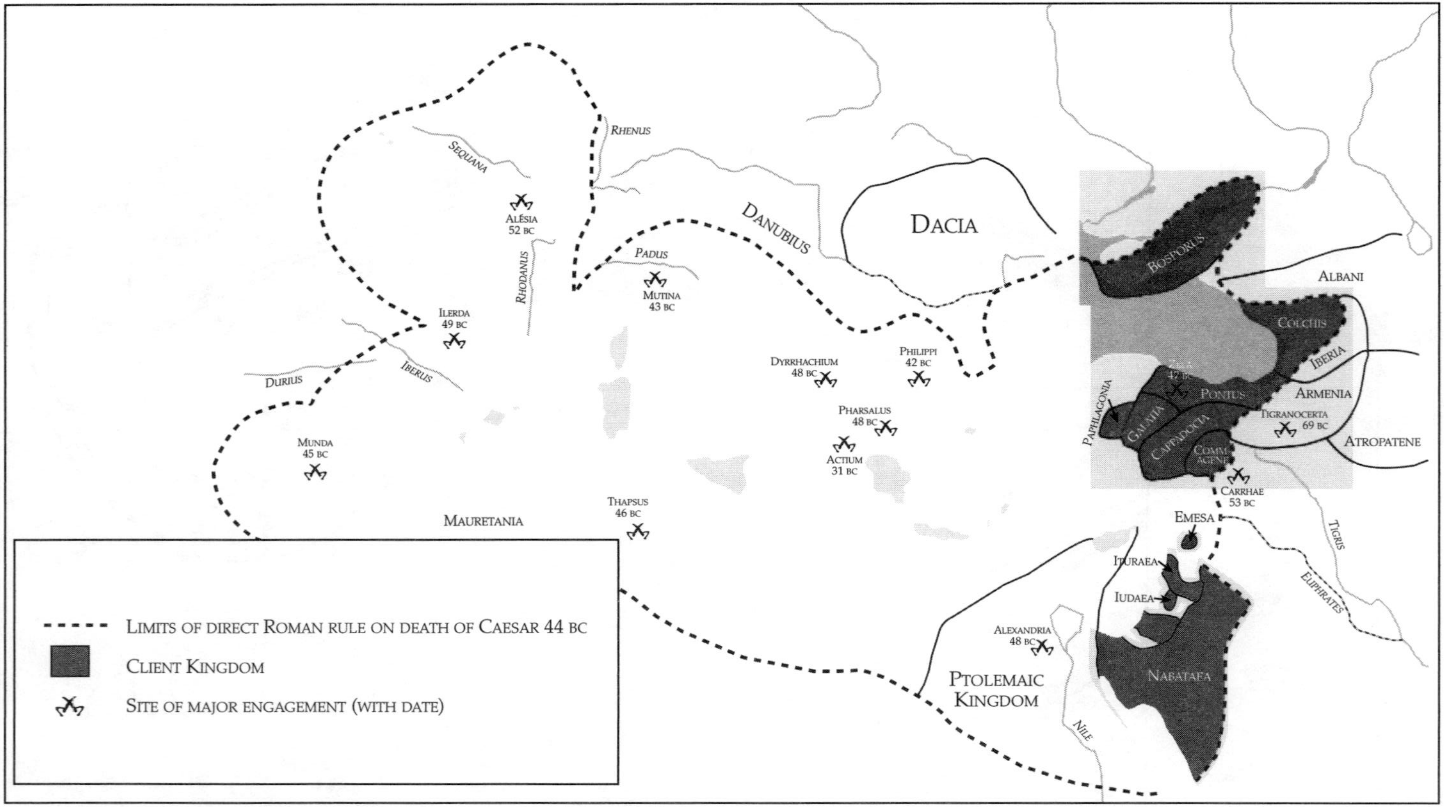

Limits of direct Roman rule on death of Caesar 44 BC

Client Kingdom

Site of major engagement (with date)

Prologue

On the night of 10 January 49 BC Caesar, with a single legion, marched into that Italy where Pompey had only to stamp with his foot upon the ground and armed legions would spring to the birth, into that Picenum where the name of Pompey was one to conjure with, and where Labienus, the sole renegade from the ranks of the invader, was known and respected. It was the depths of winter, but he resolved to swoop down, with his habitual celerity and audacity, upon Luceria, the Apulian rendezvous of the opposition. As he marched night and day along the highway that skirted the Adriatic, one town after another followed the example of Auximum and ejected its Pompeian garrison. So rapidly did the 'semi-barbarian' legions from Gaul follow their patrician generalissimo that when he turned down the Via Claudia Valeria to invest the crossroads town of Corfinium, where his would-be successor in Gaul, Domitius Ahenobarbus, was preparing resistance, the invading army numbered some 40,000 men. Cicero, paralysed with a kind of morbid fascination at the ease and speed with which the invader of Italy had progressed, wondered in a letter to his close friend and confidant Atticus: 'Is it a Roman general or Hannibal we are talking of?'[1] Speed of foot, with Caesar, stood in place of numbers.

On 21 February Corfinium fell, and Caesar, prudently magnanimous, suffered Domitius Ahenobarbus to go free, only to prepare fresh resistance in the summer at Massilia and finally to fall in the Pompeian rout of Pharsalus the following year. As for the common soldiers, drawn by the fascination of the high-bred conqueror, the majority of them promptly joined his ranks. Great was the astonishment of Caesar that Pompey should have abandoned Rome, greater still was his astonishment when he learnt that the stupefied opposition was scuttling for Brundisium, to escape from the land on which Pompey's 'prodigy' stomped. On 9 March Caesar lay before the walls of the seaport town, but for want of a fleet he could not prevent the embarkation of the Pompeian soldiers. On 15 March, the Ides, Pompey fled overseas to the east where his greatest victories had been achieved, and on 1 April Caesar met the remnants of the Senate, which were still to be found in Rome, as the undisputed master of all Italy.

Chapter 1

Republican Legions

The wars fought by early Rome consisted of hit-and-run raids and ambushes, tit-for-tat skirmishes and cattle rustling, with perhaps the occasional battle between armies. The latter were little more than warrior bands formed by an aristocrat, his kin and clients, very much like the 'private army' of the Fabii with its 306 'clansmen and companions'.[2] The clan-leader fought for personal glory, his followers out of loyalty to him and the prospect of portable booty. Livy, for instance, constantly refers to Roman plundering, and the predatory behaviour of the Romans is suitably illustrated by the raids and counter-raids conducted against the petty hill-tribes of the Volsci, Aequi, Sabines and Hernici, what he labels the frequent instances of 'neither assured peace nor open war'.[3] However, a major development came with the adoption of the hoplite phalanx, via the Greek colonies of southern Italy, probably some time in the sixth century BC.[4]

Livy, who was writing at the very end of the first century BC, attributes a major reform of Rome's socio-political and military organisation to the penultimate king, Servius Tullius (traditionally 579–534 BC). A census of all adult male citizens recorded the value of their property and divided them accordingly into classes. The archaeological record does suggest that the Romans adopted hoplite equipment some time in this century, so the annalistic tradition may be broadly accurate. Thus in Livy the Servian classes I, II and III essentially fought with hoplite arms, except that members of class I armed themselves with the *clipeus* while classes II and III used the *scutum*.[5] Classes IV and V were armed as skirmishers, the last class perhaps carrying nothing more than a sling.

This system provided the basis of the *comitia centuriata*, the assembly at which the citizens voted to declare war or accept a peace treaty, elected the consuls, praetors and censors, the senior magistrates of Rome, and tried capital cases. Gathering on the *campus Martius* (Field of Mars), an open area outside the original boundary – *pomoerium* – of the city, its structure exemplified the ideal of a citizen militia in battle array, men voting and fighting together in the same units. This assembly operated on a 'timocratic principle', that is to say, only those who could afford arms could vote, which meant the *comitia centuriata* was in effect an assembly of property-owners-cum-citizen-soldiers. However, the Servian army of Livy does not appear in his battle accounts.

The Legion

The Romans later adopted the manipular legion, either just before or during Rome's wars with the Samnite confederation.[6] Although tactically more flexible, the early legion retained many of the aspects of the hoplite phalanx from which it developed. Thus the army remained a provisional militia, and the census recorded those citizens with sufficient property to make them eligible to serve.

Originally the term *legio* – legion – had meant levy, and obviously referred to the entire citizen force raised by Rome in one year. However, as the number of citizens regularly enrolled for military service increased, the legion became the most important subdivision of the army. By the middle Republic the legion consisted of five elements – namely the heavy infantry *hastati*, *principes* and *triarii*, the light infantry *velites*, and the cavalry *equites* – each equipped differently and having specific places in the legion's tactical formation. Its principal strength was the thirty maniples of its heavy infantry, the *velites* and *equites* acting in support of these. These tactical units of some 120 men were deployed in three lines of ten maniples each. It was a force designed for large-scale battles, for standing in the open, moving directly forward and smashing its way frontally through any opposition.

The essential philosophy behind the manipular legion was that of winning a straightforward mass engagement with the enemy. A quick decisive clash with the enemy was desired, and in this role the manipular legion performed very well. The inclusion of allied troops within the armies of this period did not change the essential tactical doctrines. Many allied units were organised and equipped as legions and thus acted in a similar fashion, while the additional light-armed troops or cavalry were deployed to help achieve the same aim of breaking the enemy line. Concerning its actual organisation, we have two accounts. First, the Roman historian Livy, writing more than three centuries after the event, describes the legion of the mid-fourth century BC. Second, the Greek historian Polybios, living and writing in Rome at the time, describes the legion of the mid-second century BC.

Livian Organisation

In his account of the year 340 BC, after the close of the First Samnite War (343–341 BC), and as a preamble to the war against the Latin allies (Latin War,

340–338 BC), Livy offers a brief description of Roman military organisation. He notes that the Romans had formerly fought in hoplite style in a phalanx (introduced as part of the Servian reforms), but recently they had adopted manipular tactics with the legion being split into distinct battle lines. Behind a screen of light-armed troops (*leves*) the first main line contained maniples (*manipuli* or 'handfuls') of *hastati* ('spearmen'), the second line was made up of maniples of *principes* ('chief men'), and the third line, made of the oldest and more mature men, consisted of maniples of *triarii* ('third rank men').[7]

All three lines carried the oval-shaped Italic shield, the *scutum*, and the first and third (and perhaps also the second, but this is not made clear) had the *hasta* or spear. There is no reference to the *pilum*, which, if Livy's account is accepted, may not yet have been introduced. The earliest reference to the *pilum* belongs to 295 BC during the Third Samnite War (298–290 BC).[8] One significant problem, however, is the fact that Livy has fifteen maniples in each of the three lines, as opposed to Polybios' ten maniples. Other groups, whom Livy calls *rorarii* and *accensi*, were lightly equipped and formed a final reserve in the rear.[9]

Livy's account is pleasingly close to that of Polybios and probably derives from the latter, so that its independent value is not great. Moreover, if we choose to accept the evidence of Dionysios of Halikarnassos – namely that long thrusting-spears for hand-to-hand fighting were still being used by the *principes* during the war with Pyrrhos of Epeiros (Pyrrhic War, 280–275 BC), then Livy dates the manipular system too far back.[10] It seems, therefore, that the transformation from hoplite phalanx to manipular legion was a slow and gradual one, which for Livy was a thing over and done with by the early fourth century BC. For the organisation of the Roman legion solid ground is reached only with Polybios himself.

Polybian Organisation

Polybios breaks off his narrative of the Second Punic War at the nadir of Rome's fortunes, following the three defeats of the Trebbia, Trasimene and Cannae, and turns to an extended digression on the Roman constitution and the Roman army.[11] For us the account of the latter is of inestimable value, not least because the detailed description is provided by a contemporary, himself a former cavalry commander (*hipparchos*) in the Achaian League, who had seen the Roman army in action against his fellow-Greeks during the Third Macedonian War (171–167 BC) and had perhaps observed its levying and training during his internment in Rome (167–150 BC).

The Roman Art of War

The legion would usually approach the enemy in its standard battle formation, the *triplex acies* or 'three lines', with the normal arrangement having four cohorts in the first line, and three each in the second and third.[12] Moving ahead at a walking pace and normally deployed in four ranks, each cohort advanced alongside its neighbours under the direction of its centurions. During this advance the soldiers had to listen out for orders and make sure they never lost sight of their standards. The six centurions of each cohort were distinguished by helmets with transverse crests so the common soldiers could follow 'not only their standard, but also the centurion'.[13] The soldiers were ranged behind him by *contubernia*, the 'tentfuls' of eight men, ten per century.

It may have been necessary at some point for the advance to stop and the cohorts to align themselves before the final approach. Any gaps could be filled in at this time too. And then, at the signal, the soldiers began their attack, probably a short jog of perhaps 40 or 50 metres; running in armour, *scutum* and *pila* in hand while in formation, must have been out of the question. As they approached the enemy, they would cast their *pila*, perhaps at a distance of 15 metres or so, and then draw their *gladii* and prepare to close. This means the soldiers probably came to a near halt, perhaps involuntarily, to be sure of their neighbours. When writing of ancient warfare, Colonel Charles-Ardant du Picq puts it at its elegant best:

> At the moment of getting close to the enemy, the dash slackened of its own accord, because the men of the first rank, of necessity and instinctively, assured themselves of the position of their supports, their neighbours in the same line, their comrades in the second, and collected themselves together in order to be more the masters of their movements to strike and parry . . .[14]

According to Caesar's own words, the raising of a war-cry was usually associated with the volley of *pila* and the final charge into contact.[15] At or about the moment of impact, the narrow gaps between the cohorts were filled naturally by men from the rear ranks, and so the two opposing lines stayed face to face, so long as one did not break and allow itself to be struck in a suddenly exposed flank.

The centurions, always leading from the front, urged their men forward and pressed them to come to actual blows, crossing swords themselves when they needed to lead by example. At any place where the line thinned as soldiers pulled out from injury or exhaustion, a second-line cohort would be sent to brace them. In hand-to-hand fighting physical endurance is of the utmost importance and all soldiers in close contact with danger become emotionally if not physically exhausted as the battle proceeds. Du Picq noted the great value of the Roman system in keeping only those units that were necessary at the point of combat, and the rest 'outside the immediate sphere of moral tension'.[16] The legion, organised into three separate lines, was able to hold two-thirds of its men outside the danger zone – the zone of demoralisation – in which the remaining third was engaged. Ideally, therefore, the front-line cohorts fought the main enemy line to a standstill, but if they were rebuffed or lost momentum or the ranks thinned, the second-line cohorts advanced into the combat zone and the process was repeated. The skill of a Roman commander lay in committing his second and third lines, fresh troops who were both physically and morally fit, at the right time.

The legion had no overall commander, being officered by six military tribunes (*tribuni militum*)[17] drawn from the aristocracy. Like all senior officers of the army, these men were not professional soldiers but magistrates elected by the citizens in the *comitia centuriata.* Having served a five-year military apprenticeship – young aristocrats almost certainly fulfilled this obligation serving in the cavalry – they would be eligible for election to the rank of military tribune, although ten of the twenty-four annually elected tribunes had at least ten years' service experience.[18] These officers were responsible to the overall commander of the army, one of the two consuls, who would in many cases have only two legions of Roman citizens accompanied by an equal or larger number of *socii* – Latin and Italian allies.[19] Smaller-scale operations could be entrusted to praetors, the next magisterial college in seniority to the consuls, who were normally given an army of one legion supported by a similarly sized contingent of *socii.*

The normal strength of the legion is given at 4,200, and all citizens of military age, namely men between 17 and 46 years of age, were required to attend a selection process (*dilectus*) on the Capitol. Here the citizen-volunteers were arranged into some semblance of soldierly order according to height and age. They were then brought forward four at a time to be selected for service in one of the four consular legions identified, in a matter-of-fact way, as *I*, *II*, *III* and *IIII.* The tribunes of each legion took it in turns to have first choice, thus ensuring an even distribution of experience and quality throughout the units. The new recruits then swore an oath of obedience. It was sworn in full by one man, with the phrase *idem in me* – 'the same for me' – being sufficient for the rest.

In Polybios' day all those with property worth over 400 drachmae (= 400 denarii) were liable for service, which, although the passage is slightly defective here, was for sixteen years as a legionary or ten years as an *eques.* These figures represent the maximum that a man could be called upon to serve. In the second century BC a man would normally serve up to six years in a continuous posting, after which he expected to be released. Thereafter he was liable for call-out, as an *evocatus*, up to the maximum of sixteen campaigns or years. The legionary received an allowance (*stipendium*) at the daily rate of one-third of a denarius (120 denarii per annum), the payment going towards the cost of his equipment and rations. The *equites* received more, one denarius per diem, from which to meet the cost of maintaining their mounts.[20]

Miserly as it was, the actual amount of money was not meant to be a substitute for normal living expenses. It was well below the wages of an unskilled labourer, who commanded about 12 *asses* per day in this period.[21] But merely counting how many *asses* soldiers received misses the point. Roman society had never been broken into the three Indo-European categories, often hereditary, of military, religious and economic groups, as was common in similar civilisations. Thus throughout the republican period the soldiers fighting for Rome were its own citizens, for whom defence of the state was a duty, a responsibility and a privilege.

The legion itself consisted of 1,200 *hastati* in ten maniples of 120, 1,200 *principes* organised in the same way, and 600 *triarii* also in ten maniples. Each maniple had two centurions (*centuriones*), of which the senior held the command, two *optiones* as their subordinates, a standard-bearer (*signifer*), a trumpeter (*cornicen*), and a guard commander (*tesserarius*) who was responsible for the password, which he received each night written on a wax tablet (*tessera*). Then, as in days of old, each maniple was provided with a standard (*signum*), a simple pole with a handful of hay twisted around it that was used by the maniple commander to transmit orders and rally his men; hence the term *manipulus* came to signify a unit of soldiers belonging to the same standard. The senior centurion of the legion, who commanded the extreme right-hand maniple of the *triarii* (*centurio primi pili*, later called *primus pilus*), was included *ex officio* along with the military tribunes, in the consul's war council. The remaining 1,200 men, the youngest and poorest, served as *velites*.

As with Livy, the *hastati* were also young men, the *principes* in the prime of life, and the *triarii* veterans.[22] The *velites*, which, according to Livy, were formally created as a force in 211 BC, had a sword, a bundle of javelins, and a small round shield (*parma*).[23] The *hastati* and *principes* carried the oval *scutum*, the famous 'Iberian sword' (*gladius Hispaniensis*) and two *pila* (one heavy and one light). A Byzantine lexicographer, possibly following Polybios' lost account of the Numantine War (134–132 BC), says the *gladius Hispaniensis* was adopted from the Iberians at the time of the war with Hannibal (Second Punic War, 218–201 BC),[24] but it is possible that this formidable weapon, along with the *pilum*, was adopted from Iberian mercenaries serving Carthage during the First Punic War (264–241 BC). It was certainly in use by 197 BC, when Livy describes the Macedonians' shock at the terrible wounds it inflicted.[25]

All soldiers wore a bronze pectoral to protect the heart and chest, although those who could afford it would wear instead a mail shirt (*lorica hamata*), a bronze helmet and a pair of bronze greaves. Interestingly, Polybios clearly refers to only one greave being worn, and Arrian, writing in the second century AD, confirms this, saying the ancient Romans used to wear one greave only, on the leading leg, the left. No doubt many of those who could afford it would actually have a pair.[26] The *triarii* were similarly dressed and equipped, except they carried a *hasta* instead of the *pilum*. In order to be distinguishable from a distance, the *velites* covered their helmets with wolf skin, and the *hastati* wore tall upright feathers in their helmets, so exaggerating their height. Let us not forget, however, these short-term citizen soldiers provided their own equipment and therefore we should expect considerably more variation in clothing, armour and weapons than among the legionaries of the later, state-funded professional legions.

Each legion had 300 cavalry organised in ten *turmae* of thirty troopers each. The *turma* elected three *decuriones* ('leaders of ten'), of whom the senior commanded with the rank of *praefectus*. Each *decurio* chose an *optio* as his second-in-command. The cavalry or *equites* formed the most prestigious element of the legion, and were recruited from the wealthiest citizens able to afford a horse and its trappings. Polybios notes that the *equites* were armed in 'Greek fashion', namely helmet, linen corselet, strong circular shield, long spear and sword, but he observes that formerly (perhaps up to the Macedonian wars) they had lacked body armour and had carried only a short spear and a light shield. Being young aristocrats, the *equites* were enthusiastic and brave, but better at making a charge on the battlefield than patrolling or scouting. In short, Rome relied on its foot-soldiers.

The Professional Soldier

At first service in the Roman army entailed a citizen being away from his home – usually a farmstead – for a few weeks or months over the summer. But the need to fight overseas and to leave troops to form permanent garrisons in newly won provinces meant that men were away from home for longer periods. This interruption to normal life could easily spell ruin for the soldier-farmers who had traditionally made up the bulk of citizens eligible for military call-up. Hopkins estimates that in 225 BC legionaries comprised 17 per cent of all the adult male citizens, and in 213 BC, at the height of the war with Hannibal, 29 per cent.[27] Inevitably what had been seen as a duty and voluntary obligation took on a somewhat different character.

It is important to note here that in the middle Republic the centurions of the legion were normally elected from among the common legionaries (*milites*), the centurions in turn choosing their own *optiones*.[28] As a centurion a man received twice the pay of a legionary soldier, which would give a centurion an annual rate of 240 denarii on the normal assumption of a 360-day year.[29] That said, there existed from at least 200 BC onwards a core of near professionals, very experienced and well-trained men who liked adventure and the risks, or who had few if any home ties and were more than glad to volunteer over a number of years. A splendid example from this period must be the career of a centurion of Sabine stock, Spurius Ligustinus, in whose mouth Livy puts the following words:

> I joined the army in the consulship of Publius Sulpicius and Caius Aurelius [200 BC], and served for two years in the ranks in the army, which was taken across to Macedonia, in the campaign against King Philip [i.e. Second Macedonian War, 200–197 BC]. In the third year Quinctius Flamininus promoted me, for my bravery, centurion of the tenth maniple of *hastati*. After the defeat of Philip and the Macedonians [at Kynoskephalai, 197 BC], when we had been brought back to Italy and demobilised, I immediately left for Iberia as a volunteer with the consul Marcus Porcius [195 BC]. Of all the living generals none has been a keener observer and judge of bravery than he, as is well known to those who through long military service have had experience of him and other commanders. This general judged me worthy to be appointed centurion of the first century of *hastati*. I enlisted for the third time, again as a volunteer, in the army sent against the Aetolians and King Antiochus [i.e. Syrian War, 192–189 BC]; Marcus Acilius appointed me centurion of the first century of the *principes*. When Antiochus had been driven out and the Aetolians had been crushed [at Thermopylai, 191 BC], we were brought back to Italy; and twice after that I took part in campaigns in which the legions served for a year. Thereafter I saw two campaigns in Iberia [i.e. Iberian War, 181–180 BC], one with Quintus Fulvius Flaccus as praetor, the other with Tiberius Sempronius Gracchus in command. Flaccus brought me back home with the others whom he brought back with him from the province for his triumph, on account of their bravery; and I returned to Iberia because I was asked to do so by Tiberius Gracchus. Four times in the course of a few years I held the rank of *centurio primi pili* [i.e. centurion of the first century of the *triarii*]; thirty-four times I was rewarded for bravery by the generals; I have been given six civic crowns [*coronae civica*]. I have completed twenty-two years of service, and I am now over 50 years old.
>
> Livy, 42.34, 5–11

Ligustinus was making a plea to the consuls of 171 BC to ensure that he received an appointment appropriate to his experience and status. After his initial six years of service in Macedonia, he had re-enlisted as a volunteer, and served in Iberia, Greece, Asia and perhaps elsewhere for a further sixteen years. He was showered with military decorations by a succession of admiring commanders, including Marcus Porcius Cato (the Censor), a general Ligustinus evidently held in high regard.

Prominent among his honours were the six *coronae civica*, each an oak-leaf crown awarded for saving the life of a fellow Roman citizen in battle. Ligustinus would have worn these, as well as his other military decorations, at every public festival at home and would have commanded great respect. Such visible symbols of his valour would not be confined to the public domain, however, as it was also the Roman custom to hang up these trophies in the most conspicuous place in the house. All in all the pugnacious Ligustinus had served all but two years as a centurion, holding increasingly senior posts, culminating in that of the senior centurion (*centurio primi pili*) of the legion. As we well know, sixteen years was the maximum a man could be forced to serve, but the quintagenarian Ligustinus, now with twenty-two years' service under his belt, went on to be *centurio primi pili* again in *legio I*, serving under the consuls in the Third Macedonian War (171–167 BC).

His pattern of service would not have been much out of place in the professional standing army of the Principate. Ligustinus is presented as the ideal soldier-farmer, since Livy takes care to point out that he still farmed the plot of land he had been left by his father, where his wife had borne him six sons, four of whom were grown up, and two daughters, both of whom were married. What is intriguing is that this smallholding was not of sufficient size to have rendered him liable to military service at all, and thus his army service had been voluntary. The peasant family of three to four mouths needed a minimum of 7 *iugera* of land to survive at subsistence level. This 7-*iugera* plot (4.55 acres/1.75 ha) is very much the traditional figure for many of the *viritim* ('man-by-man') grants handed out by the state during the first half of the second century BC. Ligustinus declares that his father had left him 'one *iugerum* of land and a little hut'.[30] As this was less than the standard minimum of 2 *iugera* for landed property it is little wonder that Ligustinus had made a career out of the army.

Professional Army

Caius Marius, who held an unprecedented series of consulships during the last decade of the second century BC, and who defeated Iugurtha of Numidia and later the much more serious threat to Italy from migrating Germanic tribes, the Cimbri and the Teutones, has often been credited with taking the decisive steps that laid the basis for the professional standing army of the Principate.

Rome was now the dominant power in the Mediterranean basin and the annual levying of what was in effect a part-time citizen militia was incompatible with the maintenance of a world empire. Moreover, decades of war overseas had turned out thousands of trained soldiers and many of them would have found themselves strangers to civilian life after their years of service abroad. The army had been their life and Marius called them back home. But besides these time-expired veterans, Marius also enrolled another more numerous kind of volunteer: the men with nothing.

Those citizens who did not belong to the five classes, that is to say, those who could not declare to the censors the minimum census qualification for enrolment in Class V, were excluded from military service. Lacking the means to provide themselves with arms, these citizens were listed in the census simply as the *capite censi* or 'head count'. However, Marius was not content to supplement his army for the African campaign by only drawing upon 'the bravest soldiers from the Latin towns'.[31] Thus of all the reforms attributed to Marius, the opening of the ranks to *capite censi* in 107 BC has obviously attracted the most attention, and it incurred the unanimous disapproval of ancient writers.[32] Marius stands accused of paving the way for the so-called lawless, greedy soldiery whose activities were thought to have contributed largely to the decline and fall of the Republic a few generations later.

Yet we should not lose sight of the fact that Marius was not the first to enrol the *capite censi*. At times of extreme crisis in the past the Senate had impressed them, along with convicts and slaves, for service as legionaries. In the aftermath of the crushing defeats at the Trebbia (218 BC), Lake Trasimene (217 BC), and Cannae (216 BC), the Senate made the first of a number of alterations to the Servian constitution. In the dark days following Cannae, for instance, two legions were enlisted from slave-volunteers.[33] Marius was merely carrying one stage further a process visible during the second century BC, by which the prescribed property qualification for service in the army was eroded and became less meaningful. Now the only real prerequisites were that of Roman citizenship and a willingness to go soldiering.

Noticeably the ancient sources, unlike modern commentators, do not say that Marius swept away the qualification, or changed the law on eligibility. On the contrary, he merely appealed to the *capite censi* for volunteers, whom he could equip from state funds under the legislation drawn up by Caius Gracchus in 123 BC, by which the state was responsible for equipping soldiers fighting in its defence.[34] Even before Gracchus' *lex militaria*, there had been a progressive debasement of the property threshold for Class V from 11,000 *asses* to 4,000 *asses*.[35] In 123 BC, as one of the tribunes of the people, Gracchus himself reduced the property qualification again, setting the minimum at 1,500 *asses*.[36] This last represents a very small amount of property indeed, almost certainly insufficient to maintain an average-sized family, but the effect was an ongoing attempt to increase the number of citizens that qualified for military service.

Marius' reform should be seen as the logical conclusion to this development, something Rome's overseas ventures on increasingly far-flung fields had exacerbated. What he did was to legalise a process that had been present for about a century but that the Senate had failed to implement, that is, to open up the army to all citizens regardless of their property, arm them at state expense, and recruit them not through the *dilectus* but on a volunteer basis. None the less, his common-sense reform would bode ill for the future of the Republic. These men, the men with nothing, were willing to join for any number of reasons. While not high, there was the pay, and there was an ordered life, decent food and clothing, and, perhaps, the chance of improving one's lot in life. And so with Marius the precedent was set whereby the volunteer largely followed his general, often identifying his fortunes with him.

Maniples and Cohorts

Marius is also credited with changes in tactical organisation; namely, he abolished the maniple (*manipulus*, pl. *manipuli*) and substituted the cohort as the standard tactical unit of the legion. While maintaining the centuries and the maniples for administrative purposes, he chose to divide his legion into ten cohorts, each of which consisted of three maniples, one drawn from each of the three lines of *hastati*, *principes* and *triarii*.

The cohort (*cohors*, pl. *cohortes*) as a formation of three maniples was not entirely innovative, as it appears to have been in use as a tactical (as opposed to an administrative) expedient from the time of the Second Punic War. Polybios, in an account of the battle of Ilipa (206 BC), pauses to explain the meaning of the term *cohors* to his Greek readership.[37] Surprisingly, it receives no mention in his detailed account of army organisation, either in the sixth book or in his comparison of legion and phalanx in the eighteenth book, although it should be stated there is little on tactics in either of these. On the other hand, some have detected in Sallust's account of the operations of Quintus Caecilius Metellus (*cos.* 109 BC) against Iugurtha (109–108 BC) the last reference to maniples manoeuvring as the sole tactical unit of the battle line.[38] Hence the belief that Marius swept them away either in 106 BC or during his preparations in 104 BC for the war with the Cimbri and Teutones.

It is recognised that the battle of Pydna (168 BC) saw the triumph of the Roman maniple over the Macedonian phalanx, and this disposition was adequate until Rome came to meet an opponent who adopted a method of attack different from the slow methodical advance of the Hellenistic phalanx with its 'bristling rampart of outstretched pikes'.[39] The tactics of the Germanic and Celtic tribes, the latter armed with a long two-edged sword designed for slashing, was to stake everything upon a vigorous onslaught at the start of the battle, beating down the shields of the opposition and breaking into their formation. This was a terrifying thing, and at times could swiftly sweep away an opponent – especially a nervous one – but if it was halted the tribesmen would tend to lose their enthusiasm and retreat quickly. To counter this brutal method of attack, where the perpetrators believed that fighting power increased in proportion to the size of the mass, the Roman formation of three fixed battle lines of maniples was unsuited. The units themselves were fairly small and shallow, and an attack strongly pressed home might easily overcome their resistance. In the war against the Celtic Insubres (225 BC) the *hastati* of the front line had attempted to circumvent this difficulty by substituting their *pila* for the thrusting-spears of the *triarii* stationed in the rear.[40]

Yet the small size of the maniple was a major weakness against such a style of fighting, and Marius decided to strengthen his front line of defence by increasing the size of the individual units. Thus the cohort took the place of the maniple as the tactical unit of the Marian legion, which was now organised into ten cohorts, each of which was subdivided into six centuries. In effect the old three-fold battle array was cut into ten slices from front to back, with the cohort being a large but manageable unit of 480 men. When deployed for battle, the ten cohorts of a legion still formed up in the traditional *triplex acies*, with four in the front line, then a line of three, and finally three more at the rear.

Another sound argument for making a definite decision in favour of the cohort at the time of Marius could be that, with the lowering of the property qualification and its eventual abolition, the legionaries were now equipped by the state at public expense. Consequently, the variations in equipment that were originally linked to differing financial status now ceased to have any *raison d'être*. All legionaries were now equipped with a bronze Montefortino helmet,[41] a mail shirt (*lorica hamata*), the *scutum*, two *pila* (one heavy, the other light), and a *gladius Hispaniensis*, plus a dagger (*pugio*). Greaves disappeared, except on centurions.

The adoption of the cohort as the standard tactical unit probably also marked the elimination of the *velites*. They were assimilated into the regular structure of the centuries, which were all made the same size (i.e. eighty men, six per cohort), and armed in like fashion to the other legionaries. The last specific mention of the *velites* as such occurs in Sallust's account of Metellus' African campaigns.[42] The Roman army now provided the same function through the use of auxiliary troops, such as Numidian javelineers, Cretan archers and Balearic slingers.

Finally, although we have assumed that the size of the Marian cohort was 480 men, as it would be during the Principate, the size of the Marian legion has been a matter of controversy. It is likely that it averaged some 5,000 men all ranks, but the total complement could be higher (6,000) or, more likely, much lower (3,000). The ancient sources confuse the problem because, as Brunt points out, they normally multiply by 5,000 or so whenever they use the term *legio*.[43] In other words, *legio* is equal to 5,000 regardless of actual size. Besides, sometimes disease, hardship and occasionally desertion thinned the ranks, not to mention casualties. It is likely that casualties had reduced Caesar's legions in 49 BC to about 4,000 men each, and the following year, when Caesar embarked seven legions at Brundisium (Brindisi), he had only 15,000 men fit for duty. As Caesar himself says, 'many had been lost during all the campaigns in Gaul, the long march from Iberia had removed a great many, and the unhealthy autumn weather in Apulia and around Brundisium, after the wholesome regions of Gaul and Iberia, had seriously affected the health of the whole army'.[44]

Mules and Eagles

The legionary, like all professional foot-soldiers before his day and after, was grossly overloaded – alarmingly so according to some accounts. The renowned orator and statesman Marcus Tullius Cicero wrote of 'the toil, the great toil, of the march: the load of more than half a month's provisions, the load of any and everything that might be required, the load of the stake for entrenchment'.[45] Normally, perhaps, a legionary carried rations for three days, not the two weeks to which Cicero refers. However, it has been estimated that the legionary was burdened with equipment weighing as much as 35 kilograms, if not more. As Edward Gibbon justly says, this weight 'would oppress the delicacy of a modern soldier'.[46]

It appears, therefore, that another of Marius' apparent reforms was to reduce the size of the baggage train (*impedimenta*). The legionaries now had to shoulder much of their gear: bed-roll and cloak, three or more days' ration of grain, a bronze cooking pot (*trulleus*) and mess tin (*patera*), a metal canteen or leather flask, a sickle for cutting grain and forage, a wicker basket for earth moving, either a pick-axe (*dolabra*) or an iron-shod wooden spade (*pala*), a length of rope, and a stake (*pilum muralis*) for fortifying the overnight marching camp. This gear was slung from a T-shaped pole (*furca*), and Plutarch writes that the soldiers were nicknamed *muli Mariani*, Marius' mules, a wry description that would remain in popular currency.[47] Each *contubernium*[48] on the march was also allowed one four-legged mule to carry the heavier items such as its leather tent and millstones.

The natural implication of Marius' decision to enrol poor citizens in the army was that the newly raised legions would not all automatically cease to exist when the men were dismissed from duty. In effect, the legion became a permanent organisation into which new recruits could be added, keeping the same name and number throughout its existence. To mark this change in status, Marius gave each legion a permanent standard to represent it. The republican legion, according to the elder Pliny, originally had five standards, depicting an eagle, a wolf, a minotaur, a horse and a boar. He places the adoption of the silver eagle (*aquila*) as the supreme standard of all legions precisely in 104 BC, at the start of preparations for the war against the northern tribes.[49] This selection of the eagle, a bird of prey associated with Iuppiter, is thus firmly credited to Marius.

The new standard was carried into battle by a senior standard-bearer, the *aquilifer*, who was second only to a centurion in rank. It was under the personal care of the *primus pilus* ('first spear', formerly known as the *centurio primi pili*), the chief centurion of the legion who nominally commanded the first century in the first cohort. While its safe custody was equivalent to the continuance of the legion as a fighting unit, however depleted in numbers, its loss brought the greatest ignominy on any survivors and could result in the disbandment of the legion in disgrace, a practice that was to long continue.[50] The *aquila* not only worked to increase the loyalty and devotion of soldiers to the legion through fostering a corporate identity, but was also reflective of the sweeping away of the old class divisions within the Roman army.

Legionaries who viewed the army as a career, not simply as an interruption to normal life, came to identify very strongly with their legion, and these units developed, in the fullness of time, tremendous corporate spirit. Admittedly an old provisional legion could be a first-class fighting unit, especially if seasoned by long service, but a new professional legion was on average better trained and disciplined than its predecessors, simply because it was more permanent. At the time of Marius, the legions were probably still reconstructed every year, but by Caesar's day they had certainly begun to retain their identity. As we shall see, gifted and ambitious commanders such as Caesar would play on soldiers' pride in their legions and rivalry with other units in the army.

The Legionary's Arsenal

As we have already discussed, the soldier no longer provided his own equipment, instead being issued with weapons, armour and clothing by the state. The differences between the various property classes in the legion vanished, along with the cavalry and light-armed troops. All legionaries were now heavy infantry, armed alike with *pilum* and *gladius*.

Heavy javelin (*pilum*)

The *pilum* was employed by legionaries in battle as a short-range shock weapon; it had a maximum range of 30 metres or thereabouts, although it was probably discharged within 15 metres of the enemy for maximum effect.[51] The first authentic mention of the Roman *pilum* is a reference to legionaries in 250 BC using a *hyssos*.[52] This was probably adopted from Iberian mercenaries fighting for Carthage during the First Punic War (264–241 BC). By the end of our period the *pilum* had a pyramidal iron head on a long soft-iron shank, some 60 to 90 centimetres in length, fastened to a one-piece wooden shaft, which was generally of ash. The head was designed to puncture shield and armour, with the long iron shank passing through the hole made by the head. Once the weapon had struck home, or even if it missed and hit the ground, the shank tended to buckle and bend under the weight of the shaft. With its aerodynamic qualities destroyed, it could not be effectively thrown back, and if it lodged in a shield, it became extremely difficult to remove.[53] Put simply, the *pilum* would either penetrate flesh or become useless to the enemy. Modern experiments have shown that a *pilum* thrown from a distance of 5 metres could pierce 30 millimetres of pine wood or 20 millimetres of plywood.[54]

Plutarch attributes to Marius a modification that made it more certain that the missile would bend on impact; namely, he replaced one of the two iron rivets that held the iron-shank of the *pilum* to its wooden shaft with a wooden rivet.[55] The wooden rivet would snap upon impact, resulting in the shank bending. Archaeological evidence from one of the five Roman camps east of the Iberian stronghold of Numantia, near modern-day Burgos, indicates that it was the heavy *pilum* that was modified in this way.[56] Similar examples were recovered from the site of the siege at Alésia, showing that both types of *pilum* were still in use in Caesar's day. Whereas a long tang and two rivets were used for the heavier type, the lighter version was simply socketed on to its wooden shaft.

Experimentation with the *pilum* did not end there, however. Later it was decided to move away from Marius' adaptation by choosing to leave the iron-shank un-tempered instead. This innovation (often wrongly accredited to Caesar) meant that the head of the *pilum* retained its murderous penetrating capacity while the rest would buckle upon impact.

Shield (*scutum*)

Legionaries carried a large dished shield (*scutum*), which was oval-shaped in the republican period. To be light enough to be held continually in battle, shields were usually constructed of double or triple thickness plywood, which was made up of laminated wood strips. Covered with canvas and hide, the shield was edged with copper alloy binding and had a central iron or copper alloy boss (*umbo*), a bowl-shaped protrusion covering a handgrip. According to Polybios the *scutum* measured 120 centimetres in length by 75 centimetres in width,[57] and the one example extant from the late republican period, that found at Kasr-el-Harit in Egypt, preserved in the dry sands of Fayûm, matches his description closely.

This shield, currently held in Cairo Museum, is 128 centimetres long and 63.5 centimetres wide. It was constructed from three layers of birchwood strips, the centre layer consisting of the widest strips laid vertically, the others being horizontal and narrower. The layers were glued together and covered in lamb's wool felt, which was sewn carefully round the rim. The overall thickness was just under a centimetre at the edges, rising to 1.2 centimetres around the centre. The shield had a wooden boss and a wooden spine (*spina*), running vertically above and below the boss to the rim, which was nailed to the front. Weighing about 10 kilograms, the shield was held by a horizontal handgrip behind the boss.

Much like the riot-shield of a modern policeman, the *scutum* was used both defensively and offensively to deflect blows and hammer into the opponent's shield or body to create openings. As he stood with his left foot forward, a legionary could get much of his bodyweight behind this punch. Added to this was the considerable weight of the *scutum* itself. Weights of reconstructions range from 5.5 to 10 kilograms, and a hefty punch delivered with the weight of the body behind the left hand stood a good chance of overbalancing an opponent.

Sword (*gladius*)

Sometime in the third century BC the Romans adopted a long-pointed, double-edged Iberian weapon, which they called the *gladius Hispaniensis* ('Iberian sword'). The earliest Roman specimens date to the turn of the first century BC, but a fourth-century sword of similar shape has been found in Spain at the cemetery of Los Cogotes (Avila), while an earlier Iberian example came from Atienza some 100 kilometres north-east of Madrid. The blade could be as much as 64 to 69 centimetres in length and 4.8 to 6 centimetres wide and waisted in the centre. It was a fine piece of 'blister steel'[58] with a triangular point between 9.6 and 20 centimetres long; it had honed down razor-sharp edges and was designed to puncture armour. It had a comfortable bone handgrip grooved to fit the fingers, and a large spherical pommel, usually of wood or ivory, to help with counter-balance. Examples weigh between 1.2 and 1.6 kilograms. This basic design, with various minor modifications, continued as the weapon of choice through to the end of the second century AD.[59]

Unusually, a legionary carried his sword on the right-hand side, suspended by a leather belt (*cingulum*) worn around the waist. As opposed to a scabbard-slide, the four-ring suspension system on the scabbard enabled the legionary to draw his weapon quickly with the right hand, an advantage in close-quarter combat. By inverting the hand to grasp the hilt and pushing the pommel forward, the *gladius* could be drawn with ease.

Military dagger (*pugio*)

The dagger – a short, edged, stabbing weapon – was the ultimate weapon of last resort. However, it was probably more often employed in the day-to-day tasks of living on campaign. Carried on the left-hand side and suspended on the same waist belt that carried the sword, the *pugio* was slightly waisted in a leaf-shape and some 20 to 25.4 centimetres long. The choice of a leaf-shaped blade resulted in a heavy weapon, to add momentum to the thrust. Like the *gladius*, the Roman dagger was borrowed from the Iberians and then developed; it even had the four-ring suspension system on the scabbard, characteristic of the *gladius*.

Punch-Jab

At the battle of Aquae Sextiae (Aix-en-Provence) in 102 BC, as Plutarch records, Marius ordered his legionaries to stand firm against the Teutones and 'hurl their javelins . . . and then to draw their swords and force them backwards

The Battle of Aquae Sextiae, 102 BC

As a general Marius relied mainly on surprise and always showed a reluctance to engage in a traditional, set-piece fight. He preferred to determine the time and place and would not be hurried. Such was his victory at Aquae Sextiae. Having dogged the Teutones and Ambrones since they had crossed the Rhodanus (Rhône), Marius moved into the vicinity of the Roman colony. At the end of the day's march Marius followed his custom and began to establish a fortified camp on high ground overlooking a stream. Following the usual order of things, four military tribunes would have overseen the construction of the camp's four walls, thrown up from the *spolia* dug from the V-shaped ditches surrounding the camp. Legionaries would have carried out the manual work under the direction of their centurions while the cavalry and light-armed troops stood ready to drive off any attack.

As the soldiers laboured, servants and slaves went down the slope to the stream to fetch water. They went armed, of course, with swords, axes and spears, since the Germanic camp lay just across the stream and some of the enemy were themselves down by the water. It may not have been unusual for opponents to meet each other under such circumstances, each side tacitly ignoring the other so long as they could keep apart, but sometimes a fight must inevitably have erupted – as happened this day. The Ambrones left their camp to help their fellows at the water's edge, and some contingents of *socii* and Romans went down the hill to meet them as they splashed across the stream. Plutarch tells us that the Ambrones suffered a significant defeat, but he may have exaggerated as the larger and decisive engagement was fought two days later.[60]

This scuffle, however, meant the Romans were unable to complete their fortifications before nightfall. They still held the heights where the half-finished camp lay, and the enemy had retired, but the security the soldiers were accustomed to – and upon which the commander relied to keep his men rested and confident – was not there. Fortunately for Marius there was no attack during the night. The enemy evidently had had enough fighting during the engagement at the stream, and they spent the next day readying themselves for battle. Marius did likewise, putting a number of cohorts, perhaps five or six – they are said to have numbered 3,000 men in all – under a lieutenant of his, Marcus Claudius Marcellus, and ordering him to slip into a wooded area nearby and wait there through the night in preparation for battle the following day.

The balance of the army Marius led out the next day on the heights before the camp, sending his cavalry out ahead to skirmish with the enemy and provoke them into action. We do not know the disposition of the legionaries, though it is assumed that they were formed up in the conventional *triplex acies*. Marius is said by Plutarch to have 'sent officers all along the line ordering the soldiers to stand firm and keep their ground, to hurl their javelins when the enemy came into range, and then to draw their swords and force them backwards with their shields'.[61] Whether he instructed them this way or not, the advice reflects the usual Roman practice of disordering the enemy with *pila*, knocking them with *scuta* and closing with the *gladius*. It differed only in that the legionaries were to stand fast and receive the enemy charge instead of advancing. Obviously Marius thought it prudent to await the enemy's inevitable onslaught from his superior position and then advance down the slope once the enemy had been disordered.

The Teutones and Ambrones attacked uphill, were met and contained, and driven slowly back down the slope by the legionaries and then, while fully engaged, they were struck from behind by Marcellus' cohorts emerging from the woods. The enemy line, caught between two forces, dissolved and was utterly defeated. The usual incredible figures are given for the killed and captured,[62] but whatever the exact numbers, the Teutones and the Ambrones were finished as a threat to Rome.

with their shields'.[63] The instruction to discharge 'javelins' (*akóntion* in Plutarch's Greek) and then join battle with sword and shield is such as we might expect to be given to an army that had adopted the *pilum* and *gladius Hispaniensis*. Likewise, if this is so, the offensive use of the *scutum* tells us that the tactical doctrine commonly associated with the Roman army of the Principate was now firmly in place.[64] As we shall discover, the legionary could punch his *scutum* into the enemy as he came up quickly with a sharp, upward jab from his *gladius*.

An interesting argument for why the republican Roman army had adopted this tactical doctrine of 'punch-jab' comes from the Augustan historian Dionysios of Halikarnassos. Having derided the Gallic manner of fighting, whereby the Gauls wield their long slashing-swords 'like hewers of wood', Dionysios continues with a description of the art of swordsmanship as practised by legionaries:

> On the other hand, the Romans' defence and counter-manoeuvring against the barbarians was well practised and afforded greater safety. For while their foes were still raising their swords aloft, they would duck under their arms, holding up their shields, and then, stooping and crouching low, they would render vain and useless the blows of the others, which were aimed too high. The Romans, on the other hand, holding their swords straight out, would strike their opponents in the groin, their sides, and drive their blows through their breasts into their vitals. And if they saw any of them keeping these parts of their bodies protected, they would cut the tendons of their knees or ankles and topple them to the ground roaring and biting their shields and uttering cries resembling the howling of wild beasts.
>
> Dionysios of Halikarnassos, 14.10.2

The one major problem with Dionysios' description, packed as it is with graphic detail, is that it forms part of his narrative dealing with Marcus Furius Camillus' campaign of 390 BC against the Gauls. In other words, as is so prevalent with the annalistic tradition of Rome, the author has fallen into an anachronism.

However, Polybios does mention, in his near-contemporary account of the Gallic war of 223 BC, that legionaries used only the thrust, kept their swords straight 'and relied on their sharp points . . . inflicting one wound after another on the breast or face'.[65] In a later passage he hints that they were trained to take the first whirling blow of the Celtic slashing-sword on the rim of the *scutum*, which was suitably bound with iron.[66] He then continues with a description of the famous *gladius Hispaniensis* (*Iberikós* in Polybios' Greek), which is worn high on the right side (a Celtic tradition)[67] so as to be clear of the legs, an excellent weapon he says 'for thrusting, and both of its edges cut effectually, as the blade is very strong and firm'.[68] What we are witnessing here is the intelligent use of the sword, for a slash-cut rarely kills but a thrust allows a deep penetration of the vital organs. The use of the thrust also meant the legionary kept most of his torso well covered, and thus protected, by the *scutum*. The latter, having been used to absorb the enemy's attack, was then punched into the face of the opponent as the legionary stepped forward to jab with his *gladius*.

Needless to say, a specialised weapon required specialised training. While the *gladius* was designed for use as a stabbing weapon, it could still dismember opponents with its two-edged blade. Yet the Romans saw the advantages of using the point of a *gladius*, and in training a recruit was taught to employ the thrust and not the slash.

The training methods adopted by the Romans are well described by the fourth-century writer Vegetius. This Iberian-born bureaucrat and horse breeder devotes the whole of his first book to the selection, training and discipline of recruits, and he takes great pains to name as his principal sources the much earlier treatises of Cato the Censor, Cornelius Celsus, Frontinus and Tarrutienus Paternus, and the military regulations of Augustus, Trajan and Hadrian.[69] His military treatise, therefore, gives us an insight into the physical realities of recruit training during our period:

> 11. The ancients . . . trained recruits in this manner. They made round wickerwork shields, twice the weight that a government shield [*scutum publicum*, i.e. army issue] normally was. They also gave the recruits wooden swords, likewise of double weight, instead of real swords. So equipped, they were trained not only in the morning but even after noon against posts. Indeed, the use of posts is of very great benefit to

> gladiators as well as soldiers . . . Each recruit would plant a single post in the ground so that it could not move and protruded 6 [Roman] feet. Against the post as if against an adversary the recruit trained himself using the wickerwork shield and wooden sword, just as if he were fighting a real enemy. Sometimes he aimed as against head and face, sometimes he threatened the flanks, and sometimes he tried to cut the hamstrings and legs. He gave ground, came on, sprang, and aimed at the post with every method of attack and art of combat, as though it were an actual opponent. In this training care was taken that the recruit drew himself up to inflict wounds without exposing any part of himself to a blow.
>
> 12. Further, they learned to strike not with the edge, but with the point. For the Romans not only easily beat those fighting with the edge, but also ridicule them, as a slash-cut, whatever its force, seldom kills, because both armour and bones protect the vitals. But a thrust driven in 2 inches is fatal; for necessarily whatever goes in penetrates the vitals. Secondly, while a slash-cut is being delivered the right arm and flank are exposed; whereas a thrust is inflicted with the body remaining covered, and the enemy is wounded before he realises it . . . The wickerwork shield and wooden sword of double weight they gave out so that when the recruit took up real and lighter arms, he fought with more confidence and agility, as being liberated from the heavier weight.
>
> Vegetius, 1. 11–12

The exercises with post and swords, which were based on the system in force at the training schools for gladiators, superbly illustrate the thoroughness with which weapons training was carried out by the Roman army. As Vegetius points out, the wooden substitute for the *gladius* was intentionally much heavier so that in combat it would be easier for the fully trained legionary to wield the real weapon. Moreover, it was vitally important to develop the muscles of a recruit's shoulders so as to enhance his strength in thrusting his sword.

The mention of gladiators by Vegetius is interesting in this connection. We know from Valerius Maximus that Publius Rutilius Rufus (*cos.* 105 BC), who had already gained a reputation as a military theorist and author, introduced the methods of the gladiatorial schools into military training.[70] Moreover, Frontinus tells us that Marius, busy making preparations for the war against the Cimbri and Teutones, was so impressed by the troops trained by Rutilius that he preferred them to his own:

> When Caius Marius had the option of choosing a force from two armies already in existence, one of which had served under Rutilius, the other under Metellus and later under himself, he chose the army of Rutilius, though it was the smaller of the two, because he thought it was the better trained.
>
> Frontinus, *Strategemata*, 4.2.2

Military training was no joyride, and sword-drill of this kind alternated with running, jumping, swimming and tree-felling. Additionally, three times a month there were long route-marches for recruits on which the pace was varied from the normal marching rate to a rapid trot.[71] Once the recruit, now bulked out with muscle and bursting with stamina, had attained a proper proficiency with the dummy weapons, he would begin training with standard issue weapons. Formal training culminated in individual combat, each recruit being assigned another as adversary. This more advanced stage of weapons training was known as *armatura*, a name which itself was borrowed from the gladiatorial schools.[72]

Slash or Stab

Close-quarter combat between Roman legionary and Celtic warrior saw a clash of two very different techniques. The Celt would have required plenty of room in which to swing his long slashing-sword while simultaneously manoeuvring his flat oblong shield to block any Roman thrust.[73] He would have fought upright, aiming to slash his adversary with a downward blow to the neck and shoulders, the best sort of attack for the Celtic slashing-sword. By using the whole arm more force could be put into the blow than if it were delivered solely from the elbow. Such a blow would have been delivered diagonally downwards, either from right to left or from left to right.

The Celtic slashing-sword was certainly not contrived for finesse, but was designed to either hack an opponent to pieces or beat him to a bloody pulp. Instinctively, the legionary would have used the metal rim of his *scutum* to ward off such an attack, but if he failed in this he was not left entirely vulnerable. The narrow neck-guard projecting straight out at the back of his Montefortino helmet would have provided some protection against this type of assault, and his *lorica hamata* would have offered good protection since mail is more vulnerable to thrusts than to slashes. Furthermore, its shoulder-doubling would have given even better protection, possibly absorbing much of the stroke's kinetic energy and reducing the risk of the underlying clavicle being broken.[74]

Having drawn his *gladius*, the legionary adopted a very slight crouch, with the left foot forward, holding the *scutum* horizontally in front with the left hand and using it to cover the upper legs, the torso and lower face.[75] By keeping the *scutum* close to his body, the legionary not only gained optimum protection but also increased the range of the punch. His body would have been slightly turned in profile to his opponent to present as small a target as possible, with his elbows tucked in close to the torso so as not to expose the vulnerable underarm. His feet were roughly shoulder width apart. In this balanced position he could put all his bodyweight, which rested on the back leg, behind a punch with his *scutum*.

Punch delivered, it was now time for the swordplay. The footwork was as simple and direct as walking, for the legionary instantly stepped forward with his right foot, the weight of the body now helping to deliver an upward jab with the *gladius* held in the right hand with its edges up and down, perpendicular to the ground. It is important to note here that although the right shoulder would deliver some of the power behind the thrust, the real power of the thrust came from the rotation of the legionary's hips as he stepped forward.

Essentially two methods of combat could be employed by the legionary, namely pro-active or reactive fighting. The first necessitated striking the first blow, perhaps through overwhelming his opponent with the *scutum*: here its sheer size was a premium. The second method involved taking the opponent's sword strike on the *scutum*. This entailed moving the shield a relatively short distance to meet the incoming blow: here the metal binding around its rim was vital. The advantage here was that the parry and punch could be combined, the legionary moving in closer all the while to deliver the deadly thrust. In both cases, however, we should be aware of the fact that the final position of the legionary would have been no more than a few inches from his opponent.

Vae Victis

The Romans obviously attached a great deal of importance to training, and it is this that largely explains the success of their army. 'And what can I say about the training of legions?' is the rhetorical question aired by Cicero. 'Put an equally brave, but untrained soldier in the front line, and he will look like a woman.'[76] The basic goal of this training was to give the legions superiority over the 'barbarian' in battle, hence the legionary was taught to attack with the *gladius* by thrusting and not by slashing. As Vegetius emphasises, a thrust with the sword has penetrating power, whereas the slash, which is often difficult to aim and control, may strike a bone or the opponent's shield and thus will do comparatively little damage. The thrust or jab is delivered with the strength of the entire body, while the slash is executed solely by the elevation of the right arm and carries the weight of the weapon. On the other hand, a slashing blow can be performed more quickly than a thrust, and with the latter technique there was always the danger of getting the blade stuck. Nevertheless, raising the arm to make a slashing blow exposes the entire right side of the body. The swordplay itself had a typical scenario that pitted training and discipline against courage and individualism.

Roman swordsmanship – entirely alien to the Celtic manner of war – was the result of careful training and a comprehensive system of discipline. It was relentlessly aggressive and emphasised striking a single, deadly thrust with a minimum of effort, slicing and ripping through exposed bellies with razor-sharp sword jabs, while the Celts less successfully attempted to slash the shoulders or necks of the legionaries with hefty sword-blows. The main requirement for using the long slashing-sword was muscular strength, but the *gladius* required not only strength but science as well. Bio-mechanically sound and easy to learn, Roman swordplay was simple, direct and effective. It had only one objective: the swift demise of the enemy on the field of battle.[77] Celts, like other 'barbarians', always placed heroic deeds and a scorn of death above equipment and technique; in adopting the opposite attitude, 'civilised' Rome changed the nature and purpose of combat – and conquered triumphantly.

Chapter 2

The Forerunner

Our story starts with what the Roman nobility derisively called a *novus homo*, one who had no consuls among his ancestors. Yet despite the disadvantage of being a 'new man', the career of Caius Marius was the first one to pay scant regard to the constitutional rules of the Republic. Consequently, although conflicting and difficult to evaluate, the sources are extremely prejudiced. As he did not write his memoirs – Marius prided himself on being provincial – historians have tended to rely upon those of his contemporaries.

One important source is the memoirs of Lucius Cornelius Sulla, for instance, but Sulla thoroughly detested Marius and would become his bitterest foe. He was a patrician, not merely an aristocrat or a noble. But his branch of the Cornelii had long fallen into obscurity and straitened circumstances. Therefore it is highly likely that his history of Marius and his life reflects a strong anti-Marian tradition. A notable example of this prejudice is found in the accounts dealing with the battle of Vercellae (101 BC). On reading Plutarch, for instance, one wonders who actually won the engagement. Plutarch coolly states that Marius charged off into a cloud of swirling dust leaving his two subordinates, Sulla and Quintus Lutatius Catulus (*cos.* 102 BC), to beat the Cimbri. Perhaps here, Plutarch was using Sulla's *commentarii* as his source.[78]

Popular Politics

In many ways Marius' spectacular career was to provide a model for the great warlords of the last decades of the Republic. He was born in Cereatae into a family of the *domi nobiles*, that is, part of the local aristocracy that had considerable influence and power in nearby Arpinum (Arpino), a small, central Italian hill-town a three-day journey from Rome. The inhabitants of Arpinum had achieved full Roman citizenship only thirty-one years before Marius' birth. In 107 BC, just shy of his 50th birthday, Marius became consul for the first time; in all, he was to hold the position seven times, more than any man before. It was not simply the number that was unprecedented, but the nature, for he held five consulships in consecutive years between 104 BC and 100 BC, while the seventh he was to seize, as he had taken Rome itself, by armed force in 86 BC.

To modern eyes there is a clear-cut division between politics and warfare, even going so far as to discard war as a pivotal factor within our understanding of society. But war defined ancient Rome, so much so that no social or political aspect was divorced from events on the battlefield. Rome's expansion in the third and second centuries BC from an Italian city-state to the superpower of the Mediterranean world had been under its traditional form of government. Yet the overseas conquests led to a change in mentality among the ruling élite.

In the ancient world, wars of conquest usually showed a handsome profit for the victor. The immense wealth brought into Rome by its conquests and the opportunities and temptations offered by its empire put intolerable strains on the political and social system that had been adequate for a small city-state. As a result senatorial solidarity, which had made Rome a superpower, gave way to individualism. Increasingly generals who had achieved stunning military successes began to act on the basis of self-interest, keen as they were to acquire great personal power. The repercussions of this are not hard to guess. Internal rivalries began to emerge, leading to a power struggle that was fought out during the first century BC. As we shall discover, Sulla and Marius, Pompey and Caesar, Marcus Antonius and Octavianus were to be the leading players in the civil wars of the dying Republic.

Since the birth of the Republic the leadership of the government was firmly in the hands of the Senate, a governing body in which 300 members of the most prominent families served. Theoretically the Senate had no constitutional powers and its decrees, each known as a *senatus consultum* and passed on a majority vote, were not legally binding but merely advisory. It functioned, therefore, as a *consilium* or advisory council, advising the magistrates from its own ranks, with two annually elected consuls as the highest public officials who had equal power or *imperium*. Lesser magistrates were also appointed annually and in pairs, an expedient to allow them to veto each other and thereby prevent the concentration of power in one man's hands and preserve Rome from the ambitions of would-be tyrants. This principle of collegiality was basic to the Roman constitution.

Yet the power of the Senate was grounded in its permanence (membership was for life) and since the consuls were exclusively chosen from the senatorial families, the position of the Senate was strongly entrenched. Besides, it was a brave (or foolhardy) consul who chose to ignore the Senate's decrees. Indeed, the consulships were almost exclusively held by an even smaller group within the senatorial order, namely the *nobilitas*, the consulate not merely conferring power upon its holder and dignity for life, but also ennobling his family forever.[79] Little wonder, therefore, that the individual Roman aristocrat was under constant pressure, both of family duty and personal ambition, to emulate his ancestors by pursuing a public career and striving for the consulship.

Instruments of Power

Although not all citizens could even dream of climbing up the slippery pole of a senatorial career, let alone actually attempt to do so, all citizens could cast their votes in three popular assemblies, the *comitia tributa*, or tribal assembly, the *concilium plebis*, or assembly of the plebs, and the *comitia centuriata*, or assembly of centuries. The democratic character of the three assemblies differed significantly. In the first two assemblies, voting was done by tribes, a fabulously ancient division founded not on kinship groups but on a regional basis. It was an electoral-college 'one tribe, one vote' system in which the vote of every citizen, rich or poor, counted equally. It was here that the junior magistrates were elected: the quaestors (supervisors of the state's finances and records) and the aediles (responsible for public works and games). However, these assemblies were not entirely independent, since people's voting habits were regularly influenced by patronage ties and senatorial intimidation.

In the *comitia centuriata* the population was divided into five classes based on wealth. The wealthier citizens were in the first class and furnished the majority of the votes. In such a plutocratic system the election of praetors (responsible for the administration of justice and authorised to lead armies) and consuls (entrusted with general civil and military authority) was a matter for wealthy and well-descended Romans. In Rome's distinctive polity of 'mass' and 'élite', it was the poor inhabitants of the 'other Rome' who formed the overwhelming majority, who played no role in this assembly and were thus deprived of any real political power.

Optimates and *populares* alike were oligarchs drawn from the same exclusive group of wealthy and well-descended Romans, but they differed in the ways in which they played the complicated political system of the Republic. They were never organised into parties of a modern and parliamentary character; these are imaginary entities in the competitive arena of Roman politics. On the other hand, there was a tangible division of political approaches within the senatorial aristocracy, a partition that polarised their political methods and professed aims.

The Romans were careful to build checks and balances into their unwritten constitution. With the establishment of the Republic, the kings had been replaced not by a single officer but by a pair of annually elected consuls, coequal in power and authority. Tyranny was avoided because one consul could block the other. In a like manner, when the commons had wrested from the senatorial aristocracy the right to officers for their own protection, they grew in number until there were ten. Elected in the *concilium plebis*, the ten tribunes of the people (*tribuni plebis*) were sacrosanct (*sacer*) and had the right to veto (*intercessio*) the actions of other magistrates, including their fellow tribunes. They were even entitled to bring legislation directly before the people, without reference to the Senate, in the *concilium plebis*. A *popularis*, therefore, was an aristocratic populist who tended to bypass the Senate by enlisting the support of the tribunes and through them of the people at large.

The *optimates* were the more 'traditional' senators, self-styled 'good men', the 'best', which is the strict meaning of the term *optimates*. They were explicitly hostile to change, to challenges to the Senate's pre-eminence, to notions that matters of finance or senatorial privilege (and much else) could be taken directly to the popular assemblies and turned into legislation without any consultation, and prior approval, of the senators. In other words, these men were the defenders of the entrenched power of the Senate, and sticklers for the rules designed to uphold their dignity as senators and, most importantly, to ensure their conquering generals were prevented from using their armies to seize personal power. As our story unfolds it will become apparent that Pompey and Caesar were the penultimate pair in a succession of warlords who mobilised the Roman people as a means of winning and perpetuating political office.

Yet in the struggle for power in the closing years of the Republic, it was Caesar who took risks that his political rivals, Pompey included, were afraid to take, and that was what made him so dangerous to them. The orator and politician Marcus Tullius Cicero, a contemporary of Caesar who will loom large later in this story, reckoned 'there are two skills that can raise men to the highest level of *dignitas* [honour]: one is that of general, the second that of a good orator'.[80] Yet it was service in the army rather than a career in the courts, Cicero continues, which conferred the greatest personal status.[81] Cicero, a man not known for his military inclinations, appreciated the harsh reality that there was more glory to be won by extending the empire than by administering it. Moreover, succeeding in the arena of political life was an expensive business, but a foreign war offered unparalleled opportunities for winning glory and for enriching self and state, that is to say, the Roman people, at one and the same time.

A New Man

One of the bonds that held Roman society together was the relationship between client (*cliens*) and patron (*patronus*). This relationship came in a wide variety of forms and guises, but was always based on the mutual exchange of favours and benefits. Roman society was thus vertically structured in terms of obligation-relationships, called clientèle (*clientela*). At its crudest, a *patronus* offered protection to his *clientes*, who attended him and offered support and services in return. As the *cliens* of a privileged man might himself be the *patronus* of still less important men, *clientelae* could be mobilised as effective voting-machines. It takes little effort, therefore, for us to appreciate how much the *patronus-cliens* relationship could affect the workings of the Roman state. If a *patronus* were elected to political office his *clientela* could look forward to gaining some lucrative state contracts. The Romans saw nothing wrong or corrupt in a politician handing out state contracts to his *clientes*. It was simply how their political system worked.

Marius belonged to the *clientela* of the patrician Caecilii Metelli, one of the most prestigious families in Rome at this time, whom some, most notably Publius Cornelius Scipio Aemilianus (*cos.* 147 BC, *cos.* II 134 BC), called stupid.[82] Having risen past the Scipiones, who had held this position since the war with Hannibal, the Metelli had 'prevailed by their mass and their numbers'.[83] As early as 123 BC, when Marius became quaestor, this powerful family had taken a keen interest in his career, and it was the Metelli who helped him to gain a tribunate in 119 BC, when he was 38 years old. But he soon demonstrated that he was no flunky, successfully passing a plebiscite that allowed for the narrowing of the *pons*, the gangway across which each voter passed to fill in and deposit his ballot tablet.[84] To vote in the *comitia* a man mounted one of several bridges and walked along it to a platform, where he dropped his vote in an urn. The voters, of course, were viewed by everyone – in particular the aristocrats – and Marius was concerned about their methods of persuasion.

Little wonder, therefore, that the Metelli blocked his election to the aedileship, an office mainly concerned with public life at street level, two years later. The family intervened again when he stood for urban praetor for 115 BC, but this time they were unable to keep him out. Marius scraped in with the lowest number of votes possible, and as a consequence there were allegations of electoral bribery (*ambitus*). Whether this was a politically motivated prosecution, or one brought on merit, he prevailed at the trial, but only by the thinnest of margins. The number of votes for his guilt and innocence were equal, and he had to be given the benefit of the doubt.

In 114 BC Marius went as propraetor to Iberia, where he served as governor of Hispania Ulterior for the next two years. There he proved his competence, campaigning successfully against bandits while adding to his personal fortune by establishing the Iberian silver mines on a sound footing. On returning to Rome he married Iulia, the aunt of Caesar, which was a real political coup as the Iulii were a patrician family of the highest order.

The Ambitious Soldier

At a very early stage of his political career Marius had shown himself to be an independent man, who gained a great deal of popularity for his challenges to the *nobilitas*. However, it would be his reputation as a soldier that would make his name. Marius was by nature a soldier, as much in his later life would show, and he began his long military career as a cavalry officer, serving with distinction under Scipio Aemilianus, the greatest Roman of his generation, in the Numantine War (134–132 BC). Oddly, a young African prince called Iugurtha was also serving under Scipio Aemilianus as the leader of a Numidian contingent, made up of horsemen mostly, always the strength of that nation, and the same troops who had done such useful service for Hannibal in Italy two generations earlier. Iugurtha was an illegitimate grandson of Masinissa, who, after coming over to Rome's side during the closing stages of the war with Hannibal, had been awarded a kingdom. It was during the siege of Numantia that Iugurtha had earned Scipio Aemilianus' approval for his soldierly qualities, but it also encouraged a Roman belief that their most dangerous opponents were men whom they themselves had taught how to fight. Anyhow, the two young cavalry commanders were probably well acquainted and, like the Numidian prince, Marius was to enhance his reputation there when he killed an enemy warrior in single combat – and in full view of Scipio Aemilianus. For a man of relatively humble origins it must have looked as if the future belonged to him, unless his rivals devoured him first.

Marius went to Numidia in 109 BC as the senior legate under his *patronus*, the consul Quintus Caecilius Metellus, in the war against Iugurtha. This was the age of the Caecilii Metelli, who had held seven consulships in the last fifteen years. Obviously Marius had set himself right with the epoch-making house of the Metelli, whose sons became consuls by prerogative and were on the whole intransigent *optimates*, in the years following his provocative programme as a tribune.

The political geography of north Africa at this time was essentially quadripartite. In 146 BC, following the destruction of Carthage by Scipio Aemilianus, Rome had annexed the Carthaginian territories, creating the province of Africa (*provincia Africa*, roughly co-extensive to eastern and central Tunisia). This left to the Numidian king Micipsa much of the land his father Masinissa had appropriated from the Carthaginians, as well as his own kingdom (western Tunisia and eastern Algeria). To the west, in Mauretania (western Algeria and northern Morocco), was found the kingdom of Bocchus. In a long band along the pre-desert lived the Gaetuli, a group of tribes who lay outside the two kingdoms of Numidia and Mauretania and resisted any attempts to tax or control them.[85] In 118 BC Micipsa bequeathed his kingdom to his two legitimate sons Hiempsal and Adherbal, and also, following up an earlier recommendation of Scipio Aemilianus, to Iugurtha, the illegitimate son of his younger brother.

Ambitious and unscrupulous, Iugurtha was to put to death first one then the other of his cousins, by which he made himself master of Numidia. A senatorial commission, headed by a disreputable gentleman by the name of Lucius Opimius (*cos.* 121 BC), had been sent to settle Numidian affairs after the murder of Hiempsal. The Roman historian Sallust, who was keen to illustrate the moral decline of Rome, implies the delegation fell under the spell of Iugurtha and thus prudently recommended that the kingdom be divided between him and Adherbal. Apparently Iugurtha had discovered in Iberia the venality of many of the Romans.

Notwithstanding this settlement, four years later Iugurtha captured and sacked Adherbal's royal capital, the hill-top fortress of Cirta (Constantine, Algeria). After he had treacherously murdered both his rival and the Italian traders who had shared the defence of Cirta, the Senate as a matter of course decided on war. In spite, according to Sallust, of Iugurtha's lavish use of bribery,[86] the senators were bent on punishing the Numidian king, and after two unsuccessful campaigns (111–110 BC) they dispatched the quixotic but capable Metellus against him. Metellus repeatedly defeated him, but found it impossible to bring Iugurtha to heel. Now holed up in the Tell Atlas, Iugurtha would only skirmish with the Roman forces or fight them on his own terms. Though military incompetence was partly to blame, Sallust saw the constant failure to overcome Iugurtha as primarily down to the corruption of the senatorial aristocracy. It is interesting to note that he portrays the slippery Iugurtha both as the 'noble savage', immune against the corruption of Roman civilisation, and as the 'ignoble barbarian', a paradigm of 'Punic' perfidy.

War with Iugurtha

For our story one of the most important aspects of the war with Iugurtha was the extraordinary rise of Marius. Metellus had failed to bring the war to a swift conclusion, and seemed to be unable to physically capture Iugurtha. He therefore resorted to bribery, coupled with a policy of reducing the urban communities in Numidia, so as to deprive the king logistically. Marius was to employ the same strategy against Iugurtha, so we should be wary of any criticism of Metellus' conduct in this war. For instance, Sallust records the total massacre of the Roman garrison at Vaga (Beja, Tunisia), all bar its commander Titus Turpilius Silanus, after the town's betrayal to Iugurtha.[87] When Metellus retook Vaga he promptly put its inhabitants to the sword, and Turpilius himself was arrested and put to death. Sallust claims Turpilius was *civis ex Latio*, a Roman citizen of Latin origin, and thus could not be executed without a proper trial.[88] Yet it seems that Turpilius was only a first-generation Roman citizen and Metellus conveniently ignored his status and treated him as a non-Roman, and a treacherous one at that. Marius was to use this episode against Metellus in his campaign for the consulship.

Sallust describes how Metellus, when Marius asked permission to return to Rome to seek a consulship, exhibited the characteristic haughty arrogance of the proud, traditional, Roman nobility.[89] Sallust, who, after all, had been a partisan of Caesar before turning his hand to penmanship, suggests that Metellus was absolutely mortified that a man of Marius' background and social standing could even think of such a thing. Whatever his exact view of the matter, he flatly denied Marius' request. Sallust continues the story:

> When Marius kept on renewing his petition, he [Metellus] is alleged to have told him not to be in such a hurry to be off. 'It will be time enough', he added, 'for you to stand for the consulship in the same year as my son.'
>
> Sallust, *Bellum Iugurthinum*, 64.4

The patrician general's response was certainly spiteful, as his son was a lad only in his early twenties and currently serving on his father's staff. In other words, Marius could stand when he would be about 70 years of age. Marius could hardly have taken the jab with equanimity. Realising he could expect no support from his *patronus*, Marius started to look elsewhere. To this end he exploited the prevailing political atmosphere in Rome, thereupon making contacts of his own, particularly among the equestrians engaged in business in Africa, and building up his own reputation by claiming that he could bring Iugurtha to bay and end the war. Although elected on the equestrian and popular vote, Marius is best seen as an opportunist and not as a *popularis*.[90] He was simply exploiting popular feeling with regards to the apparent lack of swift action against Iugurtha – the war had dragged on and the expected Roman victory was not forthcoming – and thus cannot be regarded as 'anti-senatorial'. For four years Iugurtha had defied the might of Rome and many leading senators were believed to have accepted his bribes, and even some of the generals who had conducted the first campaigns against him were suspected of treason. In any event, they had been incompetent.

None the less Metellus' partisans in the Senate did not designate Numidia as a consular province, thus ensuring his continuing command there as a proconsul. It was a reasonable step on the Senate's part; the plodding but honest Metellus had done much better than his incompetent predecessors, even if his progress was slower than the people had hoped for, and he was familiar with the enemy and the army, an army hardened to campaigning in the hot wastes of Numidia. All in all he was the best choice to finish off the war and restore some of the old senatorial lustre. But it was not to be.

A tribune, Titus Manlius Mancinus, went before the people and called upon them to decide who was to take charge of the war in Numidia. And so a plebiscite was passed and the new consul Marius duly received what he wanted: the African command. There was no clear precedent for this, although it is extremely difficult to argue that his appointment was unconstitutional. In 205 BC, for example, Publius Cornelius Scipio was on the point of invading Africa when the Senate hesitated on giving him the green light. Livy records that Scipio was quite prepared to go to the people if the Senate did not give him Africa as his province.[91]

Despite being bitter, Metellus accepted the change in command – in 88 BC Sulla would not – and on his return to Rome he acquired the cognomen Numidicus for his endeavours against Iugurtha. As a matter of fact, Marius did not bring with him any new ideas on how to conduct or even win the war, but he did at least realise that to combat Iugurtha's guerrilla activities he would need more troops on the ground. Rome, however, was suffering a long-standing manpower shortage.[92] To this end, therefore, Marius took the decision to invite the *capite censi* to serve in the legions and, in the doom-laden words of Plutarch, 'contrary to law and custom he enrolled in his army poor men with no property qualifications'.[93] Volunteers flocked to join the legions and the Senate raised no protest. Yet, as we discussed at some length in the previous chapter, the fundamental nature of the Roman army was changed, transforming it from the traditional citizen-militia composed of a cross-section of the propertied classes into a semi-professional force recruited from the poorest elements of society. From now on legionaries saw the army as a career and a means of escaping poverty, rather than a duty that came as an interruption to normal life. Marius thus created, without realising it, a type of client army, bound to its general as its *patronus*.

Most of the men recruited by Marius undoubtedly were, or had been, members of the rural population, and an ex-peasant's idea of riches was his own smallholding. At the conclusion of the African campaign they would look to their wonder-general for rewards in the shape of plots of land. There is no evidence that Marius actually promised his proletariat recruits land when he enlisted them, but as consul in 103 BC he set about providing it. So, while he was training his new army for the approaching showdown with the Cimbri and Teutones, he proposed an agrarian bill seeking land in Africa for the veterans of the war with Iugurtha.

His legislation would be pushed through by the unscrupulous and brilliant tribune Lucius Appuleius Saturninus, a demagogue who frequently resorted to mob violence, and even – it was rumoured – assassination. We can, of course, argue that from now on the legions turned to their generals and not to the Senate for recompense, a case in point being when Sulla got his troops to march on Rome in 88 BC. However, such a view is far too pessimistic as not all soldiers would follow their general come what may. They would fight loyally in the defence of Rome when it was under threat, and were bound by oath to follow their appointed commanders, but they had no commitment to a political system that did little for them.

While helping the veterans was Marius' goal, it ought to have been a goal of the Senate too. Traditionally, the Senate had made no provision for discharged soldiers, letting them drift back home after their service, often to sink into poverty. But periods of service had lengthened, and it could not be ruled out that soldiers might be mobilised for years on end. Moreover, wars of conquest took armies far afield, and being uprooted in this way certainly hampered their chances of being reabsorbed into civilian society. Marius fought to see that this would not happen to the veterans of his campaigns. But ultimately it was the Senate that shirked this duty. It failed to recognise the new semi-professional army for what it was: an organisation with interests and concerns.

It is probably true that throughout Rome's history soldiers exhibited more loyalty towards a charismatic and competent commander. Therefore what we actually witness with Marius is not a change in the attitude of the soldiers but a change in the attitude of the generals. Judge for yourself. In 202 BC after Zama, if he had held revolutionary ideas, Scipio could have easily marched on Rome at the head of his victorious army. If we return to Sulla and his march on Rome, his officers were so appalled at his plan that all except one resigned on the spot, while his soldiers, though eagerly anticipating a lucrative campaign out east, followed him only after he had convinced them that he had right on his side. When envoys met Sulla on the road to Rome and asked him why he was marching on his native country, according to Appian he replied, 'To free her from tyrants'.[94] As for Marius, well, it probably never even crossed his mind at the time that Sulla would do the unthinkable. After all, a Roman army was not the private militia of the general who commanded it, but the embodiment of the Republic at war.

But let us return to our war in Africa with which we started this particular section. On assuming command there Marius soon found that it was not as easy to end the conflict as he had claimed back in Rome. Events now took an ugly turn with Marius adopting a deliberate policy of plunder and terrorism, torching fields, villages and towns and butchering the locals.[95] Moreover, he came very close to losing the war in a major battle not far from the river Muluccha (now the Moulouya, which forms the western boundary of Algeria), and Sallust hints that it was Marius' quaestor, Sulla, who saved the day.[96] We can be fairly certain that Sulla wrote this up in his *commentarii*. They are lost, but Sallust read them and made use of them in writing his account of the war. In the end Sulla befriended Bocchus, the king of the Moors[97] and father-in-law of Iugurtha, and what follows was Sulla's dramatic desert crossing, which culminated in Iugurtha's betrayal and capture. This bit of family treachery thus terminated a war full of betrayals, skirmishes and sieges. Sulla had the incident engraved on his signet-ring, provoking Marius' jealousy.[98] Nevertheless, Marius was the hero of the hour. On 1 January 104 BC he triumphed on the same day he entered his second consulship.

The war with Iugurtha had been a rather pointless, dirty affair. The king was publicly executed, but the Senate did not annexe Numidia, giving instead the western half of the kingdom to Bocchus as the reward for his treachery, and the eastern half to Gauda, Iugurtha's weak-minded half-brother. Yet it had made Marius' reputation and begun Sulla's career. More than that, it saw Marius and Sulla fall out over who was responsible for the successful conclusion to the war, a quarrel that was to cast a long sanguinary shadow on Rome.

War with the Northern Tribes

While Rome had been busy chasing Iugurtha, the Cimbri and Teutones, who were most probably Germanic peoples originally from what is now Jutland, moved south and inflicted a series of spectacular defeats upon the Roman armies. They now became Marius' next concern. Rome had always been obsessed with tribal invasions, more so in 113 BC after the consul Cnaeus Papirius Carbo was routed by the Cimbri at Noreia (Neumarkt, near Ljubljana). The Senate had dispatched Carbo to keep them out of Italy. These Germanic tribes knew something of Roman power even if they were strangers to Rome, and they agreed to pull back from the peninsula. Carbo unwisely attacked them anyway, in the hope of an easy victory over the northerners. It did not turn out that way. Iulius Obsequens, diligently recording his prodigies for that year, recounts that the 'Cimbri and Teutones crossed the Alps and made an awful slaughter of the Romans and their allies'.[99]

Following Carbo's defeat another tribe, the Celtic Tigurini (one of the tribal groupings of the Helvetii), joined themselves to the Cimbri-Teutonic alliance and ventured into Gaul with them. In 109 BC the three tribes circled back from their jaunt in Gaul. Near the frontier of Gallia Transalpina, the new Roman province, they came up against an army led by the consul Marcus Iunius Silanus. Doubting the outcome of a battle they offered to serve Rome in return for land. The Senate declined the offer, and the Tigurini then cut to pieces Silanus' army but, as with the case of Carbo four years earlier, the Celts did not follow up their advantage. The Cimbri and Teutones continued west through Gaul, while the Tigurini broke off to raid Gallia Transalpina.

In 107 BC Marius' colleague in the consulship, Lucius Cassius Longinus, advanced to recover the situation; he followed the Tigurini toward the Iberian frontier where he was defeated and killed in an ambush. The survivors were permitted to withdraw after passing under the yoke.[100] This was a complete and utter humiliation as the yoke was made of two spears fixed upright, with a third fastened horizontally between them at such a height that the defeated soldiers filing under it were obliged to stoop in token of submission. It must have been doubly galling that the Tigurini had chosen this gesture since it was an ancient Italian custom.

Although Rome's fortunes recovered somewhat in 106 BC the worst was still to come, for the following year was to witness the rout and destruction of two consular armies under Quintus Servilius Caepio (*cos.* 106 BC), now proconsul after the expiration of his consulship, and Cnaeus Mallius Maximus, one of the current consuls, at Arausio (Orange) in Gallia Transalpina. With allegedly 80,000 casualties, this was the biggest disaster to befall Roman arms since Cannae, and bickering between the two commanders was said to have been a major contributory factor here. Instead of turning east to cross the

Alps, the Cimbri and Teutones moved south into Iberia and remained there for the next three years. Italy had been spared what would no doubt have been a major invasion akin to that mounted by the Gauls in 390 BC when they briefly occupied and sacked Rome itself, all save the Capitol.

In the autumn of 105 BC a pro-Marian lobby secured for Marius a second consulship, which broke all the constitutional rules since he was not even in Rome for the election but still in Africa. Yet it does appear that Marius had the backing of the Senate as Gallia Transalpina was given to him as his consular province. Fifty years later Cicero would pose the following rhetorical question in the Senate:

> Who had more personal enemies than Caius Marius? Lucius Crassus and Marcus Scaurus dislike him, all the Metelli hated him. Yet so far from voting against the grant of the province of Gallia Transalpina to their enemy, these men supported the extraordinary command of that province to him so that he might command in the war against the Gauls [i.e. Cimbri and Teutones].
>
> Cicero, *De provinciis consularibus*, 28

Marius was to be elected consul a further four times (103–100 BC, *cos.* III–VI), thus giving him six consulships to date. Actually these other consulships were more like generalships. There are other examples of Roman generals retaining command of an army during a period of tumult, Quintus Fabius Maximus Cunctator during the initial years of the war with Hannibal, for instance. The vital difference, however, lies in the fact that when the year of their consulship ended these commanders were given proconsular rank. There was no precedent for Marius' string of back-to-back consulships, an offence to the idea of limited tenure of office.

The last four consulships can be seen as a popular measure, the people asserting that Marius was the man they wanted in command and that he should remain so for as long as they desired. Naturally Marius neatly exploited popular politics to achieve this unprecedented career because he could have had his command continued after his second consulship as a proconsul. But that meant he would only remain in command at the whim of the Senate. What is more, as was glaringly illustrated by Caepio, a *nobilis*, and Mallius, a *novus homo*, the working relationship between proconsul and consul could be fraught with danger. As a consul, Marius was firmly in charge and thus unassailable. As a matter of fact, apart from the rout of the army of his consular colleague Catulus early in the campaign, Marius was extremely successful, defeating the Teutones and their Celtic allies, the

Ambrones, at Aquae Sextiae (Aix-en-Provence) in 102 BC (*see* pp. 18–19) and, with Catulus, whose powers had been extended as proconsul, the Cimbri one year later at Vercellae (Vercelli) on the dusty plains of northern Italy.

The day was an extremely hot one, it being shortly after the summer solstice, and the adroit Marius had his soldiers advance through the dust and haze. To the consternation of the Cimbri, the Romans suddenly charged upon them from the east, with their helmets seeming to be ablaze from the shining of the sun's rays. In a ferocious struggle the Cimbri were cut to pieces, and it is reported that no fewer than 120,000 of their warriors were killed and 60,000 were captured.[101] The war leader of the Cimbri heroically fell in this battle, fighting furiously and slaying many of his opponents.

Although he consented to celebrate a joint triumph with Catulus, Marius claimed the whole credit for the victory at Vercellae. Likewise, in popular thinking all the credit went to Marius. Catulus and Sulla, on the other hand, gave very different accounts of the battle in their memoirs. The patrician Sulla, who had joined Marius and Catulus for the northern war, naturally took the latter's side. This was not only out of a personal dislike of Marius but also because of a natural bias toward the senatorial aristocracy, whose dangerous and bloody champion he would be.

With six consulships and two triumphs, Marius had created an extraordinary precedent. He was now a man above the system, a forerunner of Pompey and Caesar. However, at the time Marius' unconstitutional position did have a certain amount of logic to it as he was no revolutionary and the system had worked to his advantage. The other extraordinary aspect was the temporary nature of Marius' influence.

Political Wilderness

There is an old Latin expression *gladius cedet togae*, 'the sword gives way to the toga'. If a man would be great, he must be great at home too. After his defeat of the northern tribes, Marius was hailed by the people as the third founder of Rome, a worthy successor to Romulus himself and Camillus – the old saviour from the war with Brennos the Gaul, the sacker of Rome. However, the year 100 BC, the year of his sixth and penultimate consulship, saw the great general fail disastrously as a politician. Marius would desert the tribune who had aided him, Saturninus, and stand by as an angry mob lynched him and his supporters.[102]

The firebrand Saturninus had been re-elected as one of the tribunes for the coming year, proposing yet more radical bills, but the Senate, who saw the spectre of tribunician government raise its ugly head again, called on Marius to protect the state. Having restored public order under the terms of a *senatus consultum ultimum*, both literally and efficaciously 'the ultimate decree of the Senate', the veteran general subsequently saw his popular support slip away. The nineties BC were to be a decade of political infighting of the most extreme sort, and one of its first victims, according to Plutarch, was Marius.[103] Yet his actions in 100 BC can be seen as a bungling attempt to announce his arrival to the nobility of Rome. Of interest here are Sallust's remarks concerning the monopoly of the *nobilitas* on the consulship:

> For at that time, although citizens of low birth had access to other magistracies, the consulship was still reserved by custom for the *nobilitas*, who contrived to pass it from one to another of their number. A *novus homo*, however distinguished he might be or however admirable his achievements, was invariably considered unworthy of that honour, almost as if he were unclean.
>
> Sallust, *Bellum Iugurthinum*, 63.4

Sadly for Marius, to the *nobilitas* he would always be, despite his unprecedented six consulships and two triumphs, a *novus homo*. Despised by the inner élite and shunned by the equestrians and the people, Marius was now cast into the political wilderness. In early 98 BC Metellus Numidicus was recalled from exile – Saturninus had orchestrated this for Marius two years previously – and Marius, having tried to delay the return of his one-time *patronus*, admitted defeat and scuttled off to Asia 'ostensibly to make sacrifices, which he promised to the Mother of the Gods'.[104] The following year he did not stand, as was expected, for the censorship, a clear sign that he was not in the political spotlight.

Marius wanted to beat the *nobilitas* at their own political game, substituting self-made support for their inherited connections. Showing little flair for politics, it did not occur to him – as it would have done to Sulla and Caesar – that the rules of the game could not be changed. Though connected to the equestrians by birth and interests, and favouring the welfare of soldiers (including Italians, whom he truly valued as allies), he had no positive policies or solutions for the social problems of the day. As an individual he was superstitious and overwhelmingly ambitious, but, because he failed to force the aristocracy to accept him, despite his great military success, he suffered from an inferiority complex that may help explain his jealousy and, later, his vindictive cruelty. Yet he marks an important stage in the decline of the

Republic: creating a client army, which Sulla would teach his old commander how to use, he was the first to show the possibilities of an alliance between a war leader, demagogues and a noble faction. His noble opponents, on the other hand, in their die-hard attitude both to him and later Sulla, revealed their lack of political principle and loss of power and cohesion.

Social War

In 91 BC the tribune Marcus Livius Drusus, the son of the tribune of the same name who stirred up popular opposition to Caius Gracchus back in 122 BC, took up the cause of the Latin and Italian allies – the *socii*. A fascinating individual, Drusus had set out, much like his father before him, to gain popular support for the Senate through a whole raft of legislation designed to appease the people, including the planting of colonies. But he lost this support, and his life, when he proposed a bill that would grant Roman citizenship to the *socii*. It was now clear to the Italians at least, certainly those of the aristocracy, that Rome would not budge an inch and thereby see fit to address their grievances.

For the origins of this terrible internal conflict Appian goes back in history to a proposal of Marcus Fulvius Flaccus (*cos.* 125 BC) whereby the *socii* should be rewarded with some form of citizen status. The author then moves on to describe Gracchus' legislation, and finally comes round to that of Drusus.[105] Unfortunately, in doing so Appian has obscured the whole issue, because Flaccus did not create the desire for Roman citizenship. Secondly, as the demands of the *socii* were roundly rejected in 122 BC, why did war break out in 91 BC and not then? Thirdly, the proposals of both Flaccus and Gracchus included the granting of the right of *provocatio*, the protection against improper acts committed by holders of Roman *imperium*. This was certainly considered as a possible alternative to citizenship. However, in 91 BC no such alternative was even contemplated. This time the *socii* demanded of Rome full citizenship. Here we are dealing with a changing mood, the gradual desire for equal privileges. It was clear in the second century BC that some people in Italy wanted citizenship and could gain it by moving from their community to Rome. On the other hand, it is not at all clear that the bigger groupings of people, especially those in southern Italy, were keen to lose their own identity.

The issue of equal privileges boiled up in the one-twenties because of the Gracchan land reforms. The Gracchan commission was touring Italy and confiscating land from various Italian communities. Needless to say, to them it seemed an arbitrary mechanism as they had no means of recourse.

Therefore, some *socii* insisted on the franchise for protection and also for the gains that could be made under other Gracchan reforms. This certainly answers the case for *provocatio*. Furthermore, the number of *socii* fighting in Rome's wars overseas was increasing and, unlike their Roman counterparts, these soldiers were fighting for little or no reward. In one case at least, which is mentioned by Polybios, the *socii* received only half the battlefield spoils awarded to Roman citizen-soldiers.[106]

At some point, probably around 124 BC, the magistrates of the Latin communities certainly attained the grant of citizenship and thus the aristocracy of these communities sought similar privileges. In fact, the driving force behind the revolt of 91 BC would have been the local aristocracies. Four years previously the *lex Licinia Mucia* had established a special court of inquiry (*quaestio*) in order to prosecute those who falsely claimed Roman citizenship. It is not at all clear what particular abuse the Romans had in mind. However, we do hear of the prosecution of Titus Matrinius from Spoletium. Under Saturninus' legislation Marius had been granted the right to create Roman citizens so that new colonies could be founded. The colonies, however, were not set up, but Matrinius still claimed Roman citizenship, and Marius defended his *cliens* successfully.[107] Asconius (b. 9 BC), in his commentary on Cicero's speech *pro Cornelio*, makes an interesting comment on the effects of the *lex Licinia Mucia*:

> At a time when the peoples of Italy were fired by an enormous appetite for Roman citizenship and for that reason a large number of them were passing themselves off as Roman citizens, it seemed necessary to carry a law to restore everyone to his proper legal citizenship status in his own native place. However, so alienated were the leaders [*principes*] of the Italian peoples by this law that it was *perhaps* [my italics] the chief cause of the Social War, which broke out three years later.
>
> Asconius, 67

Although, as some would claim, this law was not the chief cause of the Social War, or *Bellum Marsicum* as the Romans knew it after the Marsi, the first people to revolt, it did make clear that Rome was going to remain exclusive, particularly with regards to the *patronus-cliens* system and the *cursus honorum*, the legal career structure that brought an ambitious Roman aristocrat a range of civil and military posts. And so Drusus made one last attempt, failed, and war was the result. This would prove to be the most dangerous war since that against Hannibal. As then, Rome found itself, quite literally, at sword's point with many of its allies.

The revolt began with the lynching of a certain Roman proconsul by the name of Quintus Servilius, along with his staff, in the theatre at Asculum Picenum (Ascoli Piceno), followed by the murder of all the Roman citizens in the said town, but the conflict itself did not commence until early 90 BC. It was then that the rebels set up the independent state of Italica (or Italia), which was centred round Corfinium – like Rome, the capital was centrally located within Italy. Two commanders-in-chief (*imperator, embratur*) were elected, as were twelve praetors (for the twelve rebel peoples), and a senate instituted. In other words, the confederation paid Rome the compliment of closely modelling the constitution of the new state along Roman lines, although some rebel coins depicted the bull, the emblem of the Sabellian peoples, trampling (or worse) the Roman she-wolf. The erstwhile allies also mustered soldiers and raised an army. Soon, it was said, 100,000 troops were under arms and ready for battle.[108] Italy was divided into two provinces, each given to a commander-in-chief in the Roman way. The north-western province (Marsic sector) was given to the Marsic noble Quintus Poppaedius Silo, who had been a close friend of the murdered tribune Drusus, and the south-eastern province (southern sector) went to the Samnite Caius Papius Mutilus; each was given six praetors as lieutenants to help them conduct the war.

Rebels

1. North-central Apennine peoples: Marsi, Paeligni, Vestini, Picentes and Marrucini (Latin speakers)
2. South-central Apennine peoples: all four Samnite groups, namely Pentri, Caudini, Hirpini and Carricini, as well as Frentani, Apulians, Lucanians and Bruttii (Oscan speakers)
3. Some Campanian towns coerced into rebellion
4. Some Etruscan and Umbrian communities (briefly in late 90 BC)

Loyalists

1. All Roman citizen communities and colonies
2. All Latin communities except Venusia (Aesernia later taken by rebels)
3. Italiote-Greek cities of southern Italy
4. Most Etruscan and Umbrian communities
5. Northern Campania and other *socii* where Roman presence was well established (e.g. among the Hernici, communities like Teanum Sidicinum)
6. Rome's northern Italian *socii* and overseas allies

By no means did all the *socii* revolt. We have already seen how the majority of their aristocrats had received Roman citizenship through the exercise of magistracies. Moreover, as the textbox shows, all but one of the Latin communities remained loyal to Rome: the rebel town of Aesernia, some 150 kilometres south-east of Rome, was strategically important as it stood astride the Via Latina at a point where it passed between the Samnite and Marsic territories. Nevertheless, the war was hard fought and can be divided into two main theatres of operation: the north, centred round Asculum Picenum, and the south, initially centred on Aesernia in central Campania but later shifting to southern Campania, Samnium and Apulia. It was a fierce struggle, fought between similarly equipped and trained armies, the rebel soldiers being legionaries in all but name. The actual fighting, which was bloody and far from one-sided, can be summarised as follows:

Year **Events**

90 BC Rome organises a large-scale mobilisation of troops in Italy, putting at least fifteen legions in the field. Marius, now 67 years old, finds himself once more in the limelight and serving the Republic in a military capacity. There are some initial Italian successes in the south, but stalemate in Campania. Publius Rutilius Lupus, one of the consuls for that year, is killed in the Marsic sector fighting against Poppaedius Silo.

89 BC The tide begins to turn and Rome slowly gains the upper hand over the rebels. The consul Cnaeus Pompeius Strabo, whose son would rise to the greatest of heights some two decades later, finally breaks the siege at Firmum. He then ends the year with the capture of Asculum Picenum, having inflicted a massive defeat on the rebel army dispatched to its relief. His colleague Lucius Porcius Cato, in contrast, suffers defeat and is killed fighting against the Marsi in central Italy. Meanwhile in the southern sector Sulla, serving as a legate, gains a string of victories over the Samnites and their allies, and is granted a triumph by the Senate for killing more than 6,000 of the rebels. This enhanced a reputation that had been steadily growing since his desert exploits in Numidia. For his actions in the field he would be voted one of the consuls for the following year.

88 BC Defeat and surrender of rebels in central Italy and Apulia (Nola, Aesernia and Volaterrae alone remain in rebel hands). Poppaedius Silo is killed in battle against the forces of Quintus Caecilius Metellus Pius, son of old Metellus Numidicus. Metellus Pius takes Poppaedius Silo's remaining contingents into his own army, and it appears that the effect of the extension of Roman citizenship is at work here. So much so, that only the Samnites remain in arms by the year's end.

Italians become Romans

Rome was faced with the prospect of the collapse of its power in the peninsula. Hence the *lex Calpurnia* apparently permitted Roman commanders to bestow citizenship as a reward to individuals and units on the field of battle, as Marius had done back in 101 BC to three cohorts of Umbrians and two of Camertians for outstanding valour at Vercellae.[109] We have an inscription recording the grant by Pompeius Strabo of Roman citizenship to thirty Iberian horsemen for such services outside Asculum Picenum, but it specifies that this was done 'in accordance with the *lex Iulia*'.[110] The *lex Iulia*, carried out at the end of 90 BC by the consul Lucius Iulius Caesar, hurriedly granted Roman citizenship en masse to the Latin and Italian communities who had stood by Rome. Lastly, in 89 BC the *lex Plautia Papiria* cleared the issue up for the others, as did the *lex Pompeia* of Pompeius Strabo, which granted Latin rights (*ius Latii*) to the inhabitants of Gallia Cisalpina.[111] And so, except for a few die-hard Samnite bands, by 88 BC this unnecessary war was virtually over. Rome had won as much by conciliation as by military force.

Virtually everybody living south of the Padus (Po) was now a full citizen of Rome, which meant the creation of ten new voting tribes in the *comitia tributa*.[112] Though these fresh tribes voted after the Romans of the thirty-five earlier tribes, making their vote often useless, this enfranchisement was to have a tremendous effect upon the socio-political life of the Republic. It was now clear to all that large numbers of former *socii* would be flooding into Rome to vote, making for a very volatile situation, which could, and did, disrupt the popular assemblies. Moreover, there was now a host of *novi homines* muscling in on the act. Also, for those Italians lower down in the social order of things, there was no longer any question of separate allied contingents in the Roman army. And indeed, the new prospects of enlistment, especially in view of the opportunities provided by Marius' military reforms, must have gone far to conciliating the aggrieved Italians.

There was, however, one immediate political repercussion of the war. The tribune Quintus Varius Hybrida proposed a law on treason (*lex Varia de maiestate*), which instituted a special court of inquiry (*quaestio Variana*) allowing the prosecution of those who had 'advised' the *socii* to revolt.[113] Obviously this manoeuvre was an orchestrated attack on the supporters of Drusus. And so, a lot of rising stars in Rome were snuffed out.

Meanwhile Out East

The kingdom of Pontus, with its royal seat at Panticapaeion, had once been an out-of-the-way satrapy of the Achaemenid Persian empire, but after the time of Alexander the Great its rulers had established themselves as an independent dynasty. The population may have contained Greek, Thracian,

The Pontic Art of War

Though Mithridates himself was of royal Persian ancestry, his army was a direct descendant of that of Alexander the Great. His power base was northern Anatolia, but his recruiting grounds extended to the north of the Black Sea and as far west as mainland Greece. Thus the Pontic army was a characteristic mélange of Near-eastern and Hellenistic elements. His cavalry included the Iranian and Cappadocian minor nobility of the inland foothills, Pontic Sarmatians, Scythian horse-archers, and Armenian *cataphractarii* and horse-archers. This was not only far superior in number to the Roman cavalry but better in quality. Above all, Roman legionaries felt extremely nervous about facing Armenian *cataphractarii*, horsemen armoured head to toe, without an obstacle such as a ditch in front. At Orchomenos Sulla took up a defensive position and set his men to digging entrenchments. As he had intended, they soon grew tired of the excavation and showed a willingness to fight.

Mithridates' infantry included Greeks from the littoral *poleis* of Anatolia, the Black Sea and mainland Greece, foothill peasants with bows, wild Galatian warriors from the hilly centre of Anatolia, and a *sarissa*-armed phalanx of freed slaves. When his Macedonian-style phalanx failed to stand up to the legions of Rome successfully, he replaced the phalangites partly with peltasts, lightly-equipped infantry, and partly with imitation legionaries of his own, trained by Marian exiles. His big battlefield speciality was the use of four-horse scythed chariots intended to be driven at speed into an enemy unit to at least break up its formation. On two occasions this worked, but on others they were successfully countered.

The Romans found that the Pontic phalangites fought well but with no better result than had earlier been achieved by other *sarissa*-armed phalanxes, such as that of Philip V of Macedon or Antiochos III Megas. Although in theory the phalanx should have a crushing superiority over legionaries, in no historical engagement did it demonstrate this, the invariable result being a slow slogging match that continued until it was settled by the phalanx falling into disorder or having its flanks exposed and then enveloped. On the other hand, the Pontic imitation legionaries do not seem to have fought any differently than their opponents, but there were never enough of them to be a decisive factor.

Finally, a word or two about scythed chariots. These 'weapons of mass destruction' could be very dangerous if allowed to get up full speed before they collided with their target. Their biggest success was against Rome's client-king of Bithynia, Nikomedes IV, when they charged a pursing Bithynian phalanx in the flank and were immediately supported by charging cavalry and peltasts. At Chaironeia they broke through one of Sulla's legions, only to be destroyed by javelins on the far side. Alternative methods of dealing with them were to counter-charge them before they had gathered speed or to plant obstacles in their path such as stakes. On the whole, a Pontic chariot charge was admirably heroic, stunning effective – and terribly costly.

Scythian and Celtic elements, but it was dominated by a well-established Iranian aristocracy, and its kings adopted, or at any rate affected, Greek culture. Mithridates VI Eupator of Pontus (r. *c.* 113–65 BC), with whom we are concerned, had presented himself as a champion of Greek civilisation, and in this role had given military protection to the Greek states dotted along the northern shores of the Black Sea, firmly imposing his authority in this region. As a result he had ready access to fertile grain-growing lands and to the resources of wealthy Greek maritime states, including a substantial navy. Mithridates, a wily opportunist, would wage a series of wars with the Romans in an effort to drive them from Asia and Greece.

In 98 BC, despite Marius having warned him to curb his territorial ambitions, Mithridates invaded Cappadocia, a land to which he had some territorial claim. Two years later the Senate sent Sulla east as propraetor to Cilicia on the southern coast of Anatolia. He had apparently gone to check piracy, a perennially favourite pastime of the Cilicians, but had also managed to install Ariobarzanes, who was a Roman friend, on the throne of Cappadocia.[114] Mithridates had already been told to give up that kingdom and Paphlagonia as well, but the Senate's command had not, by itself, proven enough. Sulla had marched off on his mission using only local levies. During his little campaign, which he played with his usual skill, Sulla's forces had clashed with those of Tigranes, king of Armenia (r. 96–*c.* 56 BC). While nothing came of it directly, Tigranes threw his lot in with Mithridates, and married his daughter.

In 91 BC Mithridates once again appeared at the head of a massive, westward-moving army. He seized Cappadocia for a second time – and Bithynia – with the aid of his son-in-law Tigranes, and the Senate, once again, ordered him out. Two years later Manius Aquillius, Marius' old comrade-in-arms during the war against the northern tribes and his colleague as consul in 101 BC, was eventually dispatched east by the Senate to confront Mithridates and drive him back to his own territories. Aquillius joined local levies with the troops of Lucius Cassius, proconsul of Asia, and threw Mithridates out of Cappadocia and Bithynia, installing Nikomedes IV as the new ruler of Bithynia. However, Aquillius went beyond his brief and, in exchange for the liberation of his kingdom, extorted a large sum from Nikomedes, who, manifestly, could not pay. Therefore, under pressure from the Roman general, the Bithynian king was encouraged to raid across the border into Pontic territory. Mithridates lodged a formal complaint to the Senate.[115]

Diplomatic niceties observed, Mithridates then exploited the foray of debt-ridden Nikomedes by invading his kingdom (First Mithridatic War, 89–85 BC).

Defeating the Roman forces four times in quick succession, he not only gained Bithynia, Phrygia, Mysia, Lycia, Pamphylia, Ionia and Cappadocia, but the Roman province of Asia too, which he started to dismantle. In the summer of 88 BC, when Rome's grip had already been loosened, 80,000 Italian inhabitants of the province – men, women and children – were reportedly massacred in one single, deadly day.[116] To crown this stunning reversal, Aquillius himself fell into the hands of the vengeful king, who, according to Sallust, had him executed by the theatrical expedient of pouring molten gold down his throat as a punishment for his rapacity.[117]

The Battles of Chaironeia and Orchomenos, 86 BC

Sulla, with an army of fewer than 15,000 legionaries and some 1,500 cavalry, confronted a Hellenistic-type Pontic army allegedly of 100,000 infantry and 20,000 cavalry – a colourful mix of eastern troops, among them Pontics, Cappadocians, Thracians and Bithynians – and 60 scythed chariots commanded by Mithridates' top general, Archelaios, a Cappadocian by birth. The battle was fought on the Boiotian plain just north of Chaironeia, a provincial town in central Greece.[118]

As Sulla marched southwards across the plain, he was obliged to turn his column left into line of battle to meet Archelaios' approach. Sulla opened the battle by attacking a Pontic detachment, whose retreat had to be covered by a chariot charge. This manoeuvre failed, but gave time for the Pontic phalanx to deploy. Although recruited from poor quality material, including freed slaves, this *sarissa*-armed phalanx managed to hold off the legionaries while the Pontic cavalry broke through to its right. Sulla ordered five cohorts from his reserve to protect their outflanked comrades, but these were encircled and soon in serious difficulties themselves. Sulla arrived in person with his cavalry from the right wing and flung Archelaios back.

The Pontic cavalry then withdrew and began to transfer to the opposite flank, while the Pontic infantry made a fresh attack on the Roman centre. Sulla reacted by dispatching four more cohorts from his reserve to aid his centre, and with three cohorts and his cavalry returned to his original position on the right wing and attacked, breaking the enemy cavalry which had returned disorganised. A general advance then pushed the Pontic army into a defile from which, it is said, only 10,000 escaped.

The second engagement was fought again on the Boiotian plain, but this time near the town of Orchomenos. As the ground was treeless and level Sulla dug entrenchments on his flanks to hinder the superior Pontic cavalry.[119] However, the cavalry attacked the Roman working parties, which Sulla had to rally in person, precipitating the battle. According to Plutarch, as Sulla pushed his way through his fleeing men he grabbed a standard and dared them to leave him to the enemy, roaring at the top of his voice: 'As for me, Romans, I can die here with honour; but as for you, when you are asked where it was that you betrayed your general, remember and say it was at Orchomenos'.[120] A similar story is told of Caesar at Munda.

The initial Pontic chariot charge, obviously designed to crack the Roman line of battle, failed when the legionaries fell back to disclose a row of stakes. Sulla then ordered a counter-attack with lightly armed troops. The chariots, their horses maddened by arrow and javelin wounds, broke, disordering their own phalanx as they swept off the battlefield. In an act of desperation, Archelaios tried to rally them by dispatching cavalry from his wings to intercept them. His weakened wings were then immediately broken by Roman cavalry charges. Though the Pontic cavalry suffered relatively light casualties in the battle, the camp in which they took refuge was carried by assault the following day and most of the fugitives perished in the nearby marshes as they attempted to escape the slaughter. Archelaios himself, however, was able to slip away.

It appears Mithridates was no ordinary enemy of Rome. Persecuted by his wicked mother as a child, the young prince had been forced to take refuge in the mountains of north-eastern Anatolia. Here he lived wild for seven years, outrunning deer and outfighting lions, or so it was said. Nervous that his mother might still have him murdered, Mithridates developed a morbid fascination for toxicology, taking repeated antidotes until he was immune to poison. Finally returning at the head of a conquering army to claim the throne, Mithridates ordered his mother killed, and then, just for good measure, his brother and sister too. Of course such legends are partly the product of mythologising, especially by Roman authors; for Mithridates became in the collective Roman psyche an archetypal enemy alongside such *bêtes noires* as Brennos and Hannibal.

Meanwhile in Rome one star that was burning brightly was the charismatic Sulla, erstwhile lieutenant to Marius but now a power in his own right, and a dangerous one at that. Thus when the Senate declared war on Mithridates, it was Sulla, as the former propraetor of Cilicia and one of the new consuls for 88 BC, who was assigned the governorship of Asia and the military command against the Pontic king.[121]

Sulla Marches on Rome

However, during that year a tribune and former associate of Drusus, Publius Sulpicius Rufus, clashed with Sulla and his colleague Quintus Pompeius Rufus over Italian voting rights. The new Romans had found their brand-new citizenship a rather dilute thing as they had been allotted to ten tribes (and hence ten votes). As their champion Sulpicius proposed to reform the tribal system and enrol the new citizens in the thirty-five old tribes so that their right to vote would not be utterly vitiated.

Up against stiff senatorial opposition and needing further support for his reforms, Sulpicius adopted a more radical stance and allied himself with Marius, who in turn wanted the tribune's help to obtain the lucrative command against the Pontic king. Violence erupted on the streets of Rome and Pompeius Rufus' son, who was related to Sulla by marriage, was one of the victims. During the rioting Sulla himself was forced to seek refuge in Marius' house, later managing to flee the city. Sulpicius was now in power and his programme of measures, including the bill transferring the eastern command to Marius, was passed by vote of the people. The septuagenarian general had stepped down from command during the later stages of the Social War pleading age and fatigue, but the glory and booty that would result from a successful campaign in the richest area of the Graeco-Roman world were undoubtedly great inducements for a second comeback.

When a tribune had done something similar in 107 BC, taking the command against Iugurtha from Metellus and handing it to Marius, Metellus had acquiesced in the decision of the people, whatever sense of outrage he may have felt. The response of Sulla, now at Nola preparing to depart for the east, was to be entirely different and revolutionary.

With his soldiers behind him, Sulla marched on Rome and after a few hours of street-fighting imposed martial law for the first time in Roman history; Sulpicius and Marius were declared *hostes*, or public enemies. Sulpicius was hunted down and killed, but Marius, after a series of hair-raising adventures that saw him outfacing contract killers, made a spectacular escape to Africa where he was *persona grata* among the settlements of his own veteran soldiers.

Sulla had earned the dubious distinction of being the first man to march his legions against Rome, and Appian recalls his justification for doing so:

> When Sulla discovered this [i.e. the transfer of the eastern command to Marius], he decided to settle the matter by force and summoned his army to a meeting, an army that was eagerly anticipating a profitable war against Mithridates and thought that Marius would enlist other men in their place. . . . [Sulla] immediately placed himself at the head of six legions. Except for one quaestor, the officers of his army made off to Rome because they could not stomach leading an army against their own country. On the way, Sulla was met by a deputation who asked him why he was marching under arms against his native land, and he replied, 'To free her from tyrants'.
>
> Appian, *Bellum civilia*, 1.57

Appian waxes lyrical here, but it is clear that the event was traumatic as all Sulla's officers bar one refused to march with him, the rest resigning their commands and hurrying to the defence of the city. What had changed was not the attitude of the army and its officers, but that of their general. Sulla had dared to do what others scarcely dared to dream.

First Civil War

The following year Lucius Cornelius Cinna, a *popularis*, and Cnaeus Octavius, an *optimate*, were returned as consuls. Octavius was a tractable man, but Cinna attempted to re-enact Sulpicius' legislation on the voting rights of the new citizens. He also recalled Marius, but was driven out of Rome along with six of the tribunes by his colleague, who supported the status quo – namely not allowing the new citizens to be fairly distributed among the voting tribes.

Washing up outside Nola, where the Social War still flickered, Cinna appealed to the one legion Sulla had left to continue the siege, and also to the rebel Italians within. In the meantime, after long months brooding in Africa, Marius had landed at Telamon in Etruria. Recruiting a personal army of slaves, he joined forces with Cinna, and then turned on Rome. There Marius quickly introduced tribal reform, and even granted the unbending Samnites full citizen rights. Psychotic with rage and bitterness, he then ordered Rome to be systematically purged of anti-Marians, including Octavius, along with six *consulares*, Marius' old campaigning colleague Catulus among them.[122] But the main opponent, his erstwhile protégé Sulla, had already gone east with five legions to fight Mithridates.

The capstone of this orchestrated bloodbath was that Cinna and Marius made themselves, without the formality of an election, consuls for the coming year. Marius had held the consulship an unprecedented six times. He liked to claim that a fortune-teller in Utica had promised him a seventh. Early in 86 BC Cinna (*cos.* II) and Marius (*cos.* VII) tightened their grip on Rome. However, Marius quickly abandoned himself to alcohol abuse and nightmares. A fortnight later he was dead.

The following year Cinna chose Cnaeus Papirius Carbo, who had been a praetor during the Social War, as his colleague, and the two would remain self-appointed consuls until 84 BC, a period known as *dominatio Cinnae*. They appointed censors so as to begin a full registration of new citizens, and a detailed reorganisation of local government in Italy now commenced, and would continue for decades.

Sulla Marches on Rome, Again

Out east in the meantime Sulla had won a number of spectacular successes against Mithridates and against the Marian commander Caius Flavius Fimbria, sent by Cinna to replace him. Fimbria had fought well against Mithridates too, but in 85 BC lost his army to Sulla and committed suicide. In 84 BC Sulla held a summit with Mithridates himself. Both men had good reason to come to an agreement. Mithridates, knowing the game was up, was desperate to keep hold of his kingdom. Sulla, nervous of his enemies back in Italy, was eager to head home. The hurried result was the Peace of Dardanus, which not only allowed Mithridates to remain on the throne of Pontus but also to retain some of his territorial gains. The cold-blooded murder of 80,000 Italians was conveniently forgotten.[123] Yet the time would come when Rome would regret that Mithridates had not been finished off for good.

Sulla's troops spent a luxurious winter in the fleshpots of Athens, binding them more closely to him. The relationship between political and military power was abundantly clear to the successful and ruthless Sulla, and it was now that the victorious proconsul dispatched an ominous letter to the Senate. The government he had established before his hurried departure had collapsed and Sulla himself had been declared a *hostis* at the behest of Marius and Cinna, his property razed, his family forced to flee. 'However', as Appian says about Sulla and his outlaw status, 'in spite of this he did not relax his authority in the least, since he had a zealous and devoted army'.[124] Now that Mithridates had been tamed, Sulla prepared to embark his loyal troops and turn his vengeance back on his native city.

At Rome events moved on apace. While Sulla was talking peace with Mithridates, Cinna (*cos.* IIII) had been stoned to death by his own troops during a mutiny, thus leaving Carbo (*cos.* II) as the sole consul for the rest of the year. Carbo, struggling with a moderate majority in the Senate and despite having pandered to the newly enfranchised communities, was eventually forced to take hostages from many towns and colonies in Italy to ensure their loyalty in the coming showdown with Sulla. As the acceptable face of the Cinnan régime, Lucius Cornelius Scipio Asiagenus and Caius Norbanus were returned as consuls for the coming year.

Early in 83 BC Sulla landed at Brundisium (Brindisi),[125] and large numbers of senators and sons of senators flocked to his side, including the young Pompey. Unlike his first march on Rome, when only a single officer had accompanied him, Sulla's entourage was now thronged with members of the *nobilitas*. By changing the rules of the political game, civil wars encouraged even more exceptional careers among those who supported the winning side and, as we shall later discover, that of Pompey was to break all records. Alas for the losers there was no such luck: Scipio Asiagenus' soldiers judged they would do better to serve under the lucky Sulla.

In 82 BC Caius Marius minor, not yet 27 years old, was consul alongside the veteran Carbo (*cos.* III), and they attempted, through a Marian–Cinnan coalition, to reassert control after a string of defeats. Despite many of his father's veterans coming to his standard, Marius was eventually holed up in the hill town of Praeneste, some 40 kilometres east of Rome. Once again the Samnites, for the last time in history, marched down from their mountains and entered the war. They joined a Marian cause already on the point of collapse, but failed to lift the siege, and then, with the sudden realisation that Rome lay unprotected to their rear, abruptly turned and marched on the capital. Abandoned by his new allies, Marius minor committed suicide, while Sulla, surprised by the Samnites' action, pursued them at frantic speed. Throwing his exhausted army into battle outside the city walls, by dawn on 2 November he emerged unbeaten from the bloodbath of Porta Collina. It had been a close call. The Samnites had marched on Rome not from loyalty to old Marius' memory, but 'to pull down and destroy the tyrant city'.[126]

Chapter 3

The Rise of Pompey

When Cnaeus Pompeius was almost 18 years old Sulla marched on Rome at the head of his legions, hardened and disciplined soldiers, demanding that he and not Marius should have command of the campaign against Mithridates of Pontus. The Senate capitulated. After a few hours of vicious street-fighting Sulla imposed martial law, and twelve men, including Marius, were declared *hostes*. Mission accomplished, Sulla then left Rome and marched against Mithridates, leaving his followers to be butchered by his political enemies. Five years later, after having driven Mithridates back to his own territory, Sulla returned to Italy and marched once more on Rome.

The Dictator

After defeating the supporters of Marius outside Rome by the Porta Collina, Sulla had himself appointed *dictator rei publicae constituendae*, 'dictator with responsibility for settling the state', reviving the old supreme magistracy, but did so without placing the six-month limit on its powers. On the day he took control of Rome he addressed the Senate. While he was speaking, terrible screams arose from the Circus Maximus where the prisoners from the battle, Samnites chiefly, were being put to death. Sulla merely said to the queasy senators that he was having some malefactors dealt with.

His reign would prove to be brief but savage. He immediately took control through the retrospective validation of his acts, or *acta*, and oversaw the first full-scale proscription in Roman history. His enemies were killed with impunity and their property confiscated and sold, thereby exacting political revenge and filling the coffers of the state at one and the same time. One man, seeing his name on the list of the proscribed, commented ironically 'I am being hunted down by my Alban estate'.[127] He had not gone far before he was apprehended and dispatched by a ruffian.

This terrible list, which was posted in the Forum, declared as outlaws some 40 senators and 1,600 equestrians initially and then more in the next few days; it was a terrifying thing and long remembered.[128] With a price to be paid for their heads, the victims were tracked down like wild beasts – in their houses, in the streets, even in the temples. Some were formally executed, some murdered by Sulla's paid killers, some lynched by mobs. 'Some were murdered after being proscribed, others proscribed after they had been murdered.'[129] Here, indeed, there was revolutionary terror. The Sullan proscription cost lives and violently transferred property, and it also meant that the sons of the proscribed were barred from holding public office.

The dictator did not stop there; indeed 'not until Sulla had glutted all his followers with wealth did the slaughter at last come to an end'.[130] For Sulla also proscribed whole communities, particularly the pro-Marian towns of Etruria, and confiscated their territories for having opposed him during the recent civil war. The territories of Volaterrae and Praeneste, for example, were confiscated and turned into *ager publicus* as if they had behaved like Rome's enemies. Sulla settled his veterans on some of the expropriated land, men loyal to himself. Thus the territory of Praeneste was shared out and allocated, while that of Volaterrae was left as it was. The same year, ominously, Quintus Sertorius' term as governor of Hispania Ulterior expired.

The following year Sulla, still as dictator, celebrated a triumph over Mithridates, passed reforms of the state, and closed the proscription. In 80 BC, as well as being dictator, he shared the consulship with a man who had led an army to victory for him, Quintus Caecilius Metellus Pius, the son of Metellus Numidicus. Impaired by the rise and domination of the Marians, the Caecilii Metelli gained power and influence again from their alliance with Sulla. Metellus Pius had earned his cognomen Pius, which means 'devoted and reverent', after he had begged the people to permit his beloved father to return from exile. This he won, in the words of Valerius Maximus, 'by his tears as others have done by their victories in war'.[131] In the meantime Pompey, over in Africa, was gaining victories for Sulla (and a name for himself) against the Marians.

At the beginning of 79 BC, however, Sulla laid down the dictatorship and retired into private life, 'fearing neither the people at home nor the exiles abroad nor the towns which he had deprived of their citadels, defences, land, money, and immunity from taxation'.[132] While Sulla gloried in his bohemian retirement, Metellus Pius was sent as proconsul to recover Iberia from the 'guerrilla' leader Sertorius. He was roundly beaten. Still, on the home front the Sullan régime had fared better. Nola had finally fallen to Roman arms, having been under siege for almost a decade, while the last rebel strongholds of Aesernia and Volaterrae were to be brought back into state control shortly after.[133]

In 78 BC Sulla, a private citizen, died in his bed – most probably of liver failure. His body was brought from Naples by a huge escort of veterans to be cremated after a public funeral in Rome, the first known for a Roman citizen. A vast procession accompanied the body to the Forum where the finest orator of the day spoke out on Sulla's deeds, and 2,000 crowns of gold were said to have been donated as gifts from various towns and from the legions that had served under him.[134] Thirty-five years later this state funeral would be excelled for the next dictator, Sulla's only superior.

More of the Same

In the days of the Soviet Union, whenever there was a stellar shake-up in the Politburo, the popular sentiment on the streets was one of 'new suits, old policies'. In a similar manner, Sulla's comprehensive programme of legislation was purely reactionary. By nature and breeding he was deeply conservative, a Roman aristocrat with very traditional views. It was the Senate that had guided Rome to greatness, prevailing over Hannibal, sweeping away great monarchies and famous empires, conquering the Mediterranean world. In looking back over the troubles of the last fifty years, Sulla wanted to re-establish the predominant power of the Senate, which meant that its predominance over the magistrates and the people must be assured. His means of accomplishing this was to suppress all possible opposition to the Senate, particularly the bogey of government by tribunes, and not to redress the evils that had led to the recent internal wars. His constitutional reforms for the restoration of the Republic – in reality a policy of re-establishing senatorial control over the state – can be conveniently summarised as follows:[135]

Lex Villia annalis

A law of 180 BC, which had set the order and minimum ages at which men could be appointed to the various magistracies, was reinforced, thereby regulating the *cursus honorum*: from quaestorship to praetorship to consulship, only a single path to the top with no possible short cuts. The principle of biennium was introduced too, in other words a two-year gap between promotions, and a rule was made that no man should be re-elected consul until an interval of ten years had elapsed since his previous consulship. By re-regulating the tenure of magistracies, dangerous iterated commands or extraordinary commands were prohibited, which in turn curbed the rise of an ambitious general, a would-be Marius.

Tribunate

The ten tribunes of the people, annually elected public officials who not only had the celebrated veto over bills they disliked but also shared with the consuls and praetors the right to propose laws in the popular assembly, lost the right to initiate legislation and trials before the people without prior consultation with the Senate. Furthermore, they were debarred from standing for any higher magistracy after the tribunate. All in all, these measures were designed to protect the state from dangerous tribunician reformers, men such as Saturninus, who was considered to have succumbed to the lure of easy popularity with the mob. The tribunes were now effectively crippled, and the tribunate a rung on a ladder leading nowhere. Quaestors and praetors might dream of the consulship, but not tribunes.

Quaestors and praetors

The number of quaestors was raised to twenty, and from now on the office would serve as the portal through which a man entered the Senate. The most junior magistracy, quaestors were either employed in Italy where they were responsible for the administration of public funds, or attached to provincial governors or generals in the field, whom they assisted by discharging day-to-day administration. Similarly the number of praetors was raised to eight, thereby providing enough of these senior magistrates to oversee the new law courts set up under the Sullan reforms.

Provinces

By now it had become customary to appoint pro-magistrates instead of magistrates as governors of the provinces. Sulla standardised this, ruling that consuls and praetors should remain in Italy during their year of office, and in the following year be sent as proconsuls and propraetors to govern the provinces. As there were now ten provinces in all, the increase from six to eight propraetors meant (with the two proconsuls) there were sufficient pro-magistrates to govern the provinces annually. As hitherto, the command of the army was to be entrusted to the provincial governors, and Sulla introduced a *lex de maiestate*, a treason law, circumscribing their military behaviour. In short, governors were now forbidden to leave their provinces or to engage in war without the proper authority of the Senate. In an ironic twist that would shadow his entire programme of constitutional reforms, Sulla's task as dictator was to ensure that in future no one would ever again do as he had done and lead an army on Rome.

Legal system

An important part of the Sullan settlement was a major shake-up of the state legal system. Seven standing courts (*quaestiones perpetuae*) were instituted or reformed with senators as the jurors. Caius Gracchus, some forty years earlier, had debarred senators from this service – and source of patronage – in the hope of securing less lenient verdicts against members of the senatorial order, especially provincial governors accused of dishonesty in their province. The seven courts, each presided over by a praetor and composed of a number of senators, were *quaestio de repetundae* (extortion), *maiestas* (treason), *ambitus* (electoral bribery), *sicariis et veneficiis* (murder and poisoning), *parricidium* (parricide), *peculatu* (embezzlement) and *falsum* (fraud). The problem of the equestrian control of the courts was thus solved, while, more importantly, the rule of law reinforced the Sullan system.

Senate

Before giving the juries back to the Senate, Sulla enlarged it by the addition of 300 newcomers. Naturally rewarding those who had supported him, Sulla put members of the equestrian order in the house also. The rift between the two orders was now healed without incurring the loss of power and *dignitas* among leading equestrians, while the losses of the recent internal wars were made good too. Moreover, as mentioned already, he made tenure of a quaestorship an automatic qualification for membership of the Senate, so it could maintain itself.

Citizens and colonies

Sulla freed 10,000 slaves of the proscribed, who become known as Cornelii after him. Appian dryly comments: 'In this way he made sure of having ten thousand men among the plebeians always ready to obey his commands.'[136] A number of pro-Marian communities in Etruria, which had evidently opposed Sulla, were disenfranchised, while colonies were planted in suspect areas (e.g. Pompeii, Fiesole, Abella, Hadria, Volaterrae, Spoletium, Capua and Praeneste), many of the colonists being none other than Sullan veterans, numbering some 120,000 men according to Appian.[137]

Public revenues

Revenue-gathering in Asia, Rome's favourite mulch-cow, was temporarily taken away from the tax-farming cartels (*publicani*). As the *publicani* paid dearly for the right to do the job and duly set the level of tribute exacted high enough to ensure themselves a healthy profit, this sensible act was intended to allow Asia to recover after the depredations of the First Mithridatic War and the war indemnity imposed by Sulla.

Politically Illiterate

Caesar, according to Suetonius, would later declare that Sulla did not know his ABC of politics.[138] Naturally Suetonius was humouring his readership here by the use of delicious irony. Both Sulla and Caesar employed military force to take over the state, but that is where the similarity ends. For Sulla used his legions to revive the Republic, Caesar to kill it. Moreover, Sulla laid down the reins of power once he had achieved his goals, Caesar, on the other hand, revelled in autocracy and after 44 BC had no notion of laying it aside. Finally, Sulla died in his bed, while Caesar came to a spectacularly violent end at the hands of men he considered friends. What Sulla realised, but Caesar did not, was that the men who joined him did so not for his benefit but for their own.

Caesar certainly stands high in the eyes (and pens) of many modern commentators. Sulla, on the other hand, is ordinarily given a bad press, being blamed for what Caesar eventually did. But Sulla marched on Rome so as to restore the Republic; not so Caesar. Naturally the case against Sulla is strengthened by the fact that he was the first Roman general to march on Rome. For that matter, Sulla earns the dubious double distinction of being the one man in history to attack both Rome and Athens. As Velleius Paterculus would later remark, Sulla was a 'man who, at the very point of victory could not be praised enough, nor after victory reviled enough'.[139] This would be the common consensus of opinion after his death.

On the whole modern opinion is fiercely anti-Sullan and tends to ignore the issue of whether or not Sulla was driven to do such a thing. Furthermore, scholars even suggest that the literary sources are tainted with Sullan propaganda and compensation should be made for this. If you want to paint Sulla as a depraved, egotistical and pretentious noble, you must also look at what he did, namely retire after the gradual dismantling of his power base. The key to this particular conundrum is relatively simple. Despite those who identify strongly with the 'great man' theory of history, nobody obtains extraordinary power without support from others, without a following. It is obtuse to talk of charismatic figures such as Alexander, Caesar, Napoléon, Hitler, or even Saddam Hussein for that matter, as having reached a position of supreme power through sheer personality alone. As the great historian Ronald Syme rightly reminds us mere mortals, 'Undue insistence upon the character and exploits of a single person invests history with dramatic unity at the expense of the truth'.[140]

We have already noticed that when Mithridates made as if to avenge the appalling Roman misdeeds in the province of Asia by butchering, it was said, some 80,000 resident Italians, Rome needed a strong commander to take charge. Sulla, who had distinguished himself in the recent fighting in Italy, was one of the consuls and accordingly was dispatched east by the Senate. Here we should note that when Marius was made consul for the first time the Senate tried to keep the province of Africa out of his hands, but the tribunate proposed otherwise and Metellus went along with this. However, in 88 BC Sulla was a consul while Marius, who had long had his greedy eye on the Mithridatic command, was only a private citizen – a mere *privatus*.[141]

There are a number of examples of ex-magistrates being awarded commands, especially during the war with Hannibal. In addition, there was a notable precedent to Mancinus' proposal to give Marius the Numidian command: that of Scipio and the command in Iberia after the deaths there of his father and uncle. It seems, therefore, that Sulla acted unconstitutionally when he marched on Rome, and the Senate certainly voiced its horror over his actions. Sulla, for his part, did try to justify his march on Rome, that is to say, 'to free her from tyrants'.[142] Therefore he did not tell his soldiers to march on their fatherland, quite the contrary; it was their patriotic duty to oust the demagogic tribunate. This they did, and Sulla instituted reforms and free elections.

We now move into territory where it is difficult for us to see what was right and what was wrong. Even for Cicero, a young contemporary, the rights and wrongs of the political situation were nigh impossible to untangle. As he was later to comment: 'It may be said that Sulla or Marius or Cinna acted rightly. Legally, perhaps; but their victorious régimes were the cruellest and most sinister episodes in our history.'[143] Yet one distinguished scholar reasons that the Cinnan régime was a period of normality, citing a passage from Cicero where the great orator claims it was a period of three years without civil war.[144] His argument rests on the fact that a number of *consulares* stayed on in Rome and cooperated with Cinna, such as the censors of 86 BC, Marcus Perperna (*cos.* 92 BC) and Lucius Marcius Philippus (*cos.* 91 BC). But no right-minded *nobilis* could resist the opportunity of holding the censorship, and Philippus eventually came over to Sulla and would become the *princeps senatus* – father of the house.

Another of those who remained in Rome was the current *princeps senatus*,

Lucius Valerius Flaccus (*cos.* 93 BC), but he tried to bring about *concordia* between Cinna and Sulla. Rome's high priest, the *pontifex maximus* Quintus Mucius Scaevola (*cos.* 95 BC) also stayed, but he certainly did not endorse the régime; in fact he was murdered during the last days leading up to Sulla's take-over.[145] It seems prominent men weathered the storm and many actually tried to distance themselves from Cinna. Cicero, when he was forced to make a choice between remaining in Italy and coming to terms with Caesar or fleeing overseas with Pompey, thought of how Philippus and others under Cinna 'had temporised when necessary, but had taken their opportunities when they came'.[146]

Sulla's Men

The young Cicero too had lived under Cinna and his associates, but what of the men who were not in Rome? Caius Scribonius Curio is a good example. His father, for all his talents, had failed to make it to the consulship, and his death while Curio was still very young explains why Curio never had a formal education and rhetorical training. Nevertheless, he still succeeded in making a name for himself as an orator in the nineties. He was drawn by his father-in-law Lucius Memmius into the circle associated with Drusus, the radical tribune of 91 BC. Following the collapse of Drusus' schemes, the outbreak of the Social War provided his opponents with an opportunity to break the careers of those who had openly supported Drusus. Having fled condemnation under the *lex Varia de maiestate*, we next hear of Curio serving with distinction with Sulla in the east. He returned to Italy with Sulla, benefited from the proscription, renewed his public career and reaped the reward with the consulship of 76 BC.

The career of Caius Aurelius Cotta, one of Curio's peers, followed much the same course; a good start as an orator, association with Drusus, prosecution in the *quaestio Variana*, flight, return with Sulla, a belated consulship in 75 BC. To this list can be added the sons of those murdered during the purge of Marius and Cinna, such as Marcus Licinius Crassus, Metellus Pius and, last but not least, Quintus Lutatius Catulus, the son of Marius' colleague of 102 BC. All were young men whose careers had been shattered and Sulla offered them new hope of high office.[147]

At the time Cicero would portray Sulla's success as a victory for the Roman *nobilitas*.[148] The dictator knew what these men wanted and thus recreated a political arena for them and laid down the ground rules for their orderly return to public office. Seen in this light Sulla's resignation from the dictatorship is no puzzle. It was assumed from the start to be a temporary post to restore order and to introduce the settlement. Once the *cursus honorum* had been restored, the men who reached the top would not tolerate the continued existence of someone with exceptional powers who might limit their *libertas*. Sulla gave them the freedom they wanted. In the following two decades those who had come over to his side would queue up to attain the climax of the republican pecking order, the consulship.

Sallust, a historian who delights in developing the themes of luxury and liberty to explain political change, devoted one of his trademark set-pieces to Sulla.[149] He describes Sulla's superior intellectual powers, and his equal appetites for glory and pleasure. He was not only a man of eloquence, shrewdness and generosity, but also one with a capacity to make friends. All these traits were combined with a gift for dissimulation, which appealed to Sallust's interest in what lies behind outward masks, because Sulla 'was deep beyond belief in his capacity for disguising his intentions'.[150] Only a man such as Sulla could have given the *nobilitas* new hope. What he appreciated, but Caesar did not, was that the men who joined him were there for their own glory and not for his.

Cursus honorum

In the days of the early Republic there was no fixed order or set age for holding magistracies. However, from the later third century BC onwards a legal career structure developed. Known as the *cursus honorum* – literally 'the course of honours' – this socio-political construction was constitutionally formalised by a law of 180 BC, the *lex Villia annalis* of Lucius Villius. For our purposes, the ladder of public offices can be best summarised as follows:

1. Early years

At the age of 17 a young aristocrat commenced his military service, perhaps first as a junior cavalry officer followed by a spell as a military tribune; he could also undertake some legal work, perhaps a minor post such as a circuit judge or supervisor for street cleaning; thence by gradually building up his *curriculum vitae*, a hopeful young man was exposed to the public eye.

2. Quaestorship

A minimum of ten years' military service was a necessary qualification for the quaestorship – *quaestor* literally means 'investigator' and reflects the pre-republican origins of this magistracy

Power: without *imperium* but did hold *potestas*, the legal sanction to allow discharge of duties
Duties: aided consuls and provincial governors, especially with financial matters; controlled the state treasury (*aerarium Saturni*), which was not only a store for public money but also for copies of statutes and other state documents
Number: originally two, but more were created as the complexity of running a world empire increased, to number twenty under Sulla – two of them served in Rome (*quaestores urbani*); one accompanied each holder of *imperium* to his province to act as financial officer; others performed administrative functions in Italy, one being in charge, for instance, of the grain supply coming to Rome from Ostia

3. Aedileship

Needed to have served as a quaestor before becoming an aedile
Power: without *imperium* but did hold *potestas* greater than that of quaestor
Duties: maintained roads and water supply; supervised traffic and markets; organised public games and festivals
Number: four – two plebeian aediles elected in the *concilium plebis*, and two curule, that is, patrician, aediles elected in the *comitia tributa* and representing the whole people
Privileges: *ius imaginum*, the right to display wax death masks of famous ancestors in atrium of house; curule aediles could use the curule seat (*sella curialis*), a special folding chair made of ivory

4. Tribunate

After the quaestorship, a plebeian could be elected a tribune of the people
Power: without *imperium* but did hold *potestas* greater than that of quaestor; had power of *intercessio* (veto over decisions of Senate or any magistrate) and *ius auxilii* (right to help), thereby able to prevent arbitrary attacks on any plebeians; could summon the *consilium plebis* and there pass resolutions called *plebiscita*
Duties: to look after the interests of the people; to protect their lives and property; to be always accessible to the people
Number: ten
Privileges: tribunes were not magistrates, and the tribunate was technically outside the *cursus honorum*; but they were protected by a religious taboo against any attacks (*sacrosanctitas*), that is to say, they were considered *sacer* (sacrosanct), which made them inviolate and anyone injuring or killing a tribune could be killed with impunity

5. Praetorship

The minimum age for the praetorship was 39, and a man also had to have been aedile before becoming a praetor
Power: held *imperium* (sovereign power in war and peace); the holder of *imperium* could compel obedience except from someone with greater *imperium*; power of life and death in battle, which was symbolised by an axe (*securis*) enclosed in a tied bundle of rods

(*fasces*) carried by the lictors, their bodyguard attendants, who walked in front; in peace only *fasces* were carried by their lictors, while *intercessio* and *provocatio* (right of appeal against arbitrary treatment by a magistrate) limited *imperium*
Duties: running civil and criminal courts; could summon assemblies and propose legislation if the consuls were busy (or dead); governing smaller provinces; leading armies (technically, of one legion only); had right to consult the gods (*auspicium*) through the auspices (*auspicia*) – the antiquarian Messalla, writing in the late Republic, appropriately describes them as 'colleagues of the consuls'[151]
Number: originally one, then two (242 BC), later four (227 BC), then six (196 BC), and eventually Sulla made the total up to eight, the senior being the urban praetor (*praetor urbanus*) responsible for the administration of private justice within the city of Rome
Privileges: accompanied by six lictors; could use curule seat; worthy of a triumph (200 BC onwards)

6. Consulship

Since 150 BC, or thereabouts, 42 years of age was the minimum age for the consulship
Power: *imperium* superior to everyone else except a dictator
Duties: summon and chair Senate and assemblies in peace; propose bills (*rogationes*) to create legislation; had right of *auspicium*; oversee the common good of the Republic; lead armies in times of war (technically, each commanded a consular army of just two legions) – 'In the elections for consuls', Cicero said in a speech when he was consul, 'it is generals that are chosen, not legal experts'[152]
Number: two
Privileges: accompanied by twelve lictors; could use curule seat; wear purple-fringed *toga praetexta*; worthy of a triumph; gave their name to the year

7. Censorship

After having held the consulship one could be elected a censor, a magistrate who was normally appointed once every five years
Power: without *imperium* but did hold *potestas* greater than that of aedile
Duties: conducting the five-yearly census, which gave information on property and wealth and thus determined military obligations, tax obligations and corresponding political rights; revising the list of the Senate to include ex-magistrates of previous five years; control of public morals (could place a mark of disgrace against anyone and expel members of the senatorial or equestrian orders for conduct unbecoming; supervise public lands (*ager publicus*) and let public contracts; had right of *auspicium*
Number: two
Privileges: use curule seat; wear *toga praetexta*

8. Dictatorship

When no consuls had been elected, an *interrex* would normally be appointed, for five days at a time, until the elections had been held. However, in times of dire emergency

the consuls themselves could appoint a dictator – full title *dictator rei gerundae causa* ('dictator for the purpose of carrying on the business of the state' – the other magistrates acting as his subordinates
Power: held double-consular *imperium*
Duties: running all military and domestic affairs in time of crisis; office lasted six months; assisted by a *magister equitum* (master of the horse)
Number: one
Privileges: accompanied by twenty-four lictors and *fasces* always included the *securis*, even within Rome

As we can now appreciate, these magistracies were of differing importance, and an ambitious Roman aristocrat had to seek them in ascending order (quaestorship, aedileship, praetorship, consulship, censorship). There had to be a gap of at least a year between magistracies, so that a magistrate could be called to account after his term of office. Candidates for public office rarely stood for election on the basis of particular policies, instead relying on their reputation for ability. It was system that heavily favoured a small clique of wealthy aristocratic families who were skilled at promoting their virtues and the successes of former generations and implying as much or more could be expected from younger members of the family. With only two posts for the consulship per annum, competition for this high honour was fierce, especially since a mixture of law and tradition prevented anyone attaining this rank before their early forties, and was supposed to prevent it being held twice within ten years.

Perilous Adolescence

The son of the thoroughly dubious and ruthless character Cnaeus Pompeius Strabo, the younger Pompey had inherited not only the largest private estate in Italy but also some of his father's unpopularity. After his father's death he was accused, unsuccessfully as it turned out, of helping himself to the spoils of Asculum Picenum. As will be recollected, Pompeius Strabo had held the consulship of 89 BC and had fought fiercely against Italian rebels in the north during the Social War, notably taking Asculum Picenum by siege. In the words of Florus:

> Pompeius Strabo made a universal waste by fire and sword, and set no end to the slaughter until by the destruction of Asculum he avenged the spirits of so many armies, consuls, and plundered towns.
>
> Florus, *Epitome*, 2.6.14

A massacre of Roman citizens at Asculum Picenum had heralded the revolt, and it was news from that same town that enabled the Romans to celebrate their first decisive victory of the war. Pompey was with his father at the time, serving on his advisory council alongside 'Lucius Sergius son of Lucius',[153] who was almost certainly the infamous Catiline.

Yet Pompeius Strabo's career was marred by duplicity and a strong suspicion that he had tried to collude with Cinna. He was also accused of a ferocious rapacity for money and was believed to have procured the assassination of a consul, none other than his kinsman and Sulla's colleague, Pompeius Rufus. He eventually sided against Cinna and Marius, but following an inconclusive engagement just outside Rome he died all of a sudden. 'Hated by heaven and the *nobilitas*',[154] one tradition says he was struck by lightning during a storm, another that he had fallen victim to a virulent disease that swept through his camp. Such was his massive unpopularity that his funeral procession was mobbed and his corpse ditched in the mud. His son Pompey may have learnt to read by studying a eulogy of his father's achievements, but he was also to learn another early lesson from the pitiless and perfidious Pompeius Strabo: the scope for dissimulation and the unprincipled use of soldiers who would become their leader's private army. Yet he himself was to serve as an example to others: the holding of senatorial office was not an essential qualification for leading Roman armies.

Pompey remained in Italy during the Cinnan régime, but discreetly retired to the ancestral lands in Picenum (Marche), on the Adriatic slopes of the Apennines, after threats were made against his life – so discreetly it was rumoured that Cinna had had him murdered. When Sulla landed at Brundisium in early 83 BC, Pompey was not slow to notice the vast number of aristocrats flocking to Sulla's standard in the hope of reviving their political careers. Thus on his own initiative he raised a private army of three legions from his father's veterans and *clientelae* in Picenum and marched south to join Sulla. Hailing the young Pompey *imperator*, the appellation traditionally awarded to a victorious general, Sulla ordered the tyro general north to clear Gallia Cisalpina of the Marians. After Sulla's victory outside the walls of Rome, his surviving opponents fled: Cnaeus Domitius Ahenobarbus, the son-in-law of Cinna, went to Africa, Carbo, who was still legally a consul, and Marcus Perperna Veiento to Sicily. Out in Iberia, meanwhile, Sertorius became a focus of anti-Sullan resistance.

Pompey was next ordered to Sicily with six legions and a senatorial grant of extraordinary *imperium pro praetore*. Once there he quickly cleared and secured the island, capturing and putting Carbo to death after a show trial – earning for himself the insulting nickname of *adulescentulus carnifex*, 'teenage butcher'.[155] However, Perperna managed to escape and joined Domitius Ahenobarbus. Pompey crossed over from Sicily to Africa and swiftly thrashed the leftover Marians, who had gained the support of a Numidian pretender named Iarbas. Pompey restored the throne to the legitimate king Hiempsal, and was hailed by his victorious troops as *imperator*. He then received instructions from Sulla ordering him to discharge all his troops save one legion, which was to stay in Africa. His army, however, had other ideas.

Returning to Rome with his legions still under orders, he hankered after a triumph but met with Sulla's stern opposition. Sulla pointed out that triumphs were for appointed praetors or consuls – at 24 years of age, Pompey had yet to hold a quaestorship – and, besides, triumphs for victories over Roman citizens were in bad taste. Unabashed, Pompey insisted, saying ominously 'that more people worshipped the rising than the setting sun'.[156] Sulla could obviously have crushed Pompey with ease if it came to a real showdown, but he probably felt that this was a quarrel that would bring him more trouble than profit. The ageing Sulla therefore yielded and even, though perhaps with a touch of sarcasm, confirmed Pompey's cognomen Magnus, 'the Great', awarded him by his army. A genius for self-promotion was to be one of the defining characteristics of Pompey's rapid and remarkable rise to power and glory.

The Triumph

On 12 March 80 BC Pompey was to celebrate the first of his three triumphs. The triumph (*triumphus*) was a procession from the *campus Martius* to the temple of Iuppiter Capitolinus on the Capitol, the most sacred spot in Rome. Here the triumphator gave thanks for his victory, which must have been substantial to merit this sort of celebration. At least 5,000 of the enemy must be dead. The campaign had to be conducted by a senior magistrate of Rome and the war concluded. The triumphator also needed permission from the Senate to retain his military rank inside the sacred boundaries of Rome (*pomoerium*), and uniquely he was to be allowed to bring his troops into the city.

On the grand day a solemn procession, headed by the Senate and including prisoners of war, entered the city. Behind this, leading his victorious army, came the triumphator himself, riding in a four-horse chariot, festooned with laurels. He wore a toga of purple and gold (*toga pica*), much like an ancient king of Rome, and held a laurel branch in his right hand and an ivory sceptre topped with an eagle in his left. His face was painted red for the day like the most sacred statue in Rome, that of Iuppiter

Capitolinus, the Best and Greatest. His troops were allowed to shout obscenities and rude remarks at him, while a slave held a crown of gold and oak leaves over his head and whispered, 'Remember you must die' (*Memento mori*) in his ear – this celebrated phrase is found only in later sources, but even if apocryphal, it is entirely true to the spirit and values of the Republic. Even at the moment of intoxicating glory, he must keep in mind he was merely mortal. He ascended the Capitol and left his laurel branch in Iuppiter's lap. In that moment the king of the gods and the semi-divine triumphator became one. His name was then entered in honour into the public records. Quite simply, for the Roman citizen there was nothing to equal a triumph. When he rode in the triumphal chariot, he knew he was the first, best and greatest.

Farcically, Pompey's chariot, pulled by four elephants he had captured in Africa, was unable to pass through the city gates. The conquering general had to give up this idea and fall back on the conventional horses.

Meteoric Rise

His flatterers, so it was said, likened Pompey to Alexander the Great, and whether because of this or not, the Macedonian king would appear to have been constantly in his mind. His respect for the fairer sex is comparable with Alexander's, and Plutarch mentions that when the concubines of Mithridates were brought to him he merely restored them to their parents and families.[157] Similarly he treated the corpse of Mithridates in a kingly way, as Alexander treated the corpse of Dareios, and 'provided for the expenses of the funeral and directed that the remains should receive royal interment'.[158] Also, like Alexander, he founded many cities and repaired many damaged towns, searched for the ocean that was thought to surround the world, and rewarded his soldiers munificently. Finally, Appian adds that in his third triumph he was said to have worn 'a cloak of Alexander the Great'.[159]

The dismal end to Pompey's life should not blind us to the masterly way in which he exploited the potential of his situation beforehand, bursting the bonds of convention to struggle free for the next episode of his career. What is more, his military reputation has suffered severely as a result of the damaging portrait of him painted by Caesar, but this should not be allowed to obscure the spectacular nature of his political ascent. In fact, as we shall discover, this was much more spectacular and far more unconstitutional than Caesar's more conventional early career. By the sixties BC Pompey would be Rome's most important war leader and politician. There are seven crucial areas of activity, both domestic and foreign, during the seventies and sixties. These activities form a backdrop to the rise of Pompey, a man whose career was utterly unprecedented, the very epitome of the problem Sulla failed to solve, that is to say, extortion by the use of armed force. Here we shall deal first with the domestic issues, covering the foreign ones in the following chapter.

Revolt of Lepidus

In 78 BC, with Sulla barely dead, one of his former lieutenants, the consul Marcus Aemilius Lepidus, attempted to undo the Sullan reforms. However, political opposition caused him to resort to armed revolt, exploiting the tension between Sullan colonists and the indigenous inhabitants in Etruria. In an effort to strengthen his power base he championed the cause of the dispossessed, promising to give back to them the land that Sulla had confiscated for the settlement of his own veteran soldiers. Lepidus sought help from the governor of Gallia Cisalpina too.

The following year Lepidus tried to emulate Sulla's march on Rome after the Senate attempted to summon him back from his large, illegal, provincial command: he had drawn Gallia Transalpina as his proconsular province and had combined this with part of Gallia Cisalpina on the other side of the Alps, a precedent on which Caesar's career would later thrive so dangerously. But Lepidus' troops were to prove less effective than Sulla's. The Senate hurriedly passed a *senatus consultum ultimum*, virtually a declaration of martial law, and asked the able and competent Quintus Lutatius Catulus (*cos.* 78 BC) to save the state. Pompey, who had lent his support to Lepidus' candidacy for the consulship and, so it was said, encouraged his subsequent subversive activities, was granted extraordinary *imperium pro praetore* by the Senate and instructed to assist Catulus. While the proconsul held Rome, Pompey advanced north to Gallia Transalpina where he vanquished Lepidus' confederate Marcus Iunius Brutus, whose son would achieve lasting fame (or notoriety) as one of Caesar's assassins. Anyhow, Brutus surrendered to Pompey on the condition his life would be spared. The 'teenage butcher' had him executed. Next he struck south, caught up with Lepidus at the port town of Cosa in Etruria and defeated him. However, as he failed to pursue him, Lepidus, with some 21,000 troops, managed to slip over to Sardinia. Soon after, Lepidus died, and his army, now commanded by an old adversary of Pompey, the Marian Perperna, sailed on to Iberia where it would eventually join Sertorius.

As a final point here, it has been cogently argued by one scholar that

Pompey was technically *legatus pro praetore*, that is, a legate with *imperium pro praetore* serving under the proconsul Catulus and thus not independent at all.[160] Indeed, in 66 BC Cicero listed all Pompey's extraordinary commands and this one against Lepidus was not reckoned among them.[161]

Social Shabbiness

The watchwords of the Senate were cohesion and consensus, and it had ruled Rome because it operated by a system of government by consensus among the senatorial oligarchy. Political competition was for the position to influence or even manipulate consensus, but never to challenge or overthrow it. There were challenges, rogue aristocrats like Lepidus who championed the poor or dispossessed, but as long as it was cohesive the Senate was strong enough and focused enough to resist these challenges. Yet one of the fundamental things wrong in this period was the constant failure of the Senate to acknowledge the social and economic problems of the day. Its members chose to believe that any Roman who did try to deal with these problems was a 'revolutionary'. Quite simply, the senatorial system had alienated the people.

It was in the year 76 BC, therefore, that a certain brave tribune, Cnaeus Sicinius, had the confidence to start agitating for the restoration of the tribunate. In his public addresses he chose to highlight the recent successes of Sertorius in Iberia. The following year Quintus Opimius did likewise. It seems that some senators started to listen, for the consul Caius Aurelius Cotta, a solid pro-Sullan, proposed that one of Sulla's most important restrictions should be rescinded. Perhaps it was a misguided concession, but the *lex Aurelia* nevertheless lifted the ban on ex-tribunes holding higher magistracies. The same year saw Cicero departing for Sicily, Rome's oldest province, to serve his term as quaestor.

In 73 BC Caius Licinius Macer, who wrote a history of Rome, continued the tribunician agitation. Sulla's settlement, he insisted, was 'wicked slavery', and the people should not be fobbed off by the token distribution of grain, recently reintroduced under the *lex Terentia Cassia*. The grain was sold at a low price, admittedly, but probably for only about 40,000 free citizens, a fraction of Rome's current total. Yet despite the scholarly Macer and his like, poor Romans continued to fight as soldiers. For many, it was a better life than struggling on a smallholding in Italy, risking debt-slavery or starvation.

By 70 BC the supremacy of the Sullan Senate was beginning to weaken, since two generals indisposed towards respect for authority, Sulla's own lieutenants Crassus and Pompey, had been elected consuls for the year.

Pompey had gained his consulship in defiance of the legal qualifications as to age and previous offices; indeed he was the first man to become a consul before he was a senator. It seems that Pompey intended to start his *cursus honorum* from the very top.

Sulla's shade would hardly have been happy, especially when Pompey oversaw during his unconstitutional consulship major changes to the Sullan constitution. The *lex Licinia Pompeia* restored all the former powers and privileges of the tribunate, while the *lex Aurelia*, the praetorian law of Lucius Aurelius Cotta, reformed the *quaestiones*: one third of the jurors were to be senators, one third *equites*, and one third *tribuni aerarii*, an obscure order below the equestrians, thereby taking away from the senators the exclusive right to sit as jurymen in the courts. The same year saw Cicero successfully prosecute Caius Verres, governor of Sicily during the previous three years, for extortion and misgovernment. This case, the *cause célèbre* of its day, truly made Cicero's reputation.

As for justice, the senators had made fine abuse of their monopoly of the jury-courts. Without the check of non-senatorial jurors, corruption became more prevalent: Sulla had promoted new men to be senators and they were even more prone to bribery, as they needed the funds for the vast expense of belonging to the senatorial order. Senators, particularly as provincial governors, were blatantly extortionate and in general could be shamefully luxurious. Corruption was endemic and the records of Rome's law courts are full of cases of returning governors facing charges of extortion. Verres, for instance, grew scandalously wealthy, raking in some 40 million sesterces in embezzlement and swindles of all kinds, or so Cicero claimed.[162] Yet to many Romans the fact that governors were more concerned to restore their personal finances at the provincials' expense was not even considered unjust. Even scrupulous governors could rake in a handsome profit from their province without breaking any laws. Cicero himself was over 2 million sesterces better off after his year as proconsul of Cilicia.[163]

Sallust knocked those senators who squandered their wealth shamefully on fantastically grandiose projects for beautifying their country estates instead of spending it honourably for the public good. The celebrated dandy Quintus Hortensius (*cos.* 69 BC), the brilliant advocate who was Cicero's only rival in the courts of Rome, was attacked for dining on roast peacock and irrigating his favourite trees with vintage wine. He was to leave 10,000 barrels of wine to his heir.[164] The very able soldier and administrator Lucius Licinius Lucullus (*cos.* 74 BC), rich through his eastern campaigns, more of which in the next chapter, owned such an extravagant villa that a picture of it was displayed to the people when his enemies were trying to get him replaced in his command. In due course Lucullus even introduced the cherry tree from Pontus and his park, a riot of follies, fountains and fabulous flora, became the envy of fellow Romans.[165] Once, when he dined alone and his steward provided him with a simple meal, the general-turned-gourmet cried out in utter indignation, 'But Lucullus is feasting Lucullus today!'[166] Enjoying *haute cuisine* was scandalous enough, but both men were accused of that ultimate extravagance, maintaining exotic fish ponds.[167]

Cicero would frequently sneer at those whom he calls *piscinarius*, 'leading men who think they have transcended the summit of human ambition if the bearded mullet in their fish ponds feed out of their hands'.[168] Hortensius and Lucullus may have been 'fish-fanciers', but what about Sallust himself? Having been installed by Caesar as the governor of Africa Nova, a province just formed from the kingdom of the pro-Pompeian Iuba of Numidia, Sallust is said to have fleeced the provincials ignominiously and to have been saved from conviction only by the good grace of his *patronus*, to whom he apparently gave a sizeable backhander. Certainly he did very well by Caesar, owning a grand villa at Tibur (Tivoli) and a splendid park at Rome, the celebrated *horti Sallustiani*, which the historian lavishly embellished from his own purse.

Cicero and Sallust may snipe enviously at their social betters, but all this private luxury was particularly controversial at a time when the few subsidised corn-distributions were not adequate to meet the needs of the poor and the price and availability of grain were being squeezed by the activities of pirates in the Mediterranean. As dictator Sulla had drastically slashed the powers of the tribunate and enhanced those of the Senate, thereby leaving the people politically ostracised. Yet Catulus (*cos.* 78 BC), one of Sulla's most distinguished associates and the very embodiment of the new régime, appears to have had second thoughts with regards to what must have seemed to many the arbitrary rule of the Sullan Senate:

> Quintus Lutatius Catulus, whose wisdom and nobility are so pre-eminent, was well aware of this. Pompey, renowned and courageous man that he is, had moved that the power of tribune be restored to them. Then Catulus was called to speak. He immediately declared, with great effect, that the senators were exercising their control in an immoral and criminal fashion; and that if only, while acting as jurors, they had seen fit to live up to Rome's expectations, the tribunes' loss of their powers would have provoked no such regrets.
>
> Cicero, *in Verrem*, 1.15.44

Cicero himself saw the tribunate as an essential part of the Roman constitution,[169] and so Pompey, with the full restoration of tribunician rights, could arguably be acting in the light of this indispensable truth. In subsequent years he was to make sure that a fair number of tribunes were his supporters and he worked through them, as Caesar was to do later, to bypass the increasingly unhappy Senate and appeal directly to the people for consent to the enlargement of his privileges and powers.

There is a sad truth in the judgement of Sallust. After Crassus and Pompey had restored the power of the tribunate, politicians, whether claiming either to be strengthening the authority of the Senate (viz. *optimates*) or to be protecting the rights of the people (viz. *populares*), were acting out a pretence: 'in reality, every one of them was fighting for his personal aggrandisement'.[170]

Conspiracy and Catiline

His great-grandfather may have been a celebrated war hero, fighting against Hannibal with a prosthetic iron hand, but politically his ancestors had been an utter embarrassment. Even so, although there had been no consul in the family for almost four hundred years, his patrician status still provided him with some social cachet. Then again, scandals clung to Lucius Sergius Catilina (Catiline). He was said to have seduced a Vestal virgin, even to have murdered his own stepson to please a mistress. His sulphurous reputation had not prevented him achieving the rank of praetor (68 BC), and in the following year he had been entrusted with the government of the province of Africa, but his first attempt to win the consulship was thwarted because he was under an indictment for extortion. Seemingly Catiline had tried to enrich himself during his term as governor of Africa and, oddly enough, Cicero offered to defend him against the extortion charges.

Thus prevented from attaining power by legitimate means, or at least so the political gossip had it, Catiline plotted to assassinate the successful candidates and make himself consul by force. But then others asserted that the chief conspirators were Crassus and Caesar. Whatever, the first so-called conspiracy of Catiline was exposed, and through Crassus' persuasion, now one of the two censors for 65 BC, the senatorial enquiry was quietly abandoned.

At the election of 64 BC Catiline stood for the consulship, with the backing of Crassus and Caesar no less, on a platform of radical debt reform. His failure – by a small number of votes – was obviously a bitter disappointment to him, especially as one of the successful candidates was Cicero, the first *novus homo* in thirty years to become consul. Cicero's whole career had been a preparation for the consulship, but Catiline, just as desperate, was attempting to make good four centuries of family failure. Cicero, from Arpinum, Marius' home-town, was now destined to achieve the rare feat of rising from a non-senatorial family to win the consulship at the first attempt and at the minimum age. Yet the senatorial oligarchy had Cicero elected partly to shut out the wild Catiline. The spectre of financial ruin stared him in the face.

Licking his wounds, Catiline made his second, and again unsuccessful, bid to be elected consul in the summer of 63 BC. Earlier in the year Cicero, as a new consul, had put forward his renowned social policy of concord between the orders, *concordia ordinum*, whereby the Roman élite recognised their obligation to serve the needs of others in society. But such a Rome had never existed and could never exist. In fact he demonstrated his true credentials by defeating a series of popular tribunician bills dealing with the chronic problems of debt and poverty, including the agrarian law of Publius Servilius Rullus, an enlightened piece of legislation for settling impoverished city folk on smallholdings. The law also provided for the establishment of a board of ten (*decemviri*) with special powers to purchase land in Italy for the settlement of veterans. Orchestrating what was essentially a smear campaign, Cicero focused largely on arousing fears of renewed rural disruption and by ascribing personal motives to the bill's sponsor. Thus he frightened his peers by representing the colonies that Rullus proposed to establish as garrisons of men ready to march on Rome at Rullus' bidding.[171]

Nowhere in his vast output of writings does Cicero actually acknowledge the existence of the social and economic problems that plebiscites like Rullus' were clearly designed to alleviate. Admittedly in one of his fine works he does say that debt is something that can endanger the state and 'it is something that can be averted in many ways'.[172] However, he cannot give any practical examples of what should be done. Little wonder then to find a growing centre of open discontent in Etruria, the same region that had been the focus of the rebellion led by Lepidus fifteen years before.

As consul Cicero was a busy man. He took the time to defend before the people the elderly senator Caius Rabirius on a charge of high treason (*perduellio*); he stood accused of having killed Saturninus, the radical tribune who had supported the great Marius himself, thirty-seven years previously. Meantime, in a Rome charged with rumours of plots and counter-plots, Cicero followed up reports of disturbances in Italy and sedition on Catiline's part. His investigations, in truth little more than amateur espionage, revealed Catiline and his co-conspirators were up to something, but what exactly? Further revelations led to the usual declaration of the *senatus consultum ultimum* on 21 October. The wording of this particular decree was intentionally vague, urging the consuls and others 'to defend the state and see that it came to no harm'. On 8 November Cicero delivered before the Senate his first blustering speech against Catiline, who himself was present, and that night the 'scoundrel' left town. From Rome he made his way to the camp of Caius Manlius, a poverty-stricken ex-centurion who had raised in Etruria a ragbag army of destitute Sullan veterans, who had either squandered their property or been deprived of it by usurers, and disaffected locals.[173] There Catiline awarded himself the consular insignia he had been unable to win back in his native city.

We may well ask ourselves why Cicero, as one of the legitimate consuls, failed to arrest Catiline when he was still at large in Rome. In a period of unmistakably heightened tensions, Catiline and Manlius were only declared *hostes* in the middle of November. Moreover, only on the morning of 3 December, after more of Cicero's predictions had come true and information had been supplied to him against other so-called conspirators, including five men of very high rank, did the Senate take action. In the afternoon of the same day Cicero delivered a third speech against Catiline, to the people. At this, Cicero received from the people, for the first time in Rome, the title *pater patriae*, 'father of his country'. The second person to receive the title would be Caesar himself.

On the evening of 5 December, in an atmosphere of hysteria, Cicero delivered his fourth speech against Catiline. He spoke about the fate of the conspirators: death or life in prison? Cicero opted for the former and the illustrious Senate, which was, technically speaking, no more than an advisory body, was turned into a lynching court. Caesar, who now held the life office of *pontifex maximus*, stood and delivered an elegant, tightly argued speech. Given that he himself was widely suspected of having instigated the earlier plot and of some complicity in the current one, this was coolly audacious of him. He pointed out that summary execution was illegal, and if it were to be carried out it would create a dangerous precedent.[174] Marcus Porcius Cato, a tribune-elect for 62 BC, later to become famous as Caesar's most determined opponent, then rose, praised Cicero, hinted that Caesar had been privy to Catiline's schemes, and remarked that leniency would embolden the rebels while severity would dishearten them. Finally he demanded a sentence of death and was wildly applauded.[175] Here, in a clash between these two men so matched in talent, so opposite in character, was the opening salvo of a titanic struggle that would eventually destroy the Republic. For now, it was Cato who emerged triumphant. The five leading senatorial conspirators were garrotted, among them Publius Cornelius Lentulus Sura (*cos.* 71 BC), stepfather of Marcus Antonius.

On 31 December an army under Caius Antonius Hybrida, uncle and father-in-law of Marcus Antonius, left Rome. This particular individual certainly had a shady reputation. He was also a born survivor. Ejected from the Senate in 70 BC by the censors, along with Lentulus Sura, he began his career again, reaching the consulship with Cicero as colleague. When news of the conspiracy broke out, he tried to remain on the fence, but was finally forced into activity to avoid charges of sympathising with the conspirators. Not only suspected of double-dealing with the rebels, he was also a coward and an alcoholic to boot. For his proconsulship he was allotted Macedonia as his province but reluctantly agreed to be temporarily in command against Catiline. Allies of Pompey began to press for the great man's recall. This in turn provoked an eruption of moral outrage from Cato, who announced that he would rather die than see Pompey given an Italian command.

In late January of the new year Caius Antonius placed himself at the head of his army and took the field. But it was his legate Marcus Petreius who was to win the crucial battle because Caius Antonius was in his tent laid low by an attack of gout. Catiline had put up a desperate resistance, and when he was eventually cornered at Pistoria (Pistoia) in Etruria, he and his 3,000 desperadoes sold their lives to a man. His head was cut off and sent to Rome. Now freed from the cares of his consulship, Cicero successfully defended Publius Cornelius Sulla, the nephew of the dictator, for his role in the conspiracy.

We rely upon two contemporary authorities for the supposed Catilinarian conspiracy, a series of four orations Cicero delivered against Catiline (*in Catilinam*), published with adjustments in 60 BC, and Sallust's monograph (*Bellum Catilinae*), which narrates the career of Catiline in the years 64 to 62 BC. A great deal of what Sallust has to say about Catiline, none of it favourable, was derived from Cicero, and Cicero painted Catiline as a perfect monster, the 'aristocratic anarchist' hell-bent on destroying the whole system, with himself playing the role of the 'heroic saviour' of the Republic, a patriot pure and simple.[176] In Rome personal abuse made the best of arguments, and Cicero was a past master at the use of revilement to further a cause, his own ordinarily. An exquisite example of this concerns the day Cicero oversaw the election for the consulships of 62 BC. Soon after the event he would boast loudly that he had appeared on the *campus Martius* wearing beneath his toga a 'broad and conspicuous cuirass, with a very strong guard of intrepid men'.[177] Hired thugs and brawlers, if the truth be known, and Catiline, too, had his personal guard, made up, according to Cicero, of 'all the gamblers, and adulterers, all the unclean and shameless citizenry'.[178]

The story was that the candidate was out to murder the consul, surely a wondrous piece of black propaganda. By presenting himself to his fellow-citizens as a 'consul in peril and danger', Cicero dashed Catiline's hopes for a consulship. As the results were announced and Catiline's defeat became known, so the usurers flocked to pick at his corpse. In a forensic speech delivered seven years later on behalf of Marcus Caelius Rufus, a wayward banker's son who had once been closely associated with him, Cicero says that Catiline was a strange blend of good and evil: a man of enormous energy, a brave soldier, popular with a wide circle of friends to whom he was intensely loyal, generous both with his money and with his time.[179] So Catiline was not a monster after all. We may ask ourselves whether or not the conspiracy of 63 BC was unvarnished fact or Ciceronian fiction. Thereafter Cicero was to regard this as his finest hour, 'a pinnacle of immortal glory',[180] as our provincial from Arpinum modestly expressed it.

The Charmed Circle

The Roman aristocracy, which made up around 2 per cent of the citizen population, was divided into two orders, the senatorial order (*ordo senatorius*) and the equestrian order (*ordo equester*). The difference was not a 'class' distinction in the Marxist sense of the word, but one of function. The Romans themselves talked in the language of status groups, which entitled them to certain privileges. If an outsider asked a Roman to what class (*classis*) he belonged, he would probably refer to one of the five property classes in the oldest of the three citizen assemblies, the *comitia centuriata*. Cicero, when he blithely claimed the Senate was open to all citizens, said the senators were members of 'the highest order'.[181] Put simply, the senatorial order supplied the members of the Senate, and was concerned with politics, while the equestrian order, made up of *equites* or 'knights', was concerned with business.

Senators were frowned upon if they carried out commercial activities (without a front-man), while equestrians on the other hand were expected to conduct business and indeed could become hugely rich by doing so. Cicero's equestrian friend Titus Pomponius Atticus (b. *c.* 110 BC), for instance, was one of the richest men in Rome. Nevertheless, there was very little upward social movement within Roman society and this charmed circle of aristocrats was extremely hard to break into. We should remember that this attitude was typical of any agrarian society – there were no self-made men in a Rome where the avowed ideas of a landed aristocracy earning wealth were both sordid and degrading. Senators were often wealthier than equestrians were, and in the late Republic a man needed 400,000 sesterces to qualify as an equestrian, but 1 million sesterces to be a senator. Just to give you some idea of what this actually represents on a practical level, consider the bill of Caesar, which doubled the pay of the legionary soldier, not the lowest of society by any means, to 900 sesterces per annum. Entrance to a cheap bathhouse in Rome at the time was a *quadrans*, a coin worth one-sixteenth of a sesterce, while an affordable prostitute at Pompeii could be had for two *asses*.

Being a senator obviously had its privileges, such as the right to wear a toga with a broad purple strip (*latus clavus*), to sit in the front-row seats in the theatre and at the games, and, of course, considerable prestige and influence. As in most walks of life, the rewards and perks grew greater the higher you moved up the ladder or, as was the case for a senator, the *cursus honorum*.

There were distinct groupings within the Senate, such as the *aedilicii* (those who had been aediles). These senators, after death, had the right to have an *imago*, a funerary mask in wax. It first served to keep the corpse from decomposing too quickly, and then was displayed in the atrium of the family home. Kept in a special cupboard, with inscriptions beneath them, the more *imagines*, the greater the family's distinction. Another group was the *consulares*, former consuls who had conferred *nobilitas* not only upon themselves but also their families through holding this high office. Here we have an extremely important social distinction. The word *nobilis*, literally 'well-known', should be viewed not as a mere adjective but as a semi-technical term, emphasising the aristocratic and personal nature of Roman politics. Livy stresses that it was *nobilitas* acquired through fathers and grandfathers having held the consulship that got a man elected.[182] The statistics speak for themselves, for over a period of three centuries and down to the late Republic only fifteen *novi homines* held the consulship. Indeed, the *nobiles* formed an increasingly exclusive clique controlling the Senate and were often referred to as the 'senatorial oligarchy'.

Generally sons of senators became senators, but there was nothing to stop an equestrian standing for election if he met the property qualification. Men with no senatorial ancestors were called *novi homines* and often had to overcome prejudice to be accepted. Only the best got beyond the lower magistracies, and it was very rare for a *novus homo* to seek the consulship.

In more ancient times the *equites* were those rich enough to pay for a horse and thus serve in the cavalry. However, by our period some 1,800 were given a horse at public expense, and it was these *equites equo publico* that formed the equestrian élite. In general a man became an *eques* through birth and by having the appropriate amount of property to be registered as an equestrian at the census. Thus free birth for three generations and a landed interest were the perquisites for social recognition. Also the law demanded physical fitness and military service.[183] It too had its privileges, like the right to wear a toga with a narrow purple strip (*angustus latus*) and a golden ring, good seats in the theatre and at the games, prestige and influence, and, above all, the opportunity to make a lot of money in the service of the state.

Generally sons of equestrians became equestrians, while within the ranks of the equestrian order itself we can distinguish three sub-groupings. First the *publicani* referred to by Cicero as the 'flower of the order',[184] the 'super-rich' who bid for state contracts for public building works and above all tax-farming, which was highly lucrative – these men were often richer than senators. Secondly, the *argentarii* or *negotiatores*, a functional not a class term as it covers bankers and commercial entrepreneurs, some of whom, especially bankers, could become extremely wealthy and influence senators who often needed ready cash in a hurry. Last the *domi nobiles* or 'nobles in their own homes', an apt Ciceronian phrase referring to country squires and landowners with enough property to qualify as equestrians; unlike the first two classes they often lived outside Rome, their wealth mainly but not exclusively in land.

The watchword of the equestrian was *otium*, peace and quiet. The non-involvement in politics was thought to bring a more secure and untroubled life, where one could get on with making money. For much of the Republic equestrians had the same social outlook and class sympathies as senators, except they preferred the pursuit of money and pleasure to political responsibility, forming what was essentially the non-political section of the aristocracy. Nevertheless, Rome's acquisition of an overseas empire changed things, and gradually the equestrians became more self-conscious as an order, forming an important part of the political equation by the turn of the first century BC. Naturally, even before that they took an avid interest in how senatorial policy decisions would affect their business interests in the provinces.

Not all equestrians pursued active careers in the cut-and-thrust world of state and private enterprise. Cicero's life-long friend Atticus, who seems never to have considered a public career, was on terms of close friendship with some of the leading *nobiles* of his day, including Cato and Brutus. Atticus' life was spent in cultural and antiquarian pursuits (he was the author of a work on Roman history and several chronicles of Roman noble families), on the management of his large fortune, and on obliging his friends such as Cicero. A true 'gentleman of leisure', he enjoyed a long period of residence in Athens, one of the cultural capitals of the Mediterranean world, where he developed a passionate love of things Hellenic, hence his cognomen Atticus.

The equestrian order was a disparate body. Round an aristocratic core composed of men like Atticus were grouped leading men from the colonies and municipal towns, as well as *publicani* and even *negotiatores*. Many were of a similar background. Thus senators and equestrians, by the time of Atticus at least, formed a plutocracy that shared both landed and business interests. Indeed, in social standing equestrians were almost equal to senators, freely intermarrying even with the patrician nobility and gaining entry to the Senate if they wanted it.[185]

Chapter 4

Pompey at War

Rome's self-ordained destiny was to conquer and dominate other people. 'That the Roman people should be slaves is not right,' Cicero publicly announces. 'On the contrary,' he continues, 'the immortal gods have granted Rome the dominion of all the nations of the earth.'[186] This quest for total domination, which made the Romans so difficult to defeat, meant that the conqueror owned everything that belonged to the conquered, even their bodies. Territory from a defeated enemy automatically devolved to the state, and it was the Roman custom to seize usually a third of their lands, sometimes half. The land, called *ager publicus*, was scattered throughout the Italian peninsula and as it was state property it was meant for distribution to the people should they ever need it. Disposition of the enemy's movable assets, on the other hand, was left to the discretion of the commander on the ground. Part of the booty had to go to the public treasury to relieve the citizens' war burden, but the soldiers almost always received a portion of it. When the partnership between the Senate and the Roman people came unstuck, the people sought and acquired a voice and an agenda of their own, with land for veterans and bread for the urban poor as the leading items.

The Senate as a whole had doubts about the necessity for either and was grudging in its response, just as it was also reluctant to acknowledge that the legions were now recruited from the poorest in society, the have-nots, the *capite censi*, and refused to take responsibility for their welfare after discharge. This naturally encouraged a closer bond between general and soldiers. Military commands brought glory, which in turn brought popularity. They also brought tribute money and ransoms and loot that could be used to buy power. Generals also had armies, which the Senate did not. Pompey had been able to raise an army at his own expense and largely from his own family's estates in spite of his youth and lack of any legal authority. He would make his way to the top by championing (or exploiting) the popular interest of Rome. Pompey was to be spectacularly successful, against both the Mediterranean pirates and Mithridates of Pontus, Sulla's old adversary who was to rise against Rome again.

Guerrilla Leaders

Out in Iberia, meanwhile, a former supporter of Marius, the talented *novus homo* Quintus Sertorius, maintained an open rebellion against the Sullan régime. Unquestionably brave, the young Sertorius had been wounded at the Roman fiasco at Arausio. Next serving under Marius against the Cimbri, he had readily disguised himself as a Celt so as to spy out their intentions. After the final defeat of the Cimbri he fought in Iberia and, as a quaestor, in the Social War, during which he lost an eye in action. Siding with Marius and Cinna during the civil war, he did not hesitate to continue the struggle against Sulla even after all others had either been liquidated or gone to ground.

In 81 BC Sertorius, serving as the governor of Hispania Ulterior, had been expelled by the pro-Sullan replacement, Caius Annius, and sought refuge in Mauretania. Here he managed to overcome the Sullan garrison. The following year Sertorius re-entered Iberia with a tiny army of 2,600 men, 'whom for honour's sake he called Romans',[187] combined with a motley band of 700 Africans, and opened a successful campaign against the Sullan forces. An inspiring, if not brilliant commander, he exploited local backing and quickly established a Marian 'government in exile'. Acting as a Roman proconsul rather than an Iberian warlord, Sertorius had his own alternative senate and a readiness to recruit able local talent and encourage them to learn Latin and proper Roman ways; he was to show how Iberians under proper leadership and discipline could hold Roman armies at bay. More importantly, opponents of Sulla's men in Rome could now escape to the far west – when Sertorius' hold was eventually broken, Pompey tactfully burnt Sertorius' letters from important people in Rome without (he said) even reading them.

In 79 BC Metellus Pius (*cos.* 80 BC), son of the man who had warred against Iugurtha, was sent to Iberia to expel Sertorius, but turned out to be no match for him and suffered a number of humiliating reverses. By the end of the following year Sertorius held much of the peninsula with influence extending into Gallia Transalpina. It was about this time that he was reinforced by Marcus Perperna Veiento and the remnants of the Marian rebels who had backed the renegade Lepidus.

In 77 BC the Senate, fearful that Sertorius, like a second Hannibal, might attempt to invade Italy, once again granted Pompey an extraordinary command, that of a propraetor, to assist the proconsul Metellus Pius. After the departure of Lepidus, Pompey had once again pulled the stunt of refusing to disband his army, and the *princeps senatus*, Lucius Marcius Philippus (*cos.* 91 BC, censor 86 BC), made his famous speech in the Senate, using the equally famous senatorial phrase that Pompey was being sent out 'not on behalf of the consul, but instead of the consuls'.[188] Both consuls, Decimus Iunius Brutus and Mamercus Aemilius Lepidus, had failed to display any enthusiasm for assuming the Iberian command and, interestingly, Plutarch says they 'were quite useless'. However, it appears that the two had Marian sympathies and were accordingly shunned by the Sullan establishment, especially as Sertorius was recognised as a real threat.[189]

Sertorius quickly took the offensive against Pompey, and the two of them promptly engaged in battle, united, as Plutarch dryly remarks, by the mutual fear that Metellus Pius should arrive before the day was decided. But Pompey had to be rescued by the man whose glory he had hoped to steal, for only the timely arrival of Metellus Pius prevented his complete and utter rout. 'If the old women had not arrived, I would have whipped the boy back to Rome,' commented Sertorius sourly afterwards.[190]

The year 76 BC was to witness further successes for Sertorius. Pompey, or 'Sulla's scholar' as Sertorius was said to have dubbed him in derision, was facing for the first time in his career a commander of real ability, albeit of the unconventional kind. Though driven by circumstances into a war against his own people, Sertorius turned out to be an adept at leading irregular forces and waging guerrilla warfare. Having served in Iberia before, he fully appreciated that even the most dangerous opponent could be defeated if gradually worn down in a series of small wars, for continuous pressure is more effective than mere brute force — hit and run, wait, lie in ambush, hit and run again, and do so repeatedly, without giving the opposition a moment's rest.

Sertorius was in sober fact following the basic guerrilla precepts of attacking when least expected and never risking defeat in a set battle. To show his irregulars they should not risk all on one large-scale engagement with the Roman army, Sertorius instructed a strong man to pull the hairs from a straggly horse's tail all at once while a weak man was to pull the hairs from a full tail one by one.[191] He had the support of the local population too, and any guerrilla war is won or lost by the relationship with the local population: once their support is lost, then so is the war and from then on it just becomes a matter of time.

In the winter of 75/4 BC, while his ill-fed legions were freezing in their winter quarters, Pompey wrote to the Senate bitterly complaining of their lack of support. According to Sallust, he closed his missive with a threat to bring back his army to Italy.[192] True or not, the desired result was achieved and reinforcements of two legions along with substantial funds were swiftly dispatched to his aid. At about the same time Sertorius hosted an embassy from Mithridates of Pontus. In return for warships and money Sertorius was seemingly prepared to concede not only Bithynia and Cappadocia but also the Roman province of Asia. Sertorius had put the matter before his senate and the general consensus of opinion was that the loss of territory not under their control was a small price to pay for aid. He also sent military advisers to train the Pontic army in Roman fighting methods.

Sertorius taught Pompey several sharp lessons, especially in their early encounters, and 'the boy' was to learn from his mistakes. Yet the Iberian campaign revealed that Pompey could be outmatched on the battlefield by a top-flight general. In the end Pompey, by campaigning with more circumspection and operating in concert with Metellus Pius, gradually backed his wily mentor into a corner. Sertorius' victories, the lifeblood of any guerrilla leader, became less frequent, and his supporters, both Roman and Iberian, began to waver in their support while he himself abandoned his previously frugal habits and turned to alcohol and women.

In 73 BC a conspiracy of senior Marian officers headed by Perperna, who resented having a mere ex-praetor as his commander and decided he could do better, resulted in Sertorius' assassination at a drunken dinner party.[193] Perperna, who came from an established, if not distinguished family of Etruscan origin, obviously possessed pride greatly in excess of his actual ability, for his military record to date was an unbroken string of defeats, several of them inflicted by Pompey himself. In any case within days of his *coup d'état* Perperna, who was no adroit guerrilla fighter like Sertorius, was ambushed, taken prisoner and promptly executed.[194]

By the following year Pompey had brought the Sertorian War to a successful conclusion. The conflict in Iberia had been long and savage, the clashes between Roman troops and their guerrilla opponents frequently marked by appalling atrocities. After its conclusion Pompey devoted much time and effort to organising the settlement of the peninsula, establishing such towns as Pompaelo (Pamplona) to encourage some of the more unruly locals to sample the benefits of Roman law and order. He also conferred Roman citizenship on a number of individuals who had served with distinction during the recent troubles. Lucius Cornelius Balbus was one such foreigner, a gentleman of Gades (Cadiz) who was, therefore, a Phoenician, a Semite. But he was a very powerful person at Gades, and had made himself indispensable to Pompey.[195] Balbus we will meet again. Anyway, it was not until 71 BC that Pompey finally took his army of seasoned veterans back to Italy. It had taken him (and Metellus Pius) nearly six years of grim fighting and he commemorated it with a trophy in the Pyrenees, topped by his own statue and inscribed to say that he had conquered no fewer than 876 cities. Aged 36, Pompey was proving to be Rome's supreme general of the moment.

The Siege of Lauron, 77 BC

Two of Pompey's legates, albeit leading small detachments, had already been defeated in their turn when the young general advanced with confidence to engage Sertorius, who was currently busy with the siege of Lauron (probably somewhere near modern Valencia).

A race for control of the high ground dominating the town was won by Sertorius, but then Pompey closed in behind him, apparently trapping his opponent between his own legions and the town. His confidence is said to have been so great that he sent messengers to the townsfolk inviting them to climb on their walls and watch as he smashed the enemy. It was only then that he discovered that Sertorius had left 6,000 men in his old camp on high ground, which was now behind Pompey's position. If he deployed his army for a full-scale attack on Sertorius' main force then he would himself be taken in the rear. Instead of ending the war in a swift victory, Pompey was forced to sit still and watch impotently as Sertorius prosecuted the siege, for he felt that to withdraw altogether would be an open admission of the superiority of the enemy.[196]

During the siege there were only a couple of areas from which Pompey could secure forage and firewood. One was only a short distance from his camp, but this was continually being raided by Sertorius' lightly armed troops. After a while Pompey decided that his foraging parties should switch their attention to the more distant area, which Sertorius had deliberately left unmolested. The time required to travel to the area, gather forage and return ensured that any expedition in this direction could not complete the task in a single day. Yet at first this did not appear to be a serious risk, as there continued to be no sign of enemy activity in this area. Finally, when Pompey's men had become complacent, Sertorius ordered Octavius Graecinus, 'with ten cohorts armed after the Roman fashion, and ten cohorts of light-armed Iberians along with Tarquitius Priscus and 2,000 horsemen' to lay an ambush in a nearby forest.[197]

To avoid detection the ambush was set at night. The following morning, around the third hour, the unsuspecting Pompeian convoy began to lumber into view loaded down with forage and firewood. The sudden violence of the assault by the Iberian light-armed troops threw the whole convoy into confusion. Before resistance could be organised to this initial assault, the cohorts armed as legionaries emerged from the forest and charged. The Pompeians were cut to pieces, their rout being harried by Priscus and his horsemen.

News of the ambush prompted Pompey to dispatch a legion under Decimus Laelius to the convoy's rescue. Priscus' cavalry pretended to give way before this new force, and then slipped round the legion to assault its rear while those who followed up the routers attacked it from the front also. As the situation went from bad to worse, Pompey rapidly got his entire army on the move in the hope of rescuing the rescuers. Sertorius deployed his army in battle order on the opposite hillside, thus forcing Pompey to look on as the ambush mopped up both the convoy and most of Laelius' command. Frontinus, our main source for this ambush, refers to a lost (and unidentifiable) passage of Livy, which claimed that Pompey suffered some 10,000 casualties during this engagement.

Once the population of Lauron realised their visible ally was unable to aid them, they surrendered to Sertorius. He permitted the townsfolk to go free, but razed the town itself to the ground in an effort to complete Pompey's humiliation. It was an extremely disappointing end to Pompey's first campaign in the peninsula, a bitter blow to the ego of the 'boy-general' who was likened, by his flatterers, to Alexander the Great.

Slave Generals

It was fortunate for Rome that Pompey got the upper hand in Iberia so decisively in 73 BC, for that year saw the outbreak of a serious upheaval in Italy itself, a slave-society's worst nightmare come true. This was the slave insurrection led by the charismatic Spartacus. For us moderns his name is synonymous with justified rebellion, the courageous underdog daring to fight back. Not only did he have the 'right stuff' for Hollywood, Spartacus also became an important *leitmotif* to typify the modern wage-slave who rebels against economic exploitation and social inequality. Most noteworthy in this respect is the radical group of German Socialists founded in March 1916 by Karl Liebknecht and Rosa Luxemburg, the *Spartakusbund*, who linked the Spartacus legend to protests against the Great War and the current economic order. Similarly, in more recent times, *Subcomandante* Marcos, the leader of the indigenous uprising in the Lacandona forest in Chiapas, Mexico, has used Spartacus, alongside Che Guevara, as a revolutionary icon for the popular fight against injustice. However, despite the Marxist reassessments of Spartacus, his uprising was not a conscious attempt at social revolution.[198]

Examples could be multiplied of Spartacus' uprising assuming a different shape according to the viewpoint of the observer: as individual hero, as leader of a significant socio-political rebellion, as potential destroyer of Rome and, of course, as inspiration for future class struggle. As it happens, we all have our own particular vision of Spartacus, be it from the perspective of political commitment or antiquarian interest. According to Plutarch, himself a Greek, Spartacus was 'much more than one would expect from his condition, most intelligent and cultured, being more like a Greek than a Thracian'.[199] The comment implies that to a Greek intellect living under the superpower of Rome, Spartacus could be considered to have overcome the natural inferiority produced by the twin handicaps of foreignness and servile status by sheer force of personality.

The historical Spartacus was a real hero, big, brave and great-hearted, and his reported actions bear out his ability to lead others and his ingenuity in battle. But views on his short career as a slave general oscillate between the improbabilities of fiction and the probabilities of fact. His followers' aim was not to attack slavery but to free themselves and return to their tribal homelands, preferably after a spree of heavy looting in Italy. Marx famously declared Spartacus 'as the most splendid fellow in the whole of ancient history'.[200] In the ancient world Spartacus was a slave who rebelled, but who ultimately did not win. Still, a punitive force equal to that with which Caesar was later to conquer Gaul was required to defeat his slave army.

It was from successive waves of prisoners of war conscripted as gladiators that the profession inherited its bizarre, exotic uniforms, which was one of the sources of public enjoyment. During Rome's brutal wars of expansion during the second and first centuries BC there was a ready supply of foreign prisoners. These were tribal warriors or trained soldiers who could be pushed into the arena with little need for preparation, being made to fight with their native weapons and in their ethnic styles. Many of these men, it is true, were simply wretched captives herded before the baying spectators, but various classes of professional gladiator likewise came from this category. These earliest trained killers appeared in the arena as prisoners of war taken from the Samnites of central eastern Italy, dressed in the heavy, resplendent armour of the Samnite warrior. Soon after the Samnites, Gauls started to appear in the arena. Again these were originally prisoners of war taken from the tribes of Gaul. By about the early seventies these two had been joined by a third type of gladiator based on another foreign foe, the Thracian. It was not until the early years of the Principate that there would be the many categories of gladiators that we are more familiar with, that is, gladiators who were distinguished by the kind of armour they wore, the weapons they used, and their style of fighting. At the time of Spartacus, however, gladiatorial contests were still in the process of becoming a prolific form of popular entertainment; the sophisticated and formalised programmes of combat and spectacle known to history had yet to be developed.

The Campanian metropolis of Capua, for centuries the main entrepot for the training and housing of gladiators, was also the city that produced the greatest gladiatorial sensation of all time. One day in the springtime of 73 BC gladiators led by the Thracian Spartacus and the Gauls Crixus and Oenomaus broke out of the gladiatorial training school of Cnaeus Lentulus Batiatus. Armed with knives and spits from the mess kitchen, they overpowered the guards and fought their way to freedom. As they raced through the streets of

Capua they found a cart loaded with gladiatorial weapons and equipment, which they seized. Once out of the city, Spartacus and the others sought refuge on the slopes of nearby Mount Vesuvius, then dormant and believed to be extinct.[201]

Little is known about this remarkable character. According to one account Spartacus had spent some years serving in the Roman army as an auxiliary, perhaps in Greece or Macedonia, but then he deserted and became a brigand.[202] He had certainly gained some experience of military command before being captured and sent to the gladiatorial school at Capua. Whatever the truth of the matter, he quickly formed an army of runaway slaves and people with little to lose, such as shepherds and herdsmen, and defeated the troops – 'forces picked up in haste and at random'[203] – under one of the praetors of 73 BC, Caius Claudius Glaber, sent to besiege his mountain stronghold. The victorious rebels then seized the Roman camp with all its possessions and supplies. Two more praetors for that year, Lucius Cossinius and Publius Varinius, as well as Varinius' legate Caius Furius and his quaestor Caius Toranius, all suffered thundering defeats in separate encounters. Cossinius, for instance, first narrowly escaped capture only to die a short while later in an engagement over his own camp, while Varinius, most ignominiously, had his very horse and lictors captured. These stunning victories encouraged many malcontents to flock to join Spartacus.

The following spring, with his army now reputed to be some 70,000 strong, Spartacus rampaged throughout Campania, with specific assaults on the prosperous cities of Cumae, Nola and Nuceria. There is also evidence that the rebellion now affected Lucania and Bruttium, the latter a region long associated with chronic brigandage. Spartacus tried to restrain the worst of this savagery, but a perilous division in the high command resulted in his colleague Crixus leaving, taking the Gauls and Germans with him.[204]

Crixus and his entire force were destroyed near Mount Garganus in north-eastern Apulia after a surprise attack by the two consular armies of Lucius Gellius Poplicola and Cnaeus Cornelius Lentulus Clodianus. Spartacus arrived before the Romans could reform and defeated both consuls in turn, who were consequently recalled to Rome in disgrace and promptly relieved of their duties by the Senate. Appian tells how, in mockery of the Roman custom, Spartacus forced 300 of his prisoners to fight as gladiators, killing their own comrades to save their own lives, to appease the spirit of Crixus.[205] Thus, in the rather fitting phrase of Orosius, 'those who had once been the spectacle became the spectators'.[206] Clearly the Thracian had a sense of irony.

Moving north again, Spartacus' intention was to cross the Alps into Gaul and then head to Thrace. Outside Mutina (Modena) on the plain of the river Po he defeated Caius Cassius Longinus (*cos.* 73 BC), the governor of Gallia Cisalpina and general of an army of two legions. The road to the Alpine passes was open and the prospects looked promising. At this point Spartacus changed his mind, and for some inexplicable reason turned back and headed south again. At one juncture he contemplated attacking Rome, yet in the event he returned to the south of the peninsula and eventually spent the winter near Thurii (Sibari) instead.[207]

Spartacus now posed an enormous (and embarrassing) threat to Rome. He and his slave army had shredded the armies of three praetors, two consuls and one proconsul with apparent ease. Marcus Licinius Crassus, who had been praetor in the previous year, was given ten legions, six of them newly raised and the rest taken over from the disgraced consuls, and entrusted with the overall command of the war against Spartacus. As the rebel slaves were making their way south, Crassus took up a position in the region of Picenum and ordered his legate Mummius to shadow but not to engage Spartacus. He disobeyed the order and attacked, and his two legions were trounced; reportedly a large number of the troops ran from the battlefield. In turn, Spartacus retreated across Lucania to the sea. Crassus must have feared his opponent, for instead of forcing a decisive battle he tried to trap Spartacus in the toe of Italy by means of an immense earthwork that stretched from sea to sea.[208] Spartacus had hoped that Cilician pirates would transport him and his men across the strait to Sicily – a recent slave war there had not long ended and could easily be rekindled – but in the event they took the money and sailed off.

In spite of these reverses, however, one wintry night, with snow falling and settling on the ground, Spartacus managed to penetrate Crassus' makeshift barrier. Again the slave army was soon at large in the open country of the mainland. Again Crassus pursued. Meanwhile the Senate, becoming impatient, called upon Pompey, who with his veteran army was returning from the Iberian campaign, to assist Crassus in quelling the rebellion. On learning of this, Spartacus set out for Brundisium in order to escape by sea to Epeiros, but when he discovered the port was garrisoned, he abandoned the attempt. After a series of escalating clashes, he was finally brought to heel in north-western Lucania by the dogged Crassus.

Marx, in the aforementioned letter to Engels, calls Pompey 'a real shit [*reiner Scheisskerl*]: got his undeserved fame by snatching the credit' from others.[209] It takes little effort for us to imagine a Crassus who now begins to fear Pompey's return, which would steal his thunder. Sometime in the spring of 71 BC a major battle was fought near the source of the river Silarus (Sele), and Spartacus was defeated and slain. His body was never found. With Spartacus dead, the remnants of his slave army were quickly hunted down and terrible examples made of them. Crassus had 6,000 prisoners crucified at regular intervals along the Via Appia from Capua, where the revolt had begun, to the very gates of Rome, as a gruesome warning to everybody passing along it.[210] Subsequently, another 5,000 of Spartacus' followers, as they attempted to escape northwards, encountered Pompey, who promptly exterminated every last one, claiming that although Crassus had won the battle, he, Pompey, had extinguished the war to its very roots.[211] Crassus' feelings can only be imagined.

The armies of Crassus and Pompey converged on Rome in a mood of mutual hostility, yet both leaders hoped for a consulship and to gain it each needed the support of the other. Crassus' assets were that he was fabulously rich, and numerous senators were indebted to him; Pompey's that he was the idol of the people. So they set their differences aside, provisionally linked arms, and were duly elected to the consulships for the following year. They then disbanded their veteran soldiers. On the pretext that they were awaiting their triumphs, the pair had maintained their armies and then had menacingly pitched up outside Rome. It should not be overlooked that Pompey received a triumph for defeating Sertorius. This was rather irregular as Sertorius had been a Roman citizen and Pompey had yet to hold public office and enter the Senate, both of which he was to do on 29 December 71 BC, the very day he rode in glorious triumph along the Via Sacra. The legitimate Crassus, on the other hand, was only voted a lesser triumph, an *ovatio* or ovation, as the defeat of a slave army was not considered worthy of the full glory of a triumph.[212]

The Third Man

Like Pompey, the young Crassus had joined Sulla during his second march on Rome. Unlike Pompey, however, Crassus had a personal feud with the Marian faction. His father had led the opposition to Marius during his bloodstained seventh consulship, and had anticipated his fate by stabbing himself to death.[213] In the resulting purge Crassus' elder brother was liquidated and the family's estates seized. Yet at the time of Spartacus' revolt Crassus, who was now in his early forties, was one of the wealthiest men in Rome and allegedly the city's greatest landlord. He had laid the foundations of his wealth at the time of Sulla's proscriptions, buying up the confiscated property of murdered men at rock-bottom prices. He had multiplied it by acquiring burnt-out houses for next to nothing and rebuilding them with his workforce of hundreds of specially trained slaves. He then did his best to increase this personal fortune by all kinds of investments and shady deals, but his primary concern was extending his political influence. A genial host, a generous dispenser of loans and a shrewd patron of the potentially useful, he ensured his money bought him immense influence. A debt taken out with Crassus always came with heavy interest.

No one, Crassus is reported to have boasted, could call himself rich until he was able to support a legion on his yearly income.[214] The cost of this is easily determinable. In 52 BC Pompey would receive from the state 1,000 talents out of which he was expected to feed and maintain his soldiers.[215] At the time Pompey's provinces were Iberia and Africa in which there were stationed six legions.[216] One talent was worth 6,000 Greek drachmae, which was equivalent to 6,000 Roman denarii or 24,000 sesterces. Thus six legions cost 6 million denarii to maintain, so the cost for one would be 4 million sesterces per annum.[217] But here we should remember that this is Crassus' minimum qualification for the epithet rich. In fact in that same passage Pliny gives Crassus' fortune as worth 200 million sesterces. Obviously Crassus could support not only a legion but a whole army.

Fleeing the bounty hunters, the young Crassus had escaped Marian Rome and made it to Iberia where his father's spell as proconsul had been immensely profitable. Despite being a fugitive, he had taken the unheard-of step of recruiting his own private army, a force of some 2,500 clients and dependants. Crassus had then led this force around the Mediterranean, sampling alliances with other anti-Marian factions, before finally sailing for Greece and throwing his lot in with Sulla. At the battle of the Porta Collina he would shatter the Samnite left wing and thereby save Sulla. Sadly, his besetting sin of avarice lost him the favour of the dictator soon afterwards when he added to the proscription lists the name of a man whose property he wanted. Sulla discovered this, and never trusted Crassus again.

Fabulously wealthy he was, but his driving ambition was military glory. He took on the command against Spartacus when many other Romans were reluctant to do so. Because of the total humiliation that would have followed from it, a defeat at the hands of a slave army would have sunk any political career. Crassus notably revived an ancient and terrible form of punishment to strike terror in his soldiers' hearts. He inflicted the fate of decimation on the reluctant members of Mummius' legions who survived. He selected 500 soldiers who had run from the battle, then divided them into fifty groups of ten. Each group of ten had to select a victim by lot from among them. Then the remaining nine were ordered to club the tenth man to death, the courageous along with the cowardly, while the rest of the army looked on.[218] Military discipline was re-imposed. At the same time a warning was sent to the opposition that they could expect no mercy from a general prepared to impose such sanctions upon his own men.

Pirate Kings

When strong kingdoms with powerful navies existed, piracy was usually reduced to a minimum. Yet the last hundred years of the Republic saw one of the most remarkable developments of piracy that the Mediterranean has known, when from mere freebooters the pirates organised themselves into a pirate-state with headquarters in Cilicia and Crete. It was the more remarkable that the sea was controlled by a single power, which, when it put forth its strength under a capable leader, had no difficulty in putting an end to the malignancy in a short space of time. The ease with which Pompey finally achieved its suppression has naturally led to a severe condemnation of Rome's negligence and apathy in permitting piracy to flourish for so long a period. This is especially so when the alliance formed between Mithridates and the pirates of Cilicia had given the Pontic king command of the Aegean, which in the First Mithridatic War had been nearly fatal to Sulla.

This was partly due to the turmoil of the times, which hindered policing of the seas, and partly due to the influence of Roman slave dealers who tolerated the pirates as wholesale purveyors of slaves. The more the economy was glutted with slaves, the more dependent it became on them, and the pirates were the most consistent suppliers. Appian writes that the pirates operated 'in squadrons under pirate chiefs, who were like generals of an army'.[219] At this level of organisation they were capable of raiding roads and besieging towns along the coasts of Italy. They even staged predatory raids into the western Mediterranean, where they were reputed to be in contact with various insurgent movements, including Sertorius in Iberia and, as already mentioned, Spartacus in Italy. 'The pirate is not bound by the rules of war, but is the common enemy of everyone,' thundered Cicero. 'There can be no trusting him, no attempt to bind with mutually agreed treaties.'[220] But most damaging of all, they were intercepting the Roman grain fleets plying between Sicily, Sardinia, Africa and the ports of Italy. As this raised the price of grain and led to shortages in Rome, it became a political question.

At any stage of economic development, navies have always been expensive to build and have required handling by specialised crews. Their construction and operation therefore demanded considerable disposable wealth. However, with the decline of cereal production in Italy over the last hundred years or so, Rome came to rely heavily on supplies from overseas. Part of the problem was that the maintenance of a navy merely for police duties seemed not worth the financial outlay, especially so when anti-piratical operations tended to be lengthy affairs and their success was not always guaranteed. In 78 BC the Senate had sent Publius Servilius Vatia (*cos.* 79 BC) against the pirates in southern Anatolia (Lycia, Pamphylia and Isauria); after three years' hard fighting in and out of the rocky inlets there and the mountain fastnesses that stretched beyond them, he earned for himself the cognomen Isauricus. Four years later Marcus Antonius (father of the Marcus Antonius), a praetor, was given wide-ranging powers and considerable resources to fight the pirates. In 72 BC Antonius was defeated by the pirates on Crete, and the fetters with which Antonius had loaded his ships were used by the victorious Cretans to bind Roman captives, 'and so he paid the penalty for his folly'.[221] The following year Antonius was compelled to conclude a humiliating peace, which the Senate later rejected. He died in office the same year and was awarded, posthumously and it seems derisively, the cognomen Creticus, which would normally signify a victorious campaign, for his pains.

In 68 BC the scourge of piracy struck at the very heart of the Republic itself. At Ostia, where the Tiber met the sea, a pirate fleet sailed into the harbour and burned the consular war fleet as it rode at anchor. The port of Rome went up in flames. By the following year the shortage of grain had become so acute that the *lex Gabinia*, the tribunician bill of Aulus Gabinius, was promulgated and passed. Its tenets granted Pompey, over the heads of existing proconsuls, *imperium pro consule* and massive military resources with which to combat the pirates. What is more, his command was not for the customary six months but for three years, and encompassed everywhere in the Mediterranean and the Black Sea and the entire coastline for a distance of 80 kilometres inland from the sea.[222] The pessimism with which the Roman people regarded even their favourite general's prospects may have been reflected in the length of his commission, but the immediate result was a fall in the price of grain.

In a wide-ranging whirlwind campaign, Pompey cleared the western Mediterranean of pirates in forty days, and the eastern Mediterranean and Cilicia in three months, and rightly added enormously to his prestige. His plan had been an able one. He first closed the Pillars of Hercules, the Hellespont and the Bosporus, and then divided the Mediterranean into thirteen zones – six in the west and seven in the east – to each of which was assigned a fleet under an admiral. All areas were swept simultaneously, in order to prevent the pirates from concentrating, and the impetus was from west to east. Pompey himself was not tied to a particular zone, but kept a fleet of sixty warships at his immediate disposal.

By the end of this remarkable campaign Pompey's forces had captured 71 ships in combat and had a further 306 handed over to them. About 90 of these were classed as warships and fitted with rams. Pompey's treatment of his 20,000 captives showed a shrewd understanding of the causes of piracy, for he knew they would swiftly resume their profession if allowed to return to their coastal communities. The old pirate strongholds were slighted or destroyed and the ex-corsairs and their families were successfully settled in more fertile regions throughout the eastern Mediterranean lands.[223] Many went to the coastal city of Soloi in Cilicia, which was revived and renamed Pompeiopolis and became a prosperous trading community. Raiding and piracy were not permanently eradicated from the Mediterranean, but they never again reached such epidemic proportions as they did in the early decades of the first century BC.

Eastern Princes

When the tribune Aulus Gabinius proposed his bill all the senators bar one, Caesar, who as a young man had been kidnapped by pirates and ransomed for 50 talents, opposed it.[224] Two tribunes, Lucius Roscius and Lucius Trebellus, were even willing to act on behalf of the Senate and attempted to intervene, but to no avail. The slick Gabinius used the tactic first employed by Tiberius Gracchus and got the tribes to vote the two pro-senatorial tribunes out of office. They unceremoniously backed down. In 67 BC it seems that Pompey lacked support in the Sullan Senate. During the seventies BC the senators had willingly handed him extraordinary commands, but now he was relying on popular support through the tribunes.

The contrast is remarkable and the shift came with Pompey's consulship of 70 BC when he restored the tribunician powers, thereby weakening the general supremacy of the Senate strengthened by Sulla. For its part the Senate thought the consulship had solved the problem of what to do with Pompey by allowing him to take his place within the establishment. But crisis followed crisis and consul after consul failed. In the end Pompey was the only man who could deal with these external threats and thus, as in his pre-establishment days, extraordinary command followed extraordinary command, namely the prestigious command against the pirates followed by that against Mithridates. The redoubtable Pontic king, whom Sulla had humbled but not destroyed, was at war again in Asia. He had been provoked by Rome's acquisition of the nearby kingdom of Bithynia, which convinced the king that only the defeat of Rome could prevent the steady erosion of his power.

In 74 BC, aware that the Romans had their hands full with Sertorius in Iberia, Mithridates had invaded Bithynia with his new model army and then driven into neighbouring Asia (Third Mithridatic War, 73–63 BC). Fortunately for Catulus and his political cronies, one of their own was serving as consul that year. Lucius Licinius Lucullus, the nephew of Metellus Numidicus and the man who as quaestor in 88 BC had been the only officer to follow Sulla on his first march on Rome, was sent against the Pontic king with five legions. He was particularly devoted to the dictator's memory and, unlike Pompey and Crassus, could be trusted to stay true to his dead commander and comrade.

The next four years were to witness a string of victories for Lucullus over Mithridates. In his first independent command Lucullus turned out to be a strategist and tactician of truly exceptional talent who, in spite of limited resources, consistently out-manoeuvred Mithridates and defeated his army either in battle or, 'making its belly the theatre of war', through starvation.[225] By the end of 70 BC the power of Mithridates had been shattered and the king himself was a fugitive, driven across the mountains into neighbouring Armenia, the kingdom of his son-in-law Tigranes.

Yet despite his enormous success, Lucullus found himself sucked further and further east with an increasingly demoralised army. Perhaps without the support of the Senate, he crossed the headwaters of the Euphrates and invaded Armenia. The kingdom was a high plateau with steep mountain ranges, which had been, until quite recently, a patchwork of petty states owing allegiance to different rulers. However, under Tigranes, the self-styled 'king of kings', Armenia began to acquire most of the surrounding territory, building a new capital, the fortress city of Tigranocerta, named after its king. This jerry-built empire did not survive its first major test, however, for outside Tigranocerta Lucullus defeated Tigranes and continued his pursuit of Mithridates.

In the past eastern armies had very successfully relied on overwhelming numbers to defeat an enemy, more often than not through a prolonged archery battle. When he saw the Romans approaching, Tigranes famously joked that they were 'too many for ambassadors, and too few for soldiers'.[226] Lucullus led an army of no more than 16,000 infantry with 3,000 cavalry, mainly Galatian and Thracian, and the Armenian king was extremely sorry he had only one Roman general to fight. The royal quip provoked much sycophantic mirth; soon afterwards Lucullus' legions cut Tigranes' great host to pieces in a matter of hours. Tigranes' show-piece capital was then stormed and literally taken apart. With their customary brutal efficiency, the Romans stripped the city bare, Lucullus taking the royal treasury, his men everything else.

In 68 BC Mithridates slipped out of Armenia and managed to return to Pontus. In the meantime Lucullus continued his campaign in the highland kingdom, much to the dismay of his exhausted troops and the Senate. As we have discussed previously, one of the Sullan laws, the *lex de maiestate*, had forbidden a governor to lead troops beyond the borders of his own province without the express permission of the Senate. What is more, Lucullus was surrounded by soldiers who had been with him for nigh on six years, men who had marched over mountains and across deserts, zigzagging backwards and

Marble bust of Pompey (Paris, musée du Louvre), dated to *c.* 70 BC. Plutarch's pen portrait emphasises the 'hair swept back in a kind of wave from the forehead' and the configuration about the eyes that 'gave him a melting look'. The resemblance of our 'Roman Alexander' to the real one, however, was 'more talked about than really apparent'. (*Esther Carré*)

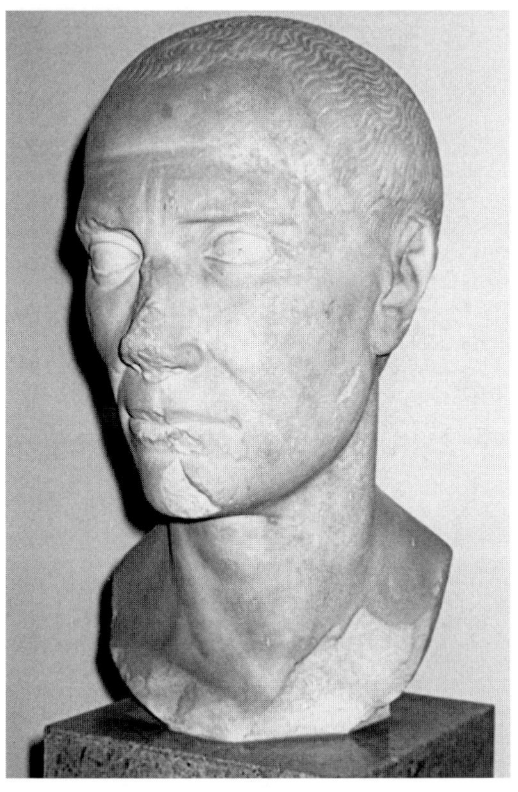

Marble bust of Caesar (Palermo, Museo Archeologico Regionale, N.I. 1967), a Iulio-Claudian copy of a first-century BC original, provenance unknown. Of all the figures of antiquity, his spectacular demise on the Ides of March would make him a household name. A genius both with the sword and the stylus, Caesar also displayed a certain amour-propre about his hair. (*Esther Carré*)

Legionaries on the Altar of Domitius Ahenobarbus (Paris, musée du Louvre, Ma 975). For many recruits enlistment in the army was an attractive option, promising adequate food and shelter, a cash income, and a hope of something more, both during their service and on their formal retirement. Furthermore, they no longer provided their own equipment, instead being issued with standard arms and armour by the state. (*Esther Carré*)

The war-god Mars on the Altar of Domitius Ahenobarbus (Paris, musée du Louvre, Ma 975) dressed in the uniform of a senior officer, most probably that of a military tribune. He wears a muscled cuirass with two rows of fringed *pteruges*, and a crested Etrusco-Corinthian helmet. Developed from the Corinthian-type, this style commonly preserved the eyeholes for decoration. (*Esther Carré*)

Straight sword and dagger (Madrid, Museo Arqueológico Nacional), from Almedinilla, Córdoba, fourth or third century BC. As well as being two-edged and sharp-pointed, the actual blade shape of these stabbing weapons nicely reminds us that Iberian straight swords and daggers were the forebears of the legionary *gladius* and *pugio*. (*Esther Carré*)

Funerary monument of Tiberius Flavius Miccalus (Istanbul, Arkeoloji Müzesi, 73.7 T), first century BC, from Perinthus (Kamara Dere). Here a legionary wields a *gladius Hispaniensis*, the celebrated cut-and-thrust sword with a superb two-edged blade and lethal triangular point. During 'boot camp' recruits underwent an exacting weapons-training programme, whereby they were taught to thrust, not slash, with this particularly murderous weapon. (*Nic Fields*)

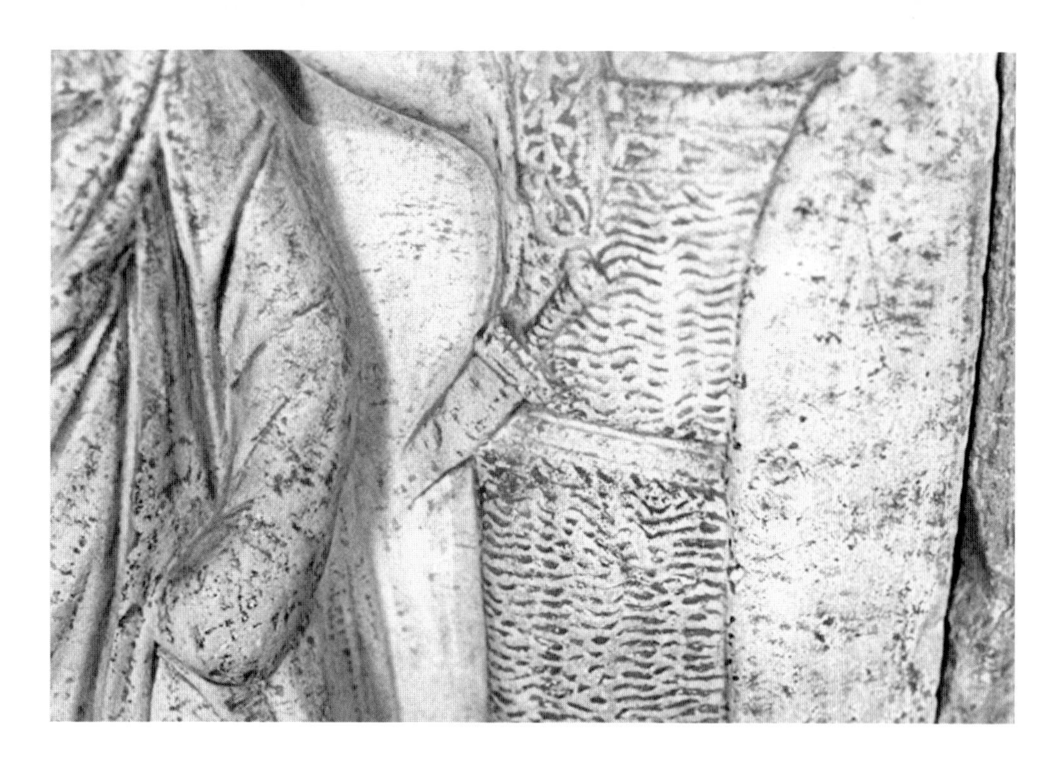

Closer view of one of the legionaries on the Altar of Domitius Ahenobarbus (Paris, musée du Louvre, Ma 975), showing the *gladius Hispaniensis*. Worn high on the right, the *gladius* was suspended from a waist belt by means of a four-ring system. By inverting the right hand and pushing downwards, the weapon was drawn in combat with ease and without the legionary exposing his sword arm. (*Esther Carré*)

Altar of Domitius Ahenobarbus (Paris, musée du Louvre, Ma 975), where a legionary holds his *scutum* by a single horizontal grip. Much like the riot-shield of today's policeman, the dished *scutum* was used both defensively and offensively, to deflect blows and hammer into the opponent's shield or body to create openings. The *scutum* itself was constructed of plywood, canvas and calfskin. (*Esther Carré*)

Reconstruction Gallic arms and armour, displayed at an archaeological open day at Bobigny, Seine-Saint-Denis. Conspicuous here is the characteristic long slashing-sword of the Gallic warrior. It was certainly not contrived for finesse, but was an end-heavy, two-edged weapon designed to either hack an opponent to pieces or to beat him to a bloody pulp. It required a fair amount of room to swing the sword effectively. (*Esther Carré*)

Based on an earlier Celtic design, the Montefortino helmet (Palermo, Museo Archeologica Regionale, 42644) was a simple hemispherical bronze bowl beaten to shape and mass-produced for the arming of soldiers by the state. With a narrow peaked neck-guard and an integral crest knob, this helmet-type often had large, scalloped cheek-pieces too. The type is named after the necropolis at Montefortino, Ancona. (*Nic Fields*)

The adoption of mail by the Romans derived from their having borrowed the idea from the Celts, among whom it had been in use at least since the third century BC, albeit reserved for use by aristocrats such as the Vachères warrior. Note that a long slashing-sword, for all to see, hangs at his right hip as he leans on his shield in characteristic Gallic fashion. *(Nic Fields)*

Marble bust of Mithridates VI Eupator (Paris, musée du Louvre, Ma 2321), depicted as Herakles or Alexander. Of all the enemies of Rome, Mithridates lasted the longest, having fought Sulla, Lucullus and Pompey. He died by his own hand in 63 BC after vigorously defying the might of Rome for some three decades. Pontus, along with Mithridates' treatise on poisons, thus became the property of Rome. *(Esther Carré)*

Marble bust of Iuba (Paris, musée du Louvre, Ma 1885) from Caesarea (Chercell, Algeria), dated *c.* 60 BC. King of Numidia and Gaetulia since before 50 BC, he supported the Pompeian side in the Second Civil War. After the defeat at Thapsus he committed suicide, and his kingdom became a Roman province. His son would marry Cleopatra Selene, daughter of Marcus Antonius and Cleopatra. (*Esther Carré*)

This curved wall is all that remains of the temple of Iulius Caesar. On 20 March his corpse was brought to the Forum, and it was probably here that the body was cremated by the mob after Antonius' funeral oration. The temple itself was dedicated by Octavianus in 29 BC in honour of Divus Iulius, and to this day continues to be a site of pilgrimage. (*Esther Carré*)

The battle site of Philippi, looking west from the acropolis (311m). It was on this plain, hemmed in by mountains to the north and marshes to the south, that the legions of the triumvirs and the Liberators clashed. The latter were camped just below and on either side of the Via Egnatia, nowadays the modern road, and traces of their extensive fieldworks can still be seen. (*Nic Fields*)

Marble bust of Octavianus (Paris, musée du Louvre). On his return to Italy from Macedonia, the stripling Octavianus would style himself Caius Iulius Caesar after his adopted father. Caesar's name would serve him well in the vicious struggles to come, and so there was certainly more than a little truth in Antonius' barrack: '*et te, o puer, qui omnia nomini debes*'. (*Esther Carré*)

forwards in pursuit of an elusive enemy. That winter the whispers were all of how Pompey's veterans, merely for fighting rebels and slaves, were already settled down with wives and children, in possession of fertile land. Their general, on the other hand, was starving his veterans of loot. Little surprise then that a mutiny and smear campaign followed, orchestrated by the young Publius Clodius Pulcher, and this was to undo Lucullus. In spite of his skills as a general, the aloof Lucullus lacked the knack of winning his soldiers' affection and was deeply unpopular with the army. Clodius, who happened to be Lucullus' brother-in-law and had joined his army hoping for promotion and profit, saw an opportunity to present himself as 'the soldiers' friend' and stirred up their passions.[227]

Lucullus was also hated by many influential groups back in Rome, in particular the equestrian businessmen, or *publicani*, whose tax-farming companies operated in the provinces. Lucullus, a humane and highly cultivated man possessing a genuine concern for the well-being of the empire's subjects, had severely curtailed the illegal activities of many of their agents, a measure that did much to win back the loyalty of the provincials to Rome. However, back home the general had become the target of violent criticism by various tribunes in the pay of the business lobby. On the point of total victory Lucullus was thus starved of troops and resources, while his command was gradually dismantled around him.[228]

The following year, while Pompey was enjoying his success at sea, the irrepressible Mithridates popped up with yet another army and won a series of quick victories over the Roman occupying forces. Near Zela (Zilleh, Turkey), for instance, a certain legate by the name of Triarius was trounced by Mithridates, his army losing no fewer than 24 military tribunes and 150 centurions. Lucullus could only watch in impotent fury as Mithridates and Tigranes recovered most of their home kingdoms. It must have seemed to him that his fierce campaigns had not brought about pacification.

As his world collapsed around him, Lucullus was given a rare moment of satisfaction when he heard the news that his pestiferous brother-in-law had been captured by Cilician pirates. Having absconded from Lucullus' camp after stirring up the mutiny, Clodius had headed west and paid a visit to another of his brothers-in-law, Quintus Marcius Rex (*cos.* 68 BC), the governor of Cilicia. Marcius, who intensely disliked Lucullus and was more than happy to cock a snook at him, had given the young mutineer the command of a war fleet, and it was while out on patrol with this that Clodius had been seized. It seems abduction by pirates had become something of an occupational hazard for young Roman aristocrats.

The Imperial Proconsul

Following the successful conclusion of the Pirate War, Pompey spent the winter with the bulk of his army in Cilicia. At the beginning of 66 BC the *lex Manilia*, the tribunician bill of Caius Manilius, granted Pompey command of the war against Mithridates. The majority of the Senate, recognising a frontrunner when they saw one, had abandoned their qualms and voted this time to award Pompey further, and even more unprecedented, powers. Not only was he to command the largest force ever sent to the east, but he was allowed to make war or peace without direct reference to the Senate, the obvious intention being that he should defeat Mithridates once and for all. Lucullus, by contrast, was left with nothing. Among the backers of the law was Cicero, now a praetor, who was to support Pompey loyally in the years to follow.

With the spadework already done by the luckless Lucullus, Pompey swiftly defeated Mithridates in his first year of operations. Making full use of his naval strength, Pompey sent his ships to guard the Asiatic coast from Syria to the Bosporus, a precaution against any attack by the Pontic navy in his rear. He then left his Cilician base to confront Mithridates in the north. The army he took with him was not unduly large, being as much as he needed, for he had already by adroit diplomacy managed to involve Tigranes against the Parthians, and the Pontic king was conveniently isolated.[229]

Mithridates encamped at first in a strong mountain fastness, in a part of his kingdom known as Lesser Armenia, but was obliged to retreat to a worse position as a result of water shortages. Pompey occupied the stronghold thus vacated, deduced from the vegetation that water existed at no great depth and successfully dug wells. Subsequently, however, despite Pompey's engineering efforts to cut him off, Mithridates slipped away eastwards with a still substantial army. Pompey pursued him as far as the upper reaches of the Euphrates and an engagement was fought there by moonlight. The low moon behind the Romans cast long shadows ahead of them and played havoc with Pontic missile fire. Mithridates' army was routed.[230]

Again, however, the wily king escaped and fled to the northernmost part of his realm in the Crimea, taking the land route round the eastern shore of the Black Sea to avoid the Roman fleet patrolling its waters. Meanwhile, Pompey pushed on to Artaxata, where Tigranes wisely negotiated a surrender, and on payment of 6,000 talents and capitulation of his conquests, was reinstated by Pompey as a 'friend of the Roman people' to hold Armenia as a docile buffer state. Soon afterwards Pompey was asked by the Parthian king, whom he had induced to attack Tigranes by the promise of territory, to recognise the Euphrates as 'the boundary between his empire and that of the Romans'. Pompey gave a deliberately evasive reply, saying that the boundary 'adopted would be a just one'.[231] As the Romans were soon to learn, the Parthians were troublesome only if disturbed on their own ground. As for the Pontic king, Pompey did not attempt to follow Mithridates northwards, but found himself involved in gruelling warfare with the Iberi and Albani of the Caucasus, virgin territory for Roman arms.

Pompey was to spend the next three years reorganising the east under Roman control. The whole coastline from Pontus to the borders of Egypt was incorporated into the empire, and the kingdoms of the interior given definitive status as Roman vassals. In the north not only Armenia, but Cimmerian Bosporus, Colchis and Iberia were also added to the area under Roman suzerainty, which extended, in theory, as far as the Albani of the eastern Caucasus. This career of eastern conquest gained for Pompey a huge patronage, but it was pointed out that he was not, in fact, doing much campaigning against Mithridates. However, Pompey had decided that Lucullus was wrong to follow the old king around his territories while his army grew ever more weary of the chase. Instead he made it diplomatically impossible for Mithridates to gather allies or find any place to rest.

Eastern Promise

In the summer of 64 BC Pompey marched into Antioch. Antiochos, the thirteenth king of that name to have sat upon the Seleucid throne and recently restored to it by Lucullus, fled into the desert, where he was ignominiously murdered by an Arab chieftain. Pompey dispatched his kingdom, a mere shade of its former glory, thereby declaring Syria a new province of the empire – probably as a bulwark against the Parthians. The following year, after abortive plans to make a comeback, Mithridates died in the Crimea. At last despairing of his ability to rebuild his shattered kingdom, he tried to commit suicide by taking poison, but in his youth he had developed an obsessive interest in toxicology and so inured himself by taking antidotes over the years that the poison would not work. He then ordered one of his Galatian officers to run him through with a sword. Indomitable to the bitter end, he had warred against Rome for twenty-four years.[232]

Meanwhile Pompey headed south to campaign in a Iudaea currently torn by civil war. There he laid siege to Jerusalem, and after three months took it by storm. The first man over the walls in the final assault was Faustus Cornelius

Sulla, the dictator's son. On entering the city Pompey and his senior officers went into the holy of holies within the Temple of Jerusalem, following the Roman urge to be the first to do anything, but out of respect took nothing from it.[233] After settling the affairs of Jerusalem, Pompey created a list of dependent minor principalities including Emesa, Ituraea, Iudaea and the extensive, if sparsely populated kingdom of the Nabataean Arabs, whose capital was at rose-red Petra. Like his hard-hitting campaign against the Mediterranean pirates, his eastern settlement was a testament to his genius for organisation.

In a sense Pompey personified Roman imperialism, where absolute destruction was followed by the construction of stable empire and the rule of law. It also, not coincidentally, raised him to a pinnacle of glory and wealth. The client-rulers who swelled the train of Rome also swelled his own. He received extraordinary honours from the communities of the east as 'saviour and benefactor of the People and of all Asia, guardian of land and sea'.[234] There was an obvious precedent for all this. As the elder Pliny later wrote, Pompey's victories 'equalled in brilliance the exploits of Alexander the Great'. Without a doubt, so Pliny continues, the proudest boast of our 'Roman Alexander' would be that 'he found Asia on the rim of Rome's possessions, and left it in the centre'.[235] Thus the notion of taking Roman dominion to 'the ends of the earth' (*ultimos terrarum fines*) reached its climax with Pompey, who, we are told, 'wanted to extend his conquests to the ocean that surrounds the world on all sides'.[236] Brilliant at self-promotion, Pompey would have made trophies and statues bearing representations of the *oikoumene*, the whole world.[237]

On a darker note, Pompey's activities went beyond any brief given by Rome. The settlement of the east was his, not the Senate's. Pompey's power and influence rested not simply upon the *imperium* given him by Rome, but on his personal influence, connections and patronage. As we will discover, in the final showdown with Caesar the east would provide Pompey with his most solid support.

In Retrospect

Pompey's eastern campaigns were to stand as his greatest achievements. These unprecedented victories had brought Rome vast accessions of territory, as well as a host of new dependent allies, a huge influx of treasure and revenue. Although, like every Roman conqueror before him, he exploited the lands he conquered, nevertheless, he gave their people peace such as they had not enjoyed since the fall of the Persian empire.

In 67 BC Pompey had finally mopped up the last of the pirate strongholds in Cilicia; he was, therefore, already in the east and thus in a perfect position to take up the war against Mithridates. At the time it seemed logical to grant him the mission against the Pontic king, especially as Lucullus, whose reputation was now in tatters, was currently winding up his shattered eastern command. Hence early in 66 BC Manilius proposed and carried through his law to grant Pompey command in the war against Mithridates, and, remarkable as it may seem, this was the occasion of Cicero's first public speech.

In his speech in favour of Manilius' law, which he later published for posterity under the august title *de imperio Cnaeo Pompeii*, Cicero dwelt on the 'sufferings' of the *publicani* in Asia as a result of Lucullus' recent reforms. There was a real danger for Cicero here, as he could not afford to identify himself too closely with a radical tribune like Manilius. He thus cloaked his support for Manilius' bill by acting in the interests of the equestrian order, the non-senators from whose ranks he came. What is more, he craftily concealed from his audience his true motives in making this speech, that is, a desire to embellish his reputation and to secure his future by ranging himself alongside Pompey, to whom the people looked then, and the Senate were presently to look, as their champion.

Cicero was to declare that Pompey possessed in abundance the four chief attributes of a great general, namely 'military knowledge, courage, authority and good luck'.[238] Though born in the same year as Pompey, Cicero was practically without military experience and was anything but a soldier.[239] Yet his inaugural speech shows him eloquently committed to supporting Pompey, faithfully reflecting the moderate opinion of the day. Fundamentally, at all times, Cicero himself was a moderate, a middle-of-the-road man, opposed both to reaction and revolution. The absolute irony, as we can now see, is that Pompey's extraordinary career showed Caesar the way ahead. Arrogant, devious and aloof, but with no autocratic intentions, Pompey fostered no revolutionary ideas. He was happy with the republican system as long as the rules could be bent almost but not quite to breaking point to accommodate his extraordinary eminence.

Members of the Roman aristocracy were constantly competing among themselves for military glory, and the political and economic rewards that accompanied it. As the stakes got higher in the late Republic, so the competition became more intense and more destructive to the political order. Pompey's career was extraordinary only in the sense that it represented, in an exaggerated form, the inherent contradictions of city-state politics played out on a Mediterranean-wide stage. Nevertheless, we should not underestimate the man as many of his contemporaries did.[240] By superb skill and timing he rose from his lawless beginnings as a warlord of Picenum to a constitutional pre-eminence in which he could discard the use of naked force. As the Caesarian Sallust said of him, he was 'moderate in everything but in seeking domination'.[241]

Chapter 5

The Rise of Caesar

Caius Iulius Caesar married Cornelia, the noble young daughter of Cinna, and they had a daughter Iulia, named after his paternal aunt, the wife of Marius. When Sulla marched on Rome for the second time and became its dictator in 82 BC, after Marius and Cinna died, he ordered the 18-year-old Caesar to divorce Cornelia as a demonstration of loyalty to the new warlord of the Republic. Caesar refused. Sulla was impressed with his courage and spared him, saying, 'In this young man there is more than one Marius'.[242] If the story is true, then Sulla must have been a remarkably good judge of character.

Caesar had been born in 100 BC, in Marius' sixth consulship. A few months before the birth, Marius had enjoyed the almost superhuman glory of his second triumph, that over the Cimbri and the Teutones. The ancestral busts in the atrium of the Iulii included ten consuls, but eight of those had been in the dim and distant days of the fifth century BC, and there was only one with a triumphal garland, Caesar's great-great-great-great-grandfather, victor in some forgotten skirmish near Brundisium in 267 BC. Thus the family had only managed to produce a single consul during the entire second century BC, at the height of Rome's overseas expansion. At the time the marriage connection with Marius was worth more to the family than its own record, and may be the reason for its revival, marked by the Iulii consuls (Caesar's uncle and two of his cousins) of 91 BC, 90 BC, and 64 BC.

Early Days

In most respects Caesar's early career was conventional, unlike that of Pompey, and it would be erroneous of us to insist that he began his ascent to power and glory with a well-orchestrated plan for achieving supremacy in Rome. Still, there is no doubt that he was keenly aware of just how to capitalise on any action that could increase his prestige. This is clear early in his political career, in 69 BC – long before his successes in Gaul – during the funeral of his aunt Iulia.[243] Roman funerals were understood as an occasion to honour both the deceased and the greatness of the clan or *gens*. Funerals were held for the living more so than the dead. And so the occasion prompted Caesar to make his first attempt at becoming the leader of the *populares* who in the past had followed Marius. Sulla had been safely dead for ten years by this time, but his followers, *optimates* in the main, still controlled Rome, and after all the dictator's entire political programme had been an attempt to scotch the *popularis* tradition. In her funeral procession Caesar displayed, besides the images of other members of the family, the image of his deceased uncle Marius, Iulia's husband and Sulla's greatest foe.

Displaying images of relatives was common, but displaying Marius' image was daring and dangerous, because the state had forbidden it. Thus Caesar's action was a deliberate challenge to some of the powerful Roman families that had sided with Sulla. His action was criticised but not punished. Four years later, as aedile in 65 BC, he would surreptitiously replace Marius' trophies on the Capitol, and again survived the attack of the Sullan faction and became the spokesman and leader of the Marians, which favoured his conduct. When he began to display images of Marius, long a non-person, no mention was made in the accompanying inscriptions of the civil war or his uncle's triumph in Numidia but rather of his victories over Rome's most serious threat in recent times – the Cimbri and the Teutones. 'And all who saw them were amazed at the daring of the man who had set them up – it was quite obvious who he was.'[244] He would prove to be the most masterly *popularis* in Roman politics, yet by birth he was a true patrician, descended from the oldest nobility in Roman history. For the Iulii claimed descent from the legendary kings of Alba Longa, and through them from the founding father Aeneas of Troy, whose mother was the goddess Venus and whose son Iulus originated the family name.

Fear was not part of Caesar's character. Back in 75 BC, while on a ship bound for Rhodes, he had been captured by Cilician pirates. They put a ransom of 20 talents on his head, an enormous sum, but Caesar thought this was too small and insolently informed them that he was worth at least 50. The pirates had a good laugh and let a few of his companions go in order to secure the ransom money. Meanwhile Caesar treated the pirates as if they were his personal bodyguard, ordering them around and leaving no doubt as to who was in charge. They played along and went on laughing even when he told them that after his release he would come back to take revenge. As soon as the ransom was paid Caesar was set ashore. He immediately went to Miletos, put together a small fleet, came back – and did exactly what he had said he was going to do. Every pirate he was able to catch was to suffer the frightful Roman punishment of crucifixion. But because they had treated him well during his captivity, he had their throats slit before they were put on the cross, in a gesture of compassion.[245]

The functionaries known as aediles sought to attract popularity by giving *ludi honorarii*, supplementary games attached to theatre and circus performances. Aediles supervised the public life of Rome at street level, and they soon learned that they could manipulate their office to improve their chances of being elected to more senior magistracies in future years. The funds provided by the state could be used by the aediles to put on adequate public festivals, but to make a real impression they had to dip into their own pockets. Such games could be very costly and, being free to the public, there was no profit to be made. So the investment was high risk, and many found themselves almost bankrupt by their year in office, but if a man went on to hold one of the more senior (and lucrative) political posts he would be able to recoup his investment and repay any money he had borrowed. It was as one of the aediles of 65 BC, writes Suetonius, that Caesar, in honour of his father who had been dead for twenty years, put on a gladiatorial show:

> But he had collected so immense a troop of combatants that his terrified political opponents rushed a bill through the Senate, limiting the number that anyone might keep in Rome; consequently far fewer pairs fought than had been advertised.
>
> Suetonius, *Divus Iulius*, 10.2

Caesar was undaunted. He made certain everyone in Rome knew it was the Senate that had robbed them of the most spectacular games of all time. All the same his diminished troupe of gladiators still amounted to 320 pairs, and each man was equipped with armour specially made from solid silver.

Caesar's show was not only a huge success but also hugely expensive. For money Caesar had turned to Crassus. As we know, it had been Crassus who had crushed bloodily the rebellion of Spartacus, but it had been Pompey who had stolen most of the credit. Magnificent Pompey was currently in the east earning more glory for himself but would soon be back in the political arena of Rome. Crassus was therefore willing to put some of his stupendous wealth into furthering the career of a potential rival to Pompey. As Sallust says, 'Crassus, it was thought, would have been glad to see Pompey's supremacy threatened by the rise of another powerful man, whoever he might be'.[246]

The post of *pontifex maximus* became vacant in 63 BC after the death of Metellus Pius, Pompey's colleague of the Sertorian War. As the highest of all priests responsible for overseeing the official auguries of the priests and magistrates at Rome, this office was the crown of a distinguished career. It was given, therefore, to retired censors and well-regarded *consulares*, illustrious men, in fact, like the senior conservative *nobilis* Catulus, the favoured candidate.

Caesar, who had risen no further than aedile, had the temerity to stand against him. On the morning of the election, Caesar kissed his mother goodbye with the remark: 'Today, Mother, you will see your son either as *pontifex maximus* or as an exile'.[247] Not implausibly, as Suetonius' version has it, the electors were bribed on a monstrous scale and thus Caesar was successful.[248] This very honourable position was held by him until his death.

Men of Honour

The Roman constitution, evolved in a tiny city-state, provided none of the machinery required to subdue, police and administer a world empire. The prosecution of foreign wars and the exploitation of all the conquered provinces required large armies and teams of officials, none of which Rome's political institutions could provide. The provinces were effectively autonomous states, far larger and frequently richer than Rome itself, with their own separate administration. The proconsuls who governed them at their own expense, and to their own profit, were often absent from Rome for years on end, acting effectively as independent rulers in their allotted territories; when they returned at last, enormously wealthy and to the adulation of the people, they had, in reality, infinitely more clout than the institutions they were supposed to serve.

When Pompey celebrated his triumph, his third, on returning from the east it was to engulf Rome for two whole days. He had defeated fourteen nations and captured 900 cities, 800 ships and 1,000 pirate strongholds. His chariot was preceded by the captive families of three conquered kings along with manacled pirate chiefs. He boasted of having killed or subjected over 12 million people and of nearly tripling Rome's public revenues. It was noted that his three triumphs commemorated victories on different continents – Africa, Europe and Asia.[249] After Pompey, anyone who aspired to be *princeps civitatis*, the leading citizen in the Republic, had to do much more than just win an ordinary triumph. The price of glory had gone sharply up. Yet there was no room, it seemed, for such a man, no legitimate channel for his influence or proper way in which he could exert his power. There were many who remembered that Pompey had begun his career as one of Sulla's lieutenants, that it was Sulla who had named him Pompey the Great. And Sulla, who had returned from defeating Mithridates to make war on Rome itself, had set a terrible precedent.

So the big issue hanging over Rome from 63 BC, the fateful pinnacle of Cicero's career, was Pompey's return to Italy and to the political scene following his impressive victories in the east. Pompey was now in an extraordinary position as he had literally turned the east upside down. Syria was now a province, local kings had flocked to him for recognition and a series of client kingdoms had thus been established; some, like the unpopular Ptolemy XII Auletes of Egypt, had come with massive bribes. In addition, the Temple of Jerusalem had been 'polluted', and Pompey, the uncrowned emperor of the east, had made numerous friends and clients, some of whom worshipped him as a semi-divine being.

Little wonder the Senate was worried, despite the dispatch Pompey had sent to its members in April 62 BC assuring them he was going to quietly retire, and the political reflex was to cut him down to size. What prompted this remarkable claim was a book-length letter Cicero himself had sent to Pompey the previous December in which he compared his own achievements as consul to those of Pompey, 'the Roman Alexander'. Naturally his boasting about the defeat of the Catilinarian conspirators alienated Pompey, and his response to Cicero had been withering to say the very least.

Notwithstanding the excitement of the Catilinarian conspiracy, poor deluded, swollen-headed Cicero had not had a happy ending to his consulship. At the time Pompey had already dispatched to Rome a representative, the newly elected tribune Quintus Caecilius Metellus Nepos – a member of the dominant family of the Caecilii Metelli – who was ordered to silence Cicero, forbidding by tribunician veto the orator's great swan-song speech in which he was going to describe the wondrous year Rome had just experienced under his consulship. By custom Cicero ought to have delivered the usual valedictory address of a consul leaving office, but this was denied him under the pretext that he had ordered the execution of Roman citizens, namely the senatorial associates of Catiline, without trial. Metellus Nepos even had the impertinence to demand that Pompey be recalled to Italy so as to finish the campaign against the Catilinarians. The Senate rejected the demand and Metellus Nepos was compelled to withdraw from Rome.[250]

Pompey's dispatch to the Senate was indeed an extraordinary document, and we can easily imagine that during its composition Pompey was probably clenching his teeth. In his next letter to Pompey Cicero expressed his delight at 'the bright prospect of a peaceful future'. Then he cattily added 'that it came as a severe blow to your old enemies, nowadays your friends; their high hopes dashed, they despond'.[251] But who are these new-found friends of Pompey?

Many modern commentators claim them to be Caesar and Crassus, but this can hardly be true. Caesar was already an ardent supporter of Pompey, while Crassus' relationship with him went back to that rather uneasy partnership of

70 BC when they were both consuls. It has been suggested, on the other hand, that the poor and discontented, the Catilinarians who had risen in Etruria under Caius Manlius, were Pompey's 'new-found friends'.[252] Pompey had given Cicero scant praise for the quashing of the Catilinarian conspiracy and it seems that he may have even disapproved of his actions. Anyhow, it appears these desperate people now hoped for Pompey to return from the east as Sulla had done before him, to carry out a proscription and dole out money and land. They were 'old enemies' because Pompey had put down the revolt led by Lepidus. As a matter of fact, this was why Cicero was so bitter towards Pompey on his return, claiming he was quite happy to crush the down-and-outs back in 78 BC, but was now friendly towards them.

Pipe-Dreams

Cicero fantasised that he and Pompey would go far in the future as the two luminaries of the Republic. At the end of the second aforementioned missive written to Pompey, in a typical piece of oratory, Cicero compared the great man to Publius Cornelius Scipio Aemilianus (*cos.* 147 BC, *cos.* II 134 BC), the destroyer of Carthage, with himself playing the role of Caius Laelius Sapiens (*cos.* 140 BC), Scipio Aemilianus' all-knowing, life-long friend. It was a dignity for which Cicero had no doubts about his suitability, but it was not to be.

In December 62 BC Pompey landed at Brundisium. He then dismissed his army and quietly entered Rome 'unarmed, with no one to escort him save a few intimate friends, for the entire world as though he were returning from a holiday abroad'.[253] At this, the cloud of fear that had hung so heavily over the capital dispersed. Intent on seeking a legitimate channel for his power he even went as far as to divorce Mucia Tertia, his third wife, despite the fact that she was the uterine sister of his close political ally, Quintus Caecilius Metellus Celer. Cicero states that this divorce was highly approved of, especially as Mucia had been two-timing the absent Pompey, having had several extramarital relationships, including one with Caesar.[254] Pompey, now Rome's most eligible bachelor, then announced he was to marry Iunia, the niece of Marcus Porcius Cato. He was hoping to be reconciled with the senatorial clique that surrounded Cato.

Though confident that the sheer magnitude of his achievements and his undoubted supremacy would facilitate his current political aims, he was also astute enough to try to smooth the path for his proposals concerning his settlement (*acta*) of the east, the treaties he had made with the eastern princes and potentates. He was to be sadly disillusioned. Cato, a stern Stoic moralist in the mould of his great ancestor Cato the Censor, stood firm and answered, 'tell Pompey that Cato is not to be captured by way of the women's apartments'.[255] In rejecting an opportunity to bind Pompey to the *optimates*, the implacable Cato appears to have done his own cause a grave disservice. The oligarchs could not see that their humiliation of this great warlord was unlikely to be overlooked by the next great warlord. Meanwhile, however, the rebuffed Pompey was politically isolated.

Pompey's eastern *acta* held out the prospect of revitalising the province of Asia. This meant that tax farming, which in the past had always been a lucrative business, once again looked very attractive. It is clear that a company of *publicani* had already paid a high price for the contract in anticipation of handsome returns. These profits did not materialise and a delegation, headed by Crassus, appealed to the Senate for compensation. Cicero was outraged but said that the Senate must give in. For a long time Cicero had been promoting his policy of concord between the orders, *concordia ordinum*, whereby the ruling élite, the Senate, of which he was a member, and the non-senatorial wealthy class, the equestrian order from whose ranks he came, should see eye-to-eye in the interests of the Republic.

This idea of harmony between the two orders, Cicero firmly believed, had been given new vitality as a consequence of the troubles of 63 BC. Despite some wishful thinking on Cicero's part, it did have a degree of practicality. Cicero did not want the Senate to alienate the equestrian order. Indeed, he got up on several occasions and waxed lyrical to his fellow senators about *concordia ordinum*, explaining how the current political strife in Rome might be terminated by securing the cooperation and recognition of common interests between the two orders, with Pompey as the leader and rallying-point acceptable to both.

Yet this idea presented no real contribution to solving the political problems of the day, and in truth was merely an attempt to shore up the status quo. In any case, the die-hard constitutionalist Cato, using the services of a tame tribune, prevented any decision being taken and in 60 BC won his case. Crassus and the *publicani*, therefore, felt alienated.

Pompey was now in desperate straits, not only over his desire for the Senate to ratify his eastern *acta* but also over the need for a land bill to settle his veterans. Thwarted by the Senate, Pompey turned to the tribune Lucius Flavius, who obligingly promulgated an agrarian law whereby the booty from Pompey's recent campaigns was used to buy up land for the Pompeian veterans. Although Cicero did not oppose the bill outright, he did try to water down its terms and conditions.[256] Others, led by the insulted consul Metellus

Celer, attacked the bill outright. Again thwarted by the leading members of the Senate, the whole issue of land for Pompey's veterans eventually turned sour and, three months later or thereabouts, Pompey allowed Flavius to drop the ambitious bill.[257]

Meanwhile his eastern *acta* were to be confirmed by a single vote in the Senate. Pompey had a lot of prestige (and wealth) riding on this issue, but Lucullus emerged alert and vindictive, and demanded, with some justification, that the terms of the *acta* should be gone through clause by clause before any decision was arrived at. He prevailed, supported by hard-line senators such as Cato and new-found allies such as the Metelli brothers, Celer and Nepos. The eastern *acta* were thus stalled, and Pompey's honour-cum-status, his *dignitas*, was once again dented. 'Thus he learned that he did not possess any real power,' mused Cassius Dio, 'and he repented of having let his legions go so soon and of having put himself in the power of his enemies.'[258] Even his victory over Mithridates was sneered at by Cato, whose achievements were a fraction of his own, as 'a war against feeble women'.[259]

The whole issue came to a head in 60 BC, and it all centred on Caesar. With hindsight at our disposal, it is easy to over-emphasise his early career, but in this year he returned from governing Hispania Ulterior having earned for himself a triumph for his highly successful policing operations against the outlying tribes along the Atlantic seaboard. The problem was that Caesar also wanted to stand for the consulship of 59 BC, and in order to be eligible the candidate had to submit his name personally (*ratio*) and thus enter Rome, that is, cross the sacrosanct bounds of the city, the *pomoerium*. Unfortunately for Caesar, the law stated that a victorious general awaiting his triumph had to remain outside the city limits with his troops until granted permission to retain his *imperium* within the city on the day of his triumph. Indeed, it was among the most essential provisions of the Roman constitution that no army should ever be brought into Rome, and that a general must lay aside his command (and the legal immunity it gave him) before entering the city.

In order not to forfeit his triumph, according to Plutarch, Caesar asked the Senate for permission to register *in absentia*. Many of the senators were willing to consent to it, but Cato opposed it. A decision had to be reached before nightfall on a certain day. On the last day remaining before the election lists closed, Cato employed his favourite tactic of filibustering, haranguing his colleagues in his booming, rasping voice until the sun went down; his speeches were generally performances of thunderous belligerence, full of devastating energy, of aggression and of righteous rage.[260] Rough and unadorned, his voice appeared to sound directly from the rugged, virtuous days of Rome in ancient times. Cicero, who admired Cato deeply, could nevertheless bitch that 'he addresses the Senate as though he were living in Plato's Republic rather than Romulus' cesspool'.[261] Whatever, the very next morning Caesar coolly laid aside his command, thereby giving up his triumph, and entered Rome to seek election, his *dignitas* dented. Yet the sacrifice of a once-in-a-lifetime triumph gives an indication of just how confident he was of gaining the highest of offices.

Caesar was duly elected consul for 59 BC along with Marcus Calpurnius Bibulus, Cato's son-in-law. Bibulus and Caesar had been aediles and praetors in the same years. As aediles, they had shared the expenses for the games put on, but Bibulus complained that Caesar, with his extravagant gladiatorial spectacle, took all the credit. The particular causes of friction in their praetorship are unknown, but may have concerned their attitudes to the Catilinarian conspirators. Being saddled with the somewhat plodding and quarrelsome Bibulus, Caesar expected stiff opposition from the *optimates* during his year of office.

Every consul, once he had completed his term of office, was subsequently appointed to a governorship as a matter of course. The Senate, according to Suetonius, so as to limit his influence, awarded Caesar not Iberia or Gaul but the humdrum provincial command of 'woods and drove roads' in Italy itself, which was normally the task of a praetor.[262] Suetonius obviously presents this as a deliberate insult to Caesar. It has been suggested that as the Gallic tribes were once again on the move the Senate wanted to keep one proconsul in Italy, stressing the fact that Caesar did gain his Gallic command later that same year.[263] However, it does appear that this was a definite political ploy by the arch-conservatives to prevent Caesar taking up a major overseas command.

The Gang of Three

The clear-sighted Caesar was quick to realise that there was an interesting possibility at hand. His plan was to be brutally simple: to carry Pompey and Crassus with him in a mutual balance of favours. Caesar had lost his triumph, Pompey his land bill and eastern *acta*, and Crassus had been snubbed, all through the machinations of Cato and the *optimates*. Crassus had the money, Pompey the veterans and Caesar the backing of the people. Caesar therefore argued that the three of them should come together and pool their resources and thereby turn the tables on the opposition by forming a *factio*. Pompey, who had wanted to become Cato's son-in-law, became Caesar's instead, marrying

Caesar's beloved only daughter Iulia (when he was 47 and she 17). And so the alliance was cemented.

Intriguingly, Cicero claims Caesar's intimate friend and agent Lucius Cornelius Balbus of Gades unexpectedly paid him a visit armed with an invitation to join the coalition. Cicero declined.[264] It was clear that Caesar preferred Cicero on the inside and not sniping from afar. Balbus, as we know, had become a Roman citizen through the agency of Pompey. Subsequently, he formed a close connection with Caesar, who, as governor of Hispania Ulterior, had employed him as a senior staff officer. At the time of his house call to Cicero, our man from Gades was playing a prominent part in the negotiations that brought Caesar, Pompey and Crassus together.

We should first understand that the triumvirate of 59 BC, unlike the so-called Second Triumvirate, had no legal authority under the constitution and that its aims were short-term. The terms of the political liaison were quite precise; Caesar would use his consulship to steamroller through a package of laws in the interests of all three, legislation that had been held up by Cato and his clique. Once this had been achieved there was no real reason to keep the coalition together, and as such it worked effectively.

Pompey got his eastern *acta* ratified *en bloc* and land for his veterans 'with no opposition'.[265] Pompey had brought his veterans – the very men who would benefit from the bill granting land – into the city, a tacit threat to anyone inclined to oppose the measure. Crassus was able to secure compensation for the *publicani*, who in turn 'extolled Caesar to the skies'.[266] A second agrarian bill, the *lex Campana*, despite Cato's usual antics, allowed for the distribution of *ager Campanus*, the rich lands behind the bay of Naples first taken as public after Roman victories over Hannibal in 211 BC, to be awarded to veterans and other needy citizens such as fathers with families of three or more children. Finally, having fulfilled his obligations toward his two colleagues, Caesar set about consolidating his own constitutional position and preparing for his proconsulship. To this end he got his tame tribune, Publius Vatinius, to propose to the people that he be given a plum provincial command.

The *lex Vatinia de Caesaris provincia* granted Caesar Gallia Cisalpina (northern Italy) and Illyricum (the region from the Adriatic to the Danube) as his proconsular province, which was chosen for two reasons. First for its political value, since it kept him close to Italy, and secondly because it nevertheless offered scope for military success against the tribes bordering the north-eastern frontier, that is, an Illyrian campaign. Furthermore the command, which came with a force of three legions, was voted for five whole years instead of the normal two. To Caesar's great good fortune, the allotted governor for

Gallia Transalpina, Metellus Celer, had suddenly died and on learning of the potential danger from surrounding tribes the Senate asked for this province to be added to Caesar's provincial command, and with it one legion. He was, after all, a proven general for what might be a major crisis, and the enlarged province would certainly keep him busy and removed from the central arena of Rome. But Caesar saw his appointment as a great opportunity for advancement, for it gave him the power not only to raise legions and gain victories that might rival Pompey's, but also to amass a fortune, which he badly needed to pay off his mounting debts and thereby avoid further dependence on Crassus.

At this juncture we should note that Caesar's ineffectual colleague Bibulus was flatly against him and adopted the ploy of remaining at home so as to 'watch the skies' for omens. To hold assemblies the auspices had to be correct and the decision was the sole responsibility of either of the two consuls. In other words, Bibulus was going to make sure that a 'bad omen' would turn up just prior to any public meeting. Caesar paid no attention to this archaic humbug and simply overrode Bibulus' pious mutterings. He called in Pompey's veterans, swept his opponents from the Forum, and in the tumult a bucket of dung was thrown over Bibulus' head and his *fasces*, the emblems of his authority, were broken and thrown after him. So well had the secret of the coalition been kept that, when this incident revealed it, the Senate was completely nonplussed. It dared not pass the ultimate decree and order Bibulus to restore order, because he had no troops at his disposal. Caesar, therefore, was master of the Forum. The joke on the streets was that there were two consuls for the year – Iulius and Caesar.[267]

'The three-headed monster' was now loose to feed at will, and it could be argued that all the legislation of 59 BC was passed under conditions of illegality (and violence). Caesar also gave teeth to his bootleg bills by adding a clause that required the senators to swear an oath of non-resistance to them on pain of exile. Intimidated and disoriented, his opponents meekly complied. Only two men held out. One of these was Metellus Celer, by now dangerously ill but still possessed of sufficient strength to continue his defiance of the man who had insulted his sister. The other, inevitably, was Cato. Cicero had to placate both men, pointing out that exile would hardly help to serve their cause, and both eventually complied. At the end of his consulate Caesar was able to boast that he had got everything he wanted to the accompaniment of his opponents' groans: now he was at liberty to dance on their heads. He then departed for Gaul, having contrived the election as one of the tribunes for the following year of his protégé Publius Clodius Pulcher.

The Street Fighter

Clodius, whose cognomen Pulcher meant 'Pretty-boy', believed he had solved the perennial problem of firm support for a revolutionary tribune aiming for long-term influence. He had built up a number of close connections among the urban plebs and thereby felt confident that he had established for himself a permanent power base. However, although he had adopted the popular spelling of his family name, Clodius was, like Caesar, born into one of the grandest patrician dynasties: namely he was a pedigree Claudii. The Claudii were notorious for their arrogance and waywardness, but they could also boast half a millennium of high achievement, a record of consistency without parallel in the Republic. Yet his lineage presented a real problem for him, for only a plebeian could become a tribune of the people. Unperturbed, Clodius attempted to get himself adopted into a plebeian family but failed.[268]

In 59 BC Caesar, as *pontifex maximus*, and Pompey, as sponsor, came to Clodius' aid and secured for him his adoption. Clodius was very much his own man and certainly did not act under the dynasts' direct orders when he was tribune. However, both Caesar and Pompey saw Clodius as a potential weapon (if they could control him) against Cicero if the orator stepped out of line while the two of them were away from Rome. Anyway, as one of the tribunes of 58 BC, the wild Clodius proved well up to the challenge and a raft of legislation was immediately laid before the people. The bills were crowd-pleasers all.

On taking office Clodius immediately restored the common people's rights to form social groups and associations, the *collegia*, which the Senate had high-handedly declared contrary to the interests of the Republic and abolished back in 64 BC. Open to everyone, citizen, freedman and slave alike, the *collegia* were institutions that represented everything from social clubs and mutual-benefit associations to neighbourhood self-defence groups, and Clodius soon set about forming them into bands of street-fighting men. Owing their new legitimacy to him, the *collegia* became Clodius' own instruments, making him, whether in or out of office, the warlord of the streets. The *lex frumentaria*, on the other hand, was standard fare for any self-respecting popular programme, the only difference being that Clodius made his distribution of grain into a free monthly allotment. This was the culmination of legislation started by Caius Gracchus, with more than 300,000 men able to claim their free measure of grain every month.

Having catered for the great unwashed, Clodius now turned his attention to the big men. By repealing parts of the *lex Aelia et Fufia* (*c.* 150 BC) he made sure that consuls were no longer allowed to announce contrary auguries, the right of *obnuntiatio*, and thus prohibit plebeian assemblies, much as Bibulus had tried to do during Caesar's consulship the year before. He also secured the passage of a law enabling the annexation of Cyprus as a Roman province, thereby conjuring up a mulch-cow to supply the much-needed cash to finance the extravagant provisions of his *lex frumentaria*. The island's ruler was to be ousted ostensibly because he had supported the pirates against Pompey, but Clodius had an old grudge against the ruler's brother, Ptolemy Auletes of Egypt. When he had been captured by Cilician pirates back in 67 BC, the young Clodius had arrogantly written to the king demanding the ransom fee, the response being a derisory 2 talents, to the immense amusement of the pirates and the fury of the captive himself.

So as to remove a most upright opponent from Rome, Clodius had the task of overseeing what was, in essence, the theft of an entire island assigned to Cato. The legislation was taken directly to the people, a brilliant manoeuvre using the tribunes and an assembly-vote, which meant the appointment was Cato's civic duty, so he could hardly refuse it. But by accepting, the punctilious and dutiful Cato was also accepting, indirectly, the legality of a whole chain of similarly approved legislation that he had bitterly contested. And so a very public figure who had the nerve and integrity to oppose Clodius was got rid of by being given a prestigious and potentially lucrative assignment. However, Cato insisted on making himself personally responsible for the sum extracted from Cyprus, and when he came to hand over his haul of scrupulously catalogued treasure it amounted to 6,000 talents.

The young political gangster was also to exorcise another demon from his past, namely Cicero. Having returned to Rome after being released by the pirates – his enemies, of whom there were many, claimed that the price of his ransom had been his anal virginity – Clodius came to public attention once again in the winter of 62 BC when he was found in the house of the *pontifex maximus*, Caesar, intent on seducing his wife, Pompeia. Caesar had left the house that night, since it was the venue of the all-female rite of the Bona Dea or Good Goddess. Clodius' devious plans to disguise himself as a female musician failed disastrously. He escaped, but Cicero exploded his alibi, perhaps because he was feuding with Clodius' eldest sister, Clodia Metelli, whom he was later to accuse of committing incest with her brother and poisoning her husband.

In the ensuing brouhaha, Caesar – now praetor, just one step removed from the consulship – calmly divorced Pompeia, the granddaughter of Sulla, claiming that it was not enough to know she was innocent of adultery as

'Caesar's wife must be above suspicion'.[269] And before anyone could press him over this singular, enigmatic comment, Caesar slipped quietly away to Hispania Ulterior. In any event, Clodius revenged his personal grudge against Cicero with a retrospective law that outlawed any citizen guilty of putting another to death without trial. There was no need to mention names as everyone knew its target. Cicero was to be run out of Rome and into exile on the pretext that the executions of the Catilinarian conspirators had been illegal.

The two consuls of 58 BC, Lucius Calpurnius Piso Caesoninus, Caesar's father-in-law, and Aulus Gabinius, he of the *lex Gabinia*, were cleverly bought off with the offer of lucrative proconsular commands, and thus turned a collective deaf ear to senatorial opposition and backed Clodius' ploy to have Cicero banished. The political climate in Rome was such that Cicero suddenly found himself out on a limb with no allies. Unwilling to antagonise the people and their radical tribune, the dynasts were prepared to see Cicero sacrificed.[270] He tried to visit Pompey, who saw him coming and fled by the back door as Cicero was shown in at the front. Caesar was apologetic, but shrugged his shoulders and said there was nothing he could do. Cicero disconsolately went off into bitter exile for eighteen long months and Clodius had his property sold off and personally tore down his house on the Palatine. Revenge was sweet, and the tribune crowned his victory by consecrating the ground to the goddess Libertas.

Thereafter, Clodius maintained his political influence through bands of heavily armed supporters, gangs made up of veteran soldiers, freed slaves, artisans and tradesmen. At one point he even had Pompey heckled cruelly in the Forum. A fight broke out between Pompey's and Clodius' men. Several people were killed and a man was caught apparently in the act of attempting to assassinate Pompey himself. Baffled and afraid, the greatest man in the Republic withdrew to his house, where he was besieged and prevented from leaving.

Urban Warfare

The year 57 BC was to witness serious rioting on the streets of Rome. Initially Clodius' gangs had the run of the city until the *optimates* found a young aristocrat, Titus Annius Milo, a curmudgeonly and cruel Pompeian who had married Fausta, the libertine daughter of Sulla. On their behalf Milo was more than happy to lead gangs of well-armed gladiators and fight fire with fire – he had assumed the cognomen Milo in honour of the half-legendary wrestler Milo of Croton. Since gladiators were not only disposable but also controllable commodities, their professional associations with violence and killing could be directed towards highly unsavoury ends. Clodius himself used the gladiators of his eldest brother Appius, who was praetor that year, as a private armed force to block the passage of a bill to recall Cicero from exile.

Conservative opinion had now turned against Clodius' banishment of Cicero, and Pompey and the *optimates* mobilised support for him, especially among the *domi nobiles* of Italy. Meanwhile Caesar, far away in Gaul, had been persuaded to give his reluctant approval to Cicero's recall, and a vote in the Senate backed it, by 416 votes to 1. The dissenting voice had, inevitably, belonged to Clodius. On 4 August the bill sanctioning the recall was passed in the *comitia centuriata*, the electorate being protected by Milo and his band from Clodius and his ruffians. Exactly a month later Cicero was back in his beloved Rome, owing Pompey his career. For a while thereafter Cicero tried to play an independent political hand, taking advantage of the stress in the coalition of the dynasts. Meanwhile, the free distribution of grain instituted by Clodius had been followed, predictably, by grain shortages in Rome, and by the late summer this had become so serious that Pompey was given a special commission by the consuls to maintain supplies.[271]

With the triumvirate apparently breaking at the seams, Cicero seized the chance to snipe at Caesar's agrarian law, the *lex Campana*, in the Senate. Pompey showed no offence as his veterans had already been provided for, but should the law be repealed it would have precluded Caesar from using the remaining land for his own veterans. In addition to Cicero's attack on Caesar, Lucius Domitius Ahenobarbus, Cato's brother-in-law, who was standing for the consulship of 55 BC, announced his intention that he would deprive Caesar of his army and provinces should he be elected. Courage came easily to the arrogant Domitius Ahenobarbus. He was a man described by Cicero, who was sensitive to such things, as having been born a consul-designate. He had another birthright to claim as well, namely Gallia Transalpina, a province that had been largely conquered and organised by his grandfather, Cnaeus Domitius Ahenobarbus (*cos.* 122 BC).

Caesar acted fast to stop the rot. In mid-April at Luca (Lucca), the southernmost town in Gallia Cisalpina, a secret conference was held so as to heal the rift between himself and his fellow dynasts and to refloat the coalition. The triumvirate was not dead, after all. They mutually agreed that Pompey and Crassus should hold consulships in 55 BC, thereby robbing Domitius Ahenobarbus of his, and at the conclusion of their term of office to govern respectively Iberia and Syria, each with armies and for a term of five years. In exchange Caesar's command was to be extended for five years. He had no intention of leaving the conquest of Gaul incomplete and besides, on returning to Rome he would face prosecution for the political violence of 59 BC and a conviction would have resulted in *infamia*, loss of citizen rights and political extinction. Three warlords now dominated the Republic, holding in their hands the most important of the provinces and some twenty legions.

After the meeting Pompey invited Cicero through his brother Quintus to cease his attacks on Caesar and withdraw his motion on the *lex Campana*. Cicero, far from trimming, was merely 'moving with the times'.[272] In truth, vulnerable and nervy, he was finally forced to behave and become an apologist for the dynasts. And that is what he did, making a number of speeches on behalf of the dynasts, including one in defence of Caesar's Punic henchman Balbus. On leaving for Gaul Caesar had taken Balbus on his staff once again. But when the triumvirate seemed to be breaking up, its enemies launched an attack on Balbus' right to citizenship, and brought their case to law.

For the first few weeks of 55 BC there were no consuls, a campaign of intimidation and violence having successfully blocked the consular elections. The orchestrator had been Clodius. Now back in league with the triumvirate, he was ensuring that the planned second consular partnership of Pompey and Crassus would be a political reality. On the morning of the election Domitius Ahenobarbus, the sole candidate to stand against them, and his supporters were attacked and routed and Pompey and Crassus were duly returned. Then, by bribery and violence, the two consuls secured most of the magistracies for their political allies, and put up one of the tribunes, Caius Trebonius. Hence the deal of Luca was promulgated under the *lex Trebonia* and, despite a speech from Cato of the utmost passion and solemnity, Caesar's command was extended for five years by a law, the *lex Licinia Pompeia*, that was taken straight to the people. Ominously Cicero, writing to his close friend and confidant Atticus, had months earlier joked joylessly that the dynasts' pocketbooks were no doubt filled with lists of the names of 'the future consuls'.[273]

The following year, despite Pompey's opposition, Domitius Ahenobarbus got his consulship at last. True, one of the consular candidates backed by Pompey had got in, but the haughty Appius Claudius Pulcher was hardly a reliable ally. However, one of the power-brokers at the Luca conference had been Appius Claudius. There he had offered the dynasts his own support and that of his rabble-rousing youngest brother Clodius, and the price was their backing in the elections for 54 BC. Indeed, both consuls brought about their own disgrace by accepting bribes to fix the forthcoming consular elections.[274] Pompey caused the scandal to be shown up and the elections had to be postponed for six months. Then Pompey's partisans began to murmur he should be made dictator. Though proconsul of Iberia, Pompey was residing in the suburban vicinity of Rome so as to protect his interests, having dispatched his legates to govern the Iberian provinces and command the seven legions stationed there.[275] Pompey, openly disavowing the dictatorship, kept his peace and deceived nobody. Yet his domestic bliss was to be shattered when, in September, his adored wife Iulia died during childbirth. Her father and husband were left equally devastated. For Caesar, however, heartbreak was compounded by consternation as the death snapped the family link between him and Pompey. Needing Pompey more than Pompey needed him, Caesar offered another marriage alliance but the great man politely declined to marry his great-niece Octavia.

Meanwhile beyond Rome Aulus Gabinius (*cos.* 58 BC), proconsul of Syria, had recently intervened in Egypt to restore Ptolemy Auletes (r. 80–58 BC, 55–51 BC) as the legitimate ruler of Egypt – he had been thrown out by his irate subjects – leaving him a body of Roman, Gallic and German troops to wring from his subjects the price of his restoration. Technically Gabinius, who was Pompey's agent, had no authority to intervene. It was illegal for him to enter Egypt at all, much less invade at the head of an army. For this bellicose act Gabinius stood trial as soon as he was back in Rome. On that charge he was acquitted, but was then promptly charged again on the grounds he had accepted bribes from Ptolemy. Cicero undertook the defence, against his will and not very well. Gabinius went into exile. On the streets at the time there was serious rioting and bloodshed, vividly depicted by Cicero in his letters to his brother Quintus serving with Caesar in Gaul.

In 53 BC Clodius was running for the praetorship, and his sparring-partner, the turbulent street-brawler Milo, for the consulship. The former was apparently sponsored by Caesar, the latter by Cato, but both were in sober fact running way out of any sponsors' control. Once a ferocious partisan of Pompey, Milo had been unceremoniously dumped by him after the Luca conference, and was therefore happy to throw his lot in with Cato, who was vainly seeking a forceful counterweight to Pompey. Yet the inevitable clashes between the two urban warlords led to a complete breakdown of law and order, with rioting preventing the election of the consuls (and praetors) for that year until July.

While Rome descended into anarchy Crassus, now in his late fifties, seized his chance for the full glory of a military triumph, denied him after his actions against Spartacus. Crassus had begun his second consulship with the express aim of going to war with Parthia, an 'ally and friend of the Roman people' (*socius et amicus Romani populi*), a very vague title indeed. Not everyone

The Parthian Art of War

The Parthian military system and philosophy were radically different from the Roman. On the field of battle the Parthians were famous for their fully armoured cavalry, or cataphracts, and their horse archers. There were Parthian infantry, most of whom were said to be archers, but they were of poor quality and receive very little mention in our sources. In effect, the Parthian army was an interesting combination of the very heaviest and very lightest types of cavalry.

The Parthian nobles made up the 'super-heavy' cavalry, protected from head to foot in scale, mail and laminated plate. They even wore helmets with scale or mail neck protectors (aventails) and solid metal face-masks. Their arms and legs were sheathed in segmented armour. The modern term cataphracts comes from the Greek word *kataphraktoi* (Latin *cataphractarii*), meaning 'covered over'.

They were mounted on large horses, which were also completely armoured in bronze and iron except for their legs. Bronze was preferred because iron tended to rust from the horse's sweat. The Parthians, like the Achaemenid Persians before them, successfully bred the Nisaean horses, which were known even in China. They trained their horses to run with a high-stepping action that carried the rider very smoothly, which was especially important for a man wearing armour *de cap-à-pied*. The Parthian method of training horses to move in this manner, which is not instinctive to horses, was to exercise them in ploughed fields, so that the horse was forced to learn to pick up its hooves in order to negotiate the furrows.

Their primary weapon was a 3.5-metre-long heavy spear (*kontos*), often held in both hands, and, 'charging' ponderously at the trot, they were capable of riding over any cavalry that tried to face them. However, they could not count on breaking steady close-formation infantry in sufficient depth, only breaking them if they were disordered or demoralised by a long period of shooting by the horse archers.

Recruited from the lesser nobility and retainers, the horse archers were unarmoured and wielded the powerful recurved composite bow. Relying on their horses' speed to keep them out of harm's way in battle, the horse archers often discharged their arrows back toward the enemy while pretending to flee. This was achieved by twisting the torso while simultaneously drawing the bow, and then firing to the rear, all in one fluid motion.[276] Firing from a moving horse did not make for accurate shooting (later Arabic manuals advised that the archer should aim to loose his arrow when his horse was in mid-stride), but the objective was to pepper the target area with as many arrows as possible so that some were bound to find a mark. Only when this constant barrage had weakened the enemy would the *cataphractarii* charge and finish the job.

If the enemy's strength and determination seemed undiminished then the Parthians simply withdrew and continued to shadow their opponents, waiting for a more favourable opportunity. The Parthians would certainly flee if the situation was unfavourable. The readiness with which they fled but then rounded on any incautious pursuers always astonished the Romans. It made it doubly difficult to inflict a decisive defeat on them in battle since it was so easy for the Parthian horsemen to escape.

Finally a few words on the composite bow. The skeleton of the bow was a lath of plain or laminated wood (ash, birch or cherry) long enough to form the solid extremities where the bowstring can be attached. To the belly of the bow (the inner face when it was reversed and strung) were glued two curved strips of ibex or antelope horn. Sinew from the neck tendon (*ligamentum colli*) of an ox was similarly attached to the back (or outer face) of the bow, and then covered with leather or birch-bark to preserve it from damp and injury. The glues, compounded of boiled-down cattle tendons and skin mixed with smaller amounts reduced from the bones and skin of fish, could take a year or more to dry. Only when all the bow's elements had indissolubly married was it strung for the first time.

Bowstrings were commonly made of twisted gut or sinew, horsehair and perhaps matter such as certain vines, and sometimes silk. Archers always carried spares, including for use in different climatic conditions. Horsehair strings, for example, are best suited to cold climates, unlike sinew strings, which absorb moisture and stretch. Drawn to the ear, thus fully stretching the sinew and compressing the horn, a composite bow had more power than a wooden self-bow. The design of a composite bow took full advantage of the mechanical properties of the animal matter used in its fabrication. Sinew has high tensile strength, approximately four times greater than bow wood, while horn has compressive strength. When released the horn belly acts like a coil, returning instantly to its original position. Sinew, on the other hand, naturally contracts after being stretched, which is exactly what happens to the convex back of the bow as it snaps back to resume its relaxed shape. Put simply, the sinew gave the bow its penetration, the horn its speed. This factor, combined with the bow's shorter span, meant it was well suited for use on a horse. Furthermore, it could be kept strung for long periods of time without losing power like a self-bow did. In fact composite bows function better when kept under tension, and the ready-strung bow in its case certainly made quick firing possible, the weapon being pretty well 'loaded' and ready for use.

approved, and a tribune attempted to arrest Crassus for breaking faith with Parthia. When that failed, as the proconsul and his entourage hurried out of Rome and clattered down the Via Appia, the same tribune cursed them with the very archaic Roman equivalent of bell, book and candle. The tribune was later prosecuted for this, having been too successful.[277] In the spring of 54 BC Crassus arrived in his province, and his early campaigns across the Euphrates met with modest success. The following summer Crassus crossed the Euphrates again, but he was barely beyond the frontier when his army was lured into defeat at Carrhae, costing him his life and most of his legions. It seemed that Pompey's eastern settlement would be overthrown by the victors, but as the Parthian king quarrelled with the chief of the Suren clan and Caesar with Pompey, the war petered out. Only Armenia and Iberia passed out of Roman control.

The Battle of Carrhae, 53 BC

Crassus had left Rome for Syria hoping to provoke a war with Parthia, thereby acquiring military glory and popular acclaim to balance that of Pompey and Caesar. In Syria he was joined by his youngest son Publius Licinius and 1,000 Gallic horse sent to him by Caesar. Leading seven legions, some 4,000 light-armed troops and as many horsemen, and relying on his long-neglected military skills, Crassus crossed the Euphrates in June and, though soon deserted by his Armenian allies, continued his advance into unfamiliar and hostile territory. So Carrhae (Harran, Turkey), a caravan town shimmering in the arid wastes of northern Mesopotamia, was set to be the scene of a Roman military disaster.

The Parthian force numbered some 1,000 *cataphractarii*, 10,000 horse archers, and a baggage-train of 1,000 Arabian camels laden with an unusually large reserve of arrows, one camel load per ten archers. This army combined the two tactical essentials of projectile power and shock. To prevent being attacked in the rear on the 'boundless plain', Crassus formed up his army in a hollow square screened by skirmishers. The *cataphractarii* charged to drive the screen in, then withdrew to let the horse archers shoot at will. Led by Publius Licinius, a counter-attack mounted by the Gallic cavalry was lured out of touch with the main body of the Roman army, surrounded and destroyed. Publius Licinius himself was decapitated, and a Parthian horseman, brandishing the head on a spear, galloped along the ranks of the Romans, jeering at them and screaming insults at Crassus. Now completely encircled, the main body doggedly held its ground until nightfall and then, when the Parthians finally drew off, Crassus abandoned his wounded and withdrew his now demoralised men to Carrhae.

The town was not provisioned, so a further retreat was ordered. The Parthians were ideally suited to harassing a retreating foe, especially one that was mostly on foot, and pursued with vigour. The Romans were soon intercepted, and Crassus and his officers were killed during truce negotiations. Now leaderless, some 10,000 of the Roman survivors surrendered, although the other remaining 5,500 fought their way out to eventual safety under the resourceful leadership of Crassus' ablest lieutenant, a quaestor by the name of Caius Cassius Longinus, later infamous as one of Caesar's assassins. The lesson of Carrhae was that in a desert environment infantry are at the mercy of an enemy who combines firepower with mobility unless they possess comparable firepower and, of course, access to water. As Napoléon was to point out, the Romans were nearly always defeated by the Parthians because the legions were unsuited to their mode of fighting.[278]

On the political front, Carrhae virtually spelt the end of the triumvirate. It upset the balance between Pompey and Caesar, and meant that from now on they would slowly but surely drift apart. Similarly Surena, a young leader of talent who was also the chief of the powerful, semi-autonomous Suren clan, was not to enjoy the fruits of his success; he was executed because the Parthian king feared him as a potential rival.

Old Enemies, New Friends

New Year 52 BC, and again there were no consuls in office. On 18 January the enemies Clodius and Milo met, apparently by chance, some miles from Rome on the Via Appia. Clodius was attended by thirty slaves carrying swords, Milo by 300 armed men, including several gladiators. In the ensuing showdown Clodius was injured and was carried into a nearby tavern, where Milo's men broke in and killed him. The next day his associates, including two tribunes, displayed the corpse, naked and battered as it was, in the Forum, and rioting again gripped Rome after Clodius' widow Fulvia's impassioned mourning helped to incite the popular mood. The exasperated mob took the corpse from its bier, carried it right into the Senate house, and attempted to cremate their champion on a bonfire of smashed furniture. The house itself and several adjacent buildings, including Rome's first permanent law court, the Basilica Porcia, were burnt down.

In the pandemonium that followed the homeless Senate had no choice but to elect Pompey sole consul, his third, to restore public order. Naturally, the appointment *consul sine collegia* gave rise to popular rumours of a dictatorship. Notwithstanding, Pompey began his rapprochement with the Senate and married Cornelia, the widow of young Publius Licinius Crassus and the daughter of the arch-constitutionalist Quintus Caecilius Metellus Pius Scipio, a vicious non-entity despite the roll-call of his illustrious names, who was then invited to serve as his colleague for the remaining five months of the year. As sole consul, however, Pompey passed new laws to create a five-year interval between magistracy and pro-magistracy, and to make election *in absentia* illegal, subsequently adding a clause exempting Caesar. Finally Pompey's command in Iberia was extended, Cassius Dio says for five years, though Plutarch says four.[279] Whatever, the crux of the matter is that Pompey's and Caesar's commands were no longer synchronous. The two remaining dynasts seemed to be drifting apart.

In many ways this was a greater subversion of the traditional republican system than any of Pompey's previous commands, but the argument for making Pompey the sole consul for 52 BC – and thus putting the Republic back on the rails – came from an unexpected quarter, namely Cato and Bibulus.[280] A dozen years previously, during the darkest days of the Catilinarian conspiracy, Cato had declared that while he lived he would never consent to Pompey being handed an Italian command. Now, hopeless, he concluded that 'any government was better than no government at all'.[281] Outwardly, it does seem rather odd that a group of dyed-in-the-wool republicans, and enemies of

Pompey to boot, should propose this idea. However, if Pompey was elected dictator there would have been no control over him at all. As sole consul, albeit with immense powers, the office would only run for one year. This option, therefore, was the lesser of two evils.

Increasingly too, Pompey began to feel that he did not need Caesar any more, especially as the system was now ready to accept him. And so his behaviour in 52 BC was truly exceptional. Pompey ordered his legions into the city. With brisk and military efficiency, he then damped down the explosive situation in Rome; the street gangs of Clodius and Milo were no match for Pompey's hardened and disciplined legionaries. Milo himself was abandoned, finally condemned and exiled to the sunshine and red mullet of Massilia. When Milo was put on trial for the murder of Clodius, Pompey's troops, ringing the place of judgement, were so numerous and so menacing that even Cicero, who had undertaken Milo's defence, lost his nerve, failed to deliver the speech he had planned and saw his client convicted for murder, bribery and corruption.

By mid-summer, which must have pleased many, Pompey proposed that another consul should share his office, namely his new father-in-law. He may have amazed the *optimates* by the propriety of his behaviour, but these are all signs that Pompey was now entering the established order of things.

It was at about this time that Caesar announced that he wished to go straight from his Gallic command into a second consulship, standing for the election *in absentia* and remaining in Gaul until he could enter Rome to celebrate his triumph and become consul on the same day, just as his uncle Marius had done back in 104 BC. As a magistrate he would be immune to prosecution, which his bitterest opponents were keen to see happen, and then could take another province and military command. There was much talk of the need to avenge Crassus' defeat at Carrhae and the subsequent Parthian raids on Syria, and it was generally felt that either Caesar or Pompey should be given control of this war.

Chapter 6

Caesar at War

Certainly the most successful Roman commander of any period, Caesar was also a gifted writer. 'Avoid an unfamiliar word', he used to say, 'as a sailor avoids the rocks.'[282] His own elegantly and lucidly written account of his campaigns gives us an invaluable picture of the Roman army in this period, albeit he generally assumes, rightly so, that his reader is well acquainted with all the necessary detailed information about the army's command structure, equipment and tactics. Caesar himself did little to reform the army, but raised the soldiers under his command to a peak of efficiency. The booty from the Gallic campaigns was lavishly distributed among his men, and conspicuous service was rewarded by decorations and rapid promotion. Newly raised legions were provided with a valuable cadre of experienced centurions promoted from junior grades in veteran units.[283] To a modern readership the technical details Caesar provides may often be disappointingly sketchy, yet his depiction of the Roman soldiers under his command is one of the most prominent and distinctive features of his narrative. Nothing in ancient literature corresponds to the prominence of these soldiers or their moral – as well as military – significance in the battle narratives.

Caesar's Legions

Caesar spent eight years, from 58 BC to 51 BC, fighting in Gaul, Germania and Britannia, and established the Roman frontier on the Rhenus (Rhine). In this period he would increase his army from four to twelve legions. Most of the new recruits were probably volunteers, and all the new formations were raised, during the winter months, from Caesar's own provinces, though some Italians presumably travelled north on their own account, with a view to enlistment. The new legions were raised by virtue, it would seem, of a proconsul's right to call out local forces in defence of his province. Unlike most proconsuls, Caesar had access to reserves of citizens in Gallia Cisalpina. At first he paid and equipped the new legions at his own expense from the profits of war. At the Luca conference in April 56 BC he was able to get recognition for *legiones XI–XIIII*, which were henceforth paid by state funds, but the later formations remained dependent for pay on Caesar himself.[284] Caesar enlisted men both south and north of the Padus (Po): those living north of the river were not full Roman citizens, but had the status of 'Latins'. Caesar ignored the distinction, and was happy to admit all to his ranks. Hence the formation of a militia from the native population of Gallia Transalpina, twenty-two cohorts in all, which formed the basis of *legio V Alaudae* that we later find among his forces. Existing legions were supplemented each year by drafts from Gallia Cisalpina, so that by the time Caesar crossed the Rubicon, his army must have possessed a unique coherence and loyalty, which were important factors in his eventual victory.

Caesar trained his men hard, but also flattered them, fostering their pride in themselves and their unit. He created an especially close bond with the veteran *legio X*, habitually placing them on the right of his line, the position of most honour, and leading them in person. When this legion, worn out by long service in foreign and civil wars, threatened to mutiny, Caesar restored order with a single, barked word, addressing them as *quirites*, civilians not soldiers. Normally commanders began addresses to their troops with *milites*, soldiers. Caesar habitually began with the more flattering term *commilitones*, comrades. To him the term *commilito* was imbued with a feeling of brotherly loyalty and a sense of responsibility for the fate of his men. This inborn feeling of fraternity did not undermine Caesar's authority as leader; on the contrary, it served to enhance it. Yet now he was addressing the battle-hardened veterans as citizens, just men off the street. He was implying, of course, that he now considered them discharged from his service.

In battle a commander must be able to exercise control over his army at all times. He must be close enough to read the battle but should not get involved in the initial fight. Therefore, in battle, Caesar rode about close behind the front line of his army. From this sensible position he encouraged his men, witnessed their behaviour and rewarded or punished them accordingly. He also had a close view of the combat zone and could appreciate the situation as the thousands battled, judging the fight by the morale exhibited and the yells made by friend and foe alike. Using this information he could feed in reinforcements from his second or third lines to exploit a success or relieve part of the fighting line that was under pressure. Put simply, Caesar had tactical *coup d'oeil*, that is to say, the ability to perceive the decisive point, even the need to intervene personally in the fight when his army was on the verge of defeat or when the moment had arrived to move in for the kill. That personal intervention in battle was not considered incompatible with the demands of leadership can be seen from Caesar's praise of the doomed

Lucius Aurunculeius Cotta for fulfilling the duties of a commander and fighting in the ranks as a common soldier.[285]

Just as the function of a soldier was to fight battles, so the function of a commander was to win battles. He therefore needed to judge where and when the crisis of battle would occur and move to that part of the fighting line, and there is no doubt that in this role Caesar took up such a prudent position to ensure he reacted positively and instinctively. Yet often we find him next to his soldiers, exposing life and limb to mortal danger. When the day's outcome was in doubt, Caesar would send away his horse, clearly demonstrating that he, like his men, could not escape from the enemy blows and that he was ready to die alongside them. Caesar understood his soldiers as few did, with the probable exception of his uncle Marius. He shared with them the glories, the rewards, but also the toils, miseries and, above all, the dangers of soldiering. He was indifferent to personal comforts or luxuries and he was a fine horseman who could even ride fast with both hands clasped behind his back. During the campaigns in Gaul he got into the habit of dictating dispatches while on horseback.[286] If Caesar was a risk-taker, he was one who carefully hedged his bets if he stepped into a fight; the decision was taken either from necessity or from the certainty that the risk was small and the promise of reward great. At the Sabis, as we shall soon discover, Caesar's army was caught totally unprepared while making camp and it would be his splendid example of bravery that would help save the day. At Alésia, in contrast, he led the final attack as the enemy were on the verge of collapse, and when his soldiers realised that Caesar himself was coming, they fought with greater vigour.

Although there was still no permanent legionary commander, and this situation would remain so until the establishment of the Principate under Augustus, there were still, as in the days of Marius, six military tribunes, *tribuni militum*, in each legion. Likewise, tribunes were still being elected by the citizens in the *comitia centuriata*, and both Caesar and Cato were elected tribunes in this fashion.[287] On the other hand, additional tribunes could be chosen by a general himself. Here the demands of *amicitia* were met by taking on to his staff family, friends and the sons of political associates, who were thus able to acquire some military service and experience that would stand them in good stead for their future excursions into politics. Cicero's friend Caius Trebatius was offered a tribunate by Caesar,[288] and for a young inexperienced blue-blood such an appointment was the swiftest way of kickstarting a political career, the *cursus honorum*.

With the increase in size of the armies under the command of one man from a nominal two or four, namely the traditional consular or double-consular army, to a strength of anything from six to twelve legions, the question of the command of individual legions became of supreme importance. Thus we note that there is no instance of a military tribune commanding a legion in action during Caesar's campaigns in Gaul. As they were invariably short-term politicos, who had an eye cast in the direction of Rome, tribunes could be rather an embarrassment at times. In 58 BC, when Caesar was preparing to march against Ariovistus of the Suebi, these young blades became so terrified that they tried to excuse themselves from duty and some even wept openly.

In their place Caesar started to appoint a senior officer, usually a legate (*legatus*, pl. *legati*), both for the command of individual legions and as commanders of expeditionary forces detached from the main army. Hence Caesar placed his quaestor and five legates in command of his six legions for the fight against Ariovistus, 'to act as witness of each man's valour'.[289] The quaestor was an elected magistrate, a senator at an early stage of his *cursus honorum*, who was supposed to administer the finances of the province and act as the governor's deputy. Similarly, in the early winter of 54 BC when his army was distributed over Gaul because of the difficulty of the food supply, the various areas were entrusted to picked legates.

Unlike military tribunes, these legates were not elected but chosen by Caesar from among his *amicitia*. Usually of senatorial rank, some of these men might be former proconsular governors or army commanders, providing the leadership, experience and stability that the legion needed to operate effectively. In Gaul the most prominent of these legates was Titus Atius Labienus, Caesar's second-in-command as a *legatus pro praetore* ('subordinate officer acting in place of a praetor'), who at times was employed as an independent army commander, and who commanded the entire army in Caesar's absence. Yet although the appointment of legates by Caesar was a makeshift, the benefit of it was so apparent that it was adopted by Augustus as a permanent solution.

The legates loom large in the military history of the late Republic, and many of them were first-rate soldiers of considerable experience. One such was Marcus Petreius, the son of a centurion under Catulus, Marius' consular colleague of 102 BC. Petreius, as you may remember, was responsible for the defeat and death of Catiline at Pistoria, and Sallust rated him as 'a good soldier, who for more than thirty years had served with great distinction as *tribunus*, *praefectus*, *legatus*, and *praetore*'.[290] Petreius' career owed much to Pompey, whom he later served as legate in Iberia over a number of years. There were many such military gentlemen, far more than our sources allow us to know, following the sort of career that Sallust by chance mentions for Petreius. For instance, when Cicero set out for Cilicia to take up the post as governor there, on his staff was a certain Marcus Anneius. 'My legatus', explains Cicero, 'is a man whose services, advice and military experience may clearly be invaluable to me and to the state.'[291] Cicero manifestly held his legate in high regard.

Caesar's Own

Possibly raised by Caesar personally when he was governor of Hispania Ulterior (61–60 BC), *legio X* was with him in Gaul (58–49 BC) and Iberia (49 BC), and fought at Pharsalus (48 BC) and Thapsus (46 BC). The survivors were discharged *en masse* after sixteen years' service (46–45 BC), but were fighting again at Munda (45 BC). The legion's emblem was the bull, perhaps reflecting its Caesarian origin as the bull was the zodiacal sign associated with Venus, legendary ancestress of the Iulii. It gained the cognomen *Equestris* after Caesar ordered some of the legion to mount up on the horses of his Gallic cavalry and accompany him to the parley with Ariovistus of the Suebi (58 BC). This prompted a wit among the soldiers to discern a further honour for this, already Caesar's favourite legion. For some time he had been treating the unit as his personal bodyguard, and now he was making all its members *equites* – the aristocratic cavalry traditionally provided by the equestrian order.[292] Of course, the *equites* had long since abandoned any military function and had turned into the social rank just below the senators. The actual cavalry (also *equites*) of Caesar's day consisted of auxiliaries, that is, non-Romans of inferior status to citizen legionaries. So by transferring the men of *legio X*, jokes the soldier, they are not being demoted but promoted.

Serve to Lead

Another important factor in preserving collected experience and skill in the army was the rise of the professional centurion. In a legion of Caesar's time there were sixty centurions, six in each of the ten cohorts. The highest centurial rank was that of *primus pilus*, 'first spear', the chief centurion of the legion who nominally commanded the first century in the first cohort. Although Polybios comments on the care taken to select determined fighters to fill the ranks of the centurionate of his day, it was only in the late Republic that these men became more prominent. In Caesar's narrative of his own campaigns the centurion more than any other grade of officer receives attention and praise, both collectively and as named individuals. They were men like Publius Sextius Baculus, *primus pilus* of the newly raised *legio XII*, who was seriously injured at the Sabis, Marcus Cassius Scaeva who received several serious wounds and lost an eye defending one of the forts at Dyrrhachium, and Caius Crastinus who died while leading the charge at Pharsalus.[293] These men are depicted as heroic figures, men who inspired the soldiers under their command through their conspicuous courage.

During the Gallic campaigns Caesar's army more than doubled in size, creating many opportunities for promotion to higher grades of the centurionate. Thus on several occasions he notes that he promoted gallant centurions from lower grades in veteran legions to higher positions in recently raised units. Scaeva, mentioned above, was transferred from 'the eighth cohort to the post of first centurion of the first cohort', that is, *primus pilus*.[294] Unfortunately, however, we have no real clue about the selection of these officers and whether they entered the army as officers or were promoted from the ranks. What is clear is that once a man joined the centurionate, he became an individual of some status and, in time, often a wealthy man from the booty he acquired and the bonuses he was paid. As well as promotion, Scaeva was rewarded with a bounty of 50,000 denarii, a princely sum equivalent to well over two hundred years' pay for an ordinary ranker.

Centurions controlled the lives of their men, the common legionary, *miles gregarius*, enforcing tight discipline with the business end of their badge of office, the *vitis*, a gnarled vine-branch held in the right hand. Besides the omnipresent *vitis*, centurions were also distinguished from their men by dress, both to denote rank and to be visible in the chaos of battle. A centurion's helmet was adorned with a transverse crest, *crista traversa*, rather than fore-and-aft like the legionary's. Centurions' armour during this period, except for their antiquated greaves, was pretty much like that of their men. They did, however, wear their *gladii* on the left rather than the right side, perhaps to keep it clear of the *vitis*.

In what he called his 'Commentaries', *commentarii*, Caesar himself emerges as the all-conquering general, but his centurions are the true heroes. They were a tough, hand-picked body of men of great dependability and courage. Referring to those celebrated rivals Titus Pullo and Lucius Vorenus, who vied with each other in exhibiting bravery, Caesar says the two centurions were 'close to entering the *primi ordines*'.[295] The six centurions of the first cohort were collectively known as the *primi ordines* ('the front rankers') and enjoyed immense prestige. Centurions *primorum ordinum* are coupled by Caesar with the military tribunes and were regarded as members of the councils of war he regularly held with his senior officers.[296] Wise commanders recognised the value of their centurions not only in leading men into battle, but also in providing valuable advice based on their experience of war. Caesar himself would have listened to their views and used them to pass on information and orders to the rank and file. Their understanding of a battle plan was vital for success simply because they were the ones leading the men on the ground. Centurions were the key to an army's success in battle, and Caesar knew it.

The Universal Soldier

In the *commentarii* the account is strictly of the campaigns themselves, and we learn almost nothing of the leisure activities of Caesar or his men, or the mundane facts of camp life, or the presence of women and camp-followers.

Caesar's Braves

Caesar names many centurions, especially the brave, but it is the epigraphical evidence that gives us a glimpse of the common soldiers. An epitaph from Capua records two brothers called Canuleius who served under Caesar in Gaul with *legio VII*. The elder, Quintus, was soon killed in action aged 18, but the younger, Caius, served throughout the campaigns – presumably including Britannia – and survived, having been recalled to the colours, to earn his honourable discharge. His military decorations included torcs (*torques*), armbands (*armillae*), medals (*phalerae*) and one crown (*corona*). He died aged 35, and the tombstone was put up by the brothers' loving father. From other tombstones we know also of a Quintus Cabilenus who served in *legio VIII*, a Vinusius in *legio IX*, and a Vettidius in *legio XII*.[297]

One of the bravest of the brave that we know of must have been the aforementioned Caius Crastinus. He was the former *primus pilus* of *legio X Equestris*, the role having gone to a younger centurion the previous year on Crastinus' retirement. On his recall, however, Caesar had welcomed Crastinus back to his legion as one of the other *primi ordines* and for the decisive encounter with Pompey at Pharsalus had placed the grizzled veteran at the head of 120 volunteers of the first cohort of *legio X Equestris*, putting them in the front line to lead the charge. Caesar had once more placed his favourite formation, now universally considered the stoutest of Caesar's legions, on the extreme right of his army, the attacking wing.

Crastinus was to fall that day, and after the battle Caesar, according to Appian, ordered his men to search carefully for his body among the carnage. Crastinus' corpse, on being recovered, was adorned with decorations of valour by Caesar, who then 'buried him with them and made a special tomb for him near the mass grave'.[298] As a norm, the Romans did not award posthumous decorations.

In most Latin literature, on the other hand, the faceless men in the ranks are characterised more by aggression, lechery, greed and boastfulness. For Suetonius, for example, lechery was a hallmark of both Caesar and his men. He offers plenty of anecdotes describing Caesar's sexual adventures, and quotes lines of an appropriately licentious song sung in Caesar's Gallic triumph, in which his men take vicarious pride in their beloved general's achievements:

> Home we bring our bald whoremonger;
> Romans, lock your wives away!
> All the gold you lent him,
> his Gallic tarts received as pay.
>
> Suetonius, *Divus Iulius*, 51.1

Naturally, there is nothing but march and battle, the fresh air of the camp and the excitement of action in his formal accounts of the Gallic campaigns. Neither Caesar nor his men are described as having anything to do with the prostitutes who were a regular part of army life. Likewise, the men are motivated by honour and loyalty – but also by financial gain. Caesar himself not only paid off his astronomical debts but became extremely wealthy too, and it is certain that many, if not most, of the legates were considerably enriched. It was well known at Rome that an appointment to Caesar's staff was a passport to wealth. The common soldiers too stood to gain, from slaves and loot. Such factors were not negligible in their support for Caesar, and he could not afford to ignore them. The baggage train, of which Caesar took the greatest care while the army was on the move, contained the soldiers' accumulated wealth, which he and they were concerned not to endanger.

Other negative characteristics such as aggression, greed and boastfulness do surface, but only in set contexts, intended to help the reader evaluate the progress of an action or anticipate its outcome. So, for example, if greed and aggression belong to the domain of Gauls or Germans, they tend to signal moral and martial inferiority to the Romans. If they are attributed to Romans, it is usually because Caesar wants to explain a setback. When the legionaries of Lucius Aurunculeius Cotta and Quintus Titurius Sabinus sought to escape from their winter quarters, much heart-searching went on over what was to be left behind. Even so, the quantity taken on the moving column was still large, and when the decision was taken to abandon everything, soldiers broke ranks to save what they could of their own possessions.[299] Similarly, when the impetuous and ill-organised attack on the walls of Gergovia came unstuck and met with a bloody reverse, Caesar reprimands the troops for disobeying the orders of their military tribunes and legates. Caesar's only criticism of them in his account is to say that they were simply too confident and eager to win his praise.[300]

It may seem surprising to find aggression appearing as a mainly negative attribute, especially as we see the Roman army as one of the most aggressive institutions in history, but throughout his writings Caesar stresses the relationship between himself and his men as one of cooperation and above all control. Uncontrolled aggression poses a threat to strategic planning and careful tactics. The proof of this comes from the Gauls and the Germans, whose random aggression is highlighted to form a vivid contrast with the channelled, organised sort displayed by the Romans.

Pen and Sword

As with many Roman military operations of the period, Caesar's invasion of Gaul was motivated by a mixture of personal self-aggrandisement, novel wealth-creation schemes for himself and his *amicitia*, furtherance of the glory of Rome and a genuine need to keep Rome's enemies at bay. Unlike Cicero, who argued that the scope of war was the search for peace, Caesar looked at the problem in a more realistic vein.[301] War was meant to conquer people and establish Roman rule. The end result was to bring glory and wealth to those in the field and the citizens back home. The conquest of Gaul was the greatest of Caesar's achievements, yet at the time it was little more than a stepping-stone in his struggle for power.

In this, as we well know, Caesar had the great advantage of being a man of letters as well as a man of war. It was a talent that enabled him to be, as the Romans said, his own herald. He wrote seven *commentarii* on his campaigns in Gaul, with a further three dealing with the subsequent war against Pompey. Additional *commentarii*, that were not written by Caesar himself but produced after his death by officers who had served under him, cover the final operations in Gaul and the remainder of the Second Civil War.[302]

By calling them *commentarii* the author meant they were not drab history but more like a general's front-line dispatches enlivened by letters exchanged between Caesar and the Senate. In all probability he wrote all seven *commentarii* on the Gallic War, the *Bellum Gallicum*, in the winter of 52/1 BC, meaning of course they were published at a particularly opportune time. The image of him revealed by the *commentarii* – soldier, statesman and strategist – surely did much to ensure the popularity he needed to win the eventual showdown with Pompey as they presented a Roman Caesar who was more than the equal of Pompey as the great conqueror of the east. Whereas Pompey was glorified by the Greek intelligentsia around him, the great man himself being somewhat ill at ease with the pen, Caesar was now glorified by his own clear Latin. Written in the third person, the artful commentaries use the proper noun 'Caesar' 775 times. With or without the assistance of Shakespeare, Caesar (as seen by Caesar) would have lived in history because, quite simply, he decided that it should be so.

Yet, although his 'manifesto of propaganda' may have been prepared for popular consumption, it is still a historical document of major importance, for it was based on Caesar's own notes and battle reports. To Caesar's own seven *commentarii*, one of his officers, Aulus Hirtius (later *cos.* 43 BC), added an eighth not long after Caesar's death, which brought the historical record up to 50 BC.[303] Hirtius, who would himself be dead within another year, combined Caesar's unpublished notes with additional material, some of which he wrote himself. Interestingly, Hirtius is nowhere mentioned as a legate in the Gallic campaigns, and was a wealthy person of scholarly taste. Apparently he was also somewhat of a gourmet, and Cicero reckons it was risky to ask him to dinner.[304]

Destroyer of Gaul

Caesar famously opens his first *commentarius* with a brief description of what he identifies as Gaul, dividing its inhabitants, culturally and linguistically, into three broad groups, the Celtae or Galli, the Aquitani and the Belgae.[305] The first were located between the Garunna (Garonne) and Sequana (Seine), the second in modern Gascony, and the third north of the Sequana and Matrona (Marne). Of the three, Caesar held that the Belgae were the most courageous. All these tribes were still largely untouched, as Caesar says, by the enervating luxuries of Mediterranean life, and they were probably mixed with Germanic peoples from east of the Rhenus (Rhine).

The Battle of the Sabis, 57 BC

At this time Caesar commanded eight legions, two of which were still *en route*, and an unknown number of auxiliaries including specialists such as Numidian javelineers, Cretan archers and Balearic slingers. The six legions were entrenching their camp for the night on rising ground above the Sabis (Sambre) when the enemy charged out of the marshland and forest some 300 metres on the other side of the river, crossed it, and raced up the slopes towards them with incredible speed. According to Caesar, and the following account is very much based upon that given by him in his second *commentarius*, his army faced at least 60,000 warriors of the Nervii, the fiercest of the Belgic tribes, along with the Artebates and Viromandui. Whatever the actual numbers may have been, there is no doubt that they outnumbered Caesar's 40,000 legionaries.

Almost wrong-footed by this sudden attack, the legionaries dropped their entrenching tools, grabbed their arms and automatically created a line-of-battle by falling in around the nearest standard instead of seeking their own cohorts. Thus a ragged improvised battle line was formed, with *legiones VIIII* and *X* holding the left wing, *legiones VIII* and *XI* the centre, and *legiones VII* and *XII* the right wing. Opposite them the Nervii created a very strong left wing, the Viromandui held the centre, and the Artebates the right wing. The two cavalry forces were already hotly engaged, with the Gauls mauling the Roman auxiliaries, many of them Gauls too.

Despite the battle line being cut up by the broken terrain, the legionaries held fast and withstood the Belgic onslaught. The Roman centre was successful and the left wing repulsed the Artebates, driving them pell-mell down the slope and across the Sabis, before chasing them up the rising ground on the far side. This success left the half-built Roman camp and the right wing of the battle line exposed and the Gauls quickly captured the camp and baggage train.

In the meantime the Nervii had outflanked the Roman right wing. Here the legionaries were in great difficulties as most of their centurions had been killed or injured and their ranks had become too closely packed together to allow them to operate effectively. The situation was critical. Caesar dismounted and grabbed a *scutum* from a man in the rear, then made his way to the forefront of the fighting line, yelling orders for the ranks to open up and the two legions to form a square so they could defend themselves from attack on all sides. His own energetic reaction and presence on foot helped to stiffen resistance until aid arrived in the form of the veteran *legio X Equestris*, which had been sent back by Labienus to assist after capturing the enemy encampment, and the two greenhorn units of the rearguard, *legiones XIII* and *XIIII*, which had finally arrived. The combined force of five legions turned the tide of battle and annihilated the Nervii, who refused to surrender or retreat.[306]

Caesar's over-confidence had led to a near-disaster, but his personal bravery and the experience of some of his legions – the knowledge, too, that defeat meant massacre – turned it into a significant victory. This successful engagement had broken the power of the Belgae to such an extent that even Germanic tribes beyond the Rhine sent envoys to Caesar offering submission.

The limited use of armour by the Gallic warriors, and the need to swing long slashing-swords, rendered them vulnerable to the relatively short stabbing swords of the legionaries, who were well protected by their *scuta*. Moreover, Gallic war bands were fragile, virtually clouds of individuals almost as much in competition with each other for glory as in conflict with the foe. They consequently lacked cohesion, which made for a fine line between success and failure. In contrast, Roman legionaries were trained to fight as teams, to trust each other and to remain steady under pressure. This difference gave the legions a decisive tactical edge.

The Celtic Art of War

The Celts had a fearsome reputation for aggressiveness, even among the militaristic Romans, and there can be no doubt that warfare played a central role in Celtic society. For the nobles, raiding offered the opportunity of wealth, prestige and reputation to further political aspirations at home. As in Germania, a retinue could only be maintained by actual fighting and they seem to have been at least semi-permanent and, added to their clients, formed a strong nucleus for the tribal army. They were far outnumbered, however, by the mass of ordinary warriors composed of all free tribesmen able to equip themselves. The latter appear to have been made up of war bands based on clan, familiar and settlement groupings, making a man's relatives the witness of his behaviour.

It is likely that the boldest (or more foolhardy) and best equipped naturally gravitated to the front rank. Body armour seems to have been very rare and the combination of shield, long slashing-sword and short spear(s) formed the equipment of most warriors. The appearance of the individual, his size, expressions and war cries, added to the din of clashing weapons and the harsh braying of the *carnyx*, or war trumpet, were clearly intended to intimidate the enemy before actually reaching them. If the enemy was persuaded he was going to lose before an actual mêlée began, then a Celtic charge would drive all before it. Tactics were simple and relied on a headlong rush by a screaming mass of warriors in a rough phalangial order headed by their war leaders. As was common in tribal armies, the warriors were poorly disciplined and lacked training above the level of the individual. And so after a violent and savage onslaught launched amid a colossal din, the individual warrior battered his way into the enemy's ranks punching with his shield, thrusting with his spear or slashing with his sword.

Cavalry provided the highest quality troops in any Celtic army. They were drawn chiefly from the nobles – the *equites* mentioned by Caesar – and their retinues and clients. Because of their recruitment from the wealthier and more prestigious warriors, equipment was of good quality and consisted of a shield, javelins, a short spear and a long slashing-sword, and often helmet and mail armour. Added to this was the four-horned saddle, later adopted by the Romans, a key technical innovation that provided a thoroughly secure seat. The morale of these horse-bands was usually very high; even when outclassed by the much heavier Parthian *cataphractarii* at Carrhae, the younger Crassus' Gallic horse fought fiercely.[307] Tactics were normally simple: a shower of javelins was thrown, and followed up by a charge using spears and swords. Naturally, discipline was normally poor, so they were difficult to rally from pursuit or rout.

In the early encounters between the Celts and the Romans, it was the two-horse war chariot that attracted most Roman interest. It appears that the main use of the chariot was for causing panic. The charioteers would drive their vehicles against the enemy lines in a rush, the warriors throwing javelins as they did so, and this, coupled with the mere speed and noise of the chariots, was often enough to unsettle the opposition. Once this initial stage had been accomplished, the warriors dismounted from the chariots and, in true 'Homeric' style, fought on foot, while the charioteers kept the chariots at the ready to effect, if necessary, a speedy retreat. Livy mentions that some 1,000 chariots took part in the battle of Sentinum (295 BC), and at Telamon (225 BC) an unknown number of chariots were stationed on the wings of the Gallic forces.[308] As their prowess and agility as horsemen increased, so the Gauls gradually gave up the chariot. Chariots were no longer in fashion when Caesar was conquering Gaul, and he was surprised to find them still in use in Britannia. Caesar was evidently fascinated by these war chariots, with their fearful clamour of hooves and wheels, and describes their role in battle at some length.[309]

Finally a few words on the Celtic slashing-sword. Cemeteries were an initial key to the archaeology of the Celts and many of the greatest surviving La Tène treasures come from graves. In common with many earlier societies, the dead were buried in full clothing, perhaps in some cases clad in especially fine ceremonial garments and accoutrements. The clothes rarely survive, although occasionally the processes of corrosion preserve impressions and even fragments of textiles on metal objects (e.g. jewellery and metal fastenings). Weapons and even food and drink were also buried, and graves can tell us much about how the Celtic warrior was dressed, armed and provisioned.

Polybios describes how some Celtic swords were made of such poor metal that they bent on impact, thereby requiring the owner to retire and stamp the blade back into shape with his foot before re-entering the fray.[310] This view is contradicted by the archaeological record, which suggests Celtic swords were very well made with a good edge and great flexibility. Polybios' story of swords that bend reads like one of those tall tales told by soldiers to while away idle moments around the camp fire. Nevertheless, other authors took up Polybios' comments and criticisms.[311] The one notable exception was Philon of Byzantium (*fl. c.* 200 BC) who, in an illuminating passage written around the time of Polybios' birth, describes how the Celts tested the excellence of their swords:

> They grasp the hilt in the right hand and the end of the blade in the left: then, laying it horizontally on their heads, they pull down at each end until they [i.e. the ends] touch their shoulders. Next, they let go sharply, removing both hands. When released, it straightens itself out again and so resumes its original shape, without retaining a suspicion of a bend. Though they repeat this frequently, the swords remain straight.
>
> Philon, *Belopeika*, 4.71

Swords exhibited various general and local fashions during the La Tène period. Blades were short from the fifth to the third centuries BC. Improvements in iron technology and changes in fighting style resulted in the two-edged sword designed for slashing, often of enormous length and round-ended, in the second and first centuries BC. Surviving examples of this period have an overall length range of about 85 to 90 centimetres, with some having a blade length of 90 centimetres without the handle. Quality varies, but few of these blades descend to the poor quality described by Polybios.

In the hands of a tall Celtic warrior with a long reach the sword could be a deadly weapon, especially against shorter opposition with shorter blades. The sword was considered the weapon of the high-status warrior, and to carry one was to display a symbol of rank and prestige. Perhaps surprisingly it was worn on the right, hanging from a waist-belt of metal chain. The chain passed through a suspension loop on the back of the scabbard and kept the weapon upright, helping to prevent the sword from becoming entangled with the warrior's legs as he walked or ran. It is in fact fairly easy to draw even a long blade from this position. As we well know, Roman legionaries, likewise, wore their swords on the right.

Caesar makes much of the Rhine as a boundary. To him, and to his readers, the river was indeed a symbolic boundary between the known and the unknown. But to say that the Rhine was the divide between the Gauls and the Germanic tribes was little more than a convenient generalisation. Archaeological evidence of settlements in northern Gaul indicates that some of the tribes known as Germanic to the Romans may well have been Celtic, or a mixture of the two. Thus it is more realistic to assume that a broad band of hybridisation extended on both sides of the river. Indeed it seems that the territory between the Seine and the Rhine shared a cultural gradient between Celtic and Germanic that was constantly being reformed by tribal movements.

Caesar does mention the Germanic antecedents of the Belgae, whose name meant 'furious ones', but the overall description of Gaul that he offers is at best a generalisation. The population of Gaul – as of the Celtic territories generally – was descended both from earlier peoples and from the Celts (and others) who had migrated there. Furthermore the Gauls were not a nation; they were a complex of tribal groups in different stages of social development. It is probably true, however, that the entire population was divided into 200 to 300 tribes, a few large and many small, and of the latter many were clients of the former. In the main these tribes, great and small, lived in settlements scattered round a central refuge to which the Romans applied the term *oppidum*.

The location and design of these *oppida* varied greatly. Many were situated on high ground, but others were on flat land, and whereas some had elaborate defences others had few or none. The usual type of defence consisted of timber palisades, but some *oppida* had substantial stone walls. Caesar's description of the typical Gallic defensive work – the *mura gallicus* – which he encountered at Avaricum (52 BC)[312] is of particular interest since the type has been recognised at a number of excavated sites both in France and Germany. The *mura gallicus* type of construction used vertical walling and horizontal timbering, with the timbers nailed on with large iron spikes. Notwithstanding this, the pattern of Gallic urbanisation, with the development of *oppida* as centres of government and economic activity, was becoming well established by the time of Caesar.[313]

His fellow Romans would have referred to these regions as Gallia Comata (Long-haired Gaul). A fourth region is usually referred to by Caesar as Provincia, the Province. Its official name was Gallia Transalpina (Gaul-across-the-Alps) in contrast to Gallia Cisalpina (Gaul-this-side-of-the-Alps). In the Italian peninsula the Rubicon (Rubicone) marked the boundary between Gallia Cisalpina and Italy proper. Gallia Transalpina, unlike Gallia Comata, was already part of the empire. It had come under Roman control in the second century BC, following the development of Roman links with the Greek trading colony of Massilia (the Latin form of Massalia, now Marseilles) and the establishment of a permanent fortified outpost at Aquae Sextiae (Aix-en-Provence), the site of Marius' victory against the Teutones in 102 BC. Gallia Transalpina gave the Romans an important land-route from north Italy to Iberia, where Roman influence had been much longer established. The control of this route, along which successive Roman armies passed, and the safeguarding of Roman economic interests were thus of major concern to the Senate. Cicero wrote 'all Gaul is filled with Italian traders, all Provincia is full of Roman citizens',[314] an exaggeration no doubt, but when the stability of Gaul was threatened by the migration of the Helvetii and the political machinations of the Germanic war leader Ariovistus, Caesar was provided with an admirable excuse to move his legions deep into uncharted territory.

Caesar's uncle had saved Italy from the threatened invasion of the Cimbri and the Teutones, whose victories inflicted on earlier Roman commanders echo ominously in the background of the *commentarii*, but the vivid memory of the near-disaster remained. Barbarian migrations were the stuff of Roman nightmares, and Caesar made good use of it by playing up the 'Germanic menace'.[315] His assessment of the Gallic political scene – Gaul would have to become Roman or it would be overrun by the fierce warlike Germanic race – was probably a gross hyperbole but as a justification for his Gallic campaigns it would have convinced many who remembered the panic of fifty years before.

The forces available to Caesar when he arrived in Gallia Cisalpina consisted of three legions, numbered in orderly sequence from *VII* to *VIIII*, with a further legion, *X*, in Gallia Transalpina. These legions were supported by an unspecified number of auxiliaries, including Iberian horsemen, Numidian javelineers and perhaps also horsemen, Cretan archers and Balearic slingers, along with a number of locally raised Gallic troops, horsemen in the main. We know nothing about the previous history of Caesar's legions, except that they were already in his provinces when he took up his command. Under the legislation appointing him to the command he was allowed a quaestor to handle the financial affairs of the provinces, and ten legates whom he could appoint directly, without reference to the Senate.

Bellum Gallicum

Caesar's writing style is that of a detailed factual report, prepared year by year, of the events as they unfold. As the French essayist Michel de Montaigne complained, 'the only thing to be said against him is that he speaks too sparingly of himself'.[316] Caesar certainly chose to ignore the triumvirate and its renewal at the Luca conference, and does not give his own account of the final deterioration of relations between himself and Pompey. Worse, he masks the war's horrendous cost in human life and suffering. In any event, what follows is a year by year skeleton of the events as recorded by Caesar (and Hirtius).

Book I 58BC

Having raised from scratch two legions (XI and XII) in Italy, thus bringing his total to six legions, Caesar campaigned against the Helvetii, a Celtic people akin to the Gauls, inhabiting what is now western Switzerland near lakes Constance and Geneva. Apparently these peoples were migrating *en masse* towards the fertile region of the Santones (Saintonge) in south-west Gaul and thus were regarded as a dangerous threat to the province of Gallia Transalpina. Also this movement westwards left their old homeland open to Germanic settlement, and unless Rome took Gaul, reasoned Caesar, the Germans would. Caesar finally defeated the Helvetii at Bibracte (Mont-Beuvray, west of Autun), which was a close-run battle indeed.

Next up were the Germanic tribes under Ariovistus of the Suebi, on whom the Senate, ironically during Caesar's own consulship, had conferred the official but rather vague title of *socius et amicus Romani populi*. Exploiting the rivalries between the Sequani and the Aedui, the latter a comparatively stable pro-Roman enclave on the fringe of Roman territory, the Germans were crossing the upper Rhenus (Rhine) to seize the lands of these Gallic tribes. Caesar understood that to succeed in Gaul he needed to eliminate this migratory element from the equation. Ariovistus, a man of marked ability, quickly outflanked Caesar and then sat squarely on his line of communications. The thunderstruck Caesar was compelled to regain his line of retreat, but finally managed to force a battle on the Germans. After a terrible contest, Caesar defeated them, destroying subsequently the whole tribe, and relentlessly drove the few survivors across the Rhine.

Caesar had made blunders, which in later campaigns he would not repeat. He left his legions in winter quarters among the Sequani well to the north of the formal boundary of Gallia Transalpina, and he himself returned to Gallia Cisalpina. It would be his habit throughout the campaigns to spend the winter months there, carrying out his judicial and administrative activities as governor as well as keeping a close eye on the politics of Rome.

Book II 57BC

By this stage it was clear that Caesar had decided on total conquest. Raising a further two legions (*XIII* and *XIIII*), Caesar, now with eight legions, turned his attention to the subjugation of the Belgae, a loose confederation of warlike tribes who occupied the territory north of the Sequana (Seine). Some of them were settled on the shores of the North Sea, and significant groups had been crossing to Britannia for several generations and establishing kingdoms there. Having beaten a substantial Belgic army near Bibrax (either Beaurieux or Vieux Laon) in the territory of the Remi, Caesar quickly moved northwards against the more remote Belgic tribes, the Nervii and the Aduatuci.

The Nervii, a fierce warrior people, proclaimed they would rather accept death than Roman domination and rebuked their fellow-countrymen for having turned to Rome. A near-defeat at the river Sabis (Sambre), after the Nervii surprised Caesar in an ambush, came close to annihilating his army. His narrow escape made him thereafter much more cautious on the march. During the same season Publius Licinius Crassus, the dashing young son of the dynast, had campaigned against the Veneti and other maritime tribes that bordered upon the Atlantic between the mouth of the Seine and the Liger (Loire) estuary. The encirclement of Gaul was thus completed, but Caesar evidently recognised that his task was not finished as the legions were kept in the north, probably along the Loire, throughout that winter.

Book III 56BC

A rumour that Caesar intended to invade Britannia prompted the Veneti to revolt. They were skilful seamen, had a powerful ocean-going fleet of oak-built sailing ships, and held the monopoly of the carrying trade with southern Britannia; Caesar says as much, and archaeological evidence confirms his statement. British goods were exchanged for luxury imports, the most significant one being Italian wine shipped to the island in large ceramic amphorae. The reverse traffic would have included metals, in particular tin, together with grain, cattle, slaves, hides and hunting dogs.[317] Anyway, whatever the immediate cause, the real reason for the revolt probably lay in the fact that the submissions extracted in the previous year by Publius Licinius were all but nominal.

Caesar's attempts to attack by land proved abortive, as many of the Venetic strongholds were built on isolated spits of land often only accessible by sea, but one of his ablest legates, Decimus Iunius Brutus Albinus, the future tyrannicide, with a fleet constructed for the occasion, overcame the Veneti at sea. Caesar, with needless cruelty it seems, put the whole of the elder council to the sword and sold the tribe into slavery. Publius Licinius, meanwhile, had subdued some of the tribes of Aquitania. Towards the end of the season Caesar himself led an attack on the Morini and the Menapii, tribes of the Belgae on the North Sea littoral who had not yet surrendered. They quickly withdrew into the forests, creating difficulties for Caesar, and the onset of bad weather forced him to pull back.

Book IV 55BC

Caesar started the season campaigning in Illyricum against the Pirustae, who had been raiding Roman territory. He then defeated the Usipetes and the Tencteri, two Germanic tribes that had been crowded across the Rhine by the Suebi, the strongest nation on the eastern bank. Caesar marched against them, and was met by an offer of peace. Caesar alleged treachery on their part in the negotiations, but his own version in the *commentarii* does not sustain this. During what was an armistice, Caesar, by a rapid and unexpected march, fell upon the tribes and utterly destroyed them. A few thousand survivors managed to escape across the river. So indignant was Cato – his bitter political opponent, to be sure – at this act of unnecessary extermination that he openly proposed in the Senate to send Caesar loaded in chains to the few survivors for just punishment.[318]

Caesar then decided to intimidate the Germanic tribes further. More a publicity stunt than a punitive sortie, this trans-Rhine campaign was directed against the Sugambri. Caesar, as much an engineering genius as a master soldier, in just ten days built a trestle-bridge across the Rhine near present-day Coblenz. The first Roman invasion of Germania lasted a mere eighteen days and the devastation wrought was little short of terrorism, indeed Caesar admits as much. Despite the season being well advanced, Caesar conducted a precarious raid against the Belgic tribes of south-eastern Britannia with two veteran legions (*VII* and *X*) and 500 cavalry. Caesar risked everything by leading an under-strength and poorly supplied force to an unknown land across a boisterous sea. He landed at a point 7 Roman miles west of modern Dover, variously identified as present-day Lympne in Romney Marsh, or between Walmer Castle and Deal.

It could be said that one of his greatest traits as a general, his *celeritas* or quickness of action, became a burden. Yet Caesar was an adventurer and showman who could not resist the lure of the unknown. Some battles were fought, some settlements burnt and some hostages taken. Back home the publicity was excellent as Britannia was represented as 'beyond the Ocean', which had certainly limited the ambitions of Alexander the Great. Even Cicero was caught up in the hype, planning to write an epic poem on the 'glorious conquest', based on front-line reports from his brother Quintus.[319]

Book V 54BC

With a much better prepared plan of campaign, Caesar returned to Britannia with five legions (over half his total army) and 2,000 cavalry. He landed unopposed somewhere between present-day Sandown and Sandwich, reached the Thames and defeated Cassivelaunus of the Catuvellauni, a Gallo-Belgic tribe and at the time one of the most powerful peoples in all of Britannia – the aggressive behaviour of the Catuvellauni towards other tribes had already become notorious.

However, on his return to Gaul in the autumn he was faced with a major revolt of the Belgae and the Treveri precipitated by the charismatic war leader Ambiorix of the Eburones, a small but hardy tribe in the Ardennes. In the flurry of events that ensued, *legio XIIII* (one of the newest formations) and five cohorts of raw recruits (perhaps the core of a new legion), under the joint command of the two legates Lucius Aurunculeius Cotta and Quintus Titurius Sabinus, were surrounded and all but annihilated. The massacre of Roman troops was a huge blow to Caesar's prestige – it is noteworthy that Caesar portrays Sabinus as an inept coward – and it demonstrated to the Gauls for the first time that Caesar was not invincible. As a result the Nervii were emboldened to mount a determined, but ultimately unsuccessful, formal siege of the winter camp held by Quintus Tullius Cicero, the orator's brother.

With the luxury of hindsight, it is easy for us to argue that Caesar, who was relying on the supposed subjection of the Gauls, had quartered his legions unwisely far apart. With his usual luck and brilliance, however, he managed to avoid disaster. Yet the troops posted in their winter camps among the Belgae must have been feeling distinctly uneasy, and the recent events were a firm reminder to all and sundry that Gaul was by no means conquered. Further rebellions, even more serious, were to follow.

Book VI 53BC

Following the disastrous winter the campaigning season's efforts concentrated on re-establishing Roman control in north-eastern Gaul. Vicious punitive strikes against the recalcitrant Nervii forced them to surrender. Next followed operations against the Menapii, which forced them to submit for the first time, and the Treveri. Caesar built a second bridge close to the first location, and led a punitive expedition over the Rhine to punish the Germanic tribes for having aided the Gauls. But supply problems and an unwillingness to face the Suebi limited the scope of Caesar's operations.[320]

An interesting aspect of this year's campaigning was Caesar's need to bring the Senones and Carnutes to heel. Both tribes occupied land south of the Seine and hitherto had been left largely unmolested. This action was probably mounted because these tribes were providing safe havens for dissidents. Moreover, Caesar tells us that the druids met annually in the territory of the Carnutes, the 'centre' of all Gaul, and they were the one force that could unite the Gauls. Anyway, to date it had been a relentless war of attrition. In the long term Roman discipline and Caesar's ability to regroup and bring up reserves could not fail against a foe distracted by jarring factions and weakened by the devastation of their crops and herds.

By the end of the year Caesar had increased his army to ten legions with the formation of two units (*XIIII* and *XV*, the former replacing the 'lost' *XIIII*) and the borrowing of another, *legio I*, from Pompey (it had been part of the latter's consular army of 55 BC). As the year drew to a close some 2,000 Sugambrian horsemen crossed the Rhine and raided Gaul. They also attacked Caesar's central supply base at Aduatuca (somewhere near modern-day Tongres) where his sick and wounded were recuperating, under the protection of the green and raw *legio XIIII*. Only the heroism of certain individuals, especially the centurions, saved the day.[321]

Book VII 52BC

Over the winter months Caesar enrolled non-citizen soldiers in Gallia Transalpina: the genesis of the famed *legio V Alaudae*.[322] In theory, Roman citizens alone were eligible for legionary service. Another legion, numbered *VI*, was brought into service a little later in the year. In his narrative Caesar would have his reader believe he was bringing stability to Gaul. But Caesar's strategy of annihilation had engendered a spirit of desperation, which detonated into a revolt of Gallic tribes under the leadership of the Arvernian noble Vercingétorix. Though the Gallic peoples shared a common language and culture, forging a coalition among the fiercely independent tribes was a virtually impossible feat, and it was a tribute to Vercingétorix's personality and skill that he achieved it.

Initially Vercingétorix's strategy was to draw the Romans into pitched battle, and major engagements were fought at the *oppida* of Niviodunum (?Neuvy-sur-Barangeon), Avaricum (Bourges), and Gergovia (La Roche Blanche, south of Clermont-Ferrand). It was at the Arvernian *oppidum* of Gergovia that Vercingétorix came within a hair's breadth of beating the Romans, who lost almost 700 men, including 46 centurions, but Caesar just managed to pull off a pyrrhic victory. The young war leader was by far the most able of Caesar's opponents. He soon realised that in pitched battle he was unable to match the Romans, who were too well trained and disciplined to be beaten in open warfare, and thus began a policy of small skirmishes and defensive manoeuvres, which gravely hampered Caesar's movements by cutting off his supplies.

In the event, by brilliant leadership, force of arms and occasionally sheer luck, Caesar stamped out the revolt in a long and brutal action, which culminated in the siege of Alésia (Alise-Sainte-Reine, north of Dijon). Alésia was to be the last significant resistance to the Roman will. It involved virtually every Gallic tribe, including the pro-Roman Aedui, in a disastrous defeat, and there were enough captives for each legionary to be awarded one to sell as a slave. Taken in chains to Rome, Vercingétorix was to languish in a cell for the next six years before being garrotted at Caesar's unprecedented quadruple triumph in 46 BC.[323] Meantime, during the winter Caesar embarked on a punitive campaign against the Carnutes, who had started the revolt.

Book VIII 51BC

The opening words of the eighth book 'The whole of Gaul was now conquered' were true to a point. Gaul was now completely under Roman control but there were still pockets of discontent that Caesar and his legates had to deal with. In the north, among the Belgae, the Bellovaci made a nuisance of themselves by threatening the clients of Rome's traditional allies the Remi. In the spring Caesar marched to Belgica to suppress the Bellovaci, and his show of strength dealt a final blow to latent Belgic resistance. Hirtius, who now takes up the story, mentions a concerted plan, but these troubles appeared to be nothing other than the backwash of Alésia.

The last remaining serious resistance was in the south-west where Drappes, a Senonian with influence among other tribes, and Lucterius, a local Cadurcan, took over the well-fortified *oppidum* of Uxellodunum (Puy d'Issolu) overlooking the Duranius (Dordogne). The stronghold fell after Caesar cut it off from its water-supply; to put a stop to further revolts, Caesar ordered the cutting off of the hands of all those who had borne arms against him. This atrocity thus brought the conquest of Gaul to its bitter end. The rest of the campaign season was spent mopping up, sometimes with great ruthlessness, the many pockets of resistance that still remained. By the end of his last year in Gaul Caesar was able to return to Gallia Cisalpina content in the knowledge that his conquests and achievements would survive.

In Retrospect

Caesar's ambition had come to fruition, yet it is important to remember that his practical military experience before he went to Gaul had been minimal. It had included that fascinating private encounter with pirates as a young man (75 BC), and a brief participation as a junior officer in Asia and Cilicia (Second Mithridatic War, 83–81 BC), where he was to win the *corona civica* for saving the life of a fellow soldier at the storming of Mytilene (81 BC). It is possible he saw some action as a military tribune sometime during the Slave War (73–71 BC). Also, a few years before his Gallic command, he had tasted warfare at first hand as propraetor in Iberia (61–60 BC).

Caesar's initial conquest of Gaul had been deceptively simple. However, many of the Gallic tribes did not remain docile for long, and their uprisings alternating with Roman reprisals soon assumed the aspect of a vicious circle. The Gallic War ended with the fall of Uxellodunum, and the price paid by the Gauls was both terrible and enormous. Caesar and his legions had been actively campaigning in Gaul for eight years, each season slaughtering large numbers of people and enslaving tens of thousands of others. In many of the campaigns whole landscapes were torched. Caesar, according to Plutarch, 'had taken by storm more than eight hundred towns, subdued three hundred nations, and of the three million men who made up the total of those with whom at different times he fought pitched battles, he had killed one million of them in hand-to-hand fighting and took as many more prisoners, with more than one million being sold into slavery'.[324] So some 3 million Gauls were lost out of a population of an estimated 12 million. Whatever their accuracy, and the population figure itself is purely conjectural, these figures reflect a perception among Caesar's contemporaries that this war against the Gauls had been something exceptional, at once terrible and splendid beyond compare. They also show Caesar's disregard for human life.

> And the tall men and the swordsmen and the horsemen,
> where are they?[325]
>
> W.B. Yeats, 'The Curse of Cromwell'

Chapter 7

Pompey versus Caesar

In March 50 BC, because of the shattering defeat suffered by Crassus, the Senate ordered that Pompey and Caesar should each send a legion to Syria. Caesar complied, and on his account sent *legio XV*, incidentally, or deliberately, one of the newest formations, which was then on hand in Gallia Cisalpina. Pompey, proclaiming submission to the Senate as a solemn duty, nominated the one, namely *legio I*, he had loaned to Caesar after the loss of one of his legions during the winter débâcle of 54 BC.[326] The contemplated expedition against Parthia apparently did not materialise and when the legions arrived in Italy they were quartered at Capua, and remained there until the outbreak of the Second Civil War, though Cassius Dio affirms that a Parthian campaign, which was now over, had actually been conducted by Caesar's erstwhile consular colleague Bibulus.[327] Whether or not a campaign across the Euphrates had actually taken place, this was all a pretext for depriving Caesar of the two legions. And so these legions were retained by Pompey, though their loyalty was somewhat questionable, and were subsequently numbered *I* and *III* in his army.[328]

Countdown to War

On 1 December 50 BC the Caesarian tribune Caius Scribonius Curio vetoed the appointment of Domitius Ahenobarbus as successor to Caesar. This young noble of keen intellect and audacity had begun the year as a champion of the *optimates* and a staunch opponent of Caesar, but since Caesar had paid off Curio's monstrous debts his loyalty had been secured. Still, that was not the only incentive, for Clodius' widow Fulvia was his wife, and Marcus Antonius his close friend. So that his change of sides might not be detected, Curio moved that, so as to avoid civil discord, both warlords should disarm. Curio's artful motion was carried by 370 to 22, but it would be a rash and factious minority that prevailed. In a rage the consul Caius Claudius Marcellus dismissed the Senate and exclaimed: 'Enjoy your victory and have Caesar for master'.[329] The following day, with a Senate desperate to avoid open war, Cicero attempted to broker a peace deal. But as if to stiffen Pompey, the rash but unstable Marcellus went out to Pompey's villa outside Rome and put a sword in his champion's hands and asked him to save the Republic and he agreed.[330] Pompey then took command of the two legions in Capua and set about raising fresh levies.

Back in the dog days of summer Cicero's articulate but raffish friend Marcus Caelius Rufus had written that the 'love-affair' between Pompey and Caesar had broken up and that there would soon be a 'gladiatorial fight' between the two of them as the former 'is determined not to allow Caesar to be elected consul, unless he has handed over his army, and his provinces', while the latter 'is convinced that there is no safety for him, if he once quits his army'.[331] As consul Caesar would have no soldiers at hand, while Pompey, as proconsul of Iberia, would continue to head a considerable army. For discerning observers like Caelius it was obvious that Caesar could not accept a second consulship on those terms. 'Pompey would tolerate no equal, Caesar no superior.'[332]

On 1 January 49 BC Marcus Antonius and Quintus Cassius Longinus, Caesarian tribunes of the people and veterans of the Gallic campaigns, attempted to force the Senate to hear a mutual disarmament proposal from Caesar but the consuls, fearing that those senators who were inclined toward peace would vote in its favour, refused to allow the letter to be read. Instead Quintus Caecilius Metellus Pius Scipio, father-in-law and colleague of Pompey in his third consulship, proposed that Caesar lay down his command at a fixed date or be declared a *hostis*, an enemy of the state. The resolution was passed and six days later Caesar's province was taken from him. Only two senators opposed this prodigious decision, namely Curio and Caelius. Antonius and Cassius, as tribunes, vetoed it. On 7 January Antonius and Cassius, their veto disregarded, were warned to quit the Senate as a *senatus consultum ultimum* was about to be passed, which would effectively introduce martial law. This was a decree that was only rarely passed by the Senate and only at times when great danger was feared. The two tribunes fled north to Caesar, then camped in winter quarters at Ravenna, and on the night of 10 January Caesar crossed the Rubicon into Italy accompanied by a single legion, *legio XIII*, apparently repeating, in Greek, a proverb of the time, 'let the die be cast'.[333]

Beyond the Rubicon

The Rubicon was an otherwise insignificant muddy stream that separated Gallia Cisalpina (Caesar's province) from Italy proper. On one side Caesar still held *imperium pro consule* and had the right to command troops, on the other he was a mere *privatus*, a private citizen. It was a frank initiation of a civil war. Yet the big issue for us to consider in the light of this bellicose action is the question of who was in the right and who was in the wrong. In attempting to justify his reasons for crossing the Rubicon, Caesar claimed that his political opponents had cheated him out of his due rights. He also claimed to be defending the rights of the tribunes, namely the fugitives Antonius and Cassius, while at the same time attempting to ruin the reputations of his enemies.

The whole scholarly debate over who was right and who was wrong stems from the pen of Theodor Mommsen, a highly learned man who idolised Caesar and thus took up the quest to pinpoint the exact expiry date for Caesar's command in Gaul.[334] In true Teutonic fashion, Mommsen declared that this would allow us to determine who was in the right and who was in the wrong in 49 BC. If Caesar was still in his province when his command terminated, as Mommsen's argument goes, then he was definitely in the wrong. After much discourse and analysis, Mommsen favoured 1 March 49 BC as the date at which Caesar's Gallic command legally expired, and what is commonly called Mommsen's *rechtsfrage*, legal issue, has become the centre of interminable debate.[335]

Since Mommsen wrote his article of faith, batteries of modern commentators have fired off a vast array of dates for that expiration, but, sadly, it is all an illusion. Quite simply, there was no specific date for the termination of Caesar's command in Gaul.[336] Down to 52 BC the tenets of the *lex Sempronia de provinciis consularibus* of Caius Gracchus (123 BC or 122 BC) laid down the rules and regulations with regards to how the consular provinces were to be governed. Under this law there could be no set terminal date for any governorship, for it was clear that a governor remained in command until the arrival of his successor. Also, Sulla's *lex de maiestate* stated that the previous governor was allowed thirty days in which to quit the province once he had been superseded. Therefore, by appointing a successor to Caesar's command in Gaul the Senate could easily have ousted him from his province anyway.

However, the *lex Vatinia de Caesaris provincia* had granted Caesar Gallia Cisalpina and Illyricum *in quinquennium* in 59 BC, while Gallia Transalpina was granted by a *senatus consultum* later in the same year. Now, the term *in quinquennium* clearly means 'for a period up to five years'. The natural assumption was that the command could be wrapped up early and the victor returned to Rome for a well-earned triumph. The idea of hanging around in some outlandish province for five years seemed absolutely absurd to the Senate. The whole question of *in quinquennium* only became an issue when

Cato and his political cronies wanted to haul Caesar before the courts for his actions during his consulship of 59 BC. Naturally, Caesar's response was to stay put in his province.

In 55 BC the *lex Licinia Pompeia* granted Caesar another five years in Gaul and thus his problems were solved for the foreseeable future.[337] Moreover, in 49 BC he could stand for his second consulship quite legally, in contrast to Pompey, who had been consul in 55 BC and again in 52 BC.[338] However, it was during this last consulship that Pompey had muddled the whole issue of Caesar's authority by making into law a senatorial decree of the previous year, for the law required a lapse of a five-year interval between the holding of the office of praetor or consul and the tenure of a provincial command. Whereas before a governor could have taken up his office immediately, the Senate could now designate the provinces to former consuls and praetors of five years previously, which thus made available for assignment a number of ex-magistrates of more than five years' standing who had not held a province.[339] As a natural consequence of this law a good number of the provinces were now in the hands of men loyal to the *optimates*, or at least not dangerous, and Gaul looked like going the same way. With the abolition of the time delay, as was permitted under the terms of the *lex Sempronia*, and the *lex de maiestate* of Sulla also ruling that consuls and praetors should remain in Italy during their year of office, the problem now for Caesar was that he faced not just being superseded in Gaul but disarmed too.

One way out for Caesar was by employing the Law of Ten Tribunes, which had also been passed in 52 BC, the year of Pompey's sole consulship. Under this law Caesar alone had the right to stand for the consulship *in absentia* and by doing so remain in his province. And so, with Caesar being permitted to progress seamlessly from Gaul to a second consulship, there would be no window of opportunity for his enemies to prosecute him in the courts of Rome for the criminal actions of his first consulship. As for Pompey, he dodged and ducked the whole issue until finally coming out with the arrogant statement that he was not in favour of Caesar being a consul in command of an army in Gaul. When asked by a questioner in the Senate what he would do if Caesar chose to be consul *and* keep his army, Rome's greatest general calmly replied: 'And supposing my son chooses to take his stick to me?'[340] Now at last the rupture between the two former allies was in the open. The master of Gaul was to be treated – and presumably punished – like a malcontent minor.

Whatever the rights and wrongs of Pompey's and Caesar's constitutional claims and counter-claims, the plain facts were that the republican machinery of government had not just run out of steam but completely broken down.

Since no one could suggest, let alone enforce, a practicable alternative, autocracy was inevitable. However, republican Rome had no room for two autocratic warlords.

Barbarians at the Gates

Crossing the Rubicon was an act of war in itself. Caesar had reached the river in the chill of the pre-dawn darkness and apparently hesitated for a long time on the north bank. A consummate politician, Caesar never underestimated the momentousness of crossing the grubby watercourse into Italy. He told his men, 'we may still draw back but once across that little bridge, we shall have to fight it out'.[341] They crossed. For Caesar's men, after crossing the Rubicon, they had to emerge victorious – otherwise they would be condemned as enemies of the state and treated accordingly.

The excuse for war had come when Antonius and Cassius, allegedly disguised as slaves, washed up in Caesar's camp as fugitives. A constitutional pretext was thus provided by the violence of his enemies. Proclaiming he had come to restore the rights of the sacrosanct representatives of the Roman people, thereby defending the liberties of the people themselves, Caesar crossed the Rubicon and marched on Rome. But the popular cause was not the cause that Caesar himself valued most. In a speech to his soldiers, all battle-hardened veterans of the campaigns in Gaul, Caesar defended his *dignitas*, the status and prestige within the state that he felt his due, though no English word really embraces the full power of this concept for a Roman aristocrat.[342] The following year, at the crucial battle of Pharsalus, Caesar puts into the mouth of one of his ex-centurions, none other than Caius Crastinus the former *primus pilus* of *legio X Equestris*, a similar speech. In a pre-battle harangue delivered to his fellow volunteers, but within earshot of Caesar himself, Crastinus says: 'This one battle alone remains; when it is over he will recover his *dignitas* and we our *libertas*'.[343] Cato and his small band of supporters wanted to extinguish Caesar's political career, but Caesar was determined not to let this happen. Caesar's *dignitas* was very much the issue here, as Suetonius makes clear, and sooner than surrender it he appealed to his loyal legions for justice.[344] 'But what is dignity', Cicero aptly commented, 'if there is no honour.'[345]

It seems that Caesar's political enemies had thrust upon him the stark choice between civil war and political extinction. Then again, Cato was not totally responsible for the war as the vital catalyst in the equation was Pompey's bellicosity. When someone had inquired of him with what forces he would defend Rome if Caesar were to march on the city, the champion of the Republic had calmly crowed: 'Whenever I stamp with my foot in any part of Italy there will rise up forces enough in an instant, both horse and foot'.[346] In other words, Pompey saw Caesar as his rival and this was to be 'a struggle for personal power at the community's risk and peril'.[347] As for the Senate, the dynastic contest would create a severe strain upon the loyalties of the senators.

In his letters to Atticus, Cicero constantly harped back to the days of Sulla when the *nobilitas* was split down the middle. In the aforementioned letter to Cicero from his devil-may-care friend Caelius, Caelius muses about choosing the winning side and in doing so equates virtue with survival. 'In peacetime while taking part in domestic politics', he writes, 'it is most important to back the side that is right – but in times of war, the strongest.'[348] The calculating Caelius had once been a close associate of Catiline, yet he was not alone in this cynical judgement. Hungry for immediate pickings, an entire generation would turn away from the cause of legitimacy. Others agreed simply because they were terrified. The only precedent for this sort of civil strife was Sulla's, a dreadful one. This terror and panic are of significance, especially among senators such as Cicero who were sympathetic rather than devoted to the cause, for in Gaul Caesar's atrocities had earned him the reputation of a ruthless warlord. As Cicero penned in a letter to Atticus, 'when I picture the barbarians marching on Rome I fear all manner of things'.[349] Yet such emotional outbursts played into Caesar's hands, for they facilitated his advance through Italy, and then, when he implemented his policy of clemency, it came as an anticlimax to his enemies' expectations. And this was not just a campaign of spin, for he proved it by a readiness to pardon his enemies.

At the Crossroads

Caesar's objective was not Rome, as Cicero and others surmised. For since it had been abandoned, the city had lost its military and political significance. Instead the first clash between the two sides occurred at the crossroads town of Corfinium, in the central Apennines, east of Rome, the very same Corfinium that the Italian rebels had made their federal capital forty years before. Domitius Ahenobarbus, whom the Senate had chosen to replace Caesar in Gaul, held the town against Caesar with some thirty cohorts under his command. On 9 February, when he learnt that Caesar was advancing upon him, he decided to evacuate Corfinium, then, a few hours later, he changed his mind and determined to hold the town at all costs.[350] This do-or-die act went against the wishes of Pompey, who wanted the very energetic but very stupid

Domitius Ahenobarbus and his troops to march south to join him and his two legions at Luceria (Lucera), a town in Apulia. When he learnt of it he immediately wrote to Domitius Ahenobarbus: 'With divided forces we cannot hope to cope with the enemy . . . Wherefore again and again I entreat and exhort you . . . come to Luceria on the first possible day, before the forces that Caesar has begun to collect can concentrate and divide us'.[351] Domitius Ahenobarbus, as a proconsul, was not under Pompey's authority. But instead of going to Gaul, he had established himself in Corfinium, and had taken command of the Pompeian levies that were being raised there.

When Caesar, now with two of his legions – *legio XII* by now had joined him – and the Pompeian cohorts that had deserted to him *en route*, encamped outside the town on 15 February, Domitius Ahenobarbus sent an urgent message asking Pompey to come to his rescue, otherwise 'he himself and more than thirty cohorts and a great number of senators and knights will be imperilled'.[352] The appeal was received by Pompey on the following day. He replied to it at once, and after he had outlined the general military situation he again earnestly begged Domitius Ahenobarbus to come with all his forces, adding: 'I cannot comply with your request for assistance, because I do not put much trust in these legions'.[353] Again, on the next day, he wrote to Domitius Ahenobarbus in similar terms, and added: 'So do your best, if any tactics can extricate you even now, to join me as soon as possible before our enemy can concentrate all his forces'.[354] Now completely invested, Domitius Ahenobarbus panicked and his raw levies mutinied. On 21 February they surrendered to the heir of Marius, that great patron of the Italians and grim enemy of Sulla. Old hatreds had doomed the proconsul's stand. Hauled before Caesar, the blue-blooded but block-headed Domitius Ahenobarbus begged for death. Caesar refused, pardoning his distinguished prisoner instead. The Pompeian levies, along with most of their officers, joined Caesar's invading army.

Throughout his three *commentarii* covering the struggle against Pompey, in what amounted to a military coup, Caesar took pains to stress the willingness of his soldiers to support his cause. A great many of his men were of course not from peninsular Italy but from Gallia Cisalpina and even Gallia Transalpina, hence Cicero's reference to the coming 'barbarians'. For these men a march into Italy would not provoke the same crisis of conscience, and we hear nothing of dissent at fighting other Romans. On the other hand, we do hear the occasional rumblings of discontent by veterans at being kept under arms for such an extended period, and it was probably now that Caesar doubled the soldiers' pay to 225 denarii a year,[355] an added factor in their adherence to his cause and, of course, that of those Pompeian troops who joined him during his irresistible advance southwards.

On 17 March, much to everyone's surprise, Pompey abandoned Italy, carrying with him several legions and a large number of senators, and crossed over to Epeiros. Pompey's hopes of support in Italy were far too optimistic, so he would gather help from the foreign princes he had settled or confirmed on their thrones. True, his troops in Italy were few compared with what Caesar both had and could raise. True, also, his military reputation was high in the east. Yet his foe was Caesar, a man who was able to turn the scales by the two great characteristics of his genius – rapidity of movement and the power of personality. Caesar was welcomed in Italy, but faced neutrality in a Rome he had not seen for ten years. On his arrival he found the people 'shuddering with recollections of the horrors of Marius and Sulla, and he cheered them with the prospect and promise of clemency'.[356] He immediately called the Senate together, that is, all the senators who had not followed Pompey, and explained that 'he had sought no extraordinary office' and had been 'waiting for the legitimate time of his consulship'.[357] Later in the year, on his return from Iberia, Caesar would be appointed dictator – by the people, not the Senate – for a brief eleven days, whereby he set up the constitutional machinery for the elections of the following year, and was duly elected consul for 48 BC.

Iberian Interlude

Now that he was master of Italy, we might expect Caesar to follow Pompey to Epeiros, for it is a maxim first to attack the most dangerous part of your enemy's divided forces. But there were seven Pompeian legions left in Iberia, all of them properly equipped and trained, and at least as many Iberian auxiliaries. So he departed for Iberia, telling his household 'I am off to meet an army without a leader; when I return I shall meet a leader without an army'.[358] Rome was but a day's sail from Epeiros, whereas in Iberia Caesar would be several hundred kilometres away. Knowing his man, Caesar was obviously relying on Pompey to remain inactive where he stood.

As Massilia, which had declared for Pompey, lay on his line of communications between Italy and Iberia, Caesar ordered Caius Trebonius to leave his legions, hasten to Italy, take command of three newly raised legions, bring them to Massilia and invest it. Caesar himself hastened into northern Iberia, where he found Pompey's legates Lucius Afranius (*cos.* 60 BC) and Marcus Petreius, both highly experienced commanders and Picene partisans to boot, occupying a prepared position near Ilerda (Lérida). Caesar, by a brilliant series of manoeuvres, defeated the Pompeians and their leaders surrendered, while some of their troops were recruited into Caesar's army and the rest disbanded. In three months, by avoiding battle and relying on manoeuvre, in an almost bloodless campaign Caesar deprived Pompey of Iberia, thereby securing both Italy and Gaul against attack when the time came for him to cross the Adriatic.

Meanwhile, in Africa Caesar's legate Curio had been catastrophically defeated and killed by the Numidians at Bagradas – the Numidians had encircled their foe, avoided hand-to-hand fighting, smothered him with missiles, and prevented him from regaining the security of his camp. Curio was young, headstrong and inexperienced in war, and two of his four legions had been formed out of the *cohortes Domitianae*, namely those Pompeian levies who had surrendered at Corfinium.[359]

Pompey's Banquet

The prime need was to prepare for a campaign against Pompey himself. By virtue of his office as consul for 48 BC, Caesar raised four new legions, with the traditional consular numbers *I–IIII*, so completing his numerical sequence, which now probably ran uninterrupted from *I* to about *XXXIII*.[360] Auxiliaries from the newly subdued Gallic tribes were added to his forces, and by December an expeditionary force of twelve legions had been assembled at Brundisium. Obviously all the veteran legions were earmarked, namely *VI–XIIII*, of which six had to march back from northern Iberia, together with the *Alaudae* and two of the younger legions – one of the latter we can identify as *legio XXVII*.

In the New Year Caesar (*cos.* II) crossed over to Epeiros with seven legions and 500 cavalry, lightly equipped and closely packed. This was a terrible gamble, because he did not have a strong enough fleet to take on Pompey's ships if he was attacked at sea. Luckily Pompey did not expect him to cross in the winter months, when the weather was likely to be bad, and Caesar did not meet any opposition.[361] Yet on landing Caesar was isolated and outnumbered, though four more legions were on their way to him under the command of the redoubtable Marcus Antonius.

By now Pompey had nine legions at his disposal, each at something like full strength, five from Italy, one from Crete, one from Cilicia, which had been formed out of veterans from two legions and called *Gemella* ('Twin'), and two from Asia newly recruited by the consul Lucius Cornelius Lentulus Crus, as well as 5,000 light-armed troops and 7,000 cavalry, bizarre-looking auxiliaries led by princes with exotic un-Roman names: Deiotarus of Galatia,

Ariobarzanes of Cappadocia, Antiochos of Commagene and so on and so forth. In addition, he expected the arrival from Syria of his father-in-law, Metellus Scipio, with another two legions. His men were well provisioned whereas Caesar's had to make do with what they could glean or steal from local communities. It was not until 10 April that Antonius managed to bring the rest of his legions across the Adriatic, yet even with eleven legions Caesar was still outnumbered and still faced supply problems.

At one point Caesar's men were reduced to digging up roots and baking them into ersatz bread. Some of these loaves they tossed into the Pompeian outposts as symbols of defiance. Pompey's men 'were thoroughly frightened of the ferocity and physical toughness of their enemies,' says Plutarch, 'who seemed to them to be like some species of wild beasts'.[362] Even so, by attacking one of the Pompeian supply centres at the port town of Dyrrhachium (Durrës, Albania), which was the western road head of the Via Egnatia, the vital link in the corridor joining Rome to Macedonia and beyond, Caesar narrowly avoided defeat after a series of three hard-fought engagements. The war could have ended there but Pompey allowed him to escape. After the battle, according to Plutarch, Caesar contemptuously remarked to his friends: 'Today the enemy would have won, if they had a commander who was a winner'.[363]

After Dyrrhachium Caesar slipped away south-east into Thessaly, chiefly to search for provisions, which his battered army sorely needed. His troops found fresh supplies and regained strength. Pompey believed he should avoid open confrontation with Caesar, instead attempting to wear him down by depriving him of supplies, but he was under tremendous pressure from the 'army' of self-serving senators in his camp to meet Caesar in battle and finish the matter once and for all. Hectored, criticised and insulted, according to Plutarch, he finally gave way and thus surrendered 'his own prudent resolution'.[364] In early August the two warlords camped near each other on the plain of Pharsalus in Thessaly. Caesar was now joined by Cnaeus Domitius Calvinus (*cos.* 53 BC), and Pompey by Metellus Scipio.

The *gladius Hispaniensis*

On the field of Pharsalus Caius Crastinus was to meet a suitably heroic death. Charging forward at the double, and followed by the 120 volunteers under his command, he was the first, according to Plutarch, to engage the enemy. He then proceeded to slice his way through the Pompeian ranks until he was finally 'stopped by a blow of a sword, which was thrust into his mouth with such force that it came out of the back of his neck'.[365]

It is a truism that technology makes warfare much more complex. However, technology does not create warfare but only heightens its effects. In our period it was the *gladius Hispaniensis* of the Roman legionary that was the main 'force multiplier', that is to say, the battlefield weapon that increased the combat effectiveness of the Roman legion. The *gladius* was an amazingly light and well-balanced double-edged weapon that was capable of making blindingly fast attacks, and was suitable for both cuts and thrusts. Yet both Tacitus (b. *c.* AD 56) and Vegetius (*fl. c.* AD 385) lay great stress on the use of the *gladius* for thrusting rather than slashing. As Vegetius rightly says, 'a slash-cut, whatever its force, seldom kills . . . But a thrust driven two inches is fatal.'[366] And so, having thrown the *pilum* and charged into contact, the standard drill for the legionary was to punch the enemy in the face with his shield-boss and then jab him in the belly with the razor-sharp point of the *gladius*.

This sword-type lacked a typical cross-guard, which immediately tells us that it was not intended as a parrying weapon. There is little doubt, therefore, that the *gladius* was designed primarily as a close-quarter thrusting weapon. As the desired intention was to deliver the fatal blow by a thrust, its blade was straight and its handle short, while the main design feature was its long point. The relative shortness of the weapon allowed for ease of control, while its comparative lightness enhanced the swordsman's reaction time. Unlike a typical cut-and-thrust sword, the *gladius* was balanced nearer to the wrist, a characteristic that discouraged the slash in favour of the thrust. By comparison, the balance point of a typical cut-and-thrust sword was some 10 centimetres above the hilt. Its fulcrum, therefore, was positioned to effectively encourage the swordsman to swing his sword, using the pommel in a pendulum-like fashion so as to add weight to his slashing blow.

Whereas the combination of shortness and lightness helped to increase the quickness of the thrust, it was the oversized pommel of the *gladius* that put force behind the thrust. Likewise, the oval-shaped cross-guard in front of the handle allowed the legionary to apply maximum pressure to his thrust, and this, combined with a snug-fitting contoured handgrip, increased the blow's overall effectiveness. Compared with medieval cross-guards, which were comparatively thin pieces of metal, the ovular cross-guard made complete contact with the sword hand. When the thrust was delivered, therefore, the legionary brought to bear, with equal force, his entire right hand and arm. The bone handgrip itself was some 7.5 to 10 centimetres in length, making it slightly longer than the width of a hand. This arrangement allowed for better efficiency and control in weapon handling.[367]

Caesar had reached the plain first, and the position in which he was camped gave him command of the fertile plain. The grain in the plain itself was not yet ripe, but he did have good lines of communication and, initially at least, an adequate food supply. Several days were spent manoeuvring and offering formal challenges to battle, an offer that Pompey repeatedly refused. It seems Caesar had gambled on being able to rely on stores of grain in the area until the crops were ripe, but the supplies had not in fact lasted out. Pompey, for his part, may also have been banking on this. On the morning of 9 August Caesar was preparing to move camp to a location where he could more easily secure supplies, when he noticed the Pompeians had advanced further from their camp than usual. He quickly ordered his men to form up in columns, wearing only their battle garb. They marched up, formed and faced the enemy.

Caesar, in his version of events, makes Pompey's decision to offer battle that day just as Caesar decided to strike camp a thing of mere coincidence. Of course much of the Caesarian account is clearly propagandist in intent. Caesar stresses the arrogant self-confidence of the Pompeian officers, and indeed of Pompey himself. It is interesting to note, however, that in Appian's account of this final stage Pompey knew that Caesar must move soon because his supplies were failing.[368] Then, one morning, it was observed by Pompeian scouts that the Caesarians were beginning to strike camp. Pompey had his men in readiness, his tactical orders issued, and at once advanced on to the plain and offered battle.

The Battle of Pharsalus, 48 BC

Caesar himself never mentions Pharsalus, the most famous engagement of the Second Civil War. In fact, in his whole narrative of events immediately preceding and following the battle, and the battle itself, he mentions no place at all except Larissa (Lárissa). Such topographical information as is given in his account and in other sources is of little help in identifying the exact location of the battlefield.

While Appian, Plutarch and Suetonius refer to 'the battle of Pharsalus', Frontinus, Eutropius, Orosius and the author of the *Bellum Alexandrinum*, believed by many to be the soldier-scholar Hirtius, give the additional detail that it was fought somewhere near 'Old Pharsalus', a stronghold on a hill in the territory of Pharsalus proper. Pharsalus is generally agreed to be the modern Fársala, about 5 kilometres south of the river Enipeios. The site of Old Pharsalus is disputed. One possibility is that the battle was fought on the north bank of the river, at the western end of the plain, which is almost entirely closed on the remaining sides by hills. Pompey was camped on a hill at the western end of the plain, Caesar in the plain further east. Old Pharsalus was across the river, not far from the site of Caesar's camp.

Caesar's battle report, on the other hand, does allow us to see the contending armies down to the level of the individual cohorts. On paper, Pompey had the equivalent of eleven legions made up of 110 cohorts, 45,000 legionaries plus 2,000 time-expired veterans (*evocati*) at Caesar's estimation. However, this ignores the fact that Pompey had left up to twenty-two cohorts on detached garrison duty, so that the two sides were more evenly matched than Caesar suggests. Caesar himself was able to field eight legions in eighty under-strength cohorts, totalling 22,000 legionaries by his own reckoning.[369]

Pompey's legions may have been stronger, but they were certainly less experienced than Caesar's. On the left were the two legions Caesar had handed over 'in obedience to the decree of the Senate at the beginning of the civil strife',[370] now numbered *I* and *III*, in the centre were his legions from Syria, on the right *legio Gemella* from Cilicia and some cohorts that had found their way under Afranius from Iberia. Domitius Ahenobarbus, hotfoot from the fall of Massilia, commanded the left, with Metellus

Scipio, Pompey's decorative father-in-law, in the centre, and the very experienced Afranius on the right. The *evocati*, who had volunteered their services, were dispersed throughout the line of battle. Having little confidence in the majority of his legionaries, Pompey ordered the cohorts to deploy ten deep and await the enemy charge at the halt, hoping to keep his raw recruits in a compact formation and prevent them from running away.[371] Pompey was relying upon his numerically superior cavalry, about 7,000 strong, from at least ten nations and supported by a host of archers and slingers, to outflank Caesar's right and roll up his line.

Like Pompey's army, Caesar's was deployed in the customary three lines, but it was vital that its front should cover much the same frontage as their opponents, so his cohorts were probably formed four or even six ranks deep. Realising the threat to his right flank, Caesar took one cohort from the third line of six of his legions and formed them into a fourth line, angled back and concealed behind his cavalry. As usual, in his order of battle, Caesar posted *legio X Equestris* on the right, and *legio VIIII* on the left, and as it had suffered heavy casualties in the Dyrrhachium engagements, he brigaded it with *legio VIII* 'so as almost to make one legion out of two, and ordered them to cooperate'.[372] The remaining five legions he posted in between them. Marcus Antonius was in command on the left, Domitius Calvinus in the centre, and Publius Cornelius Sulla, the nephew of the dictator Sulla who had been accused of complicity with Catiline, on the right. Caesar himself would spend most of the battle with *legio X Equestris*, his favourite unit, on the crucial right wing. For the battle Caesar's men were given the watchword 'Venus, Bringer of Victory' in reference to his divine ancestress, while Pompey's men put their trust in 'Hercules, Unconquered'.

Titus Atius Labienus, Caesar's former second-in-command, led Pompey's massed cavalry against the Caesarian right wing and soon put the enemy horsemen, who only numbered 1,000 or thereabouts, to flight. However, in the process these tyro-horsemen lost their order and merged into one great mass – many of the men supplied by eastern potentates were ill-trained and both Appian and Plutarch describe them as young and inexperienced.[373] Suddenly Caesar's fourth line, the back-up legionaries, burst from behind the main battle line and charged the milling throng of cavalry, stampeding them to the rear in wide-eyed flight. In the *sauve qui peut* that followed, Pompey's light-armed troops were left in the lurch and massacred or dispersed by Caesar's legionaries. Pompey's main attack had failed.

In the meantime the main infantry lines clashed, Caesar's superbly disciplined men stopping to re-form when they realised that the Pompeian cohorts were not advancing to meet them, as was the norm, and that they had begun their charge too early. Centurions having re-dressed the ranks ordered the advance to resume. When the Caesarians were within 20 metres of the enemy they discharged their *pila*, then charged into contact with drawn swords. A fierce struggle followed, and the second-line cohorts were drawn in. In other words, the Pompeians stood their ground and vindicated their general's battlefield tactics.

As the fourth-line cohorts swung round to threaten the now exposed left flank of the Pompeian legions and Caesar committed his third-line cohorts to add impetus to the main assault, Pompey's army collapsed. Casting aside his general's cloak, or so it was said, Pompey rode hard for the coast. His camp, in which victory banquets had been prepared and tents decked with laurel, was taken. That night Caesar dined in Pompey's tent, and 'the whole army feasted at the enemy's expense'.[374] When it came down to it, experience won over numbers. The Pompeians had lost the psychological advantage they would have got from making the first charge. As it was, Caesar's veterans spotted the trap. They stopped short of the Pompeian ranks to regain their breath and re-form their ranks.

Caesar claimed that he lost only 200 men but, because of their typically aggressive style of leadership, 30 centurions, including the indomitable Crastinus. Of Pompey's army, 15,000 had died on the battlefield while 24,000 now found themselves prisoners-of-war. Nine eagles were captured. Most Pompeian leaders were pardoned, among them Marcus Iunius Brutus, whose mother Servilia had been the great love of Caesar's life, and it was even claimed that Brutus was their love child. True or not, Brutus' legal father had been one of the many victims of the 'teenage butcher' during the previous civil war, but the high-principled stoical Brutus, by favouring the murderer of his mother's husband over her old flame, had chosen the cause of legitimacy. Incidentally, Caesar also mentions that in the pursuit Domitius Ahenobarbus was slain.

Death on the Nile

With the battle lost, Pompey himself escaped, fleeing to Egypt, where the great man was treacherously murdered on arrival. After describing the death of Priam, the Augustan poet Virgil dwells upon the contrast between the old king's squalid and miserable end and the glories of his former state, 'he who had once been proud ruler over so many lands and peoples of Asia', and continues, 'His mighty trunk lay upon the shore, the head hacked from the shoulders, a corpse without a name'.[375] These lines echo Pompey's end, once the greatest Roman of his day and conqueror of the east. On the morning of 28 September, as Pompey stepped ashore as suppliant of the pharaoh, Lucius Septimius, who had served under him first as a centurion, then as a military tribune during his eastern campaigns but now held high rank in the boy-king's Roman guard, stabbed him from behind.[376] And so perished Pompey the Great. His head was cut off, taken to Ptolemy XIII and later presented to Caesar upon his arrival in Egypt, while his naked body was left unburied on the beach.

Victorious at Pharsalus, Caesar then committed a foolhardy act and followed Pompey to Egypt with 3,000 men. Within a few days of his rival's death, Caesar reached Alexandria, but had to survive an unexpected siege, during which he had to rely on 'barbarian' help – Jewish soldiers, among others, arrived to rescue him – and the thrice-married Caesar succumbed to the charms of Cleopatra (the seventh to carry that name), the warring half-sister of Ptolemy XIII. 'As for the war in Egypt,' says Plutarch, 'some say it was not necessary, but due to Caesar's passion for Cleopatra, and that it was inglorious and full of peril for him.'[377] Whatever 'some say', Caesar's lack of caution certainly allowed the Pompeians a nine-month breathing-space and the opportunity of taking fresh root in Africa.

In his 'Précis des Guerres de Jules César' Napoléon pulls no punches when it comes to his verdict on the Alexandrian escapade, pointing out that the Pompeians prepared well for the campaign in Africa and a new one in Iberia. 'These two campaigns,' says Napoléon, 'which demanded all his genius and good fortune to achieve victory, need never have been fought had he after Pharsalus rapidly moved against Cato and Scipio in Africa, instead of proceeding to Alexandria.'[378] As Cicero himself wrote in a letter to Caius Cassius Longinus, 'the year that intervened tempted some to hope for victory, others to think lightly of defeat'.[379] This was the same Cassius who had performed so creditably at Carrhae, and who had gone on to become Pompey's most brilliant naval commander, before being pardoned by Caesar after Pharsalus. He was to join Caesar in the east. Meanwhile, another of Caesar's legates, Domitius Calvinus, who had been entrusted with the administration of Asia and the neighbouring provinces, was drawn into a war with Pharnaces II of Cimmerian Bosporus and was defeated in Pontus. During the distractions of Roman fighting Roman, the Pontic king, the son of the great Mithridates, was seeking to enlarge his kingdom.

In a five-day campaign during the high summer of 47 BC Caesar (*dict.* II, *in absentia*) vanquished Pharnaces at Zela (Zilleh, Turkey), near which Pharnaces' father had defeated a Roman army, before sending the famous *veni, vidi, vici* (Came, Saw, Conquered) dispatch to the Senate – but here again he committed the blunder of opening a campaign with too small a force, and came within an ace of failure during the battle itself after issuing a plethora of orders that merely served to confuse the troops.[380] Immediately after the victory, Caesar settled disputes and assigned prerogatives to the kings and states, and then returned to Italy more quickly than anyone expected.[381]

On his arrival he was confronted with the bothersome necessity of quelling a mutiny among his veterans on the *campus Martius*, with his beloved *legio X Equestris* as ringleaders. Currently concerned with Venus rather than Mars, his deputy Marcus Antonius had proved an unsafe pair of hands. Perhaps the most salacious aspect of the mutiny was his carryings-on with various courtesans and actresses. This was the sort of behaviour that bolsters the vision of Antonius as a 'drink-sodden, sex-ridden wreck' lolling in iniquitous ease in Rome, but Sallust, the future historian and then one of Caesar's officers, narrowly escaped lynching as the mutineers angrily made their demands. Their chief complaint was that they were exhausted by long service, and certainly by this date most of these soldiers would have served for sixteen plus years and could therefore quite properly complain of being kept 'unlawfully' in service. Anyway, Caesar made it clear that he would discharge them all, because of course if they were exhausted they were unfit for service. He addressed them as citizens, not comrades, as though dismissal was an accomplished fact. In calling their bluff he rapidly brought them to their senses; very soon his veterans were clamouring to fight wherever he sent them. The artful Caesar tidied up by arresting a few ringleaders and executing them.[382]

In a similar vein Caesar had to settle social unrest in Italy. This had been fanned during his prolonged absence by Caelius, Cicero's fashionable young friend who had supported Caesar for opportunistic reasons, and Milo, who had returned illegally from exile in Massilia, and, after their deaths, by Cicero's son-in-law, the debauched patrician Publius Cornelius Dolabella (later *cos. suff.* 44 BC), a sinister and disquieting character. These aristocrats were overwhelmed by debts and demanded their cancellation. They had expected harsh reprisals against the defeated Pompeians, and were disgusted by Caesar's leniency. This disgust found expression in them making common cause with the many debtors of Rome.

Republican Resistance

April 46 BC was to find Caesar (*dict.* III, *cos.* III) battling against Cato and Metellus Scipio in Africa. The previous December he had landed an expeditionary force consisting of five of the younger legions (*XXV*, *XXVI*, *XXVIII*, *XXVIIII* and perhaps *XXX*), together with one veteran formation, *legio V Alaudae*. While the Pompeians were aided by Iuba of Numidia (r. 85–46 BC), Caesar had the support of Bocchus II of Mauretania (r. 49–33 BC), who was at daggers drawn with Iuba. None the less, he still had to call for help from some of the veteran units – we can identify *legiones VIIII*, *X Equestris*, *XIII* and *XIIII* – left behind in Italy.[383]

After a hard slog Caesar was eventually victorious at Thapsus (Ras Dimasse, Tunisia). In the aftermath many of the Pompeian leaders met their deaths, most notably Metellus Scipio and Cato, both of whom chose suicide rather than capture. Metellus Scipio's end was worthy of his ancestors, jumping overboard when his fleeing ship was run down. Cato, ever the man of principle, first read, three times over, Plato's *Phaedo*, in which Socrates comforts his companions by offering them proofs of immortality of the soul before serenely drinking the hemlock, and then took his sword and succeeded at the second attempt. Thus through death he escaped the death of the Republic, which to Cato was what Caesar symbolised, and his 'martyrdom' in the cause of republicanism was to be a real embarrassment to Caesar.

An interesting footnote on the African campaign was the handiness of Caesar's legionaries in the use of entrenching tools – it seems they dug themselves to victory – the hallmark of the later professional legions.[384] Afterwards, *legio V Alaudae* gained its permanent elephant emblem for its exploits in the final battle. A few of its members, and probably other Caesarian veterans, were discharged, and began a new life in Africa, in one of a rash of small colonies quickly established by Caesar on the placid shores of the Cape Bon peninsula.

Caesar returned to Rome and on successive days celebrated four triumphs, over the Gauls, the Egyptians, Pharnaces and lastly Iuba. The final one was really over Romans, but victory over his fellow-citizens could not fittingly be the subject of a triumph. All the same, Iuba had joined the Pompeians and lost his life in the conflict, thereby providing the excuse for a triumph over a foreign enemy. The small son of the king, also called Iuba, was paraded through the streets, but then spared the execution that usually followed. In the rear came wagons laden with the spoils of war. Among them were 2,822 gold crowns weighing 20,414 Roman pounds (*librae*) and 60,500 talents of silver in cash. From this fabulous hoard, according to Appian, civilians received 300 sesterces each, soldiers more according to rank, each legionary, for instance, receiving 5,000 denarii – equivalent to an entire lifetime's pay – and each centurion double.[385]

Caesar then worked rapidly in Rome, pushing through various laws and reforms. One of his most far-reaching reforms was the reorganisation of the calendar. To put an end to the disorders of the calendar based on the lunar year, Caesar replaced it with the Egyptian calendar regulated by the sun. The old republican year had lasted 355 days, and whenever the calendar slipped out of kilter with the seasons an extra month of twenty days was added. The Julian calendar was a modified form of the Egyptian calendar of 365 days, with a leap year every four years.[386]

All the veteran legions, with the exception of *legio V Alaudae*, the most junior of the group, were now released, and land sought for them in Italy and Gallia Transalpina. The latter destination was probably a popular choice as some of the legionaries would have had fond memories of the province, while some may even have been natives of it – *legio VI* was established at Arelate (Arles), and *legio X Equestris* at Narbo (Narbonne), the provincial capital. Within Italy, *legio VII* was settled near Capua, in the small town of Calatia, and preparations, not complete by Caesar's death, were made for *legio VIII* to be established at nearby Casilinum. Many other veterans were settled in smaller groups throughout the peninsula. But for the others, one further round of fighting remained.

The Battle of Thapsus, 46 BC

Thapsus (Ras Dimasse, Tunisia) was a port town that sat on a cape overlooking the sea, and it was here, on 6 April, that Caesar's army of 20,000 legionaries, 2,000 archers and slingers and 1,200 cavalry fought a Pompeian army of 28,000 legionaries and 12,000 Gallic, Iberian and Numidian cavalry. In support were sixty-four Numidian elephants, split equally between the two wings, and large numbers of light-armed Numidians. Metellus Scipio and Labienus commanded the Pompeians, Iuba of Numidia the Numidians. Also present were those two Pompeian warhorses, Afranius and Petreius.

Caesar had his main force of legions, which were deployed in the normal three lines, screened by light-armed troops, *legiones X Equestris* and *VIIII* forming the right of the line of battle and *legiones XIII* and *XIIII* its left. Five cohorts of *legio V Alaudae*, whose legionaries had been given a crash course in elephant fighting, were posted, along with light-armed troops, as a fourth line obliquely – as at Pharsalus – in the rear of each wing. Caesar had no intention of employing his own pachyderms in battle – he is said to have considered the lumbering, tusked bull elephant a menace to both sides. The cavalry, intermingled with the newly trained light-armed legionaries, were deployed on the extreme right and left.

The battle began with an unauthorised charge by Caesar's troops. Most of the elephants were killed,[387] but those on the Pompeian left turned and stampeded through the troops lined up behind them. Caesar's famous *legio X Equestris* exploited the confusion caused, and as the Pompeian left swiftly unravelled, the rest of Metellus Scipio's line dissolved. Labienus, the irrepressible commander, escaped the carnage and reached Iberia where he joined up with Pompey's sons, Cnaeus and Sextus. Surrounded and cut down from his horse, he would die outside Munda fighting to his last breath. Likewise Afranius, Iuba and Petreius escaped, but the first was eventually captured and delivered to Caesar, who put him to death for his perfidy, and the other two, who expected no mercy from Caesar, fought a duel in which one killed the other and then killed himself. Ironically, Caesar, the architect of victory, was laid low by an epileptic fit early in the battle.[388] Even so, with this victory he had defeated the Pompeians so effectively that republican opposition in Africa ceased.

The Last Victory

In 45 BC, the penultimate year for Caesar (*dict.* IIII, *cos. sine collega*), there was another campaign in Iberia, where the remnants of Pompey's support had rallied round his two sons, Cnaeus Pompeius Magnus minor and Sextus Pompeius Magnus Pius. Caesar took *legio V Alaudae* and some of the younger formations, including *legio III* from his consular series in 48 BC, and appears to have diverted the veterans of *VI* and *X Equestris*, who were *en route* to their colonies at Arelate and Narbo. The only full account of the second Iberian campaign is the *Bellum Hispaniense*, by an unknown author, possibly a 'sturdy old centurion' who took part in it, and it is reckoned to be one of the worst books in Latin literature.[389] We are told by our enthusiastic eye-witness that Caesar fielded eight legions and 8,000 cavalry, and Cnaeus Pompeius thirteen legions, of which only four were tried and tested, and 6,000 cavalry.[390] Total victory was achieved at Munda.

The location of this, Caesar's last and hardest-fought, battle is uncertain, but was probably near the present village of Montilla, some 32 kilometres south of Córdoba. When the two battle lines were about to grip, each discharged a volley of *pila*, and we are told the Pompeians 'fell in heaps'. No doubt this was a figure of speech, and besides the advantage lay with the Pompeians because their discharge was delivered down-hill. As our anonymous soldier-historian notes, 'so furious the charging with its attendant volley of missiles, that our men well nigh lost their confidence in victory'.[391] When battle was joined, therefore, fear seized the Caesarians, and Caesar rushed forward, removed his helmet, and exhorted and shamed his men to face up to the enemy. As this did nothing to abate their fear, he seized a shield from a soldier and shouted: 'This will be the end of my life and of your campaigns'. Then 'the entire army attacked at the charge, fought all day, constantly winning and losing advantage in different parts of the field, until at the evening they just managed to secure victory'.[392]

Pursued by the victorious Caesarians, the panic-stricken Pompeians either fled to their camp or sought refuge in the fortress of Munda. In one they fought to the death, in the other they were besieged. Among the slain was the Pompeian loyalist Labienus. The Caesarian casualties were 1,000 killed and 500 wounded, while of the Pompeians some 30,000 are said to have perished.[393] Whatever the true figures, the battle would appear to have been the most stubbornly contested of the Second Civil War. Later a veteran of the battle, on standing before Caesar in Rome, would say: 'I am not surprised that you do not recognise me. The last time we met I was whole, but at Munda my eye was gouged out, and my skull smashed in. Nor would you recognise my helmet if you could see it, for it was split by a *machaera Hispana*.'[394]

As for Cnaeus Pompeius, although wounded, he managed to escape the disaster that overcame his ill-starred command. However, he failed in his attempt to escape by sea and soon after was captured by the soldiers of Caius Didius and beheaded. His head was then paraded as a trophy of war.

Meanwhile, Caesar had returned to Rome and celebrated his fifth triumph, that over 'Iberia', and as a result of his final victory Caesar paid 600 million sesterces into the *aerarium*. At this time he commissioned the first known world map, perhaps part of his great triumphal monument on the Capitol, portraying himself in a four-horse chariot with the globe of the world (*orbis terrarum*) at his feet.[395] He then began preparations for a military operation in the east against the Parthians, Crassus' recent undoing. As the poet Ovid says, with this campaign Caesar was planning to 'add the last part of the *orbis*'.[396]

Chapter 8

Caesar's Triumph

During his campaigns in Gaul Caesar's manner of waging warfare was to conquer either by physical violence or by psychological persuasion. War then as now was Janus-faced: fight a war of the mind as much as a war of blood and iron; reward those who, floored by fear, follow your goals; pacify those who, puffed by pride, do not peacefully accept your purpose. His special instrument was the army that, as he himself claimed, could storm the very heavens with or without him.[397] Here, in the mingling of the souls of Caesar and his legions, was a glimpse of a new order.

Veni, Vidi, Vici

The military theorist Clausewitz coined the term 'military genius' to describe that combination of certain mental and intellectual attributes that enabled an individual to excel as a commander.[398] Among these qualities the most important are: the cerebral ability to process large amounts of information logically and quickly and come to sound conclusions; enduring physical and moral courage; calm determination; a balanced temperament; and a sympathetic understanding of humanity. Together, they produce a commander with the intangible abilities of judging the right moment – the *coup d'oeil* – and leadership. He can quickly assess the chaotic battlefield, perceive the decisive point in a battle, and then lead his men through the trauma of combat to achieve the objective. As we will discover, Caesar was unusually well endowed with many of these qualities, but he was far from infallible.

Napoléon, the most renowned of Caesar's self-proclaimed military successors, was said to have the ability to process large amounts of information rapidly, make a decision, and then have the moral courage required to act decisively and audaciously. Likewise Caesar had this remarkable power to act normally in the abnormal conditions of battle, and among his contemporaries his nervous force in a crisis was unparalleled. For example, seeing Pompey's dispositions on the morning of Pharsalus, Caesar made impromptu changes to his own battle line and rapidly issued orders on which units were to charge on what given signal.[399]

When we consider Caesar's *coup d'oeil*, the ability to perceive the decisive point, we need look no further than the Ilerda campaign when he steered the Pompeians, almost as if they were cattle, to gain an almost bloodless victory. At the very end of this operation, with his quarry well and truly corralled, Caesar was in a position to annihilate the Pompeians in battle. But he chose not to, because he was quick to appreciate that 'a victory could not greatly promote his final success'.[400] Thus by refusing battle, Caesar left the two Pompeian commanders, Lucius Afranius and Marcus Petreius, no option but to surrender. They sent an envoy to Caesar seeking an audience with him, 'if possible, in a place out of reach of the soldiers'.[401] He consented, but the meeting was to be held within earshot of the two armies.

As a commander, Caesar displayed moral courage on a regular basis. Many men have marked physical courage, but lack moral courage. Then again, there are men who undoubtedly possess moral courage but are very cautious about physical danger. However, Caesar was not one of these. For on the wet plain of Munda, once battle was joined, it became clear that this would be the most ferocious fighting of his career. When he saw his war-trained veterans falter, he went to rally them personally, jumping from his horse and shaming them into standing firm. Here was a man who only a few months before had the world at his feet, now at risk of dying on some remote southern Iberian battlefield. His men remembered seeing the look of death on his face as he plunged into the fray, and when he left the field of the slain 'he said to his friends that he had often before struggled for victory, but this was the first time that he had had to fight for his life'.[402] The battle, in the words of Velleius Paterculus, was 'the bloodiest and most perilous Caesar had ever fought'.[403] But his sudden appearance stemmed the rout, and his favourite formation, *legio X Equestris*, dug in its heels and pushed the Pompeians back after a long, gruelling struggle. For Caesar's favourites it was all in a day's work, but for Caesar himself it must have seemed as if it was his last hour. It proved the last, instead, for Cnaeus Pompeius, although the other son of Pompey, Sextus, was left at large.

The forced march to rescue Quintus Cicero from the clutches of the Nervii, or the decision not to follow Pompey across the Adriatic but to tackle the Pompeian legions in Iberia, displayed a degree of balanced temperament. A commander should endeavour to make decisions based upon strategic logic, rather than on emotion. However, modern commentators tend to criticise Caesar for his recklessness, for failing to make adequate preparations for his landings in Britannia, for instance, or invading Epeiros against much stronger opposition, but this is to misunderstand the doctrine of the Roman army. Roman commanders habitually maintained a bold approach to their decision-making, and if they did not seek to seize the initiative and act aggressively, then it was a sign that things were going very badly. The boldness of Caesar's campaigns was not markedly greater than those of many Roman commanders of the period, and certainly no different from the campaigns of Sulla, Lucullus or Pompey, all of whom sought short and lively wars.[404]

The Way of the General

There is an ancient Chinese adage that runs something like this: 'A general who is stupid and brave is a calamity'.[405] As far as a general is concerned, courage is but one quality and his soldiers certainly ask more of him than mere bravery. Of late the distinguished military historian John Keegan has laid down what he sees as the five basic categories of command: first, kinship, the creation of a bond between the commander and his men; second, prescription, the direct verbal contact between the commander and his men; third, sanctions, the system of rewards and punishments operated by the commander; fourth, the imperative of action, the commander's strategic/tactical preparation and intelligence; and fifth, the imperative of example, the physical presence of the commander in battle and the sharing of risk.[406]

In ancient times battles were usually set-piece affairs in which the aim was to exhaust your opponent, and then either penetrate or outflank his line. A battle meant a trial of strength on open ground devoid of obstacles, and so when, as was the case in a civil war, both sides were identically equipped, trained and organised – the so-called symmetry of evenly matched armies – success largely depended on superiority of numbers. Yet, as Fuller reminds us, Caesar adapted the tactics of his day by basing his operations not on numerical disparity and punctilious preparations but on celerity and audacity.[407] Put simply, speed of foot would replace numbers of men.

Of Caesar's system of warfare Suetonius says that he 'joined battle, not only after planning his movements beforehand but also on the spur of the moment, often at the end of a march, and sometimes in miserable weather, when he would be least expected to make a move'. Appian too pinpoints the kernel, the central theme, of Caesar's concept of warfare, remarking that 'he always exploited the dismay caused by his speed of execution and the fear engendered by his daring, rather than the strength created by his preparations'.[408] So was Caesar, with his unimaginable celerity, an outstanding military commander or not? By using Keegan's theoretical categories of command as a standard to measure by, we can make an assessment, albeit rudimentary, of Caesar's own characteristics as a general.

First: kinship, whereby a commander should demonstrate to his men that he constantly thinks of their welfare and works for their benefit. For example, good rations and adequate billeting are of supreme importance in the exercise of command. Rations then as now played a very important part in a soldier's life, not just for replenishing and storing calories and energy but for the undeniable fact that hot food immediately warms him up, raising not only his body temperature but his morale as well. A good commander knows he has to work hard to earn the loyalty and comradeship of his men, and one way to achieve this is by ministering to their basic, workaday needs. Caesar himself appreciated that an army 'marches on its stomach', though his proper understanding of logistics was based on the assumption that the land would provide more than enough in lieu. In other words, dispense with cumbrous convoys and allow war to feed war. However, as we shall see, this policy could leave his men on occasions in dire straits.

Second: prescription, whereby a commander can strengthen his position through accessibility and constant visibility. This allows the commander to exercise his personal influence on the course of the battle. Here we need look no further than Caesar's famous scarlet cloak. With his hard-pressed legionaries desperately defending the siege lines outside Alésia, Caesar knew the battle had reached its final crisis. He rode to a vantage point and began directing the battle. Finally, when the fighting became more ferocious and his men were pressed to breaking point, Caesar committed himself to the fray and the 'conspicuous colour of the cloak he habitually wore in battle proclaimed his arrival'.[409] His exhausted but inspired men raised a war-cry, threw their *pila*, and then set to work with their swords.

Third: sanctions, whereby a commander must operate a just system of rewards and punishments, carefully assessing the needful balance between praise and censure to maintain the iron bonds of discipline. The best disciplinarian is he who understands his men and remembers they are human beings and treats them accordingly. Of particular relevance here is that will-of-the-wisp known as unit morale, which can be fostered through such enlightened leadership. Thus Caesar's flattery and favours towards *legio X Equestris* not only ensured its staunch loyalty to him, but made it one of the fiercest fighting formations of his army.

Fourth: the imperative of action, whereby the safety and security of his men should be a matter of continuing concern to the commander. In this regard, therefore, the commander himself must command an eagerness for victory. This will enable him to inspire his men with the will to win, an indomitable determination to defeat the enemy, and to endure every form of hardship and danger to achieve success. A commander animated by a truly martial spirit, Caesar involved himself in many of the details during the preparatory phase of a campaign, but once the actual operation was launched he pursued his objectives with unremitting daring, trusting to his troops and his own improvisational genius and good luck – an abstract quality that can be neither bought nor sold – to cope with any crisis. Of Alexandria Napoléon said 'there seems to be nothing remarkable about the campaign . . . Egypt might well have become, but for Caesar's wonderful good fortune, the very grave of his reputation'.[410] But as Napoléon himself knew well, success in war depends more than anything else on the will to win and the good favours of fortune.

Fifth: the imperative of example, whereby a commander should be endowed with stout courage and physical endurance in order to establish himself in his soldiers' eyes. A commander worth his salt ought to be able to do better anything he asks any man in his army to do. Thus he should excel above his men in all soldierly tasks. Beyond question Caesar was a leader of this calibre, inspiring his men by his own soldierly conduct and astonishing them with 'his ability to endure physical toils that appeared to be beyond the strength of his body'.[411]

Keegan's fifth category can be divided into three command styles: commanders who always, sometimes, or never enter battle. Thus at the two ends of the 'mask of command' spectrum we have the pre-state warrior chieftain of Homer exhibiting leadership in its most literal sense, and the so-called battle manager of our own age who directs as opposed to participates in combat.

The advice given by the Hellenistic engineer Philon of Byzantium to a general besieging a city is worth consideration:

> Keeping yourself out of range of missiles, or moving along the lines without exposing yourself, exhort the soldiers, distribute praise and honours to those who prove their courage and berate and punish the cowards: in this way all your soldiers will confront danger as well as possible.
>
> Philon, 5.4. 68–9

Philon highlights here the need for the general to raise morale by moving around and talking briefly to his men. The underlying rationale of this style of generalship is well expressed by Onasander, writing under the emperor Claudius, when he says the general 'can aid his army far less by fighting than he can harm it if he should be killed, since the knowledge of a general is far more important than his physical strength'.[412] To have the greatest influence on the battle the general should stay close to, but behind, his fighting line, directing and encouraging his men from this relatively safe position. Thus at Ilerda Caesar ordered up *legio VIIII* from his reserve to reinforce the fighting line, which he was himself rallying. Again, at Pharsalus Caesar spent most of the day just behind *legio X Equestris* on his threatened right wing. From this position he gave two signals after the advance had begun, the first to the six cohorts in his fourth line, which only covered the right flank, and the second to his third line, which supported his entire main infantry line.[413]

The Other Side

At the core of Caesar's success was his quickness of action at both the strategic and tactical levels, the legendary *Caesariana celeritas*. For not only did Caesar always move his forces with amazing rapidity, but he also acted quickly to take advantage of any opportunity that presented itself. His crossing of the Rubicon with just one legion was audacious in the extreme, and Caesar's general philosophy of war, as it would be for Napoléon, was uniformly simple and to the point.

Yet it could be argued that Caesar was often rash and impulsive, taking little or no interest in the general welfare of his army. Thus his swiftness of action could sink to the level of foolhardiness, resulting in his men being ill-supplied with basic foodstuffs. For his first visit to Britannia no provisions were made to carry supplies of grain with the expeditionary force of two legions. At Ilerda his men were reduced to near-starvation, and at one point during the toing and froing around Dyrrhachium they had to make shift as best they could on local roots. Indeed, in Africa his troopers were forced to feed seaweed to their emaciated mounts.[414] Often, if his genius is shown by extracting the army from a difficult situation, it was his foolhardiness which created that situation in the first place. Clearly Caesar's genius was an enigma.

Even so, compared with him Pompey was at a serious disadvantage, a man living on his past fame, whose ambition was simply to be the first man of the Republic. Whereas Caesar had spent all but one of the last nine years at war, Pompey had last seen active service in 62 BC, since when his prestige had sunk. Moreover, as a servant of the Senate, he lacked absolute command and, added to this, was saddled with two apathetic consuls. As a general he had been solid, even stolid perhaps, sensible and thorough rather than nimble-witted or inspirational. He had worked hard, trained his men hard, looked after them, and given clear orders. He gained their allegiance by proven leadership, the odd promise, but never by way of high-flown phrases or florid speeches. When he addressed his soldiers in Epeiros, he simply said: 'I have not abandoned, and would not abandon, the struggle on your behalf and in your company. As general and soldier, I offer myself to you.'[415]

A major task of an ancient general was to draw up his battle line and issue relevant orders for pre-planned moves to be executed when battle was joined. Before battle Pompey could sketch out a plan that was well-nigh always good, but he did not seem to have the knack to modify it according to circumstances. At Pharsalus, for instance, he had the advantage in cavalry and was so confident his 7,000 or so horsemen could carry the day that he seems to have almost held off his legionaries. His plan was to have all his cavalry on the left, rout their opponents, and then swing in behind Caesar's legions. But Caesar, immediately seeing through Pompey's plan, withdrew six cohorts from his third line and posted them on his right to form a fourth line, invisible to the enemy. When the cavalry attacked and routed Caesar's heavily outnumbered horsemen, these cohorts waited until they were given the signal and then attacked so vigorously that Pompey's cavalry scattered to the four winds. After cutting down some archers and slingers, the cohorts swung in behind Pompey's main infantry line and initiated the destruction of his legions. Caesar actually credited his victory to these six cohorts.[416]

Caesar out-generalled Pompey through a realistic appraisal of the circumstances that allowed him to take advantage of Pompey's mistakes and make instant, on-the-spot modifications, that is to say, he showed the essential value of flexibility and adaptability amidst the unpredictability of battle. Caesar clearly had a better grasp of his opponent's intentions than Pompey had of his. Had Pompey's multitude of oriental horsemen been more battle-hardened, in all probability he might have won the day. To make matters worse, they had been deployed too closely together and after their initial success, therefore, they lost cohesion and quickly degenerated into a stationary mob. Pompey had kept no cavalry in reserve.

It was here that Caesar showed his military genius, that genius which in the ultimate analysis Pompey lacked. Pompey's star had gone into eclipse, though we should resist any temptation to believe that he was beaten from the kick-off, so to speak. For instance, his surprise nocturnal attack by sea against an unfinished sector at the southern end of the Caesarian siege works at Dyrrhachium showed a touch of brilliance. With mounting casualties and defeat staring him in the face, Caesar broke off the action and marched off into Greece and uncertainty. The soon-to-be-defeated Pompey was hailed *imperator* by his victorious troops.[417]

Loyalty

Caesar had the unstinting loyalty of his officers – only two of the legates past and present chose to abandon his cause and join Pompey: Cicero's brother Quintus and the outstanding Titus Atius Labienus. As Caesar's right-hand man during the Gallic campaigns, Labienus had been honoured and enriched by Caesar, and was encouraged to hope for a consulship in 48 BC.[418] Typically Caesar's ego would let him make no mention in his memoirs of how his once firm friend and loyal lieutenant had defected to Pompey, and we simply find Labienus on the other side once battle was joined. Apart from his strong credentials as a professional soldier, Labienus was a wealthy, respected and influential senator whose family came from Picenum, presumably from Cingulum (Cingoli).[419] As we know, Picenum was the ancestral home of the Pompeii and it is certainly attractive to believe that Labienus was a Pompeian partisan from the beginning.

Anyway, outwardly Caesar showed nothing but contempt by dispatching 'Labienus' money and baggage after him'.[420] Yet plainly stung by Labienus' action, from this point on Caesar would only refer to his skilled deputy for eight years in the most sneering and derogatory terms. Caesar's supporters, in their subsequent writings, would complete this character assassination, with the cumulative result that Labienus would be cast into the basement of history. However, despite the overall disparaging tone, the author of *Bellum Africum* offers a fascinating anecdote concerning our 'turncoat' general:

> Labienus was riding up and down in the front line bareheaded, cheering on his own men as he did so, and occasionally addressing Caesar's legionaries like this: 'What do you think you are doing, rookie? Little fire-eater, aren't you? Are you another one who's had his wits fuddled by his nib's fine talk? I tell you, he's brought you into a desperate situation. I'm sorry for you.'
>
> Then a soldier said, 'I'm no raw recruit, Labienus; I'm a veteran of *legio X*.' 'I don't recognise the standards of *legio X*,' Labienus replied. 'You'll soon be aware what sort of man I am,' said the soldier. As he spoke, he threw off his helmet, so that he could be recognised by Labienus, then aimed his *pilum* at him and flung it with all his might. He drove it hard full into the chest of Labienus' horse and said, 'Let that show you, Labienus, that it's a soldier of *legio X* who attacks you'.
>
> Anon., *Bellum Africum*, 16. 1–2

If the bluff Labienus was within *pilum* range, then he must have been riding close to the enemy line, probably as close as 30 metres if not closer. He was plainly seeking to animate his soldiers by his repartee, and by showing himself to be confident of success and contemptuous of the enemy, as evident by him being on a horse and bareheaded.

Civil Warrior

With the advantage of hindsight we can fully appreciate why Caesar won the Second Civil War. Though the equipment, organisation and training of the two armies were identical, it was generally agreed at the time that Caesar commanded the better army. His legions (especially *legio X Equestris*, his *corps d'élite*) were made up of hardened and disciplined troops from the Gallic campaigns, veterans flushed with their success and owing loyalty only to him. Writing about the closing stages of events in Gaul, Aulus Hirtius reports that Caesar 'had three veteran legions of exceptional valour – *VII*, *VIII* and *VIIII* – and also *XI*, a legion composed of picked men in the prime of their life, who had now seen seven years' service and of whom he had the highest hopes, although they had not yet had the same experience or reputation for mature courage as the others'.[421] On the other hand, the legions of Pompey were either unsalted or composed of raw recruits. His more experienced formations had been irreparably lost in Iberia the previous year.

Better still, Caesar's opposition lacked one head, being as it was divided between the Pompeians and the die-hard *optimates* led by Cato, who, according to Caesar, complained that Pompey had betrayed the Republic by not making better preparations for war. In his prime Pompey had been a bold and brave commander, but now his position as generalissimo of the republican forces was being undermined by senators who prodded him to action that he might otherwise have delayed or not even have taken. Unity of command, Napoléon would state with absolute conviction, was 'the first necessity of war'.[422]

The absence of *commentarii* written by Pompey himself means that our knowledge of his strategy on this particular occasion is derived from three sources: his chief antagonist, skilled both with pen and sword; the biography of the scholarly Plutarch, written long after the event; and the tart comments of the un-warlike Cicero. We are justified, however, in claiming that Pompey conceded the initiative to Caesar at the start by abandoning Italy, which shocked many of his supporters. True he had only the two formations, *legiones I* and *XV*, which six months previously had been Caesar's and thus could not be wholly trusted. Of this predicament Cicero wrote to Atticus: 'The hope lies in two legions kept back not without discredit and scarcely his own'. He glumly continues, explaining that as far as the fresh levies were concerned 'the men so far are reluctant and have no stomach for fighting'.[423] It seems Pompey, having stamped his foot on the soil of Italy, had grossly over-rated the grass-roots support for his cause. The people at large were rather indifferent to the threat to senatorial rights and liberties, and there was a general perception that the Pompeians were likely to institute a Sullan-style proscription if victorious. Indeed, the people of Italy undoubtedly cared to support neither one side nor the other, and they may perhaps secretly have vowed a plague on both their houses.

The majority of Italy certainly did not want civil war, and effectively the conflict was for the choice of masters. One of the few who did not flee the country was one of Caesar's sternest critics, Cicero. There were many things that might have brought the two men together, such as a common appreciation for literature, to which Pompey was notoriously alien, and mutual friends. Yet Caesar's supporters were a frightful collection of men on the make, unprincipled time-servers, the 'army of the underworld' as Cicero and his good friend Atticus so gleefully described them.[424] But then again, Cicero had no particular fondness for Pompey. If Pompey returned from Epeiros, he would attack Italy and allow the most dreadful reprisals. Cicero suitably sums up his feelings when he discusses the options in a letter to Atticus, rightly saying, 'neither of them has our happiness as their aim, each of them wants to be king'.[425] Basically, he hated the option of war and the destruction it would bring. Remaining in Italy was a brave move.

Tacitus, in a backward glance to earlier civil conflicts and the demolition of the republican constitution, says that Pompey was thought of as 'more inscrutable, not better [than Marius and Sulla]'.[426] When Sulla marched on Rome a generation earlier, he had been ruthless with his enemies, killing them, banishing them and seizing their property. Many were convinced that Caesar would act the same way, particularly as he had already demonstrated in Gaul his disregard for human life. Hence the genuine surprise when Caesar instituted a policy of *clementia*, clemency, by which he deliberately sought to avoid the bloody cruelty that Sulla had shown to his defeated opponents.

While on the march to Brundisium Caesar dashed off a letter, sometime around 5 March 49 BC or thereabouts, to his political agents back in Rome, Caius Oppius and Lucius Cornelius Balbus. In it he reveals the secret of his civil war policy:

> Let us try whether by this means we can win back the goodwill of all and enjoy a lasting victory, seeing that others have not managed by cruelty to escape hatred or to make their victories endure, except Lucius Sulla, whom I do not propose to imitate. Let this be the new style of conquest, to make mildness [*misericordia*] and generosity [*liberalitas*] our shield.
>
> Cicero, *Epistulae ad Atticum*, 9.7c. 1

The letter was almost certainly meant for circulation – hence the copy found in Cicero's correspondence – for it advertised the *clementia* for which he became famed. But this was a double-edged virtue, for forgiveness was the prerogative of kings and tyrants.

What was different, however, was Caesar's intellectual grasp of the nature of war. Two thousand years before Clausewitz, he had appreciated that war was 'a serious means to a serious end'.[427] Caesar waged war to further his political aims, and his means to the end was to be the shortest and sharpest method available. Thus from the outset he grasped that he was faced with a civil war not a foreign war, and that each demanded a technique of its own. He saw that the merciless war of annihilation he had fought in Gaul would be out of place in Italy. He realised that in a civil war it was as important to win the goodwill of the civil population as to impose his own will on his opponent, and more profitable to subvert his opponent's fighting forces than destroy them. Moreover, he had no desire to exterminate his fellow Roman aristocrats. Caesar was going to forgive and forget, prepared to pardon all those, armies and individuals alike, who stood against him. Cruelty and clemency were but means toward gaining specific ends, and not ends in themselves. As Fuller rightly says, 'He was neither a devil nor an angel, he was a craftsman'.[428]

As a final point of interest here, Caesar, along with his fellow warlord Pompey, was to earn a place among Catullus' array of picaresque and unsavoury characters that populate his salacious tales.[429] Suetonius tells the story that the sharp-tongued Catullus later apologised for his scurrilous attacks and was immediately invited to dine with the forgiving Caesar.[430]

Nimbus of Victory

In a speech Appian records that Caesar apparently made to his soldiers prior to slipping across the Adriatic, we are given the very essence of Caesarian generalship. Even if these are not Caesar's own words, the quayside address put into his month by Appian sounds right and seems suited to both the man and the occasion:

> Comrades, my partners in this great enterprise, I shall not be prevented from starting out either by the winter season or by the slowness of other people or by the lack of the appropriate stores. In place of all these I think swiftness of action will serve. I believe that we who are the first to gather here should first leave behind our slaves, our pack-animals, our baggage, in fact everything necessary to ensure that the ships we have will accommodate us, and we should then embark immediately, on our own, and make our crossing, in order to catch the enemy off guard. Against the winter weather we can set our good fortune, against our low numbers our daring, and against our lack of supplies our enemies' abundance of them, which it is quite possible for us to seize as soon as we land if we realise that failure will mean we have none of our own. Let

> us attack their slaves and equipment and provisions while they are passing the winter under cover. Let us attack while Pompey imagines that I am spending the winter like him or am occupied with consular pomp and sacrificial ritual. You understand war, and I put it to you that the mightiest weapon of war is surprise. It will also be the most signal honour for us to pre-empt the glory of the events that are about to unfold, and to make everything over on the other side secure before the arrival of the forces which will directly follow us. Speaking for myself, at this critical moment I would rather be afloat than making a speech, so that Pompey, who imagines I am dealing with consular business in Rome, could set eyes on me; as for you, although I know you are not difficult to convince, I none the less await your answer.
>
> Appian, *Bellum civilia*, 2.53

Long before Napoléon, Colonel du Picq or Marshal Foch, Caesar had fully understood that morale counted for more than mere numbers. Needless to say, by playing on the vanity and underlying credulity of his men, Caesar's proud and violent army called to be led on to victory and glory.

The Second Dictator

But how was Caesar going to use his victory? Suetonius, citing from a Pompeian source, says he was not going to model himself on Sulla, a man 'who had proved himself a dunce by resigning his dictatorship'.[431] Though this remark of Caesar's was preserved by a hostile tradition keen to demonstrate his desire to overthrow the Republic, we do gain a foretaste of what Caesar was striving for from his own words as he surveyed the bloody aftermath of Pharsalus:

> Asinius Pollio records in his *Historiae* that when Caesar, at the battle of Pharsalus, saw his enemies forced to choose between massacre and flight, he said, in these words: 'They wanted it thus. They would have condemned me – me Caius Caesar – regardless of all my victories if I had not appealed to my army for help.'
>
> Suetonius, *Divus Iulius*, 30.4

In 44 BC Caesar shared his fifth consulship with his right-hand man Marcus Antonius, but a month before his death he was declared *dictator perpetuus*. Despite odious memories of Sulla, the choice of the dictatorship was recommended by its comprehensive powers and freedom from the tribunician veto. It was certainly a logical and executable way to hold and use *imperium*, and to some extent Caesar was acting more within the tradition of the Republic than he had in the fifties BC, when, along with Pompey and Crassus, he had controlled the affairs of state from outside the legal framework of magistracies. Even so, the fact that he intended to hold the office in perpetuity clearly caused great offence among those now deprived of their freedom, *libertas*, which depended on magistracy and *imperium*. Of course, much like democracy today, the concept of freedom was a jolly good thing and could mean anything you wanted it to mean.

At this time Caesar was planning to quit Rome for at least three years in order to fight in Parthia. A delicate and sometimes not so delicate *pas de deux* had taken place between the two empires since Carrhae. Yet there was rarely a reason needed for a fight. As we well appreciate, Rome did not need an excuse to make war, especially in the east. Rome did not play well with others and their very existence was sometimes the only trigger necessary. It should come as no surprise that the world's two military superpowers, facing each other along a frontier that was several hundred kilometres long, should come into regular conflict. And so the tug of war between Rome and Parthia continued off and on until the western border between Rome's dominions and Parthia gradually stabilised on the banks of the Euphrates. They were, as the Greek historian Herodian was later to write in the third century AD, the two greatest empires in the world, separated only by a river.[432]

The army for Caesar's next military operation was to be huge. With no fewer than sixteen legions and 10,000 cavalry, he was to invade Parthia ostensibly to punish the Parthians for wiping out his fellow triumvir Crassus and his legions almost nine years before. But the operation was to be much more than an act to restore Roman pride. It is said by Plutarch that Caesar even had his eyes on India, perhaps harbouring thoughts of becoming a second Alexander the Great with an empire 'bounded on all sides by the ocean'.[433] Whatever his military ambitions, Caesar obviously wanted his political position secured and had the consuls for the following two years already appointed.[434] The question is, however, what position was he carving out for himself?

His acceptance of the title *dictator perpetuus* demonstrates that Caesar did intend to retain power indefinitely, but this then raises two further extraordinary questions. First, was Caesar seeking a quasi-divine status, and second, was he going to convert the perpetual dictatorship into a hereditary monarchy? Even to this day both of these points are fiercely argued about by academics. Balsdon, for instance, coolly argues that the notion that Caesar hankered after divine status and kingship was the invention and elaboration of his assassins. On the other hand, others such as Taylor and Weinstock earnestly believe that Caesar was seeking divine status, that is to say, a Hellenistic-type monarch, despotic and absolute, worshipped with god-like honours.[435]

The 'Divine King'

Prior to Pharsalus Caesar had vowed to set up a temple in the new forum, the Forum Iulium, that he was having built immediately north of the existing one and close to the new Senate house. This all-marble affair was to be dedicated to Venus Victrix (Venus of Victory), but ended up being dedicated to Venus Genetrix (Mother Venus). Now *Genetrix* was not one of Venus' known manifestations; instead it was an attribute given by Caesar designating her as the one who gave birth to his illustrious family, the Iulii. This was not really exceptional, however, as Caesar could be publicly advertising, as he constantly did, his divine ancestry.[436]

The fact that the Iulii claimed descent from Aeneas and the goddess Venus made the family older than Rome itself. The goddess had given birth to Aeneas, the mythical hero who had escaped the sack of Troy to seek refuge in Italy. There his son Ascanius, the founder of the Iulii, established Alba Longa thirty-three years later. After the Romans destroyed that city some families, including the Iulii, migrated to Rome.[437] Caesar, fully aware of the importance of symbolism, lost no opportunity to stress his family's intimate connection with Venus. He carried her sculpted image on the ring he always wore, he invoked her name in the moments of highest peril, and Venus, who was, after all, the goddess of erotic love and natural beauty, had endowed him with his good looks.[438]

After Thapsus the Senate, in his absence, voted Caesar a whole series of honours. The most notable of these was a statue of him standing atop a globe inscribed with the legend *hemitheos*, 'Demi-god'. But when Caesar returned to Rome he immediately had the inscription erased.[439] It seems that a subservient Senate was falling over itself in order to flatter Caesar and went too far in doing so on this particular occasion.

With news of Munda, which was received several weeks after the battle, the Senate awarded Caesar another heap of honours in his absence. Again this included an ivory statue, which was inscribed 'To the undefeated God' and carried in procession with a statue of Victory at the opening of all games in the circus. The inscription itself had strong overtones of Alexander the Great and admittedly this is a difficult one to explain away, especially as the master of Rome did not over-rule the Senate this time. Apparently his common subjects expressed a somewhat different opinion on this particular accolade. Cicero, with a touch of bitchiness, wrote to Atticus saying the 'people are behaving splendidly in refusing to applaud Victory because of her undesirable neighbour'.[440]

Other divine honours included a temple dedicated to Clementia Caesaris and a priesthood (*flamen Dialis*) established in his name as if he were a god, with Marcus Antonius appointed as his personal priest.[441] All this would culminate in the official establishment of the cult of Divus Iulius, Caesar the God, two years after his assassination. Incidentally, the news of Caesar's victory at Munda reached Rome on 21 April, the very day the Parilia was being celebrated. This was the festival associated with Romulus and the founding of the city. The coincidence (if that is what it was) was exploited in favour of Caesar, the 're-founder' of the city, with an extra day of games added to the festival at which crowns were worn in Caesar's honour.

Naturally Caesar was worshipped in the Greek east, where Hellenistic monarchs (and powerful Romans before Caesar) had been typically granted divine status while alive, the most celebrated example being the Ptolemies of Egypt. Take, for instance, the far-famed Cleopatra and her son and co-regent Ptolemaios, honoured as living divine-sovereigns in the opening line of a decree dated to March 39 BC: 'In the reign of Kleopatra (VII), goddess [Ph]ilopat[or and of P]tolemaios, who is also the son of Kaisar, god Philometor'.[442] Ptolemaios (aka Caesarion, Little Caesar) was the alleged son of Caesar's own blood, who reigned as Cleopatra's co-ruler and heir from 44 BC until his untimely demise at the hands of Octavianus fourteen years later. As Plutarch justly observed, 'too many Caesars is no good thing',[443] particularly if one of them happened to be a living god.

We should understand that in the ancient world there was no such thing as a separation of the sacred from the secular, and a connection between the invincible leader and the gods was easily made. At Ephesus, soon after Pharsalus, the cities of Asia joined in calling Caesar 'the god manifest descended from Ares [Mars] and Aphrodite [Venus], saviour of all human life'.[444] It could be argued that Caesar did not really see himself as divine, and thus believed others did not either, but this would be naïve. It is true the Senate had voted the aforementioned honours (and others) for Caesar freely, some of which he welcomed as deserved, others merely reflecting the empty flattery of an obsequious Senate. As Cassius Dio makes clear, the Senate did so to flatter him and not out of goodwill, while Cicero says the majority of the senators in 44 BC were of Caesar's creation, perhaps rightly.[445] It could be argued, of course, that Caesar did not value such tangible trivialities when he had achieved the intangible, weighty realities of power and status.

In the Greek east civic ruler-cults and the building of temples and shrines to monarchs was commonplace. The role of the ruler in Hellenistic states and kingdoms was god-like. Apart from the fact that the ruler was hardly seen by his subjects, hence the importance of regal portraiture on coinage, the whole business involved the contractual arrangement inherent in ancient cult practices. For instance, a pilgrim could gain a hold over a particular divinity by offering regular libations or sacrifices to that god who, in turn, would offer protection, especially in times of danger. Equally, in the Greek world when an embassy stood before a king they reminded him that their city had built a temple or shrine in his honour. In other words an unspoken contract existed between monarch and subject by which the former felt duty-bound to repay the honour done to him by the latter.

Herein lies a possible solution to the question of Caesar's so-called divine status. It is certainly true that the divine worship of Hellenistic monarchs became the model for the Roman emperors, and thus we could argue that Caesar, dictator for life, was the first example of this practice. At Caesar's public funeral, as Suetonius says, Marcus Antonius 'instructed heralds to read, first, the recent decree simultaneously voting Caesar all divine and human honours, and then the oath by which the entire Senate had pledged themselves to watch over his safety'.[446] Lest we forget, even in his lifetime the Senate was quite prepared to grant him untold honours in order to placate their 'divine ruler'.

King of Rome?

But why did Caesar need the more glamorous but invidious title of *rex*, especially as he now held all the power he required by ruling Rome through the position of *dictator perpetuus*? Syme believes it is not necessary to accept that he sought to establish a Hellenistic-style monarchy, because the dictatorship was sufficient.[447]

There is the famous anecdote of the crowd hailing Caesar as *rex* when he was returning from the Latin Festival (26 January 44 BC) and he retorted with the witticism 'No, I am Caesar, not King'.[448] We next see Caesar, who had just accepted his position as dictator for life, presiding over the Lupercalia on 15 February. Known to all readers of Shakespeare, if not of the classical sources, this was an ancient and somewhat peculiar ceremony in honour of Pan when young men called Luperci, wearing the skins of sacrificed goats and their foreheads smeared with the goats' blood, ran round the foot of the Palatine striking any women they met with strips of these skins so as to assist their future fertility. The Luperci were drawn from the best families of Rome, and one of their number on this particular day was Marcus Antonius. Two men, Caius Cassius and Publius Casca, had placed a diadem bound with laurel on Caesar's knees, but Antonius stole the moment by placing it on the recipient's head. At the time Caesar was sitting in his gilded chair and wearing his purple toga and gold wreath, the dress of a *triumphator*, granted to him by the Senate along with the bodyguard of senators and equestrians that now attended him.[449] However, Caesar blatantly refused the kingly honour, throwing the diadem into the crowd with the instruction to dedicate it to Iuppiter Capitolinus, the only king in Rome, an act that was confirmed by Cicero, who was probably present.[450]

It could be said that this was Caesar's way of sounding out public opinion, which proved hostile to kingship. Equally, it might have been intended to demonstrate that he did not want the title of king, or the initiative might have been entirely Antonius'. If Cassius and Casca were already up to their necks plotting Caesar's demise we can speculate that they were out to wrong-foot the dictator. Unfortunately for them Antonius leapt in when he saw a golden opportunity to seek favour with Caesar. But Caesar, with lightning speed, stole everybody's thunder by using the moment to make a grand gesture to the populace. It was a clever move as it created an aura of negativity towards kingship.

Despite the persistence of some scholars, it is highly improbable that Caesar wanted to be called *rex*, but he certainly did not want to behave in an entirely constitutional manner. Napoléon, surely a critic as qualified as any other, said: 'If Caesar wanted to be king, he would have got his army to acclaim him as such'.[451] Yet even though Caesar spurned the title and trappings of a king, there were many who felt he was now the king of Rome in everything but name. He was certainly the first Roman to emulate the Hellenistic monarchs in having his head represented on official coinage in his lifetime, and also allowed his statue to be set up in temples with those of the gods, and made of materials, namely gold and ivory, previously reserved for the gods. So whatever his future plans may have been, his present power and conduct were sufficient to bring about his untimely death. After his victory in the civil war, Caesar lived for less than a year. His dictatorship was not characterised by a proscription and confiscations of property and wealth, but there were those who wanted the Republic back, and there was no place for Caesar there.

City of the Gods

Roman religion was characterised by scrupulous respect for the formulae of prayer and ritual. Romans, being Romans, did things by the book, and ritual was certainly no exception. The political activity of the state was heavily surrounded by ritual: assemblies needed favourable omens; magistrates could not take up office if the omens were bad, and prodigies were regularly reported and expiated by the Senate. It is difficult to stress enough how much religion impinged upon, indeed was part of, public life. For the unscrupulous, manipulation of the state religion was an easy way to manipulate politics, thus the 'sky watching' of Bibulus, Caesar's consular colleague back in 59 BC. For religious issues, therefore, the Senate could consult a number of official civic priesthoods. There were four main colleges of the Roman priesthood; however, only two of the four shall concern us here.

First, there was the college of pontiffs (*pontifeces*). Down to 300 BC the college consisted of five life-long members, all patricians, when the *lex Ogulnia* added four extra places for plebeian *pontifeces*. The college's duties were wide-ranging: they had general oversight of the state cult – sacrifices, games (*ludi*), festivals and other rituals; they advised magistrates and private individuals on the sacred law (*fas*) and kept the books (*annales maximi*) that recorded their rules and decisions; they had special areas of concern in relation to families (*gentes*) – the control of adoptions, burial law, the inheritance of religious duties (*sacra familiaria*). They had no priestly authority outside their college and their relationship with the state remained an advisory one. The leading member of the college, the *pontifex maximus*, acted as its spokesman, particularly in the Senate. This was the office Caesar had held since 63 BC.

Second, the *augures* were the official Roman diviners. There were originally four in number, all patricians, and the complement was made up to nine in 300 BC when the plebeians were admitted under the terms of the *lex Ogulnia*. Their number was further increased to fifteen by Sulla, and to sixteen by Caesar. As a college the *augures* were a body of experts whose duty was to uphold the augural doctrine, which governed the observation and application of the auspices (*auspicia*) in Roman public life. They passed decrees (*decreta*) either on their own initiative or more frequently in response to questions posed by the Senate or the magistrates (*responsa*). These 'replies' often dealt with cases of ritual fault (*vitium*), which would nullify the auspices, or the removal of *religio*, a ritual obstacle to an action. The Senate was free to accept or to reject the advice. Marcus Antonius was elected *augur* for life in 50 BC, no doubt with Caesar's monetary support and moral encouragement.

In Rome, unlike in Greece, priests were (with the exception of the Vestal virgins, see below) males, formed into colleges. Furthermore, they were not attached to particular deities or temples, but rather to special festivals or areas of religion. The *flamines* were a spectacular exception, perhaps preserving a more archaic and far closer relationship between priest and deity; they therefore provide the model for the priesthood of Caesar after his death. These priests did not constitute a separate college but were found within the college of *pontifeces*. There were three major and twelve minor *flamines*, each of them assigned to the worship of a single deity, though this did not preclude their taking part in the worship of other deities. Under the Republic the three major *flamines* were the *flamen Dialis* (Iuppiter), *Martialis* (Mars) and *Quirinalis* (Quirinus, the name of the deified Romulus), thus representing the three Indo-European functions of law, warfare and production. Each *flamen* was surrounded by archaic taboos, the *flamen Dialis*, for instance, was rarely allowed to leave his house, nor allowed to ride a horse, see weapons or even bloodshed. Just before his death, during his sanguinary seventh consulship, Marius had plans to make his young nephew the *flamen Dialis*; the post had just fallen vacant following the forced suicide of its previous incumbent. Since Caesar was only 13 years old at the time, the post had to be held open for him until he officially came of age. Three years later Cinna, Rome's current supremo and Caesar's future father-in-law, confirmed his priesthood. Following the replacement of the Cinnan régime with that of Sulla, the young *flamen Dialis* was unceremoniously removed from his office.[452] And so, thanks to Sulla, Caesar was now free to pursue an alternative career.

There were six Vestal virgins (*virgines Vestales*). All were traditionally chosen, by the *pontifex maximus*, from old patrician families at a young age, usually between the ages of 6 and 10. They would serve ten years as novices, then ten performing the actual duties, followed by a final ten years of teaching the novices. They lived in a palatial building next to the small temple of Vesta (*aedes Vestae*), the virgin goddess of hearth and home who symbolised the continuity of family and state, in the Forum. Their foremost duty was to guard the sacred fire in the temple, whose eternity symbolised the well-being and power of Rome. Other duties included performing rituals and baking the sacred salt cake (*mola salsa*) to be used at numerous ceremonies in the year. Punishments for Vestal virgins were enormously harsh. If they let the flame go out, they would be whipped. And as they had to remain virgins, their punishment for breaking their vow of chastity was to be walled up alive underground. In later life Crassus was charged with seducing a Vestal virgin. Apparently the lady in question, Licinia was her name, owned a desirable residence in the suburbs and Crassus wanted to buy it cheaply, hence the amorous attention and the subsequent scandal. 'It was his avarice that cleared him of having corrupted the lady,' Plutarch explains, 'but he did not let Licinia alone until he had acquired the property.'[453] But the honour and privilege surrounding the Vestal virgins was enormous. In fact any criminal who was condemned to death and then was lucky enough to see a Vestal virgin was automatically pardoned.

The Ides of March

In 46 BC the *optimate* hard-liner Marcus Claudius Marcellus (*cos.* 51 BC), first cousin of Caius Claudius Marcellus (*cos.* 50 BC), was pardoned by Caesar and thus allowed to return from exile. Recounting the events of what he reckoned was 'a fine day's work', Cicero writes: 'I thought I saw some semblance of reviving constitutional freedom'.[454] And so, with the return to Rome of such a prominent republican figure, Cicero, who was speaking in the Senate in gratitude for the recall, clearly saw this as the ideal time for Caesar (whom he lavishly praised) to restore the Republic.[455] Balsdon assumes that when he crossed the Rubicon Caesar was supported by a body of ambitious men who were in similar straits to those men who had flocked to Sulla when he landed at Brundisium in 83 BC. In other words, Caesar's supporters expected to be the 'top dogs' once Caesar had restored the constitution.[456]

Death

On the eve of his murder Caesar dined with friends. Over wine a discussion ensued about what was the most preferable way to die. Caesar's reply was: 'The kind that comes unexpectedly'.[457]

Although the Romans entertained many different theories concerning death and the afterlife, most prevalent was the belief that a dead person continued to exist as an independent entity in, or in the vicinity of, the tomb. It was thought that in this afterlife the spirits of the dead (*di manes*) could still influence events among the living, sometimes reappearing for example in dreams.

The dead were also believed to be subject to the same needs as the living, obliged to eat and drink, and reliant upon the living to provide for these necessities. The dead were considered to be especially likely to feel resentment if their passing had not been duly celebrated or if their needs in the grave were neglected, and so death was followed by an outburst of grief on the part of the living relatives, continued by prolonged manifestations of mourning to prove to the departed that he or she was truly lamented. The Augustan elegist Propertius expressed a common view: 'The *manes* do mean something. Death is not the end, and the pale ghost escapes the defeated pyre.'[458]

Yet for all that, the afterlife was shadowy and uncertain to most Romans, and it was fame that offered the best hope of immortality. 'Since only a short span of life has been vouchsafed us', wrote Sallust, 'we must make ourselves remembered as long as may be by those who come after us.'[459]

Down to 45 BC the new Republic had yet to materialise, but this was simply because Caesar had been rushing around the Mediterranean putting down the Pompeians. However, after Munda these men saw no evidence of a Sullan-type restoration, and they expected the worst, that is to say, Caesar had no plans to renew their liberties. Consequently, this is why many of his closest friends and supporters (many of whom had benefited from his policy of *clementia Caesaris*) were involved in the conspiracy that resulted in his assassination. Aulus Hirtius, perhaps wise after the event, told Cicero that many of Caesar's adherents held that 'clemency was his undoing, but for which nothing of the sort could have happened to him'.[460]

There is a story that while the 39-year-old Caesar was crossing the Alps on the way to assume his post as governor of Hispania Ulterior he came to a one-horse settlement. Plutarch now takes up the narrative:

> His friends were laughing and joking about it, saying: 'No doubt here too one would find people pushing themselves forward to gain office, and here too there are struggles to get the first place and jealous rivalries among the great men'. Caesar then said to them in all seriousness: 'As far as I am concerned I would rather be the first man here than the second in Rome'.
>
> Plutarch, *Caesar*, 11. 6–7

Much ink has been (and will be) spilt over Caesar's rise to power, and one of the great difficulties is to disentangle the true character and activities of this outstanding personality from the distortions of the legends that surround him. The Caesar as depicted by many scholars is in several important aspects very different from the self-revealed Caesar of the *commentarii* and the Caesar of the Graeco-Roman sources. Caesar's apotheosis as a superman emerged into the light of the Renaissance, and soon became an historical obsession. We need only think of Shakespeare's Caesar, 'the foremost man of all this world?', or Nietzsche's Caesar, 'one of those enigmatic men predestined for victory and the seduction of others'.[461]

'What drove Caius Caesar on to his own and the state's doom? Glory, ambition and the refusal to set bounds to his own pre-eminence.' So wrote Seneca.[462] The murder did not solve anything. The ailing Republic refused to stagger back on to its feet. Caesar had shown Rome what it was like to be ruled by one man, a kind of 'super-*patronus*', and the huge pressure group, his 'super-*clientelae*', would not go away. As dictator for life of the Roman state he laid the foundations for sole sovereignty. Thus the sequel, the topic of our next chapter, would be a sanguinary squabble over who was going to gain control of Caesar's legacy.

Imitation, of course, is the sincerest form of flattery. Cesare Borgia (d. 1507) was a notorious practical imitator of his ancient Roman counterpart, albeit a far less successful one. The achievements of both were praised by Niccolò Machiavelli in *Il Principe*, and in the *Arte della guerra* he repeatedly turns to Caesar the general as an exemplar of military excellence.[463]

> Thus, Iulius Caesar, Alexander of Macedon, and all such men and excellent princes always fought at the head of their own armies, always marched with them on foot, and always carried their own arms; if any of them ever lost his power, he simultaneously lost his life with it and died with the same *virtù* that he had displayed while he lived.
>
> Machiavelli, *Arte della guerra*, 7.211

A favourite term of Machiavelli, *virtù* is a necessary quality of effective generalship and statecraft. This Machiavellian concept implies what is proper to masculine and aggressive conduct, that is to say, courage, fortitude, audacity, skill and, above all, civic spirit. The archetypal product of *virtù* is the foundation of a state or an army; the archetypal figure of *virtù* is the military hero-founder, such as Romulus. However, *virtù* may be associated with the pursuit of power and self-aggrandisement by any means and at any price. Thus Caesar the tyrant was disliked by Machiavelli because he destroyed the Roman Republic and its oligarchic liberties.[464] Yet to the oppressed and dispirited, to the dispossessed, and to others under the grinding heel of poverty, Caesar became an attractive beacon.

Chapter 9

Caesar's Legacy

Caius Iulius Caesar, *dictator perpetuus*, perished at the foot of the statue of Cnaeus Pompeius Magnus, his old foe, a symbol of the Senate's *libertas*. Struck by over twenty stab wounds, he fell, covered his face with his toga, and died. At the later autopsy, Suetonius tells us, the physician Antistius concluded that a blow to the chest had been the fatal one – a blow by Marcus Iunius Brutus, Suetonius says, although Appian records that Brutus struck Caesar in the thigh.[465] The conspiracy included some sixty individuals, and not only ex-Pompeians favoured by Caesar, men such as the stoic Brutus and the saturnine Cassius, but also thorough-going Caesarians such as Caius Trebonius (*cos. suff.* 45 BC), an admirer of Cicero, and Decimus Iunius Brutus Albinus, a distant relative of the Brutus who had been a legate of Caesar in Gaul. Within days of his assassination, while the Senate was still uncertain how to react, the place of his funerary pyre had become a shrine, and a self-appointed 'priest' was honouring him as a god. The ordinary people of Rome plainly preferred Caesar to yet more 'concord' and 'liberty' from the senatorial aristocracy.

Enter the Warlord

For some four-and-a-half centuries Rome had been ruled by an elaborate aristocratic system of government, which we now know as the Republic. Under this system Rome was governed by annually elected magistrates, some of whom wielded immense power. The essence of the system was the office of consulship, which gave the holder *imperium*, the right to issue commands to people of lesser status and expect those commands to be obeyed. This *imperium* had originally been held by the kings, but they had been ousted from Rome in 509 BC, or so Roman tradition has it. However, from that date onwards no single individual would be allowed to wield power over everybody else, and this would be enforced through collegiality, limited tenure of office, accountability and the right to appeal.

Although it could be argued that any adult male citizen of Rome could seek public office, in practice magistracies were limited to a tiny wealthy élite who jealously guarded the right to hold them. Yet the extraordinary thing was the very amateurish nature of these magistracies. Holders of public office were not specialist but in fact jacks-of-all-trades able to turn their hands and minds to almost anything. Judge for yourself. As a quaestor, aged 26 or thereabouts, a man would be expected to deal with financial matters, while a couple of years later, as a tribune of the people, he was expected to deal with social matters. As a praetor, aged 39, our man was dealing with judicial matters, and three years on, as a consul, with those of an international nature. Furthermore, having served as a quaestor membership of the Senate, the advisory body few magistrates dared to ignore, became automatic and lifelong. And even though the Senate could not draw up and pass laws, the combined weight of its aristocratic membership gave it terrific influence.

Under this oligarchic system Rome came to dominate the Mediterranean world by the middle of the second century BC, establishing *provincia*, spheres in which a senior magistrate could exercise *imperium*, and by the time of Caesar it had drawn Gaul into its orbit. Beyond the boundaries of its *provincia* Rome did wield power, for example the Ptolemaic kingdom of Egypt would often sit up and take note of what the Senate said. However, is it often said that the Republic fell because its constitutional system was fit only to run a city-state, but in truth the end came because of two major factors. First, serious social and economic problems arose during the latter half of the second century BC and the Senate could not or would not deal with them, thus creating huge social and political divisions. Secondly, individuals emerged during the first century BC who wielded vast amounts of power, wealth and military muscle, which rested only in part upon the public offices they held in Rome. Such men could hardly be ignored.

When these warlords refused to accept the amateurish consular system they put their own personal interests first before those of the state, Caesar, of course, being the prime example of this autocratic phenomenon. The statement of Caius Asinius Pollio that Caesar exclaimed 'they wanted it thus'[466] when he viewed the Roman dead littering the field of Pharsalus sheds an enormous amount of light on Caesar's character and motives. Here was a man bigger than the system that had spawned him.

Yet the 'great man' theory of history has always been a puzzle to scholars, who search endlessly for reasons why. The real puzzle is why people actually follow these charismatic figures that mesmerise masses (and scholars) and leave rather large footprints in the sands of time – take, for instance, the closing chapters of Tolstoy's epic *War and Peace*. For great men to be great they need followers to make them great. So it is the motives of those surrounding Caesar that are at the crux of the matter and not those of the man himself.

In the months after Caesar's assassination his murderers advocated a return to the old republican system, where the Senate governed Rome. Yet Caesar's armies, money and the people's loyalties made it hard for them to turn the clock back as if he had not existed. Thus other men felt that the day of the autocrat was here to stay, and general factions emerged as the leading men of the state jockeyed for position.

One in particular, Marcus Antonius (*cos.* 44 BC), now saw himself as a legitimate successor to Caesar. A *nobilis* born of a prominent but notoriously improvised plebeian family, his grandfather was the great orator of the same name while his amiable father, of the same name too, suffered the double agony of being humiliated by friend and foe alike, namely the Cilician pirates and the Roman Senate. The son, however, was of a different stamp altogether. Notorious for his wine-sodden vulgarity and manic womanising, Antonius was equally undaunted upon the field of battle. He was at his best when goaded by the spur of action, and Caesar was quick to realise that his other reputation, namely for courage in battle and perseverance on campaign, was the one deserving attention. Hence Antonius' rapid promotion after the defection of Labienus. On the field of Pharsalus Caesar entrusted command of the left wing to him, and during a day of hard fighting Antonius proved to be a commander worthy of the stern veterans he had led. About the Ides of March, Cicero would write, the assassins had left a fine 'banquet' unfinished: there had been the 'leftovers', the 39-year-old Marcus Antonius.[467]

The Problems of the Late Republic

Agrarian troubles

• The Gracchi sponsor massive land distributions, but such measures are still being proposed in the sixties and fifties BC (government by tribunes)

Urban poverty and degradation

• The commons eagerly support the Gracchi *et al.*, which eventually leads to the terror of Clodius and Milo in the fifties BC (urban warlords)

The 'Italian Question'

• Caius Gracchus and Drusus propose full Roman citizenship for *socii*, but this reform is only achieved through armed rebellion (Social War)

• Rapid growth of Roman power in the Mediterranean world, leading to: an increase in the rivalry between members of the ruling oligarchy (*optimates* versus *populares*); uncontrollable generals, whose soldiers owe allegiance to the individual commander and not to the state (government by warlords); and two civil wars (Marius versus Sulla, Pompey versus Caesar).

Problems, Solutions, Problems

The late Republic was characterised by the obvious unwillingness of the ruling élite as a whole to recognise the social and economic problems of the day. Thus we witness the demagoguery of Saturninus and Sulpicius, the short-sightedness of Marius and Sulla, the high-handedness of Pompey and Caesar, the desperation of Lepidus and Catiline, the indifference of Cicero, and the mob rule of Clodius and Milo. The senatorial aristocracy simply turned in on itself, a truism that surely stands as the fundamental reason for the collapse of the Republic. The republican system itself simply did not work for the vast majority of the people who, receiving little or nothing, readily followed men like Caesar and Octavianus when they offered them an alternative dream.

Cicero's speech *contra Rullus* suitably demonstrates for us the attitude of the senatorial aristocracy at this time. The tribune Publius Servilius Rullus had sponsored a major bill of agrarian reform, a most enlightened piece of legislation proposing land distributions to the urban poor, but Cicero, as consul, played a leading part in quashing it by stirring up rumours of conspiracies. In an address to his fellow senators he denounces Rullus as 'a glutton who is stirring up the state', a 'desperado' at the ready 'to dissipate and destroy the possessions left to us by our ancestors' and 'suck dry our treasury' being, as he is, supported by a 'whole gang of the poor and criminal classes'.[468] Of course the luxury of hindsight allows us to condemn the consul not only for his total lack of sympathy but also his utter failure to understand that there were acute social problems to be solved. Similarly, if we turn to the speech Sallust puts into the mouth of Lucius Marcius Philippus (*cos.* 91 BC, censor 86 BC) we hear that those who supported the renegade Lepidus in Etruria were considered not only 'greedy' but also 'the most corrupt of all classes'.[469]

However, not everybody thought like Cicero or Philippus. In his message to the Senate, the ex-centurion Caius Manlius says: 'our object in taking up arms was not to attack our country or to endanger others, but to protect ourselves from wrong'.[470] In fact a number of popular tribunes sincerely wanted to help, in order to preserve the state, the poor and needy in Roman society. A good paradigm perhaps is Bismarck's 1884 welfare programme, which included a social insurance bill to protect the under-privileged of the unified Germany. Bismarck told dissenters that the state should always busy itself with those citizens who needed assistance, and they should not only consider it a Christian duty but also a conservative policy because even the downtrodden will support a government that looks to their welfare. For the 'Iron Chancellor' the concept of *realpolitik* always included a degree of enlightened liberalism to keep the people happy while he got on with what he considered more serious matters. Perhaps for our ailing Republic *concordia* could have been best achieved by the Senate being seen to ameliorate the social and economic ills of Rome.

But why did Cicero and others of his class turn away from such a practical, common-sense policy? Traditionally the Senate had dealt with the scourge of poverty through legislative measures such as land settlements and corn doles, but this state welfare had all ended with the Gracchi brothers. From now on the Senate was increasingly reluctant to propose major pieces of legislation in order to alleviate the plight of the poor and needy, and only through Machiavellian figures such as Caesar, for whom the end justified the means, did anything ever get done. Thus as *dictator perpetuus* Caesar pushed through a massive programme of social and economic reform through which he aimed to become all things to all men.

View from the Top

In his brilliant study on the art of government, *de re publica*, Cicero explains that the Roman state was administered in such a way that the people did not need to flex their political muscles as legislation was carried out on their behalf through the authority of the Senate.[471] In the form of a Platonic dialogue, which supposedly took place in the garden of Publius Cornelius Scipio Aemilianus (*cos.* 147 BC, *cos.* II 134 BC) sometime in 129 BC, *de re publica* is set in an epoch when the state apparatus was still sound and not threatened by autocracy. However, the political murder of the demagogic tribune Tiberius Gracchus, along with 300 of his supporters, was still fresh in people's minds.

The tribunate had been instituted way back in 494 BC and the principal speaker, Scipio Aemilianus, explains how this event was one that the circumstances of the time forced to happen: the people, now freed from the kings and living under a republican constitution, rightly demanded their own magistrates. Thus these tribunes of the people were created 'to counter the *imperium* of the consuls'.[472] By way of a reply to this assertion Cicero adds a proviso, saying it must be borne in mind that for the state to run smoothly a balance has to be struck between rights, duties and obligations. In this way the magistrates have enough power to be effective, while the Senate has influence (*auctoritas*), and the people freedom (*libertas*), the two principles of authority in theory working in perfect harmony. Scipio Aemilianus, who after all is a pragmatic statesman and not a professional philosopher, ripostes with the statement that even after the creation of the tribunate the Senate was still all powerful as the *libertas*, a vague concept at the best of times, of the aristocracy meant the continuing rule of order and the perpetuation of privilege. Hidden away in all this argument and counter-argument is the socio-political balance of power, sovereignty and rewards.

In *de officiis* Cicero tackles the age-old ethical conundrum of the relationship between means and end from the point of view of the senatorial aristocracy. Along with the *Philippics*, it stands as testament to Cicero's defiance of the destroyers of the Republic.[473] For the most part written between September and November 44 BC, it was among the last works he composed.

Cicero maintains that it is a statesman's prime duty to safeguard private property, an assertion that may have been in response to Marcus Antonius' second agrarian law of 44 BC, by which commissioners were granted the right to expropriate land. This land would then be used for settlement by Caesar's discharged veterans and also by the urban poor. Nothing is private by nature, but private property arises through custom, law and convention.[474] However, Cicero is deeply worried over this undeniably truthful statement and its obvious consequences. What happens if somebody comes along and points out that if private property is unnatural we should then share it out equally? Well, Cicero counters with the argument that each and every one of us should be thankful for what falls as our lot in life, and thus should not seek wealth in order to improve that lot.[475] Wrongful gains, that is to say, the redistribution of wealth, 'is more unnatural than death, or destitution, or pain, or any other physical or external blow'. By seeking more we violate the basic laws of human society, 'a general seizure and appropriation of other people's property would cause the collapse of the human community, the brotherhood of man'.[476] For Cicero life is a race in which there are always winners (viz. élites) and losers (viz. the masses), the losers being those who don't make it over the finishing line but none the less should be content.[477]

In fact Cicero was not so naïve as to adopt such a hard-nosed stance. We must appreciate that *de officiis* is a manual about civic duties and moral obligations, seemingly written to his son Marcus, duties to help people and obligations to one's kith and kin: 'for we do not aim to be rich for ourselves alone but for our children, relatives, friends, and, above all, for our country'.[478] Private wealth can be employed, through the *patronus-cliens* system, to aid others less fortunate, and Cicero lays down the ground rules for such beneficial deeds: first, be generous but not too generous; second, do not forget your obligations to your heirs, that is, exercise caution and do not throw your wealth away to the poor; third, what we can identify as the Victorian idea of the 'worthy poor', namely give to those who do not ask.[479]

There are limits, of course. Cicero reckoned that radical measures from tribunes were sectional and divisive. Those in public office should have respect for private property, it being morally wrong to coerce the state into redistributing wealth so as to alleviate the plight of the poor and needy. But how do we solve these social problems, Cicero? At one point he admits debt is bad and there are many ways to solve this particular problem.[480] Then he falls silent and changes the subject. In fact, he does not rule out the continuation of debt, which would be unjust to debt collectors, and he believes that the needs of the poor, the landless and the indebted are the responsibility of their patrons not the state. This is a problem, of course, because do these unfortunates actually have patrons? No, because in reality there were far fewer *clientes* than Cicero believed or wanted to believe. Moreover, the sheer scale of the social and economic problems of the late Republic was way beyond the resources of any one individual and demanded state action.

Yet over time it became more and more difficult to find solutions without infringing on the rights of others. For example, even the Gracchan proposal to hand out *ager publicus* required the eviction of others, especially as the amount of *ager publicus* now available was much less than that available during the heyday of Rome's expansion at the turn of the second century BC. Hence the violence when there was a major resettlement of people during the first century BC, particularly if it was the result of war, the settlement of Sulla's army veterans being a case in point. This was to repeat itself in the civil wars, opponents of the victorious régime being evicted from their farms.

An obvious solution was colonisation overseas, which Caesar was ultimately to pursue, but this policy had been tried before and failed, most notably with Caius Gracchus' Carthage colony. The reason for this failure was quite simple, namely consumer resistance. Furthermore Caesar also cancelled debts, but this angered men like Cicero, who as a landlord was outraged. In a nutshell, there was no quick fix to be had when it came to the poverty of the masses, and so the Senate shied away and men like Lepidus and Catiline rose against the system.

The Problems of the Solutions

1. Demagogic methods employed by the Gracchi and their followers destabilised senatorial control, thereby undermining the constitutional framework that had restricted oligarchic competition (Marius' back-to-back consulships)
2. Chaos in the city of Rome looked as though it might bring power to the urban plebs, which in turn further destabilised the established oligarchic system
3. The near-defeat of Rome in the Social War produced a large number of Italians who

were now Roman citizens, but had less say in the running of the state than the Romans themselves – note that Marian policy was favourable towards the Italians, making civil war inevitable
4. Exponential increase in the desire for money and (more dangerously) military glory in order to come out on top in Rome – note Caesar's *dignitas* as the real cause of the Second Civil War
5. Senate was now quite unable to control the likes of Sulla, Pompey and Caesar, so that, with the use of actual or potential military intervention, the business of *res publica* could be managed by extra-constitutional and non-constitutional means (rise of the warlords)
6. Each civil war made the likelihood of another more probable – Cicero makes clear, in a letter to Atticus, the bellicose attitude in the Pompeian camp: '"What Sulla could do, I can do" – that was the refrain'[481]

Caesar's Solutions

Three weeks after Caesar's murder his faithful friend Caius Matius took a grim pleasure in making the following remark to Cicero: 'For if a man of Caesar's genius could find no way out, who will find one now?'[482] Indeed, a number of Caesar's reforms do display an element of self-interest. The limiting of the tenure of office for provincial governors, for instance, was to prevent anybody else from gaining the power and amassing the wealth he had been able to do in Gaul. In a similar vein, the passing of sumptuary laws was to prevent the sort of lavish display that characterised his triumphs, though these particular restrictions were largely ignored. Likewise, determined not to be controlled by the urban mob, he abolished the *collegia*. These urban associations, lest we forget, had been the recruiting grounds for the armed gangs used by Clodius and Milo to rule the streets and assemblies of Rome back in the fifties BC.

It is certain that Caesar had no real intentions to restore the Republic; he wanted a system in which he was to be the big man. To achieve this, therefore, he looked around for the best and most workable example available for him to ape, namely the Hellenistic east. In a very real sense Caesar was the first emperor (full marks to the quiet and studious Suetonius), but this imperial experiment was to be cut short on the Ides of March 44 BC by men armed with no more than a glib reason as to why they had liquidated Caesar. Remove the tyrant and the Republic would revive. Hardly, for they had ignored the basic fact that Caesar had retained his position and power through the interests of other people, interests that he had looked after. As Cicero once wrote to a friend, Caesar had bound himself to a lot of men from all sorts of backgrounds.[483] This was one huge pressure group that had benefited from the

'Caesarian Corporation', which had been built up through a comprehensive social welfare programme, a programme that provided colonies, eradicated debt, drew up land bills, reorganised grain supplies and erected new buildings and public amenities. Under the old Republic a number of patrons had dispensed the grace and favours, now it was Caesar the super-*patronus*.

When Caesar lay murdered under the statue of Pompey the pressure group still remained. And remain it would, seeking a Caesar substitute who would take up his mantle. So when the battle lines were drawn up in the turbulent wake of Caesar's assassination, it was not really a contest between republican and Caesarian, for the Republic was already taking its last breath. In reality, the real struggle was between individuals who wanted to be that Caesar stand-in and hence control this large and influential pressure group, a sort of super-*clientelae*.

Cicero, writing towards the end of 44 BC, believed that Caesar deserved his death because to gain a throne by moral wrong was not seemly:

> Here you have a man who was ambitious to be king of the Roman People [*rex populi Romani*] and master of the whole world; and he achieved it! The man who maintains that such an ambition is morally right is a madman. For he justifies the destruction of the law and liberty and thinks their hideous and detestable suppression glorious. But if anyone agrees that it is not morally right to be king in a state that once was free and that ought to be free now, yet imagines that it is advantageous for him who can reach that position, with what remonstrance or rather with what appeal should I try to tear him away from so strange a delusion? For, by the immortal gods, can the most horrible and hideous of all murders – that of the fatherland – bring advantage to anybody, even though he who has committed such a crime receives from his enslaved fellow-citizens the title of *pater patriae*?[484]
>
> Cicero, *de officiis*, 3.83

It is thus hardly surprising that Cicero held that it was honourable to kill such a tyrant.[485] As we know, in his *de officiis* Cicero depicts the duties and obligations that a citizen should render to his friends, family and country. In what is a theoretical treatment, Cicero both presents the influential ideas of the Greek world to the Roman élite, and also employs Greek ideas to explain the Roman social and political system. However, Cassius Dio, a Roman senator from the Greek-speaking east who flourished under the absolutism of Septimius Severus (r. AD 193–211), holds an entirely different perspective:

> His slayers, to be sure, declared that they had shown themselves at once

> destroyers of Caesar and liberators of the people. Yet in reality they impiously plotted against him, and they threw the city into disorder when at last it possessed a stable government. Democracy [*demokratia*], indeed, has a fair-appearing name and conveys the impression of bringing equal rights to all through equal laws [*isonomia*], but its results are seen not to agree at all with its title. Monarchy [*monarchia*], on the contrary, has an unpleasant sound, but it is a most practical form of government to live under. For it is easier to find a single excellent man than many of them, and if even this seems to some a difficult feat, it is quite inevitable that the other alternative should be acknowledged to be impossible. For it does not belong to the majority of men to acquire virtue.
>
> Cassius Dio, 44.2. 1–2

In the late Republic the Senate and the consuls initiated hardly any major pieces of social legislation. The significant reforms came from the tribunes, often in the face of fierce opposition from their fellow senators. Many failed even to recognise the existence of the problems. On the other hand, by his refusal to come home and meekly face the destruction of his career in the law courts, Caesar precipitated a crisis. He crossed the Rubicon simply to save his skin and to defend his *dignitas*, the position he had gained in Roman public life, not to bring some new political system or panacea to an ailing Republic.

The range of purposes for which the name and life of Caesar can be utilised seems to be limitless, and in this sense he is all things to all men. He is democrat and autocrat, soldier and scholar, destroyer and achiever. After the Ides of March Cicero found a new compulsion to demonstrate his conception of a well-ordered state and to corroborate it in the light of the most recent history. In the *de officiis* Cicero's ideal statesman wears a toga rather than wields a sword. The lust for power ends in tyranny, which is the negation of liberty, the laws and all of civilised life. So much for the magnetic Caesar with all his detestable and tyrannical qualities, but on the whole the death of the Republic was welcomed.

Caesar's Solutions – and the problems they caused

1. Large-scale rebuilding of the heart of Rome – already planned in 54 BC, and financed using the booty from Gaul – including the Saepta Iulia, Forum Iulium (with its temple of Venus Genetrix and a statue of himself on horseback), Basilica Iulia, temples of Concordia and Clementia Caesaris (i.e. divine honours to personal attributes of Caesar)
   • Such grandiose building projects led to the suspicion that Caesar really wanted to be *rex* (and divine)

2. Settlement of discharged veterans and urban poor in Italy and colonies in Iberia, Africa and Gaul, and at Carthage and Corinth (cities destroyed by Rome in 146 BC)
   • Large numbers of colonists caused great resentment, especially in Italy, as a result of which Caesar brought many Italians into his Senate
3. Senate was increased from 600 to 900 members, a vast body with many new senators from Italy and even some from Gaul. Scurrilous verses did the rounds, in particular about 'long-haired' Gauls newly liberated from the national trouser and asking the way to the Senate house.[486] Gauls or not, many of the new intake seemed outrageous to the members from traditional families, what Cicero describes as 'a gang of desperadoes'.[487]
   • Caesar took over the control of the magistracies and 'arranged' the work of the Senate, thus undermining the problems with the old oligarchy but causing great resentment and hostility
4. The tenure of office for proconsuls and governors limited
   • Caesar now commands the armies of the state
5. Reduction of the number of recipients of free grain (i.e. the corn dole introduced by Clodius in 58 BC) from 320,000 to 150,000 in 46 BC. In that year Caesar, then at the height of his powers, ordered a crackdown; inspectors stood at the state granaries and only those adult men who could prove they were Roman citizens were given the grain.
6. Abolition of *collegia* (except a few ancient ones, such as Jewish synagogues)
7. Refusal to abolish debts, but some limitation of interest charges

The Consul

In the months following Caesar's death Cicero would attempt to play off Caesar's 'henchman', Marcus Antonius, against Caesar's 18-year-old grandnephew Caius Octavius, who, according to the terms of Caesar's will, had become his adopted son and heir. Cicero was not a courageous man. In the years following his consulate he had wavered between Pompey and the enemies of Pompey, and even came close to being a neutral in the Second Civil War. Yet by staking his life at this critical juncture he was at last proving himself worthy of the ideals he had for so long aimed to defend. He would fail, and the consequences of this policy were to be fatal to the Republic that Cicero held so dearly.

The Liberators, as Brutus and Cassius and their co-conspirators styled themselves, had no further plans up their sleeves, and in two days they saw any hope of the Republic reviving crash around their ears and thus retired to the Capitol. There Brutus talked to a large gathering of citizens but soon discovered, even though he eloquently justified the murder of Caesar, that the Liberators were widely unpopular.[488] In a rather despondent letter to his fellow liberators Brutus and Cassius, Decimus Brutus (Shakespeare's Decius) emphasised this lack of popular support, but he also pointed out that if their 'position were enhanced even to a moderate extent, these people would have no further part to play in public affairs'.[489] Naturally Decimus Brutus was not talking about ordinary citizens here, for 'these people' were the die-hard Caesarians like Antonius.

Yet Antonius had acted quickly. At dawn on 16 March, as the leading Caesarian, he occupied the Forum with armed men. On the following day, as sole consul, he convened a meeting of the Senate in the temple of Tellus on the Esquiline, close to his house and within hailing distance of his troops. At the meeting he discovered that the Liberators and their supporters were in total disarray and lacked any concrete ideas. Nevertheless, many present wanted to give the Liberators special honours, but Antonius quashed such a move. Yet others demanded that Caesar be declared a tyrant, denied a funeral and his body tossed into the Tiber. A compromise solution was eventually hammered out whereby the Senate would proclaim that Caesar had been slain as a tyrant by honourable and patriotic citizens. In return Caesar's unconstitutional actions as an individual would be quietly forgotten, but his acts and ordinances (*acta*) would be confirmed. Many senators, many of the Liberators themselves, had much to lose if Caesar's *acta* were scrapped. Cicero made a speech in favour of amnesty. Still to make absolutely sure of the deal, armed soldiers, Caesar's veterans, were present to clarify the senators' minds. And so with cool skill Antonius had forged an uneasy coalition of Caesarians and Liberators, which was to govern Rome through constitutional offices.

On 20 March Antonius acquired even more ammunition with which to defend Caesar's memory when, at the public funeral, he opened and read Caesar's will, revealing that the 'tyrant' had left his great gardens on the right bank of the Tiber to the people and a cash sum to each Roman citizen at Rome. Antonius then, uncovering Caesar's body, raised his bloody toga on a spear, or so tradition has it. The Roman crowd, always full of inflammable potential, broke loose and burned the body in the Forum. Prominent among them was a certain Herophilos, who sought to pass himself off as Marius' grandson. The Liberators, now finding themselves *personae non gratae*, barricaded themselves in their houses and prepared for a siege. Having slain the tyrant they had not planned a seizure of power. A military coup was out of the question for, as the pragmatic Decimus Brutus said in his letter to Brutus and Cassius, the nearest armed support they could call upon was either in Iberia or in Syria.[490] As Cicero vainly pointed out after the event, the whole affair had been performed with the 'courage of men and the counsel of children'.[491]

Early in April, continuing the policy of reconciliation between the Caesarians and Liberators, Antonius suppressed the popular demonstrations in memory of Caesar. He rounded up Herophilos, self-styled spiritual leader of the cult of Caesar, and had the impostor put to death. The Liberators, however, were finding life in Rome rather uncomfortable and one by one they quietly slipped away. Cicero too, though not among their ranks on the Ides of March, left town and retired to the Bay of Naples. It was from this idyllic location that he launched his verbal campaign against Antonius, who at the time was powerful and menacing, opening the attack with accusations of misuse of Caesar's papers. Seemingly Antonius had been producing forged decrees purporting to have been drawn up by Caesar. Meantime the Senate busied itself allotting the consular provinces for the following year, doubtless in accordance with Caesar's intentions. Though Antonius received Macedonia, and with the command went Caesar's Parthian army, six of the best of the legions, one of the Liberators, none other than Decimus Brutus, was allotted Caesar's old province Gallia Cisalpina, a territory rich in resources and recruits, already garrisoned by two veteran legions and close to Rome.

The Boy

Four weeks after the assassination Caius Octavius, Caesar's adopted heir by will and the deadliest teenager in the Mediterranean world, arrived in Italy from Macedonia, Caesar having sent him to Apollonia to study oratory and military science, for he was to take part in the invasion of Parthia. He was accompanied by a close friend and man of action, Marcus Vipsanius Agrippa, who would be the key to so many of his military successes. Octavius had served, with distinction, under Caesar during the Munda campaign and from then was marked out by the great man.[492] And so when he passed by adoption into the Iulii he acquired the new and legal designation of Caius Iulius Caesar Octavianus.[493] On landing near Brundisium, Octavianus seized one of the two most important commodities, money, which he would use at a later date to win over the other, Caesar's soldiers. In the meantime he started to sound out the leading Caesarians. Having dropped the name that betrayed his origin, he was now styling himself 'Caius Iulius Caesar', which Cicero indeed disliked.

It is worth noting Cicero's reaction on this particular occasion, the first time he made the acquaintance of Octavianus. The 'boy', as Cicero disparagingly called him, had flattered him a great deal, but the venerable old man was shrewd enough to realise that Octavianus and his entourage were not sympathetic towards the Liberators. In a letter hurriedly written to Atticus,

Cicero vented his feelings about Caesar's heir: 'My judgement is that he cannot be a good citizen. There are too many around him. They threatened death to our friends and call the present state of affairs intolerable.'[494] Cicero, although his judgement would be later clouded by events of the time, essentially saw Octavianus as the head of the Caesarians and a man who in the final reckoning would hardly tolerate the murderers of his adopted father.

Early in May, having left Cicero's Puteoli retreat, Octavianus entered Rome and addressed the people. He was quick to exploit the fact that Antonius had shown himself somewhat lenient towards the assassins, and Antonius was beginning to realise what a difficult position he had put himself in. All the same, Octavianus was treated with some disdain by Antonius, who declined to hand over either Caesar's papers or his family fortune. By the middle of the month Antonius and Octavianus were bickering over the payment of legacies from Caesar's will. Caesar had not named Antonius among the first echelons of his beneficiaries; he was only mentioned among the second recipients. Modern commentators have often said this revelation must have come as a shock to him, but this was highly improbable. Caesar, as Antonius himself surely realised, was simply ensuring the continuation of his line; Caesar had no direct male heir and his daughter Iulia had died childless. Antonius realised too that the magic name of Caesar was the making of Octavianus' fortune. As Cicero himself records, Antonius once rounded on the young man, shouting: 'And you, boy, owe everything to your name'.[495]

It was now that Octavianus started to emphasise his links with Caesar, and to put Antonius in a bad light for collaborating with the Liberators. Cicero too had hoped that Octavianus would prove a temporary phenomenon, hardly likely to last the pace of the cut-throat politics in Rome. Apparently in a memorable epigram he denigrated Octavianus as a youth to be 'praised, uplifted and lifted off'.[496] The phrase sounds innocuous enough in English translation, but in Latin it is a clever pun. The word used for 'lifted off' (*tollere*) has two meanings, one denoting elevation to fame, and the other to make away with. Just as Caesar had been, in other words. The joke spread like wildfire, and, of course, Octavianus got to hear of it too. He was to remember it well.

Antonius now made up his mind that the Liberators should quit Italy, and on 5 June summoned the Senate to a meeting in the temple of Concord during which he got Brutus and Cassius (who were praetors) appointed to an extraordinary commission for the rest of the year: they were to superintend the buying of grain in the provinces of Asia and Sicily respectively. Complimentary in appearance, the post was an honourable pretext for exile.

For the present, however, the two chief Liberators opted to remain in Italy, waiting on events. At the same time Antonius sought to obtain, in place of Macedonia previously assigned to him, Gallia Cisalpina and Gallia Comata (the wide area newly added to the empire by Caesar) as well. And so as sole consul he passed a law, some would argue irregularly, giving himself Gallia Cisalpina and Gallia Comata for five years. He also arranged for the transfer to his new province of the legions stationed in Macedonia. Of the six, four were eventually transported across the Adriatic – *legiones II*, *IIII* (from Caesar's consular series in 48 BC), *Martia* (its numeral is unknown) and *XXXV* (formed in the aftermath of Pharsalus from former Pompeians).

The enterprises of Herophilos had demonstrated what a hold the memory of Caesar had over the people, and so Octavianus busied himself with Caesarian propaganda. Games and festivals were customary devices for the organisation of popular sentiment, and in late July Octavianus personally celebrated the Games in Honour of Caesar's Victory (*ludi victoriae Caesaris*), which had been denied official celebration. When Antonius tried to intervene, the sympathies of people and veterans went to Caesar's heir. Heaven also approved. During the games a comet (Halley's Comet?) burned in the sky for seven days, and this 'star' was hailed as the apotheosis of Caesar. Caesar and Alexander are the two rulers in antiquity whose divinity was widely believed in. Octavianus placed symbols of the star on coins and on a statue of Caesar, which was dedicated in the Forum.

Early in August Antonius induced the Senate to grant Brutus and Cassius the harmless provinces of Crete and Cyrene, but they left instead for Macedonia and Syria respectively. Before quitting Italy, Brutus issued an edict. In it he affirmed the loyalty of the Liberators towards the Roman constitution, their reluctance to provide a cause of civil war, and their proud conviction that wherever they were, there stood Rome and the Republic.[497]

Cicero's Last Stand

On 1 September Antonius summoned the Senate in order to confer upon Caesar honours that far exceeded anything yet seen for an ordinary mortal, namely a feast day to be granted to Caesar as if he ranked among the immortal gods. Cicero failed to attend and Antonius uttered threats. At the meeting the following day Cicero protested he had stayed away because he could not condone such honours. In fact he had been absent for nearly six months, this being his first attendance since the tempestuous meeting of the Senate in the temple of Tellus. None the less, it was now that he went over to the offensive and attacked Antonius' policy, delivering the first of his vitriolic diatribes now known as the *Philippics*.

Unlike the succeeding thirteen *Philippics*, the *First Philippic* was different in that it was couched in fairly moderate terms, Cicero going out of his way to placate Antonius.[498] The elder statesman was quick to point out that the consul had started out with good intentions, recalling here the policy of reconciliation, only to fall down over Gallia Cisalpina and the apparent unscrupulous use of Caesar's papers. Anyway, Antonius did not take up Cicero's olive branch and asked him to attend the Senate on 19 September. When Cicero failed to be present, Antonius retorted with a bitter personal attack. Cicero replied in grand style, issuing the *Second Philippic*, a political pamphlet that cast the bibulous, womanising Antonius as the foremost enemy of the state. Rome of the Republic was not constrained by any law of libel, and a war of words ensued, which only went on for a short time but resulted in an irreparable breach between the two men. Meanwhile Octavianus, who failed to get a mention in the first two Ciceronian broadsides against Antonius, quietly consolidated his position.

Actually Cicero was outlining his new policy for saving the Republic: a break with Antonius, whom he now identified as the 'new Catiline', and the need for the Liberators to acquire some military muscle so that they could counter him. Forgetting his perceptions of six months ago, Cicero saw Octavianus as the man to champion the cause of liberty, to be discarded in the end if he did not prove pliable. However, although Cicero was punching for the Republic, the real contest was to be between Antonius and Octavianus.

Antonius had the advantages stacked high on his side. As consul he deserved the support of those who respected legitimate government, and for all Cicero's abuse and criticism Rome's best hope lay with going along with Antonius, who was trying to work out a compromise. However, the problem for him was that he had to look both ways. Octavianus none the less had one natural advantage upon which he could capitalise. He was Caesar's heir and for this simple reason alone many people would look upon him as their natural leader, as Antonius was soon to discover. The consul had journeyed to Brundisium on 9 October, proposing to greet the legions arriving from Macedonia and to arrange the details of their northwards march to their new posting in northern Italy. A month later Octavianus marched into Rome at the head of an illegal private army.

The venture had started when the young man had gone down to Campania with a convoy of wagons loaded with money and equipment. There he toured the colonial settlements and persuaded upwards of 3,000 veterans of Caesar's *legiones VII* and *VIII*, by appealing to his memory and by open bribery, to rally to his standard and return with him to Rome. Cicero, belittling 'the boy's plan' in a letter to Atticus, was not at all surprised by the fact that Octavianus had won over the veterans 'since he gives them 500 denarii apiece',[499] more than twice the annual pay of a legionary. Successful he may have been as a new Pompey at the head of his own private army, but he was to be unsuccessful playing the role of a mature Sulla.[500] Having occupied the Forum with armed men on 10 November, he hoped for a meeting of the Senate and the backing of senior statesmen. Yet he failed to rouse support to his cause, and was forced to scuttle into Etruria and lie low for a while. Antonius was fast approaching with the legions from Macedonia and many veterans, refusing to fight their fellow-Caesarians, slipped away to return their homes in the south. The coup had failed miserably.

It was, perhaps, sheer chance that in pro-Marian Etruria the rash young adventurer and his dwindling band of desperadoes received an unexpected boost. Two of Antonius' legions marching north along the Adriatic seaboard declared for Octavianus, turned westward along the Via Valeria towards Rome, and took up a position at Alba Fucens, some 100 kilometres east of the capital. Both these legions, *IIII* and *Martia*,[501] had been at Apollonia during Octavianus' sojourn there. As Keppie remarks, 'he had perhaps done his homework well, but the gap between success and political elimination had been small'.[502]

Civil war had begun once more, but winter held up warfare in the north. Not so the intrigue and politicking in Rome. On 1 January 43 BC the Senate, acting on a motion of Cicero, voted the young outsider Octavianus a place among their own number. He was awarded *imperium pro praetore*, which allowed him to command his army legally, and was instructed to cooperate with the two consuls, Aulus Hirtius and Caius Vibius Pansa Caetronianus (old partisans of Caesar), and with Decimus Brutus (one of the assassins of Caesar) to eliminate Antonius (erstwhile lieutenant of Caesar).[503] Further, by a special dispensation, he was allowed to stand for the consulship ten years before the legal age. Octavianus was now 19: he would still have thirteen years to wait.

Overnight Octavianus had turned from a boy-buccaneer bent on supreme power and revenge for Caesar's death to the boy-hero whose timely action had saved the state from the would-be tyrant Antonius. The Senate had granted before now *imperium pro praetore* to a man who had held no public office, but never before had it conferred senatorial rank on a private citizen. Such an irregularity had not been performed even for Pompey. Of course Cicero's *bon mot* of the day, namely to praise him, raise him and then kick him upstairs, nicely summed up the general feeling behind the senators' motives. To us it may seem a rather optimistic policy, but the gamble might have paid off if Octavianus, like Pompey before him, had settled down after the flattery and the applause.

Private Armies

Meanwhile, the proconsul Antonius, after trying without success to persuade the defectors to reverse their decision, resolved to hurry north to Gallia Cisalpina with his two remaining formations, *legiones II* and *XXXV*, and with the regrouped *legio V Alaudae*, its soldiers having been at hand somewhere in southern Italy awaiting their formal discharge. As the legally appointed governor of the province, he graciously invited Decimus Brutus to leave it. The Senate, on the other hand, ordered Decimus Brutus to stay where he was. Antonius, the 'legal' governor, chose to take his province, and Decimus Brutus, the 'sitting' governor, chose to barricade himself in Mutina (Modena) and wait out the winter.

With a state of emergency having been declared by the Senate, it was now possible for troops to be turned against Antonius in northern Italy. Rising from his sickbed, Hirtius hastened north up the Via Flaminia to Ariminum (Rimini), with Octavianus and his four legions nominally under his control, while Pansa raised additional troops in central Italy. Events moved on apace. Antonius decided to launch an attack on one army before the two consuls could join forces. It nearly paid off. At Forum Gallorum (Castelfranco) on the line of the Via Aemilia Antonius fell upon Pansa's four consular legions, mostly inexperienced recruits, and routed them. Pansa was mortally wounded, and died several days later. Unfortunately Antonius had no time to consolidate the victory or regroup his army. While the victorious Antonians were scattered, Hirtius came up to rescue his colleague, putting Antonius into a dangerous position. As the evening turned into night he extricated himself only after considerable loss. Octavianus' part in all this blood-letting was to guard Hirtius' camp near Mutina. He shared in the honours granted by the Senate, and along with the two consuls was hailed by the soldiers as *imperator*.[504]

Seven days later, on 21 April, Antonius was heavily defeated in a fearful battle below the walls of Mutina, which was nothing more subtle than a slogging match between Caesar's hardened veterans on each side. However, Hirtius was killed, which presented a nice opening for an ambitious Octavianus. This was the perfect moment for the Liberators to restore the

Republic, but they bungled the whole affair. Decimus Brutus was awarded a triumph and asked to assume overall command of the dead consuls' legions, while Octavianus, who was not recognised at all, was simply thanked for his assistance and effectively dismissed. This rebuff by the Senate gave Octavianus, who refused any form of rapprochement with Decimus Brutus, the excuse he needed and, backed by the soldiers of his adoptive father, he took informal command of all the consular forces. As Decimus Brutus wrote to Cicero, 'there is no giving orders to Caesar, nor by Caesar to his army – both very bad things'.[505] Meanwhile Antonius, defeated but not routed, was forced to abandon the siege of Mutina and rounded up what was left of his army. Still with the trustworthy *legio V Alaudae* intact, and with the wreckage of *legiones II* and *XXXV*, he set off along the Via Aemilia towards the west with rapidity, intending to cross into Gallia Transalpina. On the way he was joined by the loyal Publius Ventidius with three veteran legions raised in his native Picenum.[506]

Antonius had no guarantee of a friendly reception there. Marcus Aemilius Lepidus (*cos.* 46 BC), son of the Lepidus who had led the seventy-eight rebellion, proconsul of Gallia Transalpina and Hispania Citerior, and Lucius Munatius Plancus (later *cos.* 42 BC), proconsul of Gallia Comata, along with Caius Asinius Pollio (later *cos.* 40 BC) in Hispania Ulterior, had been raising fresh troops and recalling veterans in expectation of fresh fighting. In particular, Lepidus was able to reform Caesar's old *legio VI* from its colony at Arelate, and likewise *legio X Equestris* from Narbo. During the previous months it was thought these Caesarian governors might join him, or at best remain neutral, but times had changed.

From Renegade to Ruler

Back in Rome Antonius' defeat had been greeted with all but outright hysteria. In his previous speeches Cicero had tried unsuccessfully to have Antonius and his followers declared *hostes*, but the Senate had not dared to take matters that far. On one occasion it was pointed out to Cicero, perhaps with the fate of the Catilinarian conspirators in mind, that it would not do to condemn Roman citizens unheard. The Senate, led by Cicero, now did so with alacrity, and anyone who tried to speak up for Antonius was shouted down. Cicero even proposed a thanksgiving of fifty days for the victory over him, 'a number that the Romans had never decreed either for successes over the Gauls or for any other campaign'.[507] Antonius' defeat was considered decisive, and it was thought that Rome had seen the last of him.

Rome, however, had not seen the last of Octavianus. After the deaths of both consuls in the war against Antonius, the consulships were now vacant, and Octavianus meant to have one. With the power and authority of a consul he would be able to legitimise his adoption as Caesar's son and heir, pursue his condemnation of his adoptive father's murderers, and have enough clout to face Antonius on equal terms. In July there came before the Senate a bizarre embassy, some 400 centurions and common soldiers, bearing the demands of their leader, Caesar's heir. The Senate refused and one centurion revealed his sword.[508] And so it proved.

For the second time in ten months Octavianus set out to march on Rome. Crossing the Rubicon at the head of his eight legions, he then pushed on to Rome with the celerity of Caesar. A ray of hope shone upon the Senate as two veteran legions from Africa landed at Ostia. Along with a legion of recruits left by Pansa they were hurried to the defence of Rome. But Octavianus entered the city unopposed as the legions of the Senate went over to him without wavering. The senators advanced to make their peace with Octavianus, Cicero among them but not in the vanguard. 'Ah, the last of my friends,' the young man observed.[509] On 19 August Octavianus took over one of the vacant consulships. Cicero's protégé, the 'divine youth whom heaven had sent to save the state',[510] was not quite 20 years old. He then seized the treasury and awarded his soldiers a bounty of 2,500 denarii, more than eleven years' pay.[511] With a loyal army now augmented to eleven legions, the 'teenage consul' returned north.

In the north, meanwhile, events had moved on apace. Antonius entered Gallia Transalpina unopposed, reaching Forum Iulii (Fréjus) by the middle of May. The confrontation with Lepidus was not long in coming. The two armies, one fresh, the other battered, but both Caesarian, lay against each other for a time. A small stream meandered between the camps and fraternising, not fighting, was the order of the day as far as the soldiers of both sides were concerned. 'And since Lepidus was the worst of all generals', says Velleius Paterculus tartly, 'and Antonius was far his superior – while he was sober – the soldiers of Lepidus broke open their wall and took Antonius into the camp.'[512] It seems Lepidus acquiesced, and on 30 May he penned a short dispatch to the Senate explaining how his 'entire army, faithful to inveterate tendency to conserve Roman lives and the general peace, has mutinied'.[513] Peace may have blossomed between Antonius and Lepidus, but the Senate still had Decimus Brutus and Plancus.

In April the governor of Gallia Comata had mustered his army and, making a semblance of still fighting for the Senate, marched towards northern Italy.

On 26 April Plancus crossed the Rhône looking as if he intended to join up with Lepidus but, fearing a trap, he turned back and dug himself in at Cularo (Grenoble). There he waited for Decimus Brutus, who had been ordered by the Senate to pursue and give Antonius the *coup de grace*, to cross the Alps. Forlorn, with footsore troops, delayed by the raising of new levies, strapped for cash and bombarded by scratchy dispatches from Cicero, Decimus Brutus trudged westwards. He reached Plancus towards the end of June. Their combined forces, which amounted to fourteen legions, were imposing in size only. Four were veteran, the rest raw recruits, and Plancus, a political weathercock who was to enjoy a peaceful old age, knew the real value of recruits. Antonius likewise was in no hurry, and waited patiently for time, fear and propaganda to dissolve the forces of the Senate. On 28 July Plancus composed his last surviving letter to Cicero. With his usual grace and charm, he protested goodwill and loyalty to the commonwealth and explained how weak his army was. He then shifted the blame to Octavianus, saying 'the fact that Antonius is alive today, that Lepidus is with him, that they have armies by no means contemptible, that their hopes and audacity run high – for all this they can thank Caesar'.[514]

It was now that Pollio, marching up from Hispania Ulterior at the head of two veteran legions, played his part. Though a clear-sighted republican at heart, he was bound by his personal friendship to Antonius; he now reconciled Plancus and Antonius.[515] So Plancus joined the desperate band, as he had so recently called them, of the 'red-hot rebels'.[516] Wretched Decimus Brutus, duped by Plancus and betrayed by his troops, attempted to make his way to Brutus and Cassius in the east, the positions of whom the Senate had legalised, but was eventually trapped and killed in Dalmatia by a Gallic chieftain loyal to the new order.

True Colours

Octavianus had neither the desire nor the power to destroy the most powerful of the Caesarian warlords. Moreover, unlike Alexander's veterans, Caesar's veterans would never be keen to fight each other again: their one taste of blood outside Mutina was still more than enough. As he slowly moved up the Via Flaminia he instructed the other consul, Quintus Pedius, an obscure relative of good standing,[517] to revoke the decrees of outlawry against Antonius and Lepidus – for Lepidus, too, had been declared a *hostis*. More sinister was the *lex Pedia*, which enabled the Caesarians to set up a *quaestio* to condemn the murderers of Caesar.

In October Antonius and Octavianus met on an islet in a river near Bononia (Bologna): both brought their legions with them. Bringing in Lepidus, who, although Brutus' brother-in-law was a confirmed Caesarian, they agreed to be reconciled and decided to form an alliance, another threesome. The terms 'triumvirate' and 'triumvirs' are modern inventions.[518] In Latin, Antonius, Octavianus and Lepidus were titled *tresviri rei publicae constituendae*, 'three men with responsibility for settling the state'. This was a vague but alarming remit, effectively superseding the normal organs of government.

Although they were empowered to pass or annul laws and appoint the governors of all the provinces and the consuls for the coming years without reference to the Senate or the Roman people, their proconsular powers were limited to five years, a wise precaution to put some control on their thinly veiled dominance. Pompey and Caesar had shown that the way to gain and hold power was to maintain an influence or even a personal presence in Rome while at the same time commanding soldiers in one or more of the provinces. On the other hand Caesar's perpetual dictatorship had revealed that it was unwise to rob people of the hope of freedom in the future. Between them the triumvirs carved up the Roman world and shared out the legions, which numbered more than forty.[519] Lepidus, in truth a *nobilis* sleeping partner, was given control of his old province of Gallia Transalpina and the two Iberian provinces. Octavianus received Africa and the islands of Sicily, Sardinia and Corsica. Antonius, as the senior partner, was to remain governor of Gallia Cisalpina, a strong position from which he could keep watch on Italy. To advertise their rule and the effective death of the Republic, all three had coins issued bearing their official portraits. A *lex Titia*, voted on 27 November, established the pact hammered out at Bononia.

The three warlords now needed to collect cash, without which they could not hope to maintain their vast armies, and also to eradicate all actual and potential opposition. They therefore forgot the example of Caesar and remembered Marius and Sulla, for once arrived in Rome they set in train a horrendous proscription, condoning the murder of their enemies and the seizure of their property. They even included members of their own families in the list of the proscribed. Lepidus was not averse to naming his brother Lucius Aemilius Paullus (*cos.* 50 BC), who had helped to have him outlawed after he went over to Antonius, while Antonius himself put his republican uncle on the list, the elderly and honest Lucius Iulius Caesar (*cos.* 64 BC). Many potential victims fled to join Brutus and Cassius in the east or to Sextus Pompeius in the far west, the son, no less, of the great Pompey, but many more did not escape the bounty-hunters, among them Cicero, who, human to the end, hesitated and paid the price. The assassins came for him in one of his seaside villas on 7 December. His head and right hand (perhaps both hands) were hacked off and taken back to Rome where they were nailed to the rostra in front of the Senate house, the vantage point from which he had delivered many of his speeches reviling Antonius. Too late, as one contemporary rightly noted, for Cicero's inspired epithets had blackened Antonius' name forever.

Their next chief task was to eliminate Brutus and Cassius, who now controlled all Roman territory east of the Adriatic. While Cicero and the Senate had been busy with Antonius, Brutus and Cassius had acted, raising an army of 'liberation' with looting and taxation in the eastern provinces. An army of twenty-two legions was made ready, under the joint leadership of Antonius and Octavianus, and including all the re-formed Caesarian formations.[520] Over the summer of 42 BC they were ferried across the Adriatic to Dalmatia, and the two triumvirs advanced eastwards along the Via Egnatia towards Philippi (Philippoi).

The Battle of Forum Gallorum, 43 BC

If it is always hard to look into the past and obtain satisfactory answers to the questions of where people were and when, let alone why they were there, it is doubly difficult to do so for battlefields. Eye-witnesses are invariably preoccupied, trying not to succumb to one of the many invitations to death that battle offers, rather than making accurate and detailed notes for future historians. If this makes any first-hand accounts of battle of dubious reliability, it holds particularly true for accounts by contemporaries who relied on eye-witnesses. The hero returning from war is hardly likely to confess to the prodding questions of would-be historians that he spent the battle lurking in the baggage train, for example, and inevitably an element of fictionalisation creeps in. When one has to add misinformed speculation, deliberate propaganda and pure fiction into the mix, it gives some idea of the difficulty of the task of deducing what actually happened on the waterlogged plain outside Mutina.

For the first of the Mutina battles we have a letter penned to Cicero the day after the battle by his friend Servius Sulpicius Galba, who was serving on Hirtius' staff as one his legates.[521] Antonius launched a diversionary attack on Hirtius' camp, and then slipped past him so as to catch Pansa's levies coming up the Via Aemilia from the south.[522] With his back to Forum Gallorum, a settlement sitting on a waterlogged spot some 11 kilometres along the Mutina–Bononia stretch of the Via Aemilia, Antonius made contact with Pansa. Galba now takes up the story:

> Galba to Cicero greetings.
> On April 14, that being the day Pansa was to have joined Hirtius' camp (I was with him, having gone a hundred [Roman] miles to meet him and expedite his arrival),[523] Antonius led out two legions, *II* and *XXXV*, and two praetorian cohorts, one his

own and the other Silanus',[524] together with part of his reservists. In this strength he advanced to meet us, thinking that we had only four legions of recruits. But the previous night Hirtius had sent us *legio Martia*, which used to be under my command, and the two praetorian cohorts for our better security on the march to his camp.

When Antonius' cavalry came into sight, there was no holding *legio Martia* and the praetorian cohorts. We started to follow them willy-nilly, since we had not been able to hold them back. Antonius kept his forces at Forum Gallorum, wanting to conceal the fact that he had the legions; he only showed his cavalry and light-armed [troops]. When Pansa saw the legion advancing contrary to his intentions, he ordered two legions of recruits to follow him. Having traversed a narrow route through marsh and woodland, we drew up a battle line of twelve cohorts; the two legions had not yet come up. Suddenly Antonius led his forces out of the village, drew them up and immediately engaged. Both sides at first fought as fiercely as men could fight. But the right wing, where I was placed with eight cohorts of *legio Martia*, threw back Antonius' *legio XXXV* at the first charge, and advanced more than 500 [Roman] paces from its original position in the line. The cavalry then tried to surround our wing, so I started to retire, setting our light-armed against the Moorish horse to stop them attacking our men in the rear. Meanwhile I found myself in the thick of the Antonians, with Antonius some distance behind me. All at once I rode at the gallop towards a legion of recruits, which was on its way up from our camp, throwing my shield over my shoulders. The Antonians chased me, while our men were about to hurl their *pila*. In this predicament some providence came to my rescue – I was quickly recognised by our men.

On the Via Aemilia itself, where Caesar's [i.e. Octavianus'] praetorian cohort was stationed, there was a long struggle. The left wing, which was weaker, consisting of two cohorts of *legio Martia* and one praetorian cohort, began to give ground, because they were being surrounded by cavalry, which is Antonius' strongest arm. When all our ranks had withdrawn, I started to retreat to the camp, the last to do so. Having won the battle, as he considered, Antonius thought he could take the camp, but when he arrived he lost a number of men there and achieved nothing.

Having heard what had happened, Hirtius with twenty veteran cohorts[525] met Antonius on his way back to his camp and completely destroyed or routed his forces, on the very ground of the previous engagement near Forum Gallorum. Antonius withdrew with his horse to his camp at Mutina about ten o'clock at night. Hirtius then returned to the camp from which Pansa[526] had marched out where he had left two legions, which had been assaulted by Antonius. So Antonius has lost the greater part of his veteran troops; but this result was achieved at the cost of some losses in the praetorian cohorts and *legio Martia*. Two eagles and sixty standards of Antonius' have been brought in. It is a victory.
April 15, from camp.

Cicero, *Epistulae ad familiares*, 10.30

Cicero had boasted in the Senate that the Caesarian veterans were on the wane, and no match for the patriotic fervour of the levies of republican Italy.[527] Yet when it came to the blade-work outside a village called Forum Gallorum, the raw recruits were terrified by the grim sight of battle-hardened veterans 'locked together with their swords as if in a wrestling contest'.[528] To a thoughtful, experienced soldier, it was no time for rejoicing. 'Some may be rejoicing at the moment, because the Caesarian leaders and veterans appear to have perished, but they will soon be sorry when they contemplate the desolation of Italy. For the flower of our soldiers, present and to come, has perished,' wrote the despondent Pollio from Hispania Ulterior to Cicero in Rome.[529] The butchery had been horrendous.

Epilogue

Cicero's severed extremities were taken to Rome and exposed to the public, a clear signal to the men of understanding. Caesar, ever willing to forgive and forget, had pardoned him and welcomed him to his Senate; the followers of the magnanimous Caesar, the avengers of his blood, had no room in their new order for an independent spirit and a pre-eminent genius. The pale face and the pale hand nailed to the rostra outside the Senate house were a bloody sign that the Republic was as good as dead, but the elder statesman was spared the agony of seeing it actually die finally, for ever, on the plain of Philippi.

It was just west of this Macedonian town, haunted by the memories of the great Alexander's father, astride the Via Egnatia, that the two champions of what was called *libertas*, Brutus and Cassius, assembled their forces, which amounted to nineteen legions and numerous levies from the dependent potentates of the east. A ditch and palisade connected their two camps, cutting the road but equipped with a central gateway to allow soldiers from either camp to be deployed in the plain beyond. This plain was flanked by mountains inland to the north and by marshes southward towards the sea. And so, firmly entrenched and well supplied, the two Liberators, the assassins of Caesar, awaited the anticipated approach of the two triumvirs, his heirs. Like earlier battles, such as Pharsalus, this was going to be an encounter between battle-hardened legionaries. There could be no expectation of easy victory, or of favours from the other side.

Around the death of the Republic, as around its birth, have gathered innumerable legends that invest the hard and bitter facts with a certain humanity. The triumvirs had appeared some time in October, intent on a speedy action because the Liberators commanded the seas and thus had access to seaborne supplies and reinforcements, while they themselves in the manner of Caesar came in fighting order to settle the campaign with one swift decisive blow. On the eve of the battle Brutus, philosopher and dreamer as he was, had retired to his tent to read and meditate and possibly to snatch a hurried sleep before the military tribunes should come in the autumn dawn for their final orders. Plutarch picks up the story. In the glimmer of the lamplight Brutus saw a terrible and strange appearance of an unnatural and frightful body standing by him without speaking. Brutus boldly asked it, 'What are you, of men or gods, and upon what business come to me?' The figure answered, 'I am your evil genius, Brutus; you shall see me at Philippi'. To which Brutus, not at all disturbed, replied, 'Then I shall see you'.[530]

A hazardous frontal assault by Antonius forced the first engagement, his vintage legions breaking through Cassius' front and pillaging his camp. Cassius despaired too soon. Believing that all was lost he fell upon his sword and died. But the legions of Brutus, without waiting for orders, swept over the Caesarian lines and captured Octavianus' camp; he himself was not there but hiding in a nearby bog.[531] Both sides drew back, damaged and resentful.

Nearly three weeks later the restiveness of his men compelled the 'last republican' to try the fortunes of battle once again. It appears Antonius was attempting to execute a dangerous infiltration between Cassius' camp, now occupied by Brutus, and the marshes, but after a tenacious and bloody contest Brutus' men were swept away. The poet Horace joined in the 'headlong rout, his poor shield ingloriously left behind'.[532] Escaping from the field Brutus persuaded his slave Strato to run him through with a sword. This time the decision was final and irrevocable. The dying embers of the Republic were quenched in Roman blood; its last defenders, like itself, perished not by the sword of the enemy, but by their own. After the victory, Brutus' body was brought to Antonius' camp. Wittingly emulating Alexander's gesture towards the dead Dareios, Antonius took off his own scarlet cloak and cast it over the pale corpse and ordered an honourable funeral for his erstwhile comrade. Philippi had completed what Pharsalus had begun.

Notes

Abbreviations

AE	*L'Année épigraphique* (Paris, 1888–)
CIL	T. Mommsen et al., *Corpus Inscriptionum Latinarum* (Berlin, 1862–)
ILS	H. Dessau, *Inscriptiones Latinae Selectae* (Berlin, 1892–1916)
OGIS	W. Dittenberger, *Orientis Graeci Inscriptiones Selectae* (Leipzig, 1903)
SIG³	W. Dittenberger, *Sylloge Inscriptionum Graecarum 3* (Leipzig, 1915–24)

1. Cicero to Atticus, Formiae, 21 January 49 BC, in Cicero, *Epistulae ad Atticum* 7.11.1.
2. In Latin: *cognati et sodales*, Livy, 2.49.4.
3. In Latin: *nec certa pax nec bellum fuit*, Livy, 2.21.1. Many of the heroic tales of Rome's early history recorded by Livy may have their origins in the ballads composed to celebrate the deeds of these aristocratic clans.
4. Diodoros (23.2.1), on the other hand, believes that the phalanx came by way of the Etruscans.
5. Livy, 1.42.5–14. The *clipeus* was essentially the *aspis* carried by Greek hoplites, a round, soup bowl-shaped shield, approximately 90 centimetres in diameter. Built on a wooden core, the shield was faced with a thin layer of stressed bronze and backed by leather. Because of its great weight, about 6.8 to 9.1 kilograms, the shield was carried by an arrangement of two handles, the armband (*porpax*) in the centre through which the forearm passed and the handgrip (*antilabê*) at the rim. Held across the chest, it covered the hoplite from chin to knee. However, being clamped to the left arm it only offered protection to his left-hand side. The *scutum*, on the other hand, was very much like the oblong *thureos* common to peltasts of later Hellenistic armies.
6. Livy, 8.8.3, Sallust, *Bellum Catilinae*, 51.38. Livy (4.59.11) suggests the phalanx was abandoned after the war with the neighbouring Etruscan city of Veii, that is, early in the fourth century BC, whereas Diodoros (14.16.5) only refers to the introduction of annual pay (*stipendium*) to the soldiers for their service at this time.
7. Livy, 8.8.
8. Ibid. 10.39.12, cf. Plutarch, *Camillus*, 40.5, 41.4.
9. See here Varro, *de lingua Latina*, 7.57–8, where he defines *rorarii* as light-armed troops and (quoting the lost *de re militari* of Cato the Censor) *accensi* as military servants.
10. Dionysios, 20.11, where he mentions the heavy 'cavalry-spears' carried by the *principes*.
11. Polybios, 6.11–42.
12. Caesar, *Bellum Gallicum*, 1.24.2, 49.1, 4.14.1, *Bellum civile*, 1.83.2, cf. 3.89.7.
13. Vegetius, 2.13.
14. Du Picq 1946: 86.
15. Caesar, *Bellum Gallicum*, 6.8.8, 7.88.6, *Bellum civile*, 3.92.7.
16. Du Picq 1946: 53.
17. A term obviously derived from *tribunus* or tribal leader.
18. Polybios, 6.19.1. This would remain so even in the late Republic, for both Caesar and the younger Cato were elected military tribunes in this fashion (Plutarch, *Caesar*, 5.1, *Cato minor*, 8.2, 9.1).

19 Polybios, 3.109.12.

20. Ibid. 6.39.12, 15. In Polybios' day the denarius, a silver coin, was worth ten *asses*, the *as* being a copper coin. At the time of the Gracchi, the *as* was retariffed at sixteen to the denarius.
21. Cicero, *pro Roscio Comoedo*, 28.
22. The same order for the three lines appears in Polybios' narrative (14.8.5, 15.9.7), and in Livy's also (30.8.5, 32.11, 34.10) as well as in other antiquarian sources (Varro, *de lingua Latina*, 5.89, Ovid, *Fasti*, 3.128–32), and is implied by the order of seniority among centurions of the army of the Principate

where *pilus* is the most senior followed by the *princeps* and then the *hastatus*. Note Vegetius, 2.2, 15–17, 3.14, where he places the *principes* in the front line, then the *hastati*, while the *triarii* are armed like the other two lines with *pila* – in his defence he does say (1.8) that he used Cato the Censor as a source (e.g. Vegetius 2.6 is closely related to Cato fr. 11 Jordan).

23. Livy, 26.4.4–10. The term *velite* literally meant 'cloak-wearer', that is to say, he lacked any body armour.
24. *Souda* s.v. 'Sword', Polybios fr. 79. The lost monograph is mention by Cicero (*Epistulae ad familiares* 5.12.2).
25. Livy, 31.34.4.
26. Arrian, *Ars Tactica*, 3.5.
27. Hopkins 1978: 35.
28. Polybios, 6.24.1 (centurions), Varro, *de lingua Latina*, 5.91 (*optiones*).
29. Polybios, 6.39.12, taking the Polybian drachma as the equivalent of the denarius.
30. Livy, 42.34.2.
31. Sallust, *Bellum Iugurthinum*, 84.2.
32. Ibid. 86.2, Aulus Gellius, *Noctes Atticae* 16.10.10, Florus, *Epitome*, 1.36.13, Plutarch, *Marius*, 9.1.
33. Livy, 22.57.11, 23.32.1.
34. Plutarch, *Caius Gracchus*, 5.1.
35. Livy, 1.43.8, cf. Polybios, 6.19.2.
36. Gabba, 1976: 7–10.
37. Polybios, 11.23.1, cf. 33.
38. Sallust, *Bellum Iugurthinum*, 49.6.
39. Plutarch, *Aemilius Paullus*, 19.1. See Polybios 18.30–2 for the comparison between the Macedonian phalanx and Roman manipular legion.
40. Polybios, 2.33.4.
41. Derived from Celtic helmets of the fourth and third centuries BC, the Montefortino helmet was a high domed pattern that gave good protection to the top of the head. It also had hinged cheek-pieces, but had only a stubby nape-guard. The type is named after the necropolis at Montefortino, Ancona, in northern Italy.
42. Sallust, *Bellum Iugurthinum*, 46.7.
43. Brunt 1971: 687–93.
44. Ibid. 690. Caesar, *Bellum civile*, 3.2.4.
45. Cicero, *Tusculanae disputationes*, 2.16.37.
46. Gibbon, *Decline and Fall*, I.1.28.
47. Plutarch, *Marius*, 13.1. For the continued use of the term, see Frontinus, *Strategemata*, 4.1.7.
48. Literally 'tentful', a mess-unit of eight infantry, ten per century.
49. Pliny, *Historia Naturalis*, 10.5.16.
50. For example, at the start of his reign Vespasianus disbanded four legions (*I Germanica*, *IIII Macedonica*, *XV Primigenia* and *XVI Gallica*), disgraced for having either surrendered or lost their eagles (Cassius Dio, 55.24.3).
51. Junkelmann 1991: 188.
52. Polybios, 1.40.12.
53. Caesar, *Bellum Gallicum*, 1.25.3.
54. Bishop-Coulston 1993: 48.
55. Plutarch, *Marius*, 25.1–2.
56. Camp V, which is tentatively dated to the period of Pompey's campaigns against Sertorius in the later seventies BC. For the archaeological evidence, see Bishop-Coulston 1993: 50.
57. Polybios, 6.23.1.
58. It is controversial whether the Romans used steel. According to Manning (1976: 148) 'there is no evidence for widespread, regular, intentional production of steel in the Roman Empire'. The problem is that the only essential difference between iron and steel is the amount of carbon in the metal. Regular wrought iron has a carbon content of about 0.5 per cent and steel has a carbon content of 1.5 per cent. It is possible that this much carbon was imparted to the blade by the charcoal used to heat the metal as the smith forged the blade. This contact between the metal and charcoal created a sort of outer layer of steel in a process called carburisation. It is doubtful that the Romans were aware that this process was

taking place, but the end product was 'blister steel', so called because of its blistered surface.

59. Based on *gladii* found at Pompeii and on several sites along the Rhine-Danube frontier, Ulbert (1969) has been able to show that there were two models of *gladius*, the one succeeding the other. First was the long-pointed 'Mainz' type, whose blade alone could measure 69 centimetres (Connolly 1997: 49–56) and is well-evidenced in the Augustan period and the first half of the first century AD. The 'Pompeii' type, a short-pointed type, replaced it, probably during the early part of Claudius' reign. Weighing around a kilogram, this pattern was shorter than its predecessor, being between 42 and 55 centimetres long, with a straighter blade 4.2 to 5.5 centimetres wide and a short triangular point.
60. Plutarch, *Marius*, 20.1.
61. Ibid. 20.5.
62. Plutarch says (*Marius*, 21.7) 100,000 were killed or taken prisoner, including their kith and kin, while Livy (*Periochae*, 68) gives the more amazing figures of 200,000 killed and 90,000 captured.
63. Plutarch, *Marius*, 20.5.
64. See, for example, Tacitus, *Annales*, 2.14, 21, 14.36, *Historiae*, 2.42, *Agricola*, 36.2.
65. Polybios, 2.33.6.
66. Ibid. 6.23.4.
67. The wearing of the sword on the right side goes back to the Iberians, and before them, to the Celts. The sword was the weapon of the high-status warrior, and to carry one was to display a symbol of rank and prestige. It was probably for cultural reasons alone, therefore, that the Celts carried the long slashing-sword on the right side. Usually a sword was worn on the left, the side covered by the shield, which meant the weapon was hidden from view. The Vachères Warrior, a statuette dating to the end of the first century BC, shows the characteristic mail shirt, a heavy cloak, a tubular torc and sword-belt of the Celtic warrior. A long slashing-sword, for all to see, hangs at his right hip as he leans on his shield in characteristic Gallic fashion.
68. Polybios, 6.23.6–7. With its sharp point and four-ring suspension arrangement, the Delos sword, firmly dated to 69 BC, shows all the characteristics of the *gladius Hispaniensis* described a century earlier by Polybios. Another such example is the Mouriès sword, found in a tomb in association with a group of pottery and metal artefacts that can be dated to the last years of the second century BC or the very early part of the first century BC. See especially, Bishop-Coulston 1993: 53, Feugère 2002: 79.
69. Vegetius, 1.8.
70. Valerius Maximus, 2.3.2.
71. Vegetius, 1.26–7, 2.3.
72. Ibid. 1.13.
73. Polybios, 2.33.5, 3.114.3, Tacitus, *Agricola*, 36.2.
74. Varro (*de lingua Latina*, 5.116) believes that the Romans acquired their knowledge of mail making from the Gauls, who were also its original fabricators. Early Gallic mail was made of alternate lines of punched and butted rings. The Romans replaced the butted rings with much stronger riveted rings, one riveted ring linking four punched rings. Such shirts weighed some 9 to 15 kilograms, depending on the length and number of rings (at least 30,000).
75. Connolly (1991) suggests that the crouch stance was a standard fighting position, but Goldsworthy (1998: 219) believes this was impractical, as it negated the protection of the *scutum* and left the legionary's head and shoulders exposed to downward blows. However, by adopting a very slight crouch the legionary not only kept the full protection of his shield but also gained an optimum position of balance. Here I shall take the opportunity to acknowledge Brian Marshall for his important input on the bio-mechanical details.
76. Cicero, *Tusculanae disputationes*, 2.16.37.
77. Here it is important to note that the Roman style of fighting required less room to execute, which resulted in a much tighter tactical formation. In practical terms this meant when up against Celts, who required a fair amount of room to swing their long slashing-swords effectively, at least two legionaries could face one Celt on the field of battle.
78. Plutarch, *Marius*, 26.3–5.
79. *Nobilitas*, which gives us our word 'nobility', was a technical term meaning the possession of consular ancestors. See especially, Gelzer 1969: 32.
80. Cicero, *pro Murena*, 30.

81. Ibid. 38.
82. Cicero, *de oratore*, 2.267.
83. Syme 1956: 20.
84. Cicero, *de legibus*, 3.38.
85. Strabo 17.3.9, cf. Anon., *Bellum Africum* 25.2, Appuleius, *Apologia*, 24.1.
86. See especially, Sallust, *Bellum Iugurthinum*, 35.10: 'A city for sale and doomed to speedy destruction if it finds a purchaser!' This is repeated almost verbatim by both Florus (*Epitome*, 1.36.18) and Appian (*Numidica*, fr. 1), but how fair this accusation is we cannot say, though it is probably exaggerated.
87. Sallust, *Bellum Iugurthinum*, 66.3–67.3, cf. Plutarch, *Marius*, 8.1.
88. Sallust, *Bellum Iugurthinum*, 69.4.
89. Ibid. 64.2–3.
90. See especially, ibid. 85.4–40, Marius' consular speech – the manifesto of the *novus homo*.
91. Livy, 28.40.1–2.
92. Asconius, 68.
93. Plutarch, *Marius*, 9.1, cf. Sallust, *Bellum Iugurthinum*, 86.4.
94. Appian, *Bellum civilia*, 1.57.
95. Sallust, *Bellum Iugurthinum*, 91.6–7, 92.3, cf. 54.6, 55.4–6.
96. Ibid. 95.1.
97. Greek *Maurousiai*, Latin *Mauri.*
98. Pliny, *Historia Naturalis*, 37.1.9, Plutarch, *Marius*, 10.14.
99. Iulius Obsequens, *Ab Anno Urbis Conditae DV Prodiiorum*, 38.
100. Caesar, *Bellum Gallicum*, 1.7.5, 12.5–6.
101. Both Livy and Plutarch agree on the prisoners, but Plutarch (*Marius*, 27.5) gives 120,000 killed while Livy (*Periochae*, 68) 140,000. Of course these numbers should be reduced drastically, but it is of interest to note that Tacitus says, in a passage written some time before AD 98, the Cimbri were 'now a small people, but great in memories' (*Germania*, 37.1).
102. Appian, *Bellum civilia*, 1.32.
103. Plutarch, *Marius*, 30.4–5.
104. Ibid. 31.1.
105. Appian, *Bellum civilia*, 1.34–36.
106. Polybios, 41.13.8.
107. Cicero, *pro Balbo*, 48.
108. Appian, *Bellum civilia*, 1.39.
109. Plutarch, *Moralia*, 202C-D (Umbrians), Cicero, *pro Balbo*, 46, Valerius Maximus 5.2.8 (Camertians).
110. In Latin: *ex lege Iulia*, *ILS* 8888.
111. Sisenna fr. 17 (*lex Calpurnia*), Cicero, *pro Balbo*, 21, Aulus Gellius, *Noctes Atticae*, 4.4.3, Appian, *Bellum civilia*, 1.49 (*lex Iulia*), Cicero, *pro Archia Poeta*, 7 (*lex Plautia Papiria*), Asconius, 3 (*lex Pompeia*).
112. Appian, *Bellum civilia*, 1.49.
113. Interestingly, Valerius Maximus reckons Varius owed his cognomen Hybrida to the obscurity of his right to Roman citizenship. He adds, with a sneer, that 'when he had ceased to be tribune, his own law caught him in the trap of his own making' (8.6.4).
114. According to Strabo (12.2.11), the Romans had offered the Cappadocians their freedom, but they declined this offer and asked Rome to name a king for them.
115. Appian, *Mithridatica*, 36.
116. Ibid. 22, Valerius Maximus 9.2. Plutarch (*Sulla*, 24.14) puts the figure at 150,000. On the numbers, see Brunt 1971: 224–7.
117. Sallust, *Historiae*, 4 fr. 67, cf. Velleius Paterculus, *Historiae Romanae*, 2.18.3, where Aquillius is simply held captive until later freed by Pompey.
118. For the Roman forces see Plutarch, *Sulla*, 16.3, which is probably based on Sulla's own memoirs, while the size of the Pontic army is given by Appian, *Mithridatica*, 21. As a matter of interest, Chaironeia was Plutarch's home town.
119. Frontinus, *Strategemata*, 2.3.17.
120. Plutarch, *Sulla*, 21.5. As this episode is repeated virtually verbatim in Appian, *Mithridatica*, 49, the original source for these heroics was almost certainly Sulla's memoirs.

121. Appian, *Bellum civilia*, 1.55.
122. Ibid. 1.71–5 has a long list of atrocities.
123. Appian, *Mithridatica*, 55, Plutarch, *Sulla*, 24.1–3.
124. Appian, *Mithridatica*, 51. For the details of Sulla's letter to the Senate see Appian, *Bellum civilia*, 1.77.
125. According to Appian (*Bellum civilia*, 1.79), Sulla came with his five legions, 6,000 cavalry (eastern?), and levies from the Peloponnese and Macedon, altogether some 50,000 men. Elsewhere he says (*Mithridatica*, 63) Sulla left Licinius Murena with two legions, those formerly commanded by Fimbria, to tidy matters up in the province of Asia.
126. Velleius Paterculus, *Historiae Romanae*, 2.27.2.
127. Plutarch, *Sulla*, 31.7.
128. Appian, *Bellum civilia*, 1.95.
129. Orosius, 5.21.
130. Sallust, *Bellum Catilinae*, 51.34.
131. Valerius Maximus 5.2.7, cf. Cicero, *post reditum in senatu*, 25, Diodoros, 36.16, Appian, *Bellum civilia*, 1.33.
132. Appian, *Bellum civilia*, 1.103.
133. Livy, *Periochae*, 89.
134. Plutarch, *Sulla*, 38.3, Appian, *Bellum civilia*, 1.106.
135. For a comprehensive collection of the primary sources covering the Sullan legislation, see Stockton 1981: 187–97.
136. Appian, *Bellum civilia*, 1.100.
137. Ibid. 1.104.
138. Suetonius, *Divus Iulius*, 77.
139. Velleius Paterculus, *Historiae Romanae*, 2.17.1.
140. Syme 1956: 7.
141. For the theory that Marius had long had his eye on a war with Mithridates, see Luce 1970.
142. Appian, *Bellum civilia*, 1.57.
143. Cicero to Atticus, Formiae, 18 March 49 BC, in Cicero, *Epistulae ad Atticum*, 9.10.3.
144. Badian 1962: 52, citing Cicero, *Brutus*, 308. For the alternative view, see Paterson 1985: 24.
145. Appian, *Bellum civilia*, 1.88, Livy, *Periochae*, 86.
146. Cicero to Atticus, Cales, night of 18/19 February 49 BC, in Cicero, *Epistulae ad Atticum*, 8.3.6.
147. See especially, Paterson 1985: 23.
148. Cicero, *pro Roscio Amerino*, 136, 149.
149. When Caesar crosses the Rubicon, one of his companions is the 36-year-old Caius Sallustius Crispus – Sallust. He had recently fled to Caesar after being expelled from the Senate for immorality, and would prove to be a poor soldier, only to become famous as a writer of influential style.
150. Sallust, *Bellum Iugurthinum*, 95.4.
151. Messalla, *ap.* Aulus Gellius, *Noctes Atticae*, 13.15.4.
152. Cicero, *pro Murena*, 38. For the functions of a consul, see Polybios, 6.12.
153. *ILS* 8888.
154. Cicero, quoted by Asconius, 70. Incidentally, a number of slingshots have turned up at Asculum Picenum, dating to the time of the siege, with various inscriptions on them, including FERI POMP (*eius Strabonem*), 'Strike Pompeius!' (*CIL* 12: 848, 853, 858).
155. Valerius Maximus 6.2.8., cf. Pseudo-Sallust, *ad Caesarem* 1.4.1.
156. Plutarch, *Pompey*, 14.5.
157. Ibid. 36.2.
158. Appian, *Mithridatica*, 113.
159. Ibid. 117.
160. Smith 1960: 9–10.
161. Cicero, *de imperio Cnaeo Pompeii*, 10.27: Italy (82 BC), Sicily (81 BC), Africa (81 BC), Gallia Cisalpina (77 BC), Iberia (77–72 BC), the Slave War (71 BC) and the Pirate War (67 BC).
162. Cicero, *in Verrem*, 1.18.56.
163. Cicero to Mescinius Rufus, outside Rome, 5 January 49 BC, in Cicero, *Epistulae ad familiares*, 5.20.9.
164. Macrobius, *Satura*, 3.13.10 (trees), Varro, *de re rustica*, 3.6.6 (peacocks), Pliny, *Historia Naturalis*, 14.96 (cellar).

165. Pliny, *Historia Naturalis*, 15.10.
166. Plutarch, *Lucullus*, 41.2.
167. Varro, *de re rustica*, 3.17.5.
168. Cicero to Atticus, Antium, 3 June 60 BC, in Cicero, *Epistulae ad Atticum*, 2.1.7.
169. Cicero, *de legibus*, 3.26.
170. Sallust, *Bellum Catilinae*, 38.3.
171. Cicero, *de lege agraria*, 2.16.
172. Cicero, *de officiis*, 2.84.
173. Despite a state ban on the resale of land plots, explains Cicero (*de lege agraria*, 2.78), a small number of owners had concentrated land in their hands. He also claims that among Catiline's partisans were some veterans who had ended in debt, and doing so by their own irresponsibility: 'building like nabobs, with choice estates and large households, wining and dining in style . . . their only hope of rescue is to raise Sulla from the dead' (*in Catilinam*, 2.20, cf. *pro Murena*, 49, Sallust, *Bellum Catilinae*, 28.4).
174. Sallust, *Bellum Catilinae*, 50.4–51.35.
175. Ibid. 52.2–53.32
176. See especially, Juvenal, *Satura*, 10.122: 'O fortunate Roman State, born in my great consulate!' – this was a line taken from the much derided poem *de suo consulatu*, which Cicero composed in 60 BC to glorify the events of his consulate. Marcus Antonius, during his own turbulent consulate, would mock Cicero's line 'Let toga be mightier than sword' (Cicero, *Philippics*, 2.8). It seems Romans did not think much of Cicero the poet.
177. Cicero, *pro Murena*, 52.
178. Cicero, *in Catilinam*, 2.20.
179. Cicero, *pro Caelio*, 12–14.
180. Cicero to Atticus, Rome, 15 March 60 BC, in Cicero, *Epistulae ad Atticum*, 1.19.5.
181. Cicero, *pro Sestio*, 137.
182. Livy, 4.44.
183. Plutarch, *Pompey*, 22.6.
184. Cicero, *pro Plancio*, 23.
185. See, for example, Cicero, *pro Sestio*, 97.
186. Cicero, *Philippics*, 6.19.
187. Plutarch, *Sertorius*, 12.2.
188. In Latin: *non pro consule, sed pro consulibus*, Cicero, *Philippics*, 11.18. For his reputation as a wit, see Cicero, *Brutus*, 173, as a gourmet, see Varro, *de re rustica*, 3.3.9.
189. Plutarch, *Pompey*, 17.4. On Marian sympathies, see especially Leach 1986: 44.
190. Plutarch, *Sertorius*, 19.8, cf. *Pompey*, 18.3.
191. Valerius Maximus 7.3.6, Frontinus, *Strategemata*, 1.10.1.
192. Sallust, *Historiae*, 2 fr. 98 Maurenbrecher.
193. Ibid. 3 fr. 83 Maurenbrecher.
194. Plutarch, *Pompey*, 20.13.
195. His citizenship was ratified by the *lex Gellia Cornelia* of that year, in common with other enfranchisements conferred by Pompey. Balbus probably took his name Cornelius from Lucius Cornelius Lentulus Crus (later *cos.* 49 BC) who must have recommended him for citizenship.
196. Plutarch, *Sertorius*, 18.7–14.
197. Frontinus, *Strategemata*, 2.5.31. See also Goldsworthy 2004: 163–5.
198. 'Spartacus means fire and spirit, the heart and soul, the will and deed of the revolution of the proletariat': these words by Liebknecht were inscribed on a pillar commemorating the *Spartakusbund*, on Chausseestrasse, Berlin. Of particular interest here is the novel *The Gladiators* by the Hungarian-born Spanish Civil War veteran Arthur Koestler, first published in 1939 – a few months after the author had left the *Kommunistische Partei Deutschlands* (German Communist Party), the successor of the *Spartakusbund*.
199. Plutarch, *Crassus*, 8.2.
200. Marx to Engels, London, 27 February 1861, in Karl Marx-Frederick Engels, *Correspondence 1846–95* (New York, 1934), 126.
201. A group of some 200 gladiators, mainly Thracians and Gauls, resentful of their owner's inhumane

treatment, hatched a plan to escape. Fewer than half seem to have succeeded – seventy-eight in Plutarch (*Crassus*, 8.2), about seventy in Appian (*Bellum civilia*, 1.116), sixty-four in Velleius Paterculus (*Historiae Romanae*, 2.30.5), and a few more than thirty in Florus (*Epitome*, 2.8.3).

202. Florus, *Epitome*, 2.8.8.
203. Appian, *Bellum civilia*, 1.116.
204. Plutarch, *Crassus*, 9.6.
205. Appian, *Bellum civilia*, 1.117.
206. Orosius 5.24.
207. Plan to leave Italy, Plutarch, *Crassus*, 9.5–6. Assault on Rome, Appian, *Bellum civilia*, 1.117.
208. Plutarch, *Crassus*, 10.5–6.
209. See n. 200 above.
210. Appian, *Bellum civilia*, 1.120.
211. Plutarch, *Pompey*, 21.5.
212. On these events, see especially Greenhalgh 1980: 64–71.
213. Cicero, *de oratore*, 3.10.
214. Pliny, *Historia Naturalis*, 33.134. Then again Cicero (*de officiis*, 1.25), giving Crassus' definition of the money a Roman statesman required, specifies an army not a legion, which is repeated by Plutarch (*Crassus*, 2.9).
215. Plutarch, *Pompey*, 55.7. The talent (Latin *talentum*) was a fixed Greek weight of silver equivalent to 60 *minae* (Attic-Euboic *tálanton* = 26.2kg, Aiginetan *tálanton* = 43.6kg), the *mina* being a unit of weight equivalent to 100 Attic drachmae or 70 Aiginetan drachmae.
216. Ibid. 52.3, with Appian, *Bellum civilia*, 2.24.
217. The brass sesterce (= four copper *asses*) was the Roman unit of account, while 4 sesterces made a denarius, the silver coin.
218. Plutarch, *Crassus*, 10.2–3, Appian, *Bellum civilia*, 1.118.
219. Appian, *Mithridatica*, 92.
220. Cicero, *de officiis*, 3.107.
221. Florus, *Epitome*, 3.7.2.
222. Velleius Paterculus, *Historiae Romanae*, 2.31.2.
223. Appian, *Mithridatica*, 115.
224. Plutarch, *Pompey*, 25.4.
225. Plutarch, *Lucullus*, 11.2.
226. Ibid. 27.5.
227. Ibid. 34.4.
228. Ibid. 20, Appian, *Mithridatica*, 83.
229. Tigranes had spent part of his youth as a hostage in the court of the Parthian king Mithridates II (r. 123–88 BC), and secured his freedom by ceding to him part of his kingdom (Justin 38.3.1). Once safely established back home, Tigranes made war against the Parthians and annexed northern Mesopotamia.
230. Frontinus, *Strategemata*, 2.1.12, Plutarch, *Pompey*, 32.
231. Plutarch, *Pompey*, 33.6.
232. Mithridates' famous treatise on cures for poisons was translated into Latin on Pompey's orders.
233. Josephus, *Antiquitates Iudaicae*, 14.29–79, *Bellum Iudaicum*, 1.127–57.
234. *ILS* 9459.
235. Pliny, *Historia Naturalis*, 7.95, 99.
236. Plutarch, *Pompey*, 38.2.
237. Diodoros, 37.12.2.
238. In Latin: *scientam rei militaris, virtutem, auctoritatem, felicitatem*, Cicero, *de imperio Cnaeo Pompeii*, 28.
239. During the Social War, aged 17, Cicero had served for a short time in the army of Pompey's father Pompeius Strabo against the Italian rebels in the northern theatre (Cicero, *Philippics*, 12.27).
240. See, for example, Caelius Rufus' comments on Pompey written in a letter to Cicero, Rome, April 50 BC, in Cicero, *Epistulae ad familiares*, 8.1.3.
241. Sallust, *Historiae*, 2 fr. 14 Maurenbrecher.
242. Plutarch, *Caesar*, 1.4.
243. His first wife Cornelia died in the same year, and he used her funeral as an occasion to pronounce a

public speech in praise of her, a tradition at the funerals of elderly matrons but not usually the done thing in the case of a young woman. Apparently Caesar was the first to do this, and it 'was an action that made him popular' (Ibid. 5.7).

244. Ibid. 6.2.
245. Suetonius, *Divus Iulius*, 74.
246. Sallust, *Bellum Catilinae*, 17.7.
247. Plutarch, *Caesar*, 7.2.
248. Suetonius, *Divus Iulius*, 13.
249. Plutarch, *Pompey*, 45.3, Velleius Paterculus, *Historiae Romanae*, 2.40.
250. Plutarch, *Cicero*, 23, Cassius Dio, 37.38.2.
251. Cicero to Pompey, Rome, April 62 BC, in Cicero, *Epistulae ad familiares*, 5.7.1.
252. Gruen 1970.
253. Plutarch, *Pompey*, 43.6.
254. Cicero to Atticus, Rome, 1 January 61 BC, in Cicero, *Epistulae ad Atticum*, 1.12.
255. Plutarch, *Cato minor*, 30.6.
256. Cicero to Atticus, Rome, 15 March 60 BC, in Cicero, *Epistulae ad Atticum*, 1.19.4.
257. Cicero to Atticus, Antium, 3 June 60 BC, ibid. 2.1.5.
258. Cassius Dio, 37.50.5–6.
259. Cicero, *pro Murena*, 31.
260. Plutarch, *Cato minor*, 31.2–3, cf. 5.2.
261. Cicero to Atticus, Antium, 3 June 60 BC, in Cicero, *Epistulae ad Atticum*, 2.1.6.
262. Suetonius, *Divus Iulius*, 19.2.
263. Balsdon 1939.
264. Cicero to Atticus, Rome, December 60 BC, in Cicero, *Epistulae ad Atticum*, 2.3.3.
265. Cassius Dio, 38.7.5.
266. Appian, *Bellum civilia*, 2.13.
267. Suetonius, *Divus Iulius*, 20.2.
268. This was a legal process known as *transitio ad plebem*. In the early Republic political power was in the hands of a fairly small number of patrician *gentes* or families such as the Iulii, Claudii and Fabii, whose leaders monopolised the chief offices of state, including the priesthood. Deriving from the noun 'fathers' (*patres*), this was probably a group of families who originally formed the king's council. The *gentes* that were excluded from power were called plebeian, indicating that they were members of the plebs, the term applied to the whole of the non-patrician citizen population of Rome. In the fifth century BC they formed a 'state within a state' so as to put pressure on patrician aristocracy. By this means they elected their own officers (tribunes of the people and plebeian aediles). Its resolutions were called *plebiscita*, and a *lex Hortensia* of 287 BC enacted that all decrees of the plebs should be legally binding, and equivalent to *leges* passed in the *comitia centuriata*.
269. Plutarch, *Caesar*, 10.9. See also Cicero, *Epistulae ad Atticum*, 1.12.13. He had married Pompeia in 67 BC, two years after the death of Cornelia. In 59 BC Caesar would marry his third wife Calpurnia, the daughter of Lucius Calpurnius Piso Caesoninus.
270. Cicero, *pro Sestio*, 18.40.
271. Cicero to Atticus, Rome, 10 September 57 BC, in Cicero, *Epistulae ad Atticum*, 4.1.6–7.
272. Cicero to Lentulus Spinther, Rome, December 54 BC, in Cicero, *Epistulae ad familiares*, 1.9.9.
273. Cicero to Atticus, Antium, 17 November 56 BC, in Cicero, *Epistulae ad Atticum*, 4.8a.2.
274. Cicero to Atticus, Rome, 27 July 54 BC, ibid. 4.15.7.
275. Because he was in possession of *imperium pro consule*, that is, the right to raise troops, Pompey was excluded from staying in the city itself.
276. Arousing special attention among Roman poets, this equestrian feat is the origin of the phrase 'a Parthian shot' (Ovid, *Fasti*, 5.591–2, Virgil, *Georgics*, 3.31–2, cf. 4.291, 313–14, *Aeneid*, 12.856–8, Lucan, *Pharsalia*, 1.261). So a 'Parthian shot' became, by analogy, a 'parting shot', a final hostile remark or gesture delivered in such a way that your opponent has no chance of responding: 'You wound, like Parthians, while you fly. And kill with a retreating eye' (Samuel Butler, *An Heroic Epistle of Hudibras to his Lady*, 173–4).
277. Plutarch, *Crassus*, 16.7–15.

278. Napoléon, *Correspondance*, XXXII.29.
279. Cassius Dio, 40.56.2, Plutarch, *Pompey*, 55.7.
280. Plutarch, *Pompey*, 54.4.
281. Plutarch, *Cato minor*, 43.6.
282. Aulus Gellius, *Noctes Atticae*, 1.10.4.
283. There were sixty centurions to a legion, in twelve grades including *primi ordines* and *primus pilus*. Seniority was usually determined by length of service, the six *primi ordines* being the most senior centurions of a legion, all serving in the first cohort. The most important of the six *primi ordines* (the 'front rankers') was the *primus pilus* ('first spear'), the chief centurion of the legion who commanded the first century in the first cohort and was personally responsible for the unit's eagle-standard (*aquila*). In other cohorts, the centurions were ranked as *pilus prior*, *pilus posterior*, *princeps prior*, *princeps posterior*, *hastatus prior* and *hastatus posterior*.
284. Cicero, *de provinciis consularibus*, 28, *pro Balbo*, 61.
285. Caesar, *Bellum Gallicum*, 5.33.2.
286. Plutarch, *Caesar*, 17.11, cf. Suetonius, *Divus Iulius*, 57.
287. Plutarch, *Caesar*, 5.1, *Cato minor*, 8.2, 9.1.
288. Cicero to Caesar, Rome, April 54 BC, in Cicero, *Epistulae ad familiares*, 7.5.3, and Cicero to Trebatius, Rome, end of June 54 BC, ibid. 7.8.1.
289. Caesar, *Bellum Gallicum*, 1.52.1.
290. Sallust, *Bellum Catilinae*, 59.6.
291. Cicero to Minucius Thermus, Laodicea, early April 50 BC, in Cicero, *Epistulae ad familiares*, 13.57.1.
292. For the cognomen *Equestris*, literally 'Knightly', *CIL* 3.508. For the soldier's witticism, Caesar, *Bellum Gallicum*, 1.42.8–10.
293. Baculus: Caesar, *Bellum Gallicum*, 2.25.3. Scaeva: Caesar, *Bellum civile*, 3.53.3–4, Valerius Maximus, 3.2.23, Plutarch, *Caesar*, 16.4. Crastinus: Caesar, *Bellum civile*, 3.99.2.
294. Caesar, *Bellum civile*, 3.53.5.
295. Caesar, *Bellum Gallicum*, 5.44.1.
296. Ibid. 1.41.3, 5.28.3, 37.1, 6.7.8.
297. Canuleius brothers, *ILS* 2225. Cabilenus, *ILS* 2239. Vinusius, *ILS* 2242. Vettidius *ILS* 2240.
298. Appian, *Bellum civilia*, 2.82.
299. Caesar, *Bellum Gallicum*, 5.33.3–5.
300. Ibid. 7.52.
301. Cicero, *de officiis*, 1.35.
302. Caesar's three *commentarii* on the Second Civil War, the *Bellum civile*, covers the period from the beginning of 49 BC down to the beginning of the Alexandrian War in the autumn of 48 BC. The rest of the civil war is covered in three separate works by other hands, the *Bellum Alexandrinum*, the *Bellum Africum* and the *Bellum Hispaniense*.
303. Suetonius, *Divus Iulius*, 56.1. Hirtius was probably responsible for the *Bellum Alexandrinum* too.
304. Cicero to Papirius Paetus, Rome, August 46 BC, in Cicero, *Epistulae ad familiares*, 9.20.2.
305. 'Celts' was a name applied by ancient writers (*Keltai* and *Galatai* by the Greeks, *Celtae*, *Galli* and *Galatae* by the Romans) to a population group occupying lands mainly north of the Mediterranean region from Galicia in the west to Galatia in the east. Its application to the Bretons, the Welsh, the Scots and the Irish is modern. Their unity is recognisable by common speech and common artistic traditions. The artistic unity is most apparent in the La Tène style (named after the Swiss type-site), which appears in 500 BC or thereabouts. It is a very idiosyncratic art of swinging, swelling lines, at its best alive yet reposeful. For the designation *Keltai*, see especially Pausanias, 1.3.5 (quoting Hieronymos of Kardia), Strabo, 4.1.14, and Dionysios of Halikarnassos, 14.1.3. The name *Galatae* was given especially to those Celts in the East. This was a native Celtic term for warriors, being based on the word *gal* ('ability' or 'valour'). The Romans, however, tended to call the Celts by a corruption of this name, that is, *Galli*, which slang-form came into increasingly wider usage and is Anglicised as 'Gauls'.
306. The Nervii ('people of Nerios' – Nerios being a Celtic god whose name meant 'the strong one') were reputedly the bravest of all the Belgae and had a particular reputation for ferocity among the Gallic tribes. Their territory covered the plain of what is now Belgium as far as the Sambre, and the modern department of Nord in France. Their tribal centre was Bagacum (Bavai).

307. Plutarch, *Crassus*, 25.
308. Livy, 10.30.4, cf. 28.2. For Telamon, see Polybios, 2.22–31.
309. Caesar, *Bellum Gallicum*, 4.24, 33, 5.16.2.
310. Polybios, 2.33.3, cf. 30.8.
311. E.g. Plutarch, *Camillus*, 41.4, Polyainos, 8.7.2.
312. Caesar, *Bellum Gallicum* 7.23.
313. Caesar himself writes of 'states' (*civitates*), 'senates' (*senatus*), 'leading citizens' (*principes*, *primores*), 'magistrates' (*magistratus*), 'factions' (*factiones*), and 'dependants' (*clientelae*).
314. Cicero, *de re publica*, 3.16, cf. *in Verrem*, 2.5.166–7, Caesar, *Bellum Gallicum*, 4.2.1, 20.5.
315. Caesar, *Bellum Gallicum*, 1.33.5–6, 40.6, 2.4.2, 29.5, 7.77.16–18.
316. Montaigne 2.10, 'Des livres'.
317. On trade, see especially Strabo, 4.4.1, 5.2.
318. Plutarch, *Caesar*, 22.3.
319. In June 54 BC, just before his second expedition to Britannia, Caesar wrote to Cicero, who then told Atticus, 'there isn't a grain of silver on the island nor any prospect of booty apart from captives, and I fancy you won't expect any of *them* being highly qualified in literature or music!', Cicero to Atticus, Rome, 1 July 54 BC, in Cicero, *Epistulae ad Atticum*, 4.16.7. Of the second expedition Cicero, again using his brother's campaign summary, was to write to Atticus that 'they had settled Britannia, taken hostages but no booty (tribute, however imposed), and were bringing back the army from the island', Cicero to Atticus, Rome, between 24 October and 2 November 54 BC, ibid. 4.18.5.
320. Caesar's forays into Germanic territory were much like the medieval *chevauchée*, a raid to intimidate your opponents, demonstrate the power of your soldiers and convince those sitting on the fence to support your side.
321. Chief among them was the *primus pilus* Publius Sextius Baculus, left sick in bed, who seized arms and armour from the nearest soldiers and barred the entrance to the camp. His example was followed by the centurions of the garrison cohort, and this was enough to inspire some confidence in the rookie soldiers (Caesar, *Bellum Gallicum*, 6.38).
322. Reflecting its formation in Gallia Transalpina, *Alaudae*, Larks, is a plural noun of Celtic, not Latin, origin (cf. French *alouette*) – legionary titles are ordinarily declinable adjectives. It could also be a sign of the Celtic custom of wearing bird-crests or feathers attached to the helmet (Pliny, *Historia Naturalis*, 11.121). The nickname is first attested in 44 BC by Cicero (*Philippics*, 1.20, 4.12, 13.3, 37), and it may have been one which these Gallic legionaries conferred on themselves. Caesar did not have to obtain Senate permission to raise units of auxiliaries, non-citizens, which could be disbanded at any time. But then, says Suetonius (*Divus Iulius*, 24.2), Caesar unilaterally granted every man in the new unit Roman citizenship, giving them rights under Roman law. Certainly by 47 BC the unit was legally organised as a *iusta legio*, complete with number and eagle-standard or *aquila* (Anon., *Bellum Africum*, 1.5).
323. See especially, Cassius Dio, 43.19.4.
324. Plutarch, *Caesar*, 15.3.
325. W.B. Yeats, *New Poems* (1938).
326. Caesar, *Bellum Gallicum*, 8.54.1–3, cf. 6.1.3. See also, Caelius Rufus to Cicero, Rome, 1 August 51 BC, in Cicero, *Epistulae ad familiares*, 8.4.4. While Cicero was out in Cilicia as the province's (unwilling) governor, Caelius served as his political informant in the capital.
327. Cassius Dio, 40.65–6.
328. Caesar, *Bellum civile*, 3.88.2.
329. Appian, *Bellum civilia*, 2.30.
330. Ibid. 2.31.
331. Caelius Rufus to Cicero, Rome, 8 August 50 BC, in Cicero, *Epistulae ad familiares*, 8.14.2. Cicero had grudged every minute spent away from Roman politics, and although he embarked on his return journey from Side, Pamphylia, five days before this letter was written by Caelius, he would not put into Brundisium until 24 November.
332. Florus, *Epitome*, 2.13.14.
333. So says Plutarch (*Pompey*, 60.1, *Caesar*, 32.8), though usually quoted in Latin – *iacta alea est' inquit*. Others suggest, as recorded by Suetonius (*Divus Iulius*, 32), Caesar quoted a line from his favourite Greek playwright Menandros, 'the die is cast', likewise usually quoted in Latin – *alea iacta est*. Dice was the most

popular game and the betting was heavy. Either way, it is clear he had now consigned his future into the hands of the fates.

334. Mommsen's Caesar, 'the entire and perfect man', is the man who saw in advance that a monarchy was the necessary cure for Rome's ills, and became a democratic ruler by overthrowing a corrupt and arrogant oligarchy, which was closely identified by the towering liberal scholar with the Prussian Junkers whom he hated. However, it is the Caesar of Meyer (1922) that lives on, an *idée fixe* that has a Caesar who fought tooth-and-nail for power, which he intended to legitimise by becoming another Alexander the Great, ruling as a god and king over a world empire.
335. Mommsen 1857: 92. See also Rice Holmes 1923: 2.299–310, where the English scholar vindicates Mommsen's argument.
336. Seager 1979: 193–5.
337. Cicero to Atticus, Formiae, 19 December 50 BC, in Cicero, *Epistulae ad Atticum*, 7.6.2.
338. Sulla's *lex de maiestate* stipulated that there had to be a gap of ten years between consulships.
339. Cicero was among those affected and was packed off, much against his will, to govern Cilicia, which comprised at this time a huge mountainous area of central and southern Anatolia.
340. Caelius Rufus to Cicero, Rome, October 51 BC, in Cicero, *Epistulae ad familiares*, 8.8.9.
341. Suetonius, *Divus Iulius*, 31.2.
342. Caesar, *Bellum civile*, 1.7.7, cf. 8.3, 9.2.
343. Ibid. 3.91.2.
344. Suetonius, *Divus Iulius*, 30.4.
345. Cicero to Atticus, Formiae, 21 January 49 BC, in Cicero, *Epistulae ad Atticum*, 7.11.1.
346. Plutarch, *Pompey*, 57.5.
347. Cicero to Atticus, Trebula, 9 December 50 BC, in Cicero, *Epistulae ad Atticum*, 7.3.5.
348. Caelius Rufus to Cicero, Rome, 8 August 50 BC, in Cicero, *Epistulae ad familiares*, 8.14.3.
349. Cicero to Atticus, Minturnae, 23 January 49 BC, in Cicero, *Epistulae ad Atticum*, 7.13.2.
350. Pompey to Cicero, Luceria, 10 February 49 BC, ibid. 8.11a. In this short letter Pompey hails its recipient *imperator*, the title Cicero had been awarded by his troops for some trifling success over some hill-bandits while governor of Cilicia (ibid. 5.20.4).
351. Pompey to Domitius Ahenobarbus, Luceria, 11 February 49 BC, ibid. 8.12b.
352. Caesar, *Bellum civile*, 1.17.1.
353. Pompey to Domitius Ahenobarbus, Luceria, 16 February 49 BC, in Cicero, *Epistulae ad Atticum*, 8.12c.5.
354. Pompey to Domitius Ahenobarbus, Luceria, 17 February 49 BC, ibid. 8.12d.2. A few days after the arrival of *legio XII*, another veteran formation, *legio VIII*, arrived to join Caesar in the siege lines outside Corfinium, 'together with twenty-two cohorts from the latest levies in Gaul' (Caesar, *Bellum civile*, 1.15.3, 18.5).
355. Suetonius, *Divus Iulius*, 26.3.
356. Appian, *Bellum civilia*, 2.41.
357. Caesar, *Bellum civile*, 1.32.1.
358. Suetonius, *Divus Iulius*, 34.2.
359. Caesar, *Bellum civile*, 1.25.1, 30.2, cf. 2.23.1.
360. Keppie 1998: 105, 199–200.
361. Cassius Dio, 41.44.1, Appian, *Bellum civilia*, 2.52. Between the months of November and March the Mediterranean was *mare clausum*, meaning it was closed to shipping because of the weather conditions.
362. Plutarch, *Caesar*, 39.1.
363. Plutarch, *Pompey*, 65.5 cf. Suetonius, *Divus Iulius*, 36.
364. Plutarch, *Pompey*, 47.4.
365. Plutarch, *Caesar*, 44.4.
366. Vegetius, 1.12.
367. Again special thanks are due to Brian Marshall for his assistance on the bio-mechanical front.
368. Appian, *Bellum civilia*, 2.66.
369. Caesar, *Bellum civile*, 3.88.5, 89.1. Pompey had left fifteen cohorts behind at Dyrrhachium, while on the day he detailed seven cohorts to hold his camp.
370. Ibid. 3.88.1.
371. Frontinus, *Strategemata*, 2.3.22.

372. Caesar, *Bellum civile*, 3.89.1–2., cf. 93.8.
373. Appian, *Bellum civilia*, 2.76, Plutarch, *Caesar*, 45.4.
374. Appian, *Bellum civilia*, 2.81.
375. Virgil, *Aeneid*, 2.557–8.
376. Caesar, *Bellum civile*, 3.104.3, Plutarch, *Pompey*, 78.1. Ironically, Pompey's assassin was part of the Roman forces that had been left by Gabinius, the Pompeian proconsul of Syria, to prop up the ailing Ptolemaic monarchy.
377. Plutarch, *Caesar*, 48.3.
378. Napoléon, *Correspondance*, vol. XXXII, p. 63.
379. Cicero to Caius Cassius, Brundisium, February 47 BC, in Cicero, *Epistulae ad familiares*, 15.15.2. After Pharsalus, Cicero returned to Italy to spend eleven miserable months at Brundisium, in bad health and nerves, amid the ruins of his political dreams and the collapse of his marriage.
380. Anon., *Bellum Alexandrinum*, 75.1, Suetonius, *Divus Iulius*, 37.2, Plutarch, *Caesar*, 50.2. 'Came, Saw, Conquered' must rate as one of the great military epigrams.
381. Anon., *Bellum Alexandrinum*, 78.5.
382. Plutarch, *Caesar*, 51.3, Suetonius, *Divus Iulius*, 70, cf. 69.
383. Anon., *Bellum Africum*, 1.1, 5, 60.
384. For example, Frontinus, governor of Britannia (AD 73/4–77/8) and engineer of note, would quote with approval the maxim of Cnaeus Domitius Corbulo, a near-contemporary general renowned for his realistic training methods: 'Domitius Corbulo used to say that the pick-axe (*dolabra*) was the weapon with which to beat the enemy' (*Strategemata*, 4.7.2).
385. Appian, *Bellum civilia*, 2.102.
386. The Julian calendar was in use until 1582, when Pope Gregory XIII reformed it. The calendar was advanced ten days, to compensate for the slippage of the equinoxes. After that, centuries, though divisible by four, would no longer be leap years, unless they were divisible by 400. A further refinement making every year divisible by 4,000 a non-leap year will keep the Gregorian calendar accurate to within a day for 20,000 years. The Gregorian calendar was adopted by the Italian states, Spain, Portugal and the Catholic states of Germany the following year. Protestant German states adopted it in 1699, England and its colonies in 1752, Sweden in 1753, Japan in 1873, China in 1912, the Soviet Union in 1918 and Greece in 1923. Muslim countries retain the Islamic calendar, rather than the solar calendar. It has 354 days for eleven years and 355 days for the other nineteen years of a thirty-year cycle.
387. After the battle Caesar would grant *legio V Alaudae* the right to bear an elephant emblem on its shields and standards, and according to Appian (*Bellum civilia*, 2. 96, cf. Anon., *Bellum Africum*, 84) the legion would still bear elephants on its standards in his day some two centuries later. The fear that elephants evoked in the hearts of the Romans cannot be underestimated. Since the time of Alexander the Great the so-called civilised world had been terrified by what these huge beasts could do.
388. Plutarch, *Caesar*, 53.5–6.
389. Rice Holmes 1923: 3.298.
390. Anon., *Bellum Hispaniense*, 30.1.
391. Ibid. 31.2.
392. Appian, *Bellum civilia*, 2.104. Livy says, 'Caesar at length gained a signal victory, after a most desperate engagement at Munda' (*Periochae*, 65).
393. Anon., *Bellum Hispaniense*, 31.7. Plutarch (*Caesar*, 56.2) gives the same figures for the dead but makes no mention of the wounded.
394. Seneca, *de beneficiis*, 5.24.
395. Diodoros, 43.14.6, 21.2.
396. Ovid, *Ars amatoria*, 1.177.
397. Anon., *Bellum Hispaniense*, 42.6.
398. Clausewitz, *Vom Krieg*, I.3.
399. Caesar, *Bellum civile*, 3.89.2.
400. Ibid. 1.82.4.
401. Ibid. 1.84.1.
402. Plutarch, *Caesar*, 56.3. Repeated almost verbatim in Appian, *Bellum civilia*, 2.104.
403. Velleius Paterculus, *Historiae Romanae*, 2.55.3.

404. See Goldsworthy (1998: 76–115) for an analysis of the doctrine of the offensive in all forms of Roman warfare.
405. Tu Mu (AD 803–52), commentating on Sun Tzu 8.18.
406. Keegan 1987: 315–38.
407. Fuller 1998: 321. Speed was a pivotal and primordial element in Caesar's art of war, and in his *commentarii* it appears as a stellar leitmotiv. For instance, in *Bellum Gallicum* he uses the concept of celerity twenty times – once in the first book, six times in the second book, twice each in the third and fourth books, three in the fifth book, and six in the sixth book.
408. Suetonius, *Divus Iulius*, 60.1, Appian, *Bellum civilia*, 2.34.
409. Caesar, *Bellum Gallicum*, 7.88.1, cf. Suetonius, *Divus Iulius*, 64. This, of course, is a reference to the scarlet *paludamentum* customarily worn by those generals who have been hailed *imperator* by their triumphant troops (Pliny, *Historia Naturalis*, 22.3).
410. Napoléon, *Correspondance*, vol. XXXII, p. 63.
411. Plutarch, *Caesar*, 17.5.
412. Onasander, *Stratêgikos*, 33.1.
413. Caesar, *Bellum civile*, 1.45.1 (Ilerda), 3.93.1–94.1 (Pharsalus). See also Goldsworthy 1998: 156–63.
414. Plutarch, *Caesar*, 39.1 (roots), Anon., *Bellum Africum*, 24.3 (seaweed).
415. Appian, *Bellum civilia*, 2.51.
416. Caesar, *Bellum civile*, 3.94.4.
417. Ibid. 3.71.4.
418. Caesar, *Bellum Gallicum*, 8.52.3.
419. Cicero, *pro Rabirio*, 22 (Picenum), Caesar, *Bellum civile*, 1.15.2 (Cingulum). On his defection, see Cicero, *Epistulae ad Atticum*, 7.11.1, 12.5, Cassius Dio, 41.4.4.
420. Plutarch, *Caesar*, 34.3.
421. Caesar, *Bellum Gallicum*, 8.8.3. Hirtius, remember, added an eighth to Caesar's own seven *commentarii.*
422. Napoléon, *Correspondance*, vol. XXXI, p. 418 note 40.
423. Cicero to Atticus, Minturnae, 23 January 49 BC, in Cicero, *Epistulae ad Atticum*, 7.13.1.
424. Ibid. 9.10.7, 18.2. The great Oxford classicist Syme (1956: 78) calls Caesar's adherents 'a ghastly and disgusting rabble'.
425. Cicero to Atticus, Formiae, 27 February 49 BC, in Cicero, *Epistulae ad Atticum*, 8.11.2, cf. 9.7.3, 10.2, 10.7.1.
426. Tacitus, *Historiae*, 2.38.
427. Clausewitz, *Vom Krieg*, I.1.23.
428. Fuller 1998: 182.
429. For the vicious attacks on Caesar, see Catullus, 29, 54, 57, 93. Of course in the moral value system of pagan antiquity, what mattered was not the gender of a partner but the nature of the sexual act. Thus in a culture founded on conquest, which measured social standing through military prowess, to be penetrated was to be humiliated. Lampooning the great Caesar was a popular pastime among Catullus' trendy circle, and Suetonius (*Divus Iulius*, 49.1) quotes a snatch of an epigram about Caesar's sexual promiscuity by Catullus' friend Calvus. Again Caesar is portrayed as the passive partner – the ultimate taboo for a Roman male.
430. Suetonius, *Divus Iulius*, 73.
431. Ibid. 77.
432. Herodian, 4.10.2.
433. Plutarch, *Caesar*, 58.8.
434. Aulus Hirtius and Caius Vibius Pansa Caetronianus were to be consuls for 43 BC, and Decimus Iunius Brutus Albinus and Lucius Munatius Plancus for 42 BC.
435. Balsdon (1967), Taylor (1931), Weinstock (1971).
436. See, for instance, Caesar on his ancestry in his eulogy to his beloved aunt Iulia (Suetonius, *Divus Iulius*, 6.1).
437. Cassius Dio, 43.43.2. Ascanius, literally 'tentless', had a second name, Iulus (Greek Ilos). Ilos was the eldest son of Tros (ancestral king of Troy), the father of Laomedon, grandfather of Priam (whence Ilios, Homer's alternative name for Troy, the city of Ilos). Ilos' brother was Assarakos, the great-great-grandfather of Ascanius (*Iliad*, 20.230–40).

438. Cassius Dio, 43.43.3–4. See also Weinstock 1971: 25.
439. Cassius Dio, 43.14.6, 21.2.
440. Cicero to Atticus, Tusculum, 28 July 45 BC, in Cicero, *Epistulae ad Atticum*, 13.44.1, cf. 12.45.2, 48.1.
441. Cicero, *Philippics*, 2.43.1, Cassius Dio, 44.6.4, Appian, *Bellum civilia*, 2.106. On these honours and more, see especially Weinstock 1971: 386–98.
442. *OGIS* 194.
443. Plutarch, *Marcus Antonius*, 81.6. According to Suetonius (*Divus Iulius*, 52.1) Marcus Antonius informed the Senate that Caesar had acknowledged Caesarion as his son.
444. *SIG*[3] 760.
445. Cassius Dio, 43.15.1, Cicero, *de divinatione*, 2.23.
446. Suetonius, *Divus Iulius*, 84.2. Or as Ovid would sing, 'Caesar is a god in his own city' (*Metamorphoses*, 15.921).
447. Syme 1956: 59.
448. In Latin: *non sum rex sed Caesar*, Suetonius, *Divus Iulius*, 79.2, cf. Cassius Dio, 44.9.2.
449. Cassius Dio, 44.6.1. Of course, in Cassius Dio's Greek Caesar is awarded the dress of a *basileía*, a king.
450. Cicero, *Philippics*, 2.85–7, cf. Suetonius, *Divus Iulius*, 79.3, Cassius Dio, 44.11.2, Appian, *Bellum civilia*, 2.109.
451. Napoléon, *Correspondance*, vol. XXXII, p. 88.
452. Suetonius, *Divus Iulius*, 1.1, cf. Plutarch, *Caesar*, 1.3–4.
453. Plutarch, *Crassus*, 1.6.
454. Cicero to Servius Sulpicius Rufus, Rome, late September or early October 46 BC, in Cicero, *Epistulae ad familiares*, 4.4.3.
455. Cicero, *pro Marcello*, 5.15, 8.23.
456. Balsdon 1958.
457. Plutarch, *Caesar*, 63.4. The same anecdote is told by Suetonius (*Divus Iulius*, 87) and Appian (*Bellum civilia*, 2.115).
458. Propertius, *Elegies*, 4.7.1–4.
459. Sallust, *Bellum Catilinae*, 1.1.
460. Cicero to Atticus, Puteoli, 14 May 44 BC, in Cicero, *Epistulae ad Atticum*, 14.22.1.
461. Shakespeare, *Julius Caesar*, I.ii.133, Nietzsche, *Jenseits von Gut und Böse: Vorspeil einer Philosphie der Zukunft*, §200.
462. Seneca, *Epistulae*, 94.65.
463. Machiavelli, *Il Principe*, 7, 16, *Arte della guerra*, 1.17, 2.55–6, 4.111, 120, 123, 124, 5.146–7, 6.178, 179.
464. Machiavelli, *Discori*, 1.10, cf. 17, 29, 34, 37, 3.24.
465. Suetonius, *Divus Iulius*, 82.3, Appian, *Bellum civilia*, 2.117. Seeing a steely glint in Brutus' hand, Caesar said not *Et tu, Brute?* ('And you, Brutus?') in Latin, as Shakespeare (*Julius Caesar*, III.i.77) would have us believe but *Kai su, Technon?* ('You too, my child?') in Greek (Suetonius, *Divus Iulius*, 82.3, Cassius Dio, 44.19.5). Caesar had loved Brutus like a son, and rumour had it that he was indeed Caesar's son. His mother Servilia had been the great love of Caesar's life, and thus the claim was that Brutus himself was their love child. True or not, his legal father Marcus Iunius Brutus senior, tribune of the people in 83 BC, had supported Marcus Aemilius Lepidus during the abortive seventy-eight rebellion, losing his life in the process. He had been executed on the orders of Pompey.
466. Pollio, *ap.* Suetonius, *Divus Iulius*, 30.4.
467. Cicero to Caius Trebonius, Rome, 2 February 43 BC, in Cicero, *Epistulae ad familiares*, 10.6.1. Cicero dispatched this letter to Asia, of which Trebonius had been appointed governor, but the recipient was never to read it, having been murdered in Smyrna by Cicero's son-in-law Publius Cornelius Dolabella. Cf. *Epistulae ad Atticum*, 15.11.2, when Cicero, in the presence of Brutus, studiously represses his pet topic, the failure to liquidate Antonius.
468. Cicero, *de lege agraria*, 2.16.
469. Sallust, *Historiae*, 1 fr. 77.1 Maurenbrecher.
470. Sallust, *Bellum Catilinae*, 33.1.
471. Cicero, *de re publica*, 2.56.
472. Ibid. 2.58.
473. The term *officium* (pl. *officia*) is commonly translated as 'duty', but strictly speaking it meant 'appropriate

action'.
474. Cicero, *de officiis*, 1.2.
475. Ibid. 1.25.
476. Ibid. 3.21.
477. Ibid. 3.42.
478. Ibid. 3.63.
479. Ibid. 1.42.
480. Ibid. 2.73, 85 (tribunes), 83 (debt).
481. Cicero to Atticus, Formiae, 18 March 49 BC, in Cicero, *Epistulae ad Atticum*, 9.10.2.
482. Cicero to Atticus, Matius' house near Rome, 7 April 44 BC, ibid. 14.1.1.
483. Cicero to Papirius Paetus, Rome, late August or early September 46 BC, in Cicero, *Epistulae ad familiares*, 9.17.2.
484. The title bestowed on Cicero for 'saving the Republic' (63 BC) and on Caesar for 'overthrowing it' (45 BC).
485. Cicero, *de officiis*, 3.19, 32.
486. Suetonius, *Divus Iulius*, 80.2, Cassius Dio, 43.47.3.
487. Cicero to Atticus, Formiae, 28 March 49 BC, in Cicero, *Epistulae ad Atticum*, 9.18.2.
488. Appian, *Bellum civilia*, 2.137–43.
489. Decimus Brutus to Marcus Brutus and Caius Cassius, Rome, 17, 21 or 22 March 44 BC, in Cicero, *Epistulae ad familiares*, 11.1.1. The dating of this crucial letter has been much disputed by scholars, and good cases have been made out for all three dates.
490. Ibid. 11.1.3.
491. Cicero to Atticus, Puteoli, 11 May 44 BC, in Cicero, *Epistulae ad Atticum*, 14.21.3.
492. Caesar drew up his will, naming the principal heir, in mid-September 45 BC (Suetonius, *Divus Iulius*, 83.1).
493. The form Caius Iulius Caesar Octavianus would have been the regular way of indicating that he was a Caesar by adoption and an Octavius by birth. The republican aristocracy were usually known by cognomen alone (thus Cicero, Caesar, Brutus), or if a man did not have a cognomen, the family name was used in the same way (thus Antonius, Octavius, Hirtius). The cognomen Octavianus, commonly anglicised as 'Octavian' by scholars, was quickly and conveniently abandoned by him in favour of the more illustrious name of his great-uncle-cum-surrogate-father.
494. Cicero to Atticus, Puteoli, 22 April 44 BC, in Cicero, *Epistulae ad Atticum*, 14.12.2.
495. In Latin: '*et te, o puer, qui omnia nomini debes*', Cicero, *Philippics*, 13.24.
496. Decimus Brutus to Cicero, Eporedia, 24 May 43 BC, in Cicero, *Epistulae ad familiares*, 11.20.1. Of course Cicero may have never said so, but he does not actually deny it in his reply to Decimus Brutus (ibid. 11. 21.1).
497. Velleius Paterculus, *Historiae Romanae*, 2.62.3.
498. So called, first by Cicero himself, as a joke, in imitation of the speeches that his silver-tongued hero, the Athenian orator Demosthenes, had delivered against Philip II of Macedon back in the mid-fourth century BC.
499. Cicero to Atticus, Puteoli, 2 or 3 November 44 BC, in Cicero, *Epistulae ad Atticum*, 16.8.1.
500. Much later, having metamorphosed into 'the revered one' or *Augustus*, Octavianus would write in his political will that he had levied an army so as to champion 'the liberty of the Republic when it was oppressed by the tyranny of a faction' (*Res Gestae Divi Augusti*, 1.1). Like Sulla before him, Octavianus justifies his march on Rome with the subtle assertion that he is going to free it from tyrants. Unlike Sulla, who was a legitimate consul with a legitimate army, Octavianus was a private citizen with a private army. Of course tyrannicide was not a crime, but the duty of a Roman citizen.
501. Cicero, in his *Philippics* (3.6, 39, 4.5, 5.53, 12.8, 14.32), took great pains to extol the merits of this legion as a counterweight to *legio V Alaudae*, currently the backbone of Antonius' army. Indeed, such was Cicero's preoccupation with the cognomen itself that we do not know the legion's numeral. The legion was probably present during Caesar's campaign in Africa (Valerius Maximus, 3.2.19, cf. Appian, *Bellum civilia*, 2.95, Plutarch, *Caesar*, 52.16) and, excluding the veteran formations, *legiones XXV*, *XXVI*, *XXVIII*, *XXVIIII* and another, perhaps *XXX*, were then there (Anon., *Bellum Africum*, 60.1). However, we have no way of knowing which of these five fledgling legions carried the cognomen *Martia*. For a

discussion on the numeral, see Keppie 1991: 116–18.

502. Keppie 1998: 115.

503. *Res Gestae Divi Augusti*, 1.2–3, Livy, *Periochae*, 118, Cassius Dio, 46.29.2. For Cicero's proposal to legitimise Octavianus' position, see Cicero, *Philippics*, 5.16–17.

504. This, the first battle, was fought on 14 April according to the report dispatched on the following day from the camp at Mutina by Servius Sulpicius Galba to Cicero in Rome (Cicero, *Epistulae ad familiares*, 10.30.1).

505. Decimus Brutus to Cicero, Dertona, 5 May 43 BC, ibid. 11.10.4.

506. Captured as a boy by Pompeius Strabo at Asculum Picenum, Ventidius had been carted through the streets of Rome as part of the human spoils adorning the consul's triumph (Valerius Maximus, 6.9.9). From the obscurity of his early manhood – it was even rumoured that he had served as a common soldier – Ventidius rose to be an army contractor and attached himself to Caesar as a logistics expert (Aulus Gellius, *Noctes Atticae*, 15.4.3, Cassius Dio, 43.51.4–5). Perhaps because of his origins and profession, Ventidius was ungraciously called by some of his contemporaries a muleteer, Lucius Munatius Plancus (Cicero, *Epistulae ad familiares*, 10.18.3) and Cicero (Pliny, *Historia Naturalis*, 7.135) notable among them. Yet, as Pliny says, 'by a strange irony of fate, Publius Ventidius . . . became the only Roman general to celebrate a triumph over the Parthians' (ibid.). Pliny's words are repeated by Plutarch, with the added remark that Ventidius' 'origins were humble, but his friendship with Antonius gave him the opportunities to achieve great things' (*Marcus Antonius*, 34.12).

507. Appian, *Bellum civilia*, 3.73.

508. Suetonius, *Divus Augustus*, 26.1. Plutarch (*Pompey*, 58.5) tells a similar tale concerning one of Caesar's centurions.

509 Appian, *Bellum civilia*, 3.92 as quoted by Syme (1956: 186).

510. Cicero, *Philippics*, 5.43.

511. Appian, *Bellum civilia*, 3.94, cf. 74.

512. Velleius Paterculus, *Historiae Romanae*, 2.63.

513. Lepidus to the Senate, Pons Argenteus, 30 May 43 BC, in Cicero, *Epistulae ad familiares*, 10.35.1.

514. Plancus to Cicero, camp in Gaul, 28 July 43 BC, ibid. 10.24.5. Plancus was a *novus homo* from a respectable family from Tibur (Horace, *Odes*, 1.7.21), 'consul [42 BC], censor [22 BC], acclaimed *imperator* for a second time [40 or 39 BC]' (*ILS* 886). He had served with Caesar in Gaul and Iberia as one of his legates (Caesar, *Bellum Gallicum*, 5.24.3, 25. 5, *Bellum civile*, 1.40.7, Anon., *Bellum Africum*, 4.1), briefly flirting with the Pompeians before returning to Caesar's camp (Anon., *Bellum Hispaniense* 19.3). He would remain loyal to Antonius until 32 BC, when he went over to Octavianus. A natural born survivor, Plancus would propose the decree that conferred on Caesar's heir the appellation *Augustus* (Suetonius, *Divus Augustus*, 7.2). Cicero knew him as one who was 'too much at the service of the times' (Cicero, *Epistulae ad familiares*, 10.3.3).

515. As a loyal partisan of Caesar, Pollio was also one of those present when Caesar had crossed the Rubicon, was with him at Pharsalus, and may have been still with him at the last battle in Iberia. In 40 BC, as Antonius' man, Pollio would make it to the consulship. Pollio wrote a history in seventeen books beginning with the establishment of the 'first triumvirate' and continuing down to the double engagement at Philippi when the Republic finally expired in a welter of Roman blood – this great work, sadly lost to us, was used by Plutarch and Appian.

516. Plancus to Cicero, Cularo, 6 June 43 BC, in Cicero, *Epistulae ad familiares*, 10.23.2.

517. Pedius was either a nephew or grandnephew of Caesar and a beneficiary of his will; he had been a legate during the Gallic and Second Civil wars. He was aedile in 54 BC and served as the proconsul of Hispania Citerior, after which he triumphed at the end of 45 BC (Caesar, *Bellum Gallicum*, 2.2.1, 11.4, Anon., *Bellum Hispaniense*, 2.3, 12.1, Suetonius, *Divus Iulius*, 83.2, Appian, *Bellum civilia*, 3.22, *CIL* 1.50). He slips out of history until his consulate, August 43 BC.

518. 'Triumvir' comes from *tres* (three) and *vir* (man), and this construction is often used to describe a number of Romans working together in some official capacity, such as the *decemviri*, a board of ten commissioners set up for various purposes, the most notable being the *decemviri legibus scribundis* (451–449 BC) who drew up the earliest Roman code of laws, the Twelve Tables. Contemporary Romans had different terms to describe the triumvirate, many of them unprintable.

519. Livy, *Periochae*, 120.

520. Only *legio IIII* (probably now with its title *Macedonia*) is named in the literary sources as being at Philippi (Appian, *Bellum civilia*, 4.117), but according to Keppie (1998: 119) the other Caesarian formations were *legiones VI* (later *VI Ferrata*), *VII*, *VIII* (later *VIII Augusta*), *X Equestris* and *XII* (later *XII Antiqua*, afterwards *XII Fulminata*), and among the younger units, *legio III* (perhaps now with its title *Gallica*), and probably *legiones XXVI*, *XXVIII*, *XXVIIII* and *XXX*, all of which provided soldier-colonists at Philippi after the battle (e.g. *AE* 1924.55). Among Caesar's Gallic veterans we should include *legio V Alaudae* too; it is certainly counted among the eight experienced legions that remained with Antonius after Philippi (Appian, *Bellum civilia*, 5.3). Ironically, having been stationed in the east by Caesar after Pharsalus, *legiones XXVII*, *XXXI* and *XXXIII* now found they were fighting against their old comrades and on the side of the Liberators. Alongside them we should also include *legiones XXXVI* and *XXXVII*, formations created by Caesar from Pompey's beaten army.
521. An experienced and successful soldier, Galba had served for several years with Caesar in Gaul as one of his legates (Caesar, *Bellum Gallicum*, 3.1–6). Even so, he can be reckoned among those Caesarians who conspired to assassinate their leader; allegedly he held a personal grudge against Caesar, namely that he had not been made consul. Back in 49 BC, as a legitimate candidate, he had been 'robbed of the consulship, despite his far greater popularity and larger number of votes, because he was closely associated with Caesar both as a friend and as a legate' (ibid. 8.50.6).
522. According to Keppie (1998: 199) Pansa's consular series consisted of *legiones I* (later *I Germanica*), *II Sabina* (later *II Augusta*), *III* (later *III Augusta*) and *IIII Sorana*, and *legio V Urbana* (later *V Macedonica*), which was left to defend Rome.
523. A Roman mile (1.48 kilometres) marked 1,000 paces (*mille passus*) of a Roman legionary. The Romans measured a double pace, that is, the interval between the first foot leaving the ground to when the second touches it again.
524. Marcus Iunius Silanus, a legate sent by Lepidus, along with Lepidus' praetorian cohort, to assist Antonius. Under the Republic a magistrate on campaign could have a small escort and bodyguard, called a *cohors praetoria*. Later Octavianus would form a peacetime bodyguard, the one we know as the praetorian guard.
525. Besides *legio Martia*, Hirtius had thirty veteran cohorts under his command, namely *legiones IIII*, *VII* and *VIII*. According to Cicero (*Philippics*, 14.27), speaking a few days later after receiving reports of the engagement, *legiones VII* and *VIII* were under Hirtius' command that day.
526. Galba had yet to learn that Pansa had been carried out of the battle back to Bononia, fatally wounded in the side by a javelin (Appian, *Bellum civilia*, 3.69).
527. Cicero, *Philippics*, 11.39.
528. Appian, *Bellum civilia*, 3.68. Appian makes a penetrating point in the following chapter, namely these recruits 'were just as Italian as the men of *legio Martia*: so much more difference than racial origin does training make to bravery'. Incidentally *Martia* literally meant 'sacred to Mars' and, according to Appian, the legion 'took its cognomen from its reputation for valour' (ibid. 4.115).
529. Pollio to Cicero, Corduba, June 43 BC, in Cicero, *Epistulae ad familiares*, 10.33.1. In the same letter Pollio mentions he has received news that 'Pansa's army has been cut to pieces, Pansa is dead of his wounds, and *legio Martia* has been destroyed' (ibid. 4). Severely cut up, *legio Martia* in fact survived the day only to come to a tragic end the following year. During a crossing of the Adriatic, allegedly on the very day of the first battle at Philippi, the transports carrying the legion were intercepted by warships and its personnel mostly drowned or killed despite 'all sorts of brave deeds by the men in danger' (Appian, *Bellum civilia*, 4.115).
530. Plutarch, *Brutus*, 36.7–9.
531. That he was otherwise engaged during the first skirmish was even admitted by the partisan Velleius Paterculus (*Historiae Romanae*, 2.70.1), and, according to the elder Pliny (*Historia Naturalis*, 7.148), even Agrippa did not deny that his comrade-in-arms had lurked in a bog for three days.
532. Horace, *Odes*, 2.7.9–10.

Bibliography

Adcock, F.E., 1940. *The Roman Art of War under the Republic.* Cambridge, MA: Harvard University Press
Adcock, F.E., 1956. *Caesar as a Man of Letters.* Cambridge: Cambridge University Press
Adcock, F.E., 1966. *Marcus Crassus: Millionaire.* Cambridge: Heffer & Sons
Badian, E., 1958. *Foreign Clientelae.* Oxford: Clarendon Press
Badian, E., 1959. 'Caesar's *cursus* and the intervals between offices'. *Journal of Roman Studies* 49: 81–9
Badian, E., 1962. 'Waiting for Sulla'. *Journal of Roman Studies* 52: 47–61
Badian, E., 1968 (2nd edn). *Roman Imperialism in the Late Republic.* Ithaca: Cornell University Press
Badian, E., 1970. *Lucius Sulla: The Deadly Reformer.* Sydney: Sydney University Press
Badian, E., 1972. *Publicans and Sinners: Private Enterprise in the Service of the Roman Republic.* Dunedin: University of Otago Press
Ballesteros-Pastor, L., 1999. 'Marius' words to Mithridates Eupator (Plutarch, *Marius*, 31.3)'. *Historia* 48: 506
Balsdon, J.P.V.D., 1939. 'Consular provinces under the late Republic'. *Journal of Roman Studies* 29: 57–73
Balsdon, J.P.V.D., 1951. 'Sulla Felix'. *Journal of Roman Studies* 41: 1–10
Balsdon, J.P.V.D., 1958. 'The Ides of March'. *Historia* 7: 80–94
Balsdon, J.P.V.D., 1967. *Julius Caesar: A Political Biography.* New York: Athenaeum
Barker, P., 1981 (4th edn). *Armies and Enemies of Imperial Rome.* Worthing: Wargames Research Group
Beard, M. & Crawford, M.H., 1999 (2nd edn). *Rome in the Late Republic: Problems and Interpretations.* London: Duckworth
Bell, A.J.E., 1997. 'Cicero and the spectacle of power'. *Journal of Roman Studies* 87: 1–22
Bell, M.J.V., 1965. 'Tactical reform in the Roman republican army'. *Historia* 14: 404–22
Bishop, M.C. & Coulston, J.C.N., 1993. *Roman Military Equipment from the Punic Wars to the Fall of Rome.* London: Batsford
de Blois, L., 1987. *The Roman Army and Politics in the First Century before Christ.* Amsterdam: J.C. Gieben
Bradford, E., 1984. *Julius Caesar: The Pursuit of Power.* London: Hamish Hamilton
Bradley, K.R., 1989. *Slavery and Rebellion in the Roman World, 140–70 BC.* Bloomington: Indiana University Press
Brown, R.D., 1999. 'Two Caesarian battle descriptions: a study in contrast'. *Classical Journal* 94: 329–57
Brunt, P.A., 1971 (repr. 1987). *Italian Manpower 225 BC–AD 14.* Oxford: Oxford University Press
Brunt, P.A., 1982. '*Nobilitas* and *Novitas*'. *Journal of Roman Studies* 72: 1–17
Brunt, P.A., 1986. 'Cicero's *Officium* in the Civil War'. *Journal of Roman Studies* 76: 12–32
Brunt, P.A., 1988. *The Fall of the Roman Republic and Related Essays.* Oxford: Clarendon Press
Burns, A., 1966. 'Pompey's strategy and Domitius' last stand at Corfinium'. *Historia* 15: 74–95
Camps, G., 1962. *Aux origines de la Berbérie: monuments et rites funéraires protohistoriques.* Paris: Arts et métiers graphiques
Carney, T.F., 1960. 'Plutarch's style in the *Marius*'. *Journal of Hellenic Studies* 80: 24–31
Carney, T.F., 1961. 'The flight and exile of Marius'. *Greece & Rome* 8: 98–121
Carney, T.F., 1970 (2nd edn). *A Biography of C. Marius.* Chicago: Argonaut
Castellvi, G., Nola, J.M. & Rodà, I., 1995. 'La identificación de los trofeos de Pompeyo en le Pirineo'. *Journal of Roman Archaeology* 8: 5–18
Cawthorne, N., 2005. *Julius Caesar.* London: Haus Publishing
Chapman, M., 1992. *The Celts: The Construction of a Myth.* New York: St Martin's Press
Chrissanthos, S.G., 2001. 'Caesar and the mutiny of 47 BC'. *Journal of Roman Studies* 91: 63–75
Clarke, M.L., 1981. *The Noblest Roman: Marcus Brutus and His Reputation.* Ithaca: Cornell University Press
Coarelli, F., 1968. 'L' "ara di Domizio Enobarbo" e la cultura artistica in Roma nel II secolo a.C.'. *Dialoghi di Archeologia* 2: 302–68
Colledge, M.A.R., 1986. *The Parthian Period.* Leiden: E.J. Brill
Connolly, P., 1991. 'The Roman fighting technique deduced from armour and weaponry', in V.A. Maxfield & M.J. Dobson (eds), *Roman Frontier Studies 1989* (Proceedings of the Fifteenth International Congress of

Roman Frontier Studies). Exeter: Exeter University Press, 358–63
Connolly, P., 1997. '*Pilum*, *gladius* and *pugio* in the late Republic'. *Journal of Roman Military Equipment Studies* 8: 41–57
Connolly, P., 1998. *Greece and Rome at War*. London: Macdonald
Crawford, M.H., 1992 (2nd edn). *The Roman Republic*. London: Fontana Press
Cunliffe, B.W., 1979. *The Celtic World*. London: Bodley Head
Cunliffe, B.W., 1988. *Greeks, Romans and Barbarians: Spheres of Interaction*. London: Batsford
Cunliffe, B.W., 1997. *The Ancient Celts*. Oxford: Oxford University Press
Cunliffe, B.W., 2001 (repr. 2004). *Facing the Ocean: The Atlantic and its Peoples*. Oxford: Oxford University Press
Cunliffe, B.W., 2003. *The Celts: A Very Short Introduction*. Oxford: Oxford University Press
Dando-Collins, S., 2002. *Caesar's Legion: The Epic Saga of Julius Caesar's Elite Tenth Legion and the Armies of Rome*. New York: John Wiley & Sons
David, J.-M., 1994 (trans. A. Nevill 1996, repr. 1997). *The Roman Conquest of Italy*. Oxford: Blackwell
Debevoise, N.C., 1938 (repr. 1969). *A Political History of Parthia*. Chicago: University of Chicago Press
Dixon, S. (ed.), 1992. *The Roman Family*. Baltimore: Johns Hopkins University Press
Dodge, T.A., 1889 (repr. 2002). *The Great Captains*. Stevenage: Strong Oak Press
van Driel-Murray, C. (ed.), 1989. *Roman Military Equipment: The Accoutrements of War* (Proceedings of the Fifth Roman Military Equipment Conference). Oxford: British Archaeological Reports (BAR S–336)
Epstein, D.F., 1987. *Personal Enmity in Roman Politics, 218–43 BC*. London: Croom Helm
Evans, R.J., 1994. *Gaius Marius: A Political Biography*. Pretoria: University of South Africa
Everitt, A., 2001. *Cicero: A Turbulent Life*. London: John Murray
Ezov, A., 1996. 'The "Missing Dimension" of C. Julius Caesar'. *Historia* 45: 64–94
Fentress, E., 1979. *Numidia and the Roman Army*. Oxford: Oxford University Press
Feugère, M., 1993 (trans. D.G. Smith 2002). *Weapons of the Romans*. Stroud: Tempus
Feugère, M., 1994. 'L'équipement militaire d'époque républicaine en Gaule'. *Journal of Roman Military Equipment Studies* 5: 3–23
Fields, N., 2007. *The Roman Army of the Punic Wars, 264–146 BC*. Oxford: Osprey (Battle Orders 27)
Fields, N., 2008. *The Roman Army of the Civil Wars, 90–30 BC*. Oxford: Osprey (Battle Orders 34)
Frank, E., 1955. 'Marius and the Roman nobility'. *Classical Journal* 50: 149–52
Frederiksen, M.W., 1966. 'Caesar, Cicero and the problem of debt'. *Journal of Roman Studies* 56: 128–41
Fuller, J.F.C., 1965 (repr. 1998). *Julius Caesar: Man, Soldier and Tyrant*. Ware: Wordsworth Editions
Gabba, E., 1973 (trans. P.J. Cuff 1976). *Republican Rome: The Army and Allies*. Oxford: Blackwell
Garnsey, P.D.A. & Saller, R.P., 1987. *The Roman Empire: Economy, Society and Culture*. London: Duckworth
Gelzer, M., 1912 (trans. R.J. Seager 1969). *The Roman Nobility*. Oxford: Blackwell
Gelzer, M., 1921 (trans. P. Needham 1968, repr. 1985). *Caesar: Politician and Statesman*. Oxford: Blackwell
Gilbert, C.D., 1973. 'Marius and Fortuna'. *Classical Quarterly* (new series) 23: 104–7
Gilliver, K., 2002. *Caesar's Gallic Wars, 58–50 BC*. Oxford: Osprey (Essential Histories 43)
Goldsworthy, A.K., 1996 (repr. 1998). *The Roman Army at War, 100 BC–AD 200*. Oxford: Clarendon Press
Goldsworthy, A.K., 2000. *Roman Warfare*. London: Cassell
Goldsworthy, A.K., 2003. *The Complete Roman Army*. London: Thames & Hudson
Goldsworthy, A.K., 2003 (repr. 2004). *In the Name of Rome: the men who won the Roman Empire*. London: Phoenix
Gowing, A.M., 1992. *The Triumviral Narratives of Appian and Cassius Dio*. Ann Arbor: University of Michigan Press
Grant, M., 1972. *Cleopatra*. London: Weidenfeld & Nicolson
Grant, M., 1979. *Julius Caesar*. London: Weidenfeld & Nicolson
Greenhalgh, P.A.L., 1980. *Pompey: The Roman Alexander*. London: Weidenfeld & Nicolson
Greenhalgh, P.A.L., 1981. *Pompey: The Republican Prince*. London: Weidenfeld & Nicolson
Gruen, E.S., 1970. '*Veteres hostes, novi amici*'. *Phoenix* 24: 237–43
Gruen, E.S., 1974. *The Last Generation of the Roman Republic*. Berkeley & Los Angeles: University of California Press
Harmond, J., 1969 (Diss.). *L'armée et le soldat à Rome, de 107 à 50 avant notre ère*. Paris: Éditions A. et J. Picard et Cie
Harris, W.V., 1979 (repr. 1985, 1986). *War and Imperialism in Republican Rome, 327–70 BC*. Oxford: Clarendon Press
Henderson, J., 1998. *Fighting For Rome: Poets and Caesars, History and Civil War*. Cambridge: Cambridge University Press
Hildinger, E., 2002. *Swords Against the Senate: The Rise of the Roman Army and the Fall of the Republic*. New York:

Da Capo Press
Hillman, T.P., 1988. 'Strategic reality and the movements of Caesar, January 49 BC'. *Historia* 37: 248–52
Hillman, T.P., 1998. 'Pompey's *imperium* in the war with Lepidus'. *Klio* 80: 91–110
Holland, T., 2003 (repr. 2004). *Rubicon: The Triumph and Tragedy of the Roman Republic*. London: Abacus
Holliday, V.L., 1969. *Pompey in Cicero's Correspondence and Lucan's* Civil War. The Hague: Kluwer Academic
Hopkins, K., 1978. *Conquerors and Slaves*. Cambridge: Cambridge University Press
Hopkins, K., 1983. *Death and Renewal*. Cambridge: Cambridge University Press
Hughes-Hallett, L., 1990. *Cleopatra: Histories, Dreams and Distortions*. London: Fourth Estate
Huzar, E.G., 1978 (repr. 1986). *Mark Antony: A Biography*. London: Croom Helm
James, S., 1998. *Exploring the World of the Celts*. London: Thames & Hudson
Jones, P. & Sidwell, K. (eds.), 1997. *The World of Rome: An Introduction to Roman Culture*. Cambridge: Cambridge University Press
Junkelmann, M., 1991. *Die Legionen des Augustus: Der romische Soldat im archaologischen Experiment*. Mainz-am-Rhein: Philipp von Zabern
Keaveney, A., 1982. *Sulla: The Last Republican*. London: Croom Helm
Keaveney, A., 1987. *Rome and the Unification of Italy*. Totowa: Barnes & Noble
Keaveney, A., 1992. *Lucullus: A Life*. London: Croom Helm
Keegan, J., 1976 (repr. 1988). *The Face of Battle*. London: Barrie & Jenkins
Keegan, J., 1987. *The Mask of Command*. London: Jonathan Cape
Keppie, L.J.F., 1983. *Colonisation and Veteran Settlement in Italy 47–14 BC*. London: British School at Rome
Keppie, L.J.F., 1984 (repr. 1998). *The Making of the Roman Army*. London: Routledge
Keppie, L.J.F., 1991. 'A centurion of *legio Martia* at Padova?' *Journal of Roman Military Equipment Studies* 2: 115–21
Knight, D.W., 1968. 'Pompey's concern for pre-eminence after 60 BC'. *Latomus* 27: 878–83
Kromayer, J. & Veith, G., 1928. *Heerwesen und Kriegführung der Griechen und Römer*. München: C.H. Beck
Lacey, W.K., 1978. *Cicero and the End of the Roman Republic*. London: Hodder & Stoughton
Lazenby, J.F., 1959. 'The conference at Luca and the Gallic War: a study in Roman politics, 57–55 BC'. *Latomus* 18: 67–76
Leach, J., 1978 (repr. 1986). *Pompey the Great*. London: Croom Helm
Le Bohec, Y., 1998. 'Vercingétorix'. *Rivista storica dell'antichità* 28: 85–120
Levick, B.M., 1982. 'Sulla's march on Rome in 88 BC'. *Historia* 31: 503–8
Lewis, R.G., 1998. 'P. Sulpicius' law to recall the exiles, 88 BC'. *Classical Quarterly* (new series) 48: 195–9
Lintott, A.W., 1967. 'P. Clodius Pulcher – Felix Catilina?'. *Greece & Rome* 14: 157–69
Lintott, A.W., 1968 (repr. 1999). *Violence in Republican Rome*. Oxford: Clarendon Press
Lintott, A.W., 1999. *The Constitution of the Roman Republic*. Oxford: Clarendon Press
Luce, T.J., 1970. 'Marius and the Mithridatic command'. *Historia* 19: 161–94
McGing, B.C., 1986. *The Foreign Policy of Mithridates VI Eupator King of Pontus*. Leiden: E.J. Brill
Manning, W.H., 1976. 'Blacksmithing', in D. Strong & D. Brown (eds.), *Roman Crafts*. New York: Duckworth, 143–53
Marshall, B.A., 1976. *Crassus: A Political Biography*. Amsterdam: Hakkert
Mattingly, D.J., 2000. 'War and peace in Roman North Africa: observations and models of state-tribe interaction', in R.B. Ferguson & N.L. Whitehead (eds), *War in the Tribal Zone: Expanding States and Indigenous Warfare*. Oxford: James Currey, chapter 2
Matyszak, P., 2003. *Chronicle of the Roman Republic: The Rulers of Ancient Rome from Romulus to Augustus*. London: Thames & Hudson
Meier, C., 1982 (trans. D. McLintock 1995). *Caesar*. London: Harper Collins
Meyer, E., 1922 (3rd edn). *Caesars Monarchie und das Principät des Pompejus: Innere Geschichte Roms von 66 bis 44 v. Chr.3*. Stuttgart-Berlin: J.G. Cotta
Millar, F.G.B, 1981 (2nd edn). *The Roman Empire and its Neighbours*. London: Duckworth
Millar, F.G.B, 1998. *The Crowd in Rome in the Late Republic*. Ann Arbor: University of Michigan Press
Millar, F.G.B, 2002. *The Roman Republic in Political Thought*. Hanover: University Press of New England
Milner, N.P., 1996 (2nd edn). *Vegetius: Epitome of Military Science*. Liverpool: Liverpool University Press
Mitchell, T.N., 1979. *Cicero: The Ascending Years*. New Haven: Yale University Press
Mitchell, T.N., 1991. *Cicero: The Senior Statesman*. New Haven: Yale University Press
Mommsen, T., 1857. *Die Rechtsfrage zwischen Caesar und dem Senate*. Breslau: M. & H. Marcus
Morgan, L., 1997. '*Levi quidem de re* . . . Julius Caesar as tyrant and pedant'. *Journal of Roman Studies* 87: 23–40

Morgan, L., 2000. 'The autopsy of C. Asinius Pollio'. *Journal of Roman Studies* 90: 51–69
Morstein-Marx, R., 2004. *Mass Oratory and Political Power in the Late Roman Republic.* Cambridge: Cambridge University Press
Mouritsen, H., 2001. *Plebs and Politics in the Late Roman Republic.* Cambridge: Cambridge University Press
Nicolet, C. (ed.), 1984. *Des Ordres à Rome.* Paris: Presses universitaires de France
Nicolet, C., 1995 (8e édn). *Rome et la conquete du monde méditerranéen, 264–27 avant J.-C. Tome 1: Les Structures de l'Italie romaine.* Paris: Presses universitaires de France
Nicolet, C., 1997 (5e édn). *Rome et la conquete du monde méditerranéen, 264–27 avant J.-C. Tome 2: Genèse d'un empire.* Paris: Presses universitaires de France
Nillson, M.P., 1929. 'The introduction of hoplite tactics at Rome'. *Journal of Roman Studies* 19: 1–11
Oakley, S.P., 1993. 'The Roman conquest of Italy', in J.W. Rich & G. Shipley (eds), *War and Society in the Roman World.* London: Routledge, 9–37
ó hógáin, D., 2002. *The Celts: A History.* Cork: Collins Press
van Ooteghem, J., 1964. *Gaius Marius.* Brussels: Latomus
Ormerod, H.A., 1924 (repr. 1969). *Piracy in the Ancient World.* Liverpool: Liverpool University Press
Parker, H.M.D., 1926. 'A note on the promotion of the centurions'. *Journal of Roman Studies* 16: 45–52
Parker, H.M.D., 1928 (repr. 1958). *The Roman Legions.* Cambridge: Heffer & Sons
Parker, H.M.D., 1932. 'The *antiqua legio* of Vegetius'. *Classical Quarterly* 26: 137–49
Paterson, J.J., 1985. 'Politics in the Late Republic', in T.P. Wiseman (ed.), *Roman Political Life, 90 BC–AD 69.* Exeter: Exeter University (Exeter Studies in History 7), 21–43
Patterson, J.R., 1993. 'Military organisation and social change in the later Roman Republic', in J.W. Rich & G. Shipley (eds), *War and Society in the Roman World.* London: Routledge, 92–112
Pelling, C.B.R., 1973. 'Pharsalus'. *Historia* 22: 249–59
Pelling, C.B.R. (ed.), 1988. *Plutarch: Life of Antony.* Cambridge: Cambridge University Press
Pelling, C.B.R., 1996. 'The triumviral period', in A.K. Bowman et al. (eds), *Cambridge Ancient History* vol. 10. Cambridge: Cambridge University Press, chapter 1
Du Picq, Charles-Ardant, 1903 (trans. Col. J. Greely & Maj. R. Cotton 1920, repr. 1946). *Battle Studies: Ancient and Modern.* Harrisburg: US Army War College
Pleiner, R., 1993. *The Celtic Sword.* Oxford: Oxford University Press
Powell, T.G.E., 1980 (2nd edn). *The Celts.* London: Thames & Hudson
Ramage, E.S., 1991. 'Sulla's propaganda'. *Klio* 73: 93–121
Rankin, H.D., 1987. *Celts and the Classical World.* London: Croom Helm
Rawlings, L., 1999. 'Condottieri and Clansmen: early Italian raiding, warfare and the state', in K. Hopkins (ed.), *Organised Crime in Antiquity.* London: Duckworth, 97–127
Rawson, B.M. (ed.), 1986. *The Family in Ancient Rome: New Perspectives.* London: Croom Helm
Rawson, E., 1971. 'The literary sources for the pre-Marian Roman army'. *Papers for the British School at Rome* 39: 13–31
Rawson, E., 1983 (2nd edn). *Cicero: A Portrait.* Bristol: Bristol University Press
Rawson, E., 1994. 'Caesar: civil war and dictatorship', in J.A. Crook et al. (eds), *Cambridge Ancient History* vol. 9. Cambridge: Cambridge University Press, chapter 11
Reddé, M. (ed.), 1996. *L'armée romaine en Gaule.* Paris: éditions Errance
Rice, E.E., 1999. *Cleopatra.* Stroud: Sutton Publishing
Rice Holmes, T., 1911 (2nd edn). *Caesar's Conquest of Gaul.* Oxford: Clarendon Press
Rice Holmes, T., 1923. *The Roman Republic and the Founder of the Roman Empire*, 3 vols. Oxford: Clarendon Press
Ritchie, W.F. & Ritchie, J.N.G., 1985. *Celtic Warriors.* Princes Risborough: Shire (Shire Archaeology 41)
Rubinsohn, W.Z., 1980 (trans. J.G. Griffith 1987). *Spartacus' Uprising and Soviet Historical Writing.* Oxford: Oxbow Books
Sabin, P. 2000. 'The face of Roman battle'. *Journal of Roman Studies* 90: 1–17
Saller, R.P., 1984. '*Familia, domus*, and the Roman conception of the family'. *Phoenix* 38: 336–55
Saller, R.P., 1994. *Patriarchy, Property and Death in the Roman Family.* Cambridge: Cambridge University Press
Salmon, E.T., 1962. 'The causes of the Social War'. *Phoenix* 16: 112–13
Santosuosso, A., 2001 (repr. 2004). *Storming the Heavens: Soldiers, Emperors and Civilians in the Roman Empire.* London: Pimlico
Seager, R.J. (ed.), 1969. *The Crisis of the Roman Republic.* Cambridge: Heffer & Sons
Seager, R.J., 1994. 'Sulla', in J.A. Crook et al. (eds), *Cambridge Ancient History* vol. 9. Cambridge: Cambridge University Press, chapter 6

Seager, R.J., 1994. 'The rise of Pompey', in J.A. Crook et al. (eds), *Cambridge Ancient History* vol. 9. Cambridge: Cambridge University Press, chapter 7

Seager, R.J., 2002 (2nd edn). *Pompey the Great: A Political Biography*. Oxford: Blackwell

Shackleton-Bailey, D.R., 1971. *Cicero*. London: Duckworth

Shatzman, I., 1975. *Senatorial Wealth and Roman Politics*. Brussels: Latomus

Shaw, B.D. (ed.), 2001. *Spartacus and the Slave Wars: A Brief History with Documents*. Boston: Bedford/St Martin's Press

Sherwin-White, A.N., 1973 (2nd edn). *The Roman Citizenship*. Oxford: Oxford University Press

Sherwin-White, A.N., 1984. *Roman Foreign Policy in the East*. London: Duckworth

Sherwin-White, A.N., 1994. 'Lucullus, Pompey and the East', in J.A. Crook et al. (eds), *Cambridge Ancient History* vol. 9. Cambridge: Cambridge University Press, chapter 8a

Shokat, Y., 1980. *Recruitment and the Programme of Tiberius Gracchus*. Brussels: Latomus

Sidebottom, H., 2004. *Ancient Warfare: A Very Short Introduction*. Oxford: Oxford University Press

Smith, R.E., 1958. *Service in the post-Marian Roman Army*. Manchester: Manchester University Press

Smith, R.E., 1960. 'Pompey's conduct in 80 and 77 BC'. *Phoenix* 14: 1–13

Smith, R.E., 1964. 'The significance of Caesar's consulship'. *Phoenix* 18: 303–13

Smith, R.E., 1966. *Cicero: The Statesman*. Cambridge: Cambridge University Press

Southern, P., 1998. *Mark Antony*. Stroud: Tempus

Southern, P., 1999. *Cleopatra*. Stroud: Tempus

Southern, P., 2001. *Julius Caesar*. Stroud: Tempus

Southern, P., 2002. *Pompey the Great*. Stroud: Tempus

de Souza, P. 1999. *Piracy in the Graeco-Roman World*. Cambridge: Cambridge University Press

Stanton, G.R., 2003. 'Why did Caesar cross the Rubicon?' *Historia* 52: 67–94

Stockton, D.L., 1971. *Cicero: A Political Biography*. Oxford: Oxford University Press

Stockton, D.L., 1973. 'The first consulship of Pompey'. *Historia* 22: 205–18

Stockton, D.L., 1979. *The Gracchi*. Oxford: Oxford University Press

Stockton, D.L. (ed.), 1981. *From the Gracchi to Sulla: Sources for Roman History, 133–80 BC*. London: London Association of Classical Teachers (LACTOR 13)

Syme, R., 1939 (repr. 1952, 1956). *The Roman Revolution*. Oxford: Clarendon Press

Syme, R., 1964 (repr. 2002). *Sallust*. Berkeley & Los Angeles: California University Press

Tarn, W.W., 1932. 'Antony's legions'. *Classical Quarterly* 26: 75–81

Tatum, W.J., 1999. *The Patrician Tribune: Publius Clodius Pulcher*. Chapel Hill: University of North Carolina

Taylor, L.R., 1931. *The Divinity of the Roman Emperor*. Middletown: American Philological Association (Philological Monographs 1)

Taylor, L.R., 1949. *Party Politics in the Age of Caesar*. Berkeley & Los Angeles: University of California Press

Taylor, L.R., 1966. *Roman Voting Assemblies*. Ann Arbor: University of Michigan Press

Thompson, E.A., 1965. *The Early Germans*. Oxford: Clarendon Press

Ulbert, G., 1969. '*Gladii* aus Pompeji: Vorarbeiten zu einem Corpus römischer *Gladii*'. *Germania* 47: 97–128

Urbainczyk, T., 2004. *Spartacus*. London: Bristol Classical Press

Walker, S. & Higgs, P., 2001. *Cleopatra of Egypt: From History to Myth*. London: British Museum Press

Ward, A.M., 1972. 'Cicero's fight against Crassus and Caesar in 65 and 63 BC'. *Historia* 21: 244–58

Ward, A.M., 1977. *Marcus Crassus and the Late Roman Republic*. Columbia: University of Missouri Press

Warry, J., 1980. *Warfare in the Classical World*. London: Salamander Books

Weigel, R., 1992. *Lepidus: The Tarnished Triumvir*. London: Routledge

Weinstock, S., 1971. *Divus Julius*. Oxford: Oxford University Press

Welch, K. & Powell, A. (eds), 1998. *Julius Caesar as Artful Reporter: The War Commentaries as Political Instruments*. London: Duckworth

Wirszubski, C., 1968. Libertas *as a Political Idea at Rome During the Late Republic and Early Principate*. Cambridge: Cambridge University Press

Wiseman, T.P., 1971. *New Men in the Roman Senate, 139 BC–AD 14*. Oxford: Oxford University Press

Wiseman, T.P., 1994. 'The Senate and the *Populares*, 69–60 BC', in J.A. Crook et al. (eds), *Cambridge Ancient History* vol. 9. Cambridge: Cambridge University Press, chapter 9

Wiseman, T.P., 1994. 'Caesar, Pompey and Rome, 59–50 BC', in J.A. Crook et al. (eds), *Cambridge Ancient History* vol. 9. Cambridge: Cambridge University Press, chapter 10

Wistrand, M., 1979. *Cicero* Imperator*: Studies in Cicero's Correspondence, 51–47 BC*. Göteborg: Acta Universitatis Gothoburgensis

Woolf, G., 1998. *Becoming Roman: The Origins of Provincial Civilization in Gaul.* Cambridge: Cambridge University Press
Yakobson, A., 1999. *Election and Electioneering in Rome: A Study of the Political System of the Late Republic.* Stuttgart: Franz Steiner
Yavetz, Z., 1969. *Plebs and Princeps.* Oxford: Oxford University Press
Yavetz, Z., 1983. *Julius Caesar and his Public Image.* London: Thames & Hudson
Yavetz, Z., 1988. *Slaves and Slavery in Ancient Rome.* Oxford: Transaction Books
Zhmodikov, A., 2000. 'Roman republican heavy infantrymen in battle (IV–II centuries BC)'. *Historia* 49: 67–78

Index